Ian Marcousé

AQA BUSINESS STUDIES for AS

Andrew Gillespie

Malcolm Surridge

Orders: please contact Bookpoint Ltd, 130 Milton Park, Abingdon, Oxon OX14 4SB. Telephone: (44) 01235 827720. Fax: (44) 01235 400454. Lines are open from 9.00 to 5.00, Monday to Saturday, with a 24-hour message answering service. You can also order through our website www.hoddereducation.co.uk

If you have any comments to make about this, or any of our other titles, please send them to educationenquiries@hodder.co.uk

British Library Cataloguing in Publication Data
A catalogue record for this title is available from the British Library

ISBN: 978 1444 12246 6

First edition published 2008
This edition published 2011
Impression number 10 9 8 7 6 5 4 3 2 1
Year 2014, 2013, 2012, 2011

Cover photo © Lew Robertson/Corbis
Typeset by Fakenham Prepress Solutions, Fakenham, Norfolk NR21 8NN
Printed and bound in Italy by Printer Trento

Contents

Acknowledgements

Every effort has been made to trace the copyright holders of material reproduced here. The authors and publishers would like to thank the following for permission to reproduce copyright illustrations:

Fig. 1.1 © AP/Press Association Images; fig. 2.3 © CorporateFocus/Alamy; fig. 3.2 Lloyds TSB Bank plc; fig. 3.3 from *esp@cenet* service/EPO; fig. 4.1 © Yuri Arcurs – Fotolia; fig. 5.1 © AP/Press Association Images; fig. 5.2 © Phase4Photography – Fotolia; fig. 6.1 © 2008 Peter Dressel/Blend Images RF/Photolibrary Group; fig. 7.1 © Transtock Inc./Alamy; fig. 8.1 © ygrek – Fotolia; fig. 9.2 © PA Archive/Press Association Images; fig. 10.1 © keith morris/Alamy; fig. 10.2 © Bohi – Fotolia.com; fig. 11.2 © Adrian Sherratt/Alamy; fig. 11.3 © The Gourmet Chocolate Pizza Co; fig. 12.4 © Tim Gainey/Alamy; fig. 14.1 © Rex Features; fig. 15.1 © Jeff Skopin – Fotolia; fig. 16.1 © Chris Elwell – Fotolia; fig. 17.2 © Stuart Clarke/Rex Features; fig. 18.2 © Corbis Premium RF/Alamy; fig. 19.1 © PA Archive/Press Association Images; fig. 20.2 © diego cervo – Fotolia; fig. 21.1 © PA Archive/Press Association Images; fig. 21.2 © Juice Images/Alamy; fig. 22.1 © Kzenon – Fotolia; fig. 24.1 © Monkey Business – Fotolia; fig. 25.1 © Gina Sanders – Fotolia; fig. 28.1 © Andia/Alamy; fig. 30.2 © Kirill Zdorov – Fotolia; fig. 32.1 © Ivan Kruk – Fotolia; fig. 33.2 © Mark Mainz/Getty Images; fig. 34.3 © PCL/Alamy; fig. 35.1 © Art Kowalsky/Alamy; fig 35.2 © Michael Conway/Alamy; fig. 36.1 © diego cervo – Fotolia; fig. 37.2 © AP/Press Association Images; fig. 37.3 © PA Archive/Press Association Images; fig. 38.3 © Mark Newton/Alamy; fig. 39.2 courtesy of Waitrose; fig. 40.1 © ABACA/Press Association Images; fig. 41.5 © Mackie's of Scotland; fig. 42.1 © Realimage/Alamy; fig. 43.4 © AP/Press Association Images; fig. 44.2 © PSL Images/Alamy; fig. 45.1 © CORRADO RIVA – Fotolia; fig. 46.1 © AP/Press Association Images; fig. 46.2 © Gareth Byrne/Alamy; fig. 47.1 © Jon Arnold Images Ltd/Alamy.

Enterprise and entrepreneurs

Definition

Enterprise is the combination of attitudes and skills that helps an individual turn an idea into reality. Many people think 'if only . . .' but do nothing about it; entrepreneurs show the enterprise to stop dreaming and get working.

Introduction

Most **entrepreneurs** see the opportunities that others see, but have the courage and initiative to act quickly. The past ten years have seen two clear trends: an increasing desire for travel and more and more thrill-seeking, such as extreme sports. Many people could see that both trends pointed to a gap for a new service: space tourism (i.e. individuals going into outer space – just for the fun of it). Richard Branson saw the same opportunity and started Virgin Galactic, which plans to charge £150,000 per trip. It hopes to make its first flight before 2012.

A successful entrepreneur needs the following characteristics:

- understanding of the market – to know what customers want, and to see how well or badly current companies are serving them
- determination – to see things through if the going gets tough
- passion – not just to make money, but to achieve something, such as to design a more efficient solar panel, or to transform rooms from shabby into bright and freshly painted
- persuasive abilities – entrepreneurs need to persuade others to do things like provide planning permission, supply goods on credit or work harder/faster to get things completed on time. They also may need to persuade staff to take a chance by joining a brand new, risky venture
- the ability to cope with risk.

Figure 1.1 Virgin founder Richard Branson

A-grade application

From sixth form to squillionaire

Aged 17, Andrew Michael turned an A-level project into an internet business start-up. He recently sold the company, receiving a cheque for just over £46 million. His business was Fasthosts, which provides email and other services for small companies. It grew rapidly, earning a listing in *The Sunday Times* as the second fastest-growing technology company in Britain.

Andrew's business was famous for the parties he threw for his staff. At different Christmases he hired Girls Aloud, The Darkness and The Sugarbabes. Now he's sad to have sold his business, but looking forward to a lifetime ambition of owning a helicopter.

Risk-taking

Business decisions are always about the future. Therefore they always involve uncertainty, because no one can be sure about the future. The oil giant BP's management had a wonderful reputation until safety issues in America in 2005 and 2006 made its halo slip. Then came the 2010 Gulf oil catastrophe (11 deaths and America's worst ever oil spill). Similarly, phone companies such as '3' forecast huge growth from person-to-person video phoning, yet this has not happened.

Good entrepreneurs consider what they think will happen, but also about what might happen differently. Someone opening a restaurant may expect 60 customers a day, each spending £25. In fact, one month after opening, there may just be 40 customers spending £20 each. Receiving £800 instead of £1,500 may make it hard to survive financially and there may be a risk of closure. This possibility should have been foreseen so that plans could be made.

An entrepreneur looks at the risks, compares them with the possible rewards and makes a cool decision. If there's a good chance of making £1,000 a week, but also a (small) chance of losing £500 a week, it is worth carrying on. Risk-takers accept that sometimes they will take a loss; that is part of business.

Table 1.1 What makes an entrepreneur?

People who aren't entrepreneurs	Bad entrepreneurs	Good entrepreneurs
are very cautious – never want to take any risks	ignore risks – assume that their own charisma/skill will guarantee success	take calculated risks, weighing up the potential risks and rewards
assume that things are the way they have to be	rush to bring in something new or make huge changes	launch new ideas in response to changing consumer tastes or attitudes
like to be sure of next month's pay cheque – and the one after, until retirement	trust that things will go as planned, spend freely at the start as they're sure the cash will start flowing tomorrow	accept that the early days of a new business may be very tough, so try to spend as little as possible

Motives for becoming an entrepreneur

Although 20 per cent of entrepreneurs have money as their prime motive, most are looking for more. Typically they are looking for 'a challenge' or 'to prove myself'. In other words, people are looking for greater satisfaction than they can get from a regular job. A recent NatWest Bank survey of 1,400 entrepreneurs names the top start-up motive as 'to gain more control and avoid being told what to do'. Just 6 per cent said that they started their venture 'to make money'.

In some cases, starting a business can be hugely challenging, satisfying, absorbing and profitable. One example is Matteo Pantani, whose passion for ice cream led him to start 'Scoop' in 2007, opening his second London outlet in 2010 and a third planned for Spring 2011. Yet some people kid themselves about enterprise. They assume it is more satisfying, glamorous and profitable than it often is. Many shopkeepers work very long hours for quite poor rewards. Many small builders speak bitterly about their experiences in dealings with customers, suppliers and employees; they feel it would be easier to just earn a wage. Furthermore, government figures show that 30 per cent of new businesses fail within their first three years.

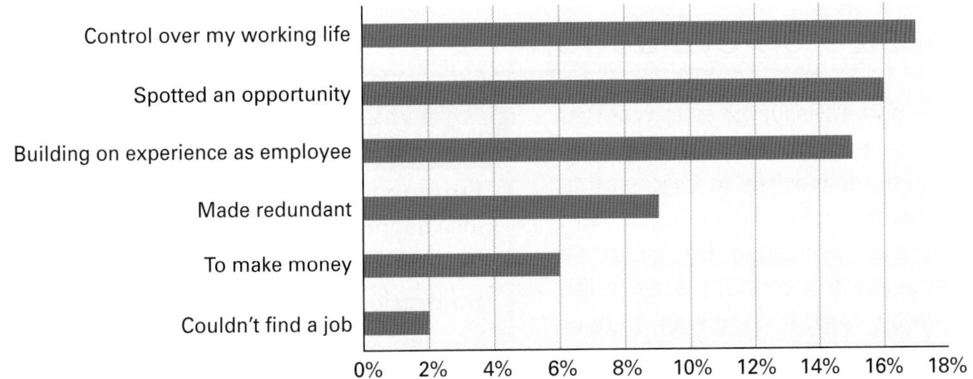

Figure 1.2 Key motivators for entrepreneurs
(Source: NatWest Bank, IFF Research, May 2007)

Government support for enterprise

Novice entrepreneurs believe that the government will be behind them all the way but they soon find out that life is not like that. Over 40 per cent of those thinking about starting a business believe that they will get a grant; in fact only 2 per cent get funding in this way – one new business in 50.

The government's main expenditure to support new business has been funding the Business Link network. This offered advice for all those starting up in business, plus a free consultation with an expert nominated by Business Link. Unfortunately the quality of the advice was very variable. Accordingly, the new coalition government decided in 2010 to replace Business Link with an online-only advice service. This decision to cut expenditure on business start-up was criticised by some organisations representing owners of small businesses.

The new government wants to continue the long-standing policy to encourage an 'enterprise culture'. In effect, create a spirit among young people that being enterprising is 'cool'. The argument runs that if lots of people want to start their own businesses, perhaps the British economy will develop as dynamically as in America – the heart of the enterprise culture.

A-grade application

From £40 to £80 million

In the 1980s the government operated an 'Enterprise Allowance' worth £40 a week to any young person starting their own business. Julian Dunkerton used this allowance to start up a market stall in Cheltenham. Later he was able to open his first shop, called Cult. The business built up steadily until he saw the opportunity to launch a new range of clothing aimed at young, fashionable men. 'Superdry' took off when David Beckham started to wear its jeans and jackets. By 2010 Dunkerton's business employed more than 1,000 staff and when floated on the London stock market in March of that year, it yielded him a cheque for £80 million. Not a bad return on a government investment of £40 a week.

Issues for analysis

Some people think that real entrepreneurs are born that way (i.e. that they have the right skills, self-confidence and attitudes from birth). Others say that all the skills can be learnt – sometimes quite late in life. Research points clearly to the second argument – that the skills can be learnt.

A second important issue is whether entrepreneurs tend to be school underachievers whose success comes from their reaction against their school 'failure'. Businesspeople such as Richard Branson and Duncan Bannatyne did badly at school, often due to dyslexia. Countering that, however, is any glance at Britain's 'Rich List'. Most of the business multi-millionaires came from wealthy families and had a good education.

Enterprise – an evaluation

Perhaps the most important issue of all is whether the government does enough to help entrepreneurs. Business representatives like to suggest that 'red tape' (government regulation) makes it hard to start up. This is largely nonsense; Britain is one of the easiest, quickest and cheapest places in the world to start up a new firm. It comes as a shock to many, though, to discover how little help there is out there. Overwhelmingly, people starting a new business need to use their own savings and plenty of their own time. Government rarely provides a magic wand.

Key terms

Entrepreneur: someone who makes a business idea happen, either through their own effort, or by organising others to do the work.

Innovations: new ideas brought to the market.

Mentor: an experienced advisor, to be there when needed.

Revision questions *(25 marks; 25 minutes)*

1 Why is 'initiative' an important quality in an entrepreneur? (2)

2 Section 1.1 lists the characteristics needed to be a successful entrepreneur. Outline which two from this list seem of greatest importance to:

a) a new firm facing a collapse in demand due to local flooding (4)

b) a 19-year-old entrepreneur wanting to start her own airline (4)

3 Explain two actions the government could take to encourage more people to become entrepreneurs. (4)

4 Briefly explain one argument for and one against the idea that entrepreneurs are born, not made. (5)

5 Having read this unit, explain briefly how successful or unsuccessful you think you would be as an entrepreneur. Take care to explain your reasoning. (6)

Revision exercises

Data response

Travis Sporland is a surfer who believes he has come up with a revolutionary design for surfboards. His father was made redundant from a Devon boatyard two years ago, so Travis thinks they can start up a small manufacturing business together. The Travis surfboard is designed for children up to the age of 11. He believes the size of the world market may be as high as 1.5 million. These are some of his forecasts about the business:

	Year 1 figures (surfers under 11)		
	UK market only	US market only	Rest of the World
Surfer population	22,000	580,000	460,000
Forecast year 1 sales	2,200	29,000	23,000
Surfboard selling price	£120	$200	$150

Questions *(20 marks; 20 minutes)*

1 If you were asked to advise Travis, identify four questions you would like to ask him about his business plans. (8)

2 Explain your reasoning behind *one* of those questions. (3)

3 Discuss two main factors you think Travis should also consider before going ahead. (9)

Case study

Tips for start-up success

These tips from the US website www.entrepreneur.com focus on people starting a business from home.

1 **Begin with a plan.** Not all home businesses need an official business plan, but every home business owner must spend some time planning. Sit down and determine how much money you need to invest, your goals (short- and long-term), your marketing plan and all those pesky details.

2 **Find a mentor.** You may know someone who has successfully created a home business and feel comfortable asking for advice. Seek help from other small businesses, professionals, government agencies, employees and trade associations. Be alert, ask questions, and learn everything you can.

3 **Money in the bank.** Don't quit your day job just yet. For those of you considering the full-time freelance plunge – set up a savings account with enough funds to cover at least six months' worth of bills. This will give you a buffer to help with your budget. While hunger might be a good motivator, it's easier to work when you have electricity and your house isn't being repossessed.

4 **Keep competitive.** Even if you think your business is unique, you need to conduct a competitive analysis in your market, including products, prices, promotions, advertising, distribution, quality and service. Be aware of the outside influences that affect your business. Know what makes the difference between you and your competitors. Is it service, price or expertise?

5 **All systems grow.** Word of mouth is the best way to grow your business. Ask your satisfied clients for referrals, offer free consultations to new referrals, and consider a referral or finder's fee. Get your name out to build your brand.

(Source: www.entrepreneur.com/article/207270 with permission of Entrepreneur Media, Inc.)

Questions *(20 marks; 20 minutes)*

1 Outline two pieces of advice that attempt to reduce the risks of start-up. (4)

2 Explain why 'every business owner must spend some time planning'. (4)

3 Explain the risks involved when an entrepreneur wrongly thinks that the business is unique. (6)

4 The text suggests ways to exploit 'word of mouth'. Explain how it can be created among customers of a new pizza takeaway business. (6)

Mini case study

Nearly Crusshed

In 1998, the same year that Innocent Drinks was launched, three men started Crussh, London's first smoothie bar. Whereas Innocent targeted the market for packaged soft drinks (and now has sales of over £100 million a year), Crussh would produce fresh smoothies or juices. James Learmond saw the need in London for drinks that were both delicious and healthy. He also saw that Starbucks had broken through various customer price ceilings. It was perfectly possible to get people to pay £2 or £3 for a drink.

James invested £100,000 to start the first Crussh bar, and then needed further capital in 1999 to buy out his other founding shareholders. In 2001, over-expansion plus an economic dip forced him to borrow £500,000 from the bank. Today James owns 40 per cent of the business.

Current managing director Chris Fung points out that many of the early juice bar and smoothie start-ups went under because they could not cope with the seasonality of the business. In a typical July week in the City of London, Monday might be rainy, causing sales to be poor; Tuesday warm, creating strong sales; Wednesday hot, causing high demand, long queues and grumpy customers; and Thursday could see thunderstorms. Worse still, the winter months would see trade dry up. A profitable summer followed by a terrible winter can be very tough on **cash flow** for a new business.

Fortunately Crussh survived its early scares and by 2006 made £500,000 profit on sales of £5 million. By the end of 2007 there were 20 Crussh smoothie bars in London, and plans were in hand for spreading them throughout the country. This success was built on a re-think of the **business model**. Nowadays, hand-made smoothies no longer form the bulk of the business. Chris Fung says that they 'capture the imagination' of consumers, who may then order an organic bread sandwich, a ham and pea soup or a cup of coffee. This is how sales have been adjusted to allow for the British weather. The Crussh start-up has become a great success, but don't suggest to James Learmond that it was easy.

Questions *(30 marks; 30 minutes)*

1 Explain what is meant by the terms:

a) cash flow (3)

b) business model (3)

2 Crussh received no government support during its set-up phase. Should the government invest in the business now? Explain your answer. (6)

3 Discuss which of the qualities listed in Section 1.1 were important in James Learmond's case. (10)

4 a) Why did Crussh change its product range over the period 1998–2007? (4)

b) How did it do so? (4)

2 Identifying business opportunities

Definition

Business opportunities must be spotted and acted upon before someone else gets there first.

Generating business ideas

At the heart of successful entrepreneurship is spotting a good business idea. This is usually based on a good understanding of consumer tastes and/or the needs of the retail trade. Both qualities were shown by Martyn Dawes, who spotted the opportunity for machines that could automatically make high quality coffee. His 'Coffee Nation' machines in motorway service stations and Tesco Express stores have made him a millionaire.

The main sources of business ideas are as follows:

- Observation – Martyn Dawes had seen similar machines in New York delis, and saw their potential use in Britain.
- Brain-storming can be useful; this is where two or more people are encouraged to come up with ideas, without anyone criticising anyone else's ideas, no matter how bizarre; the appraisal process comes later.
- Thinking ahead – perhaps about the new opportunities that will arise if the weather continues to get warmer (air conditioning, ice cream, etc.).
- Ideas from personal or business experience, for example, 'there are no ice cream parlours for miles around' or 'in my company we need quality sandwiches delivered at lunchtime'.
- **Innovations** – these may come from new science, such as Pilkington's self-cleaning glass (used in skyscrapers worldwide) – or from clever re-workings of existing knowledge, such as James Seddon's 'Eggxactly' waterless egg cooker.

Spotting an opportunity

It would be easy to get gloomy and to think that all the great business ideas and opportunities have already gone – the hamburger chain, the fizzy cola and so on. In fact, this is completely wrong. Society changes constantly, with different attitudes or fads that mark out the generations. In the 1990s most people went on 'packaged holidays' – trips to Spain run by big holiday companies, for example. Today, far more people do things independently, giving opportunities for new discount airlines, independent hotels and small car hire companies. If people want a packaged holiday, it is more likely to be a specialist one, such as diving in Egypt, and it will probably be run by a small, independent travel company.

The keys to spotting new business opportunities are to:

- think about changes to society, for example, more concern about the 'body beautiful' (cosmetic surgery, anti-ageing creams, fashion clothing, etc.)
- think about changes to the economy, for example, whether a continuing economic boom in China will provide opportunities for British brands such as Burberry, Cadbury and Superdry
- think about the local housing market: are people moving into or out of your area? Are prices moving up or down? Many local business opportunities may rise or fall depending on these factors
- use the techniques outlined below: small budget research and careful market mapping.

Small budget research

Even before using market research (see Unit 7) good entrepreneurs take the time to gain a general understanding of the market. Someone thinking of buying into a Subway franchise for Brighton might:

- walk around the town, mapping where sandwich bars and other fast food outlets are located (this is called **geographical mapping**). Figure 2.1 shows how plotting the existing suppliers can help identify a suitable place to start up (perhaps on Grand Parade?)
- while they're walking around the town, they might check on prices, special deals, student discounts, etc.
- ask Subway to arrange for them to spend a day at their franchise in a nearby town, to help understand the customer and the way the service is provided
- based on the knowledge gained by the above, produce a **market map** of fast food in Brighton; this will help identify whether Subway will have a **market niche** to itself (see Figure 2.2).

Small budget research may also point towards new business opportunities. Buying *The Grocer* magazine provides many useful insights as each week it highlights one consumer market place. For example, the 19 December 2009 issue highlighted that sales of Cadbury's Trident gum had fallen by 27 per cent in its third year on the UK market. This poor performance by Trident fruit-based chewing gums encouraged Cadbury to launch its Trebor Extra Strong gum – going back to basics with a strong mint-flavoured gum.

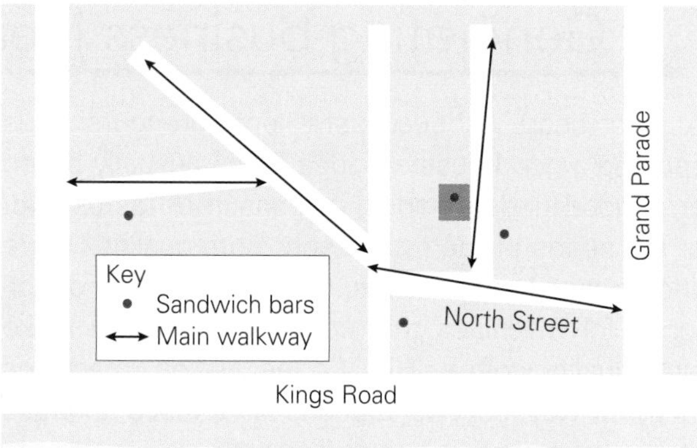

Figure 2.1 Geographical mapping of existing outlets

Market mapping

Market mapping is carried out in two stages:

1. Identify the key features that characterise consumers within a market; examples in the market for women's clothes would be young/old and high fashion/conservative.
2. Having identified the key characteristics, then every brand should be placed on a grid such as that shown in Figure 2.2; this will reveal where the competition is concentrated, and may throw up some gaps in the market.

Using this approach could help in identifying a product or market niche that has not yet been filled. In the map shown in Figure 2.2 there appears to be an available niche for healthy eating for younger customers within the fast food sector. The market map points to this possibility, but it would be up to the entrepreneur to investigate further. In particular, the niche may be present, but too small to provide an opportunity for a profitable business.

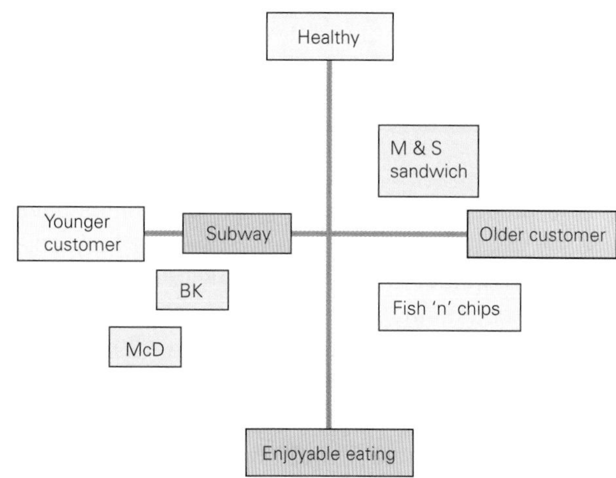

Figure 2.2 Market map: fast food

Franchises

Starting a new business with a new idea requires a huge amount of planning, skill and perhaps luck on the part of the businessperson. Government figures suggest that only 70 per cent of new businesses will survive for three years. The reasons for a failure rate of nearly a third are easy to see:

- the business idea may not be good enough
- even a good idea can be copied by other firms rushing into the market
- a good idea can be wrecked if the product or service disappoints the customer (e.g. slow service, late delivery, inconsistent product or poorly trained staff).

Many of these problems can be avoided if the entrepreneur goes for a half-way house towards running their own business: a franchise. NatWest Bank suggests that 93 per cent of franchises survive their first three years (i.e. the failure rate is only 7 per cent).

For example, if you start up an independent optician service, you have to:

- design and decorate a store that will create the right customer image
- create systems for staff training, stock control and accounting
- do your own advertising to bring in customers and to make them willing to pay the high prices charged by opticians.

Alternatively, you could start up your own, 100 per cent independent limited company, and then sign up for a Specsavers franchise. This would mean, for example, access to the specially written Specsavers store management software. From a scan of a sold pair of glasses, the software ensures that all the necessary stock ordering and accounting actions are taken. The franchise owner (Specsavers) also provides full training for the **franchisee** (the entrepreneur), plus advice and supplier contacts for store decoration and display and, of course, the huge marketing support from a multi-million pound TV advertising campaign. If you start up J Bloggs Opticians, how many people will come through the doors? If you open up Specsavers, customers will trust the business from day one.

Founding a franchise

To start selling franchises in your own business only becomes possible when its success is clear and quite long-established. Fred deLuca, aged 17, borrowed $1,000 in 1964 to open a sandwich shop. He built his business up to a chain of successful stores and then, in 1975, started offering franchises to others who wanted to buy into his Subway business. By 1995 there were 11,000 Subway outlets and in 2010 there were over 33,000 (2,000 in the UK).

The franchise owner (also known as the **franchisor**) then needs to establish:

- a training programme so that franchisees learn to do things 'the Subway way'
- a system of pricing that is profitable without putting off potential franchisees; usually

A-grade application

Specsavers

Specsavers was started by Doug and Mary Perkins in Guernsey in 1984. They opened branches in Devon and Cornwall, each run by a manager within their own Specsavers chain. In 1988, the company decided to speed up its growth by getting individuals to open their own Specsavers franchise outlets. Now the finance needed to open each new branch (approximately £140,000) would come from the franchisee, not Doug and Mary. Also, the founders would no longer have to manage each store on a day-to-day basis. Each franchisee has every incentive to run his/her store well, because all the outlet's revenues are kept locally – apart from the royalty rate of 5 per cent that must be paid to Specsavers' Head Office. Doug and Mary also receive a start-up fee from each new franchisee, which is a sum of between £25,000 and £50,000 depending upon the location.

This approach has allowed Specsavers to develop into the largest privately-owned opticians in the world, with more than 1,500 branches. Annual turnover for 2010 is estimated at more than £1,300 million.

the franchise rights are bought for £10,000–£100,000, then the franchisee must buy all store fittings and equipment via the franchise owner (this may cost £50,000–£250,000) and then buy all supplies from the franchise owner. In addition, a 5 per cent royalty is usually paid on all income and a fee of 3–5 per cent to contribute towards the national advertising campaign

- a system of monitoring, so that poorly-run franchises do not damage the reputation of the brand.

Becoming a franchisee

For those starting their first business, full independence means the freedom to make all decisions, including many mistakes. Buying into a franchise makes the start-up much safer. Instead of struggling to establish a local reputation, the business has a national reputation from day one (e.g. KFC, Subway or Specsavers). All marketing decisions will be handled by Head Office, not by the franchisee.

The franchisee will be an independent business, but working within the rules laid down by the franchise owner. These will cover the store decoration, the staff uniforms, the product range, the product pricing and much else. Yet the franchisee will still have to manage staff recruitment, training and motivation; stock ordering; quality control and management; and effective customer service.

Pitfalls of running a franchise

It is important to be clear that really independent-minded people might hate to be franchisees. After all, they may want to start their own business to 'be their own boss'. A franchisee is the boss of the business, but without the normal freedoms of decision making. This could be very frustrating. It will also be important to choose the right franchise. On the fringes of franchising are some dubious businesses that sell the promises of training and advertising support, but supply very little after they have pocketed the franchise fee. As with anything in business, careful research is essential; better franchise operators are members of the British Franchise Association (BFA). It should also be borne in mind that the franchise owner's slice of your income may make it difficult to make good profits from 'your' business.

Benefits of running a franchise

A young businessperson could treat being a franchisee as a wonderful training towards becoming a full entrepreneur: 'Today I'll open a Subway; in five years I'll sell it and open my own restaurant.' Very few people have the range of skills required of the independent business owner. Who is expert at marketing, buying, store design, window display, staff management, sales, stock control and accounting? This is why the failure rate for new independent businesses is so much higher than for franchise businesses.

Due to the different failure rates, the attitude of bankers is very different when you seek finance for a franchise start-up. Ask NatWest for £50,000 to start J Bloggs, sandwich shop, and the door will quickly be closed; ask for £50,000 to help finance a Subway outlet and the response will be far more positive. Franchisees find finance easier and cheaper to get. The interest rate charged by a bank for a potential Subway franchisee will be lower than the rate they would charge to the founder of an independent business start-up.

Figure 2.3 Specsavers is a franchise with a national reputation

Issues for analysis

When thinking of a new business idea, it is important to not only think about its unique features and the response of customers, but also how easy is it to copy? Opening the first Polish restaurant in Luton may look like a licence to print money, but how will the business do when the second and then the third Polish restaurants are opened down the road?

Buying into a franchise can be seen as business-made-easy. The difficulties should not be underestimated, though. Above all else, most entrepreneurs gain most of their satisfaction from the challenge of creating and marketing a unique business idea. What they least look forward to is the everyday slog of running a shop or managing semi-interested part-time staff. The life of a franchisee is a long way from the life of a full entrepreneur; it will only suit a certain type of person.

Identifying business opportunities – an evaluation

Every aspect of starting a business is challenging. If something looks easy, it is probably only due to naivety on the part of the observer. Anyone who has started a successful business deserves respect. If their start-up seems to have been smooth, probe and question whether the whole story is being told. If it is, then the entrepreneur(s) were probably incredibly well organised and perhaps a bit lucky. Most entrepreneurs are willing to accept that luck plays its part – for instance, in how intelligently competitors react to your start-up. Starting a business is fascinating precisely because not all the factors can be controlled – every start-up is a bit of a stab in the dark.

Key terms

Franchisee: a person or company who has paid to become part of an established franchise business (such as Subway or Specsavers).

Franchisor: the owner of the holding company and franchise (e.g. KFC).

Geographical mapping: plotting on a map the locations of all the existing businesses in your market to show where all your competitors are.

Market map: a grid plotting where each existing brand sits on scales based on two important features of a market (e.g. in the car market: luxury/economy and green/gas guzzling).

Market niche: a gap in the market (i.e. no one else is offering what you want to offer).

Revision questions *(30 marks; 30 minutes)*

1 Explain how 'observation' might help a business-minded person to come up with a great new idea for starting a firm. (3)

2 The UK population is growing older, with a rising proportion of over 60s. Outline two business opportunities that might arise as the population gets older. (4)

3 Explain in your own words the purpose of geographical mapping. (3)

4 Identify three markets where age is a crucial factor in drawing up a market map. (3)

5 Examine two reasons why a successful, growing business might choose not to sell franchises in the business. (6)

6 Why are good franchise owners keen to inspect their franchisees regularly, even though they have no ownership stake in the franchisee businesses? (3)

7 Why should a potential franchisee be very careful to research fully the background of the franchise owner? (4)

8 The evaluation talks about the importance of luck in business start-ups; outline how bad luck might damage the start of a small bakery. (4)

Revision exercises

Data response

Cara Phelps has worked in Sainsbury's personnel department for eight years and is getting bored. She owns her own flat in Leeds, has managed to save £18,000 and wants to start her own business. Her passion is shoes (she has 70 pairs!) so she wants to start a shoe shop. She has been eyeing a site close to Harvey Nichols, as she wants to target those willing to pay £50–£200 a pair. She was going to start up an independent shop, but her father has asked her to look at the franchise opportunities being offered by an upmarket London shoe shop.

Figure 2.4 is a profile of Cara, drawn up by friend who is a business consultant. Each skill has been rated out of 10, where 10 is perfect.

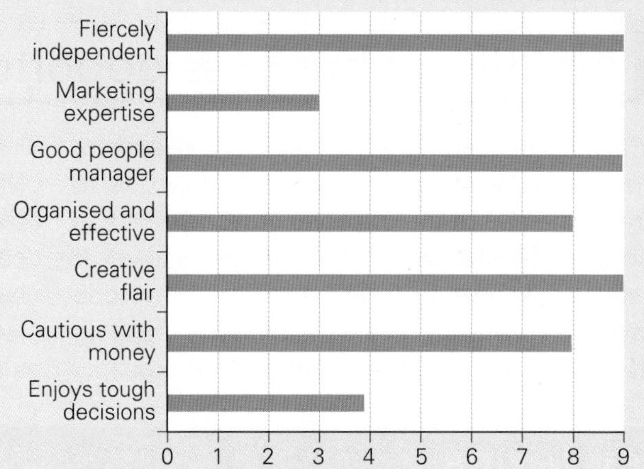

Figure 2.4 Personal skills analysis

Questions *(25 marks; 25 minutes)*

1 Outline two pieces of small budget research Cara should carry out before taking things any further with her upmarket shoe shop in Leeds. (6)

2 a) Outline one possible benefit to Cara of opting to become a franchisee. (3)

b) Outline one aspect of the London shoe shop franchise that Cara should examine more carefully before signing any agreements. (4)

3 Use the text and the graph to discuss whether Cara is better suited to running a franchise or an independent shoe shop. (12)

Data response

Why franchise?

After many years as a call centre manager, Malachy Miller looked into starting his own business. He quickly decided that franchising would be the right route for him: 'Unless you have an idea or product that will turn everything upside down then this is better than simply going it alone ... franchises allow you to minimise the risk and you're buying into something that's already there.'

When Mal went to a franchising exhibition in Birmingham, he was impressed by the O'Brien's stand. This chain of 300 franchise sandwich bars has been going for over 15 years. The exhibition stand was being run by existing franchisees who were very happy with their relationship with O'Briens.

O'Briens required an investment of £80,000, of which half had to be from Mal's own pocket. This would pay for all the shopfitting on new premises in Northampton. In addition to this initial outlay, O'Briens takes 9 per cent of the weekly turnover in fees and advertising support charges. As it can be hard to charge high prices for sandwiches, will there be enough profit for Mal to make a good living? By Googling 'O'Briens' it soon becomes clear that quite a few are up for sale, including one in Glasgow on sale for £50,000. Should Mal proceed?

Not everyone has had good experiences with franchising. Mark Simmonds was a franchisee of the restaurant chain Pierre & Victoire, when it went into liquidation. He has this advice for potential franchisees:

- Don't rely on financial information given – get it checked out.
- Speak to other franchisees to validate the information given, especially profits.
- Make sure the revenue statistics are achievable.
- Validate start-up costs.
- Make sure the location is good if it's a food franchise.

Questions *(30 marks; 30 minutes)*

1 Explain why Mal wanted to start a franchise, not an independent business. (4)

2 Examine why the views of the franchisees at the exhibition may not have been typical of those of all O'Brien's franchisees. (5)

3 Apart from the franchise fee, suggest three other business costs Mal would have to pay to run the sandwich shop. (3)

4 Consider the list of advice given by Mark Simmonds. Discuss which aspects of that would be especially useful for Mal. (9)

5 Recommend whether Mal should proceed or not with the O'Brien's franchise. Explain your thinking. (9)

Protecting business ideas

Definition

An idea cannot be protected, but patents and copyright are methods of preventing others from copying an actual invention or piece of creative work.

Intellectual property

Intellectual property (IP) is the general term for assets that have been created by human ingenuity or creativity. These would include music, writing, photographs and engineering or other inventions. Around the world, governments are keen to protect IP because otherwise there would be no financial incentive to create anything. Why should JK Rowling spend years writing about Harry Potter if others could simply photocopy the books? She is protected by **copyright**. To get fully up-to-date information, go to the website of the Intellectual Property Office (formerly the Patent Office): www.ipo.gov.uk.

Patent

The *Patents and Designs Journal* lists a series of patent applications that have recently been granted. One is by a British inventor, Michael Reeves, for a 'Lightning-protected Golf Cart'. It is easy to see that if this invention works (and can be produced at reasonable cost), it should sweep every other golf cart off the market.

The purpose of a patent is to provide a window of up to 20 years in which the work of an inventor cannot be copied by anyone else. The 20-year period starts from the moment the patent is applied for. However, the IP Office itself admits that applications take at least two and a half years to process, and can take up to five years! In Michael Reeves' case, he probably has about 17 years after the patent has been granted to get his lightning-protected golf cart to the market.

The patent system acts as an incentive to the inventor; nevertheless it can mean higher prices for the consumer. Mr Reeves' golf cart might prove significantly more expensive than his rivals', just because Mr Reeves has the **monopoly power** that comes from the patent.

For a small firm, obtaining a patent can be expensive, perhaps costing between £1,000 and £4,000 for the UK alone. Then, if the product has worldwide potential, patent applications will be required in the USA, Japan, China and so on. The total cost could be £50,000+. Then, if a competitor breaks your patent, you cannot call the police, because breaking a patent is not a criminal offence. It is a civil offence, so the patent owner has to sue the competitor. If a small firm is to take a giant such as Nike to court, there is a real risk that the cost of the court proceedings might ruin the small firm's finances.

Despite these shortcomings, the system of patents has proved an excellent way to give inventors

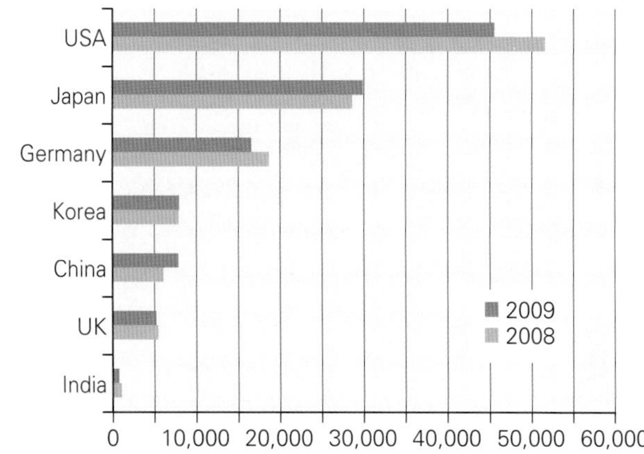

Figure 3.1 Patent applications: top five countries plus UK and India

(Source: WIPO Statistics Database)

the incentives they need. Figure 3.1 shows how patent applications are leaping ahead in China (up by 30 per cent in 2009). It also shows Britain slipping back (down 4 per cent in 2009) and the continuing dominance of the USA and Japan.

Copyright

Copyright applies to original written work such as books, newspaper articles, song lyrics and so on. Unlike patents, it occurs automatically, so there is no need to spend time and money applying for it. Copyright in a literary work lasts for the lifetime of the author plus 70 years.

Clearly copyright is at the heart of industries such as publishing and music. Less obvious is that it is also at the heart of computing and the internet. The high prices charged by Microsoft for its Office software are bound up in the copyright protection it enjoys. If Microsoft catches anyone breaking its copyright, it will sue immediately. As with patents, it can be argued that this is crucial to the development of the industry. Whereas the cost of developing a Playstation 1 game was said to be around £500,000 and Playstation 2 around £5 million, today the cost of a Playstation 3 game is more like £20 million. To justify such huge expenditure, the software producer needs to be confident that the game will sell millions of copies; being copied by millions will not pay the bills!

Trademarks

The Intellectual Property Office describes a trade mark as: 'Any sign that can distinguish the goods and services of one trader from those of another'. It goes on to say that 'These signs can be words, logos, pictures, sounds, smells, colours ... or any combination of these'. This makes a trademark a 'badge of origin': a way to spot one product or brand in a herd of competitors.

To have any force in law, a trademark must be registered at the Intellectual Property Office. To get registered, the mark must be truly distinctive and original. You would not get 'Coffee Shop' registered just because the font is bright purple, but 'Zaydor Coffee Shop' could be registered. Magners Cider was launched in 2005 with the image of cider poured over ice; it asked whether advertising cider poured over ice could be trademarked, and was told no. By 2009 Magners' sales were slumping because Bulmer's had unashamedly stolen Magners' 'over-ice' approach.

The importance of trademarks becomes most obvious when you think of the iconic ones such as the Coca-Cola logo, the black horse within the Lloyds TSB logo, the Heinz Salad Cream label and Cadbury's 'glass and a half' (of milk).

Registering a trademark costs relatively little, perhaps £1,000–£2,000, but it is not something that a small business would think much about until it starts to succeed. For businesses such as Innocent Drinks, however, early registration of their trade-marks was crucial to the company's success.

Figure 3.2 The black horse within the Lloyds TSB logo – an iconic trademark

Issues for analysis

Consumers often ignore intellectual property. They will download music tracks without paying, or photocopy an article without paying the author. However, many businesses rely hugely on tightly regulated IP. The problem is that everyone can see the long-term potential benefits of IP, but no one wants to pay higher prices in the short term.

Business success relies on building a distinctive market position and consumer image. BMW does not want its products called cars; they are 'the ultimate driving machine'. The more that patents, copyright and trademarks can help a firm achieve distinctiveness, the more secure it will become compared with its rivals.

Intellectual property protection – an evaluation

Fifty years ago, most people bought products and services with little thought for who had made them. In today's brand and fashion-conscious world, the logo on the back pocket of a pair of jeans can double its selling price, as can a tick on a pair of trainers (Nike even calls it a 'Swoosh' to try to differentiate it). With products and services making ever-greater appeals to our senses, trademarks become increasingly important. The only time when trademarks matter less is when a firm has made a genuine technical breakthrough, perhaps from a patented product. If golfers want a 'lightning-protected golf cart', they will quickly move away from the company that has supplied them in the past. Intellectual property is a huge twenty-first century business issue.

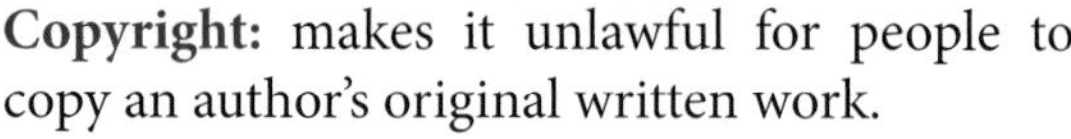

Key terms

Copyright: makes it unlawful for people to copy an author's original written work.

Monopoly power: the ability to charge high prices because you are the sole supplier of a product.

Patent: provides the inventor of a technical breakthrough with the ability to stop anyone copying the idea for up to 20 years.

Trademark: any sign that can distinguish the goods and services of one trader from those of another.

A Revision questions (25 marks; 25 minutes)

1 Briefly explain why Mr Reeves should be able to build a very successful business, based on the patent explained in Section 3.2. (4)

2 Explain why an entrepreneur may struggle if the success of new business relies on a patented invention. (4)

3 Look at Figure 3.1 and identify:
   a) Two countries where the number of patent applications rose in 2009 (2)
   b) Two countries where the number of patent applications fell in 2009 (2)

4 Briefly explain why it might disappoint the British government to see that the number of patent applications in Britain has been falling. (3)

5 For each of the following, identify whether the IP issue relates to patent, copyright or trademark:
   a) Galaxy has designed a new pack for its 'Celebrations' brand. (1)
   b) Burberry has come up with a new way to get solar power from a tartan cap, sufficient to keep an iPod powered all day long. (1)
   c) Lacoste has developed a new, completely distinctive scent for men. (1)
   d) You have just copied a tennis game from your friend's Wii console. (1)

6 Why may intellectual property be more important today than 50 years ago? Briefly explain your answer. (6)

Revision exercises

Data response

The transport sensation of the late Victorian period was the bicycle. A practical problem, though, was that women wore long dresses, not trousers, making a bicycle difficult to ride, with risks ranging from dirtied dresses to tangled spokes and sudden stops. British inventors set to work on this problem, with more than 50 patents registered with reference to 'ladies' and 'cycling'. One example of such a patent was for the 'lady's rational or divided skirt for cyling', by Oretta Bywater of Glamorgan, in 1903. The main drawing is shown in Figure 3.3.

Figure 1 in the application shows the harness for bunched up skirts; Figure 5 is the 'overdress' to protect the wearer's modesty. It is not known whether Bywater had a commercial success with the cycling skirt, because although a patent grants monopoly rights for up to 20 years, it does not guarantee that people will buy the product.

Questions *(20 marks; 20 minutes)*

1 Explain in your own words the meaning of the word patent. (3)

2 Examine the likely reasons why Oretta Bywater applied for a patent on the technical innovations within the bicycle dress. (7)

3 Discuss whether Oretta was likely to lose out as a result of focusing on the patent application rather than her target market. (10)

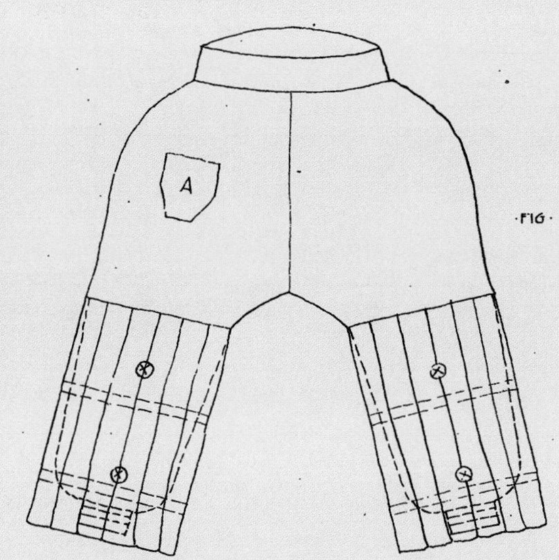

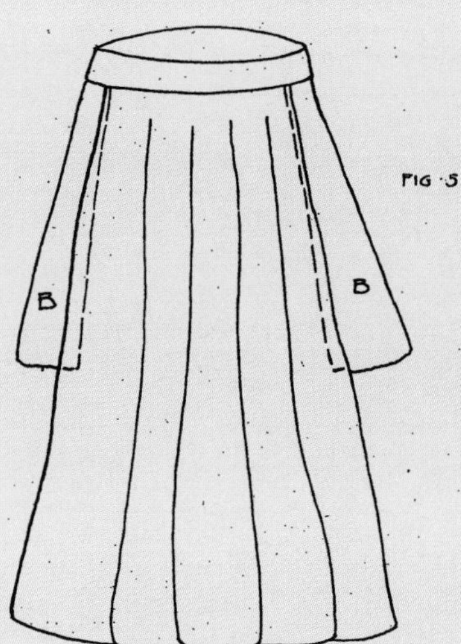

Figure 3.3 Patent application drawing

B2 Data response

In its fourth annual Digital Music Survey, research consultancy Entertainment Media Research found that just under half of the 1,700 people it questioned were illegally downloading music tracks. This was a third more than in 2006 and 40 per cent more than in 2005. Legal downloading was found to be in decline.

Young people were found to be the worst culprits with twice as many 18 to 24 year olds admitting to illegally downloading music as those aged between 25 and 34. The price of legal downloads was cited as the key factor for this after 84 per cent of those questioned said that older digital downloads should be cheaper to buy than new releases.

John Enser, head of music at law firm Olswang, agreed. He said: 'As illegal downloading hits an all-time high and consumers' fear of prosecution falls, the music industry must look for more ways to encourage the public to download music legally.'

However, music industry association the BPI disagreed with the research claiming that both legal and illegal downloads had risen within the past year as a result of a 25 per cent growth in broadband penetration.

A spokesman for the BPI told Computeractive: 'Consumers must also understand that by downloading songs free they are denying an artist of money and rights which could cause the industry to collapse.'

Questions *(25 marks; 25 minutes)*

1 Explain whether the above issue is about breaking copyright or trademark law. (4)

2 Outline two possible reasons why 18–24 year olds may be the 'worst culprits'. (4)

3 Discuss whether John Enser is right to urge the music industry to cut its prices for officially downloaded music. (8)

4 Evaluate whether young people are likely to listen to the appeal by the BPI spokesman against 'downloading songs free'. (9)

4 Developing business plans

Definition

A business plan is a document setting out the business idea and showing how it is to be financed, marketed and put into practice. It is likely to be a crucial part of an attempt to raise finance from outside sources such as a bank.

Purpose

Starting a business is quite complex, as it requires a lot of different tasks to come together in a coordinated way at the right time. For example, if you are opening your first restaurant, all the following must be ready on the day before your opening night: building work, decoration, kitchen equipment bought and fitted, staff hired and trained, menu chosen and printed, wines chosen, delivered and wine list printed, food supplies bought, tills and credit card-reading equipment in place, and so on. For this to work without a clear plan is asking for the impossible. Therefore, a business plan seems essential for start-up success. Yet most entrepreneurs treat a business plan as something banks ask for (i.e. something for others, not for themselves).

Government figures show that, on average, new business entrepreneurs are white, male, in their mid 30s and have a university degree. As a consequence, many have built up the capital to start up without needing any external finance. Therefore they do not *need* a full business plan. As a result, the same government figures show that most businesses start up without a formal plan.

For a young entrepreneur, this would be virtually impossible. The need to find the capital to start up would make it crucial to have a plan persuasive enough to obtain funding. For most, that is the sole purpose of the plan: to obtain capital. This is a pity, because a good plan can act as the 'Satnav to success', steering the novice businessperson towards his or her goals.

The contents of a good plan

A good plan should be persuasive to an outside investor and useful to the entrepreneur. It should explain what makes the business special and help the entrepreneur to never lose sight of what he or she is trying to achieve. Despite this, it is clear that a business that needs capital will concentrate mainly on the outside investor. This might be a bank or (less likely) a 'dragon' type of investor who will buy an ownership stake in the business. A bank's main concern is that the start-up will be a safe investment, whereas a 'dragon' is mainly interested in the upside potential (i.e. the chance of making a huge profit).

The heart of the business plan should be based around **competitive advantage**. This means identifying the features of your own product/service that will make it succeed against competitors. This might be based on a unique idea, a better product/service or the protection provided by a patent or copyright. On the other hand, a business might decide to strip a product or service down, to make it possible to be the cheapest in the market. Ryanair's competitive advantage is based on being Europe's lowest-cost airline; this allows it to charge the lowest prices, yet still make a profit.

Every business plan should contain the following sections:

1 **Executive summary**: this should be short, but compelling enough to persuade the busy

banker to want to read on. It should say who you are, what the customer's pain is and how you will relieve it, why your team is ideal for the task, how much capital you need for the start-up, and how much you are putting in yourself.

2 The product/service: explain it from the customer's point of view – for example, with smoothies, don't say 'we'll crush fruit and put it in bottles', but instead say 'it'll provide busy people with two portions of fruit in an enjoyable, unmessy way'. If others already offer the service, you must explain what is different about your idea.
3 The market: focus on market trends rather than market size – whether the market is growing and, if so, how rapidly. You also need to provide a brief analysis of key competitors.
4 Marketing plan: how do you plan to communicate to the customers you are targeting? How expensive will this be? Within this section should be an explanation and justification for the prices you plan to set, plus a forecast of likely sales per month for the first two years.
5 Organisational plan: to explain who will be in the team and how they will be managed and organised. A CV should be provided for all key managers.
6 Operational plan: how will the product/service be produced and delivered? This might involve production in China, in which case you will need to have already made contact with willing suppliers.
7 Financial plan: the heart of this will be a cash flow forecast (i.e. a prediction of monthly cash out and cash in from the start of the business until at least two years after the firm has started trading). This will give an idea of the bank balances over the start-up period, and therefore the financing needs.
8 Conclusion: this will include some idea of the longer-term plans for the business, including any 'exit strategy', such as a plan to sell the business within five years.

A-grade application

Tom Doyle worked as a motor auctioneer for ten years before deciding to set up his own car dealership at the age of 28. He would specialise in German cars, especially BMWs, Audis and Volkswagen. He knew all the local garages and felt confident that he could get cars serviced, reconditioned and valeted to maximise the value added. The business model was simple: buy slightly run-down German cars at auction, get them revamped, then sell them at a higher price. He thought that he could make £300–£500 net profit per car.

Tom wrote up his plans with care, using a blank business plan from NatWest Bank. He made his sales forecasts and cash flow projections and committed himself to putting in half the £100,000 to start up the business. When he went to see the Regional Business Bank Manager, the conversation went well until it came to the financial needs. The Bank Manager thought Tom had underestimated the finance needed to run the day-to-day business. Tom was turned down because he'd asked for £20,000 too little!

Advantages and disadvantages of business plans

The key thing to remember is that the business plan is only as good as the information it contains. Since much of this will have to be estimated or guessed, it is clear that no one should treat a business plan as a factual document. Although a business plan may help steer the business in the right general direction, it would be an exaggeration to see it as a guarantee of success. Table 4.1 shows some of the advantages and disadvantages associated with business plans.

Table 4.1 Advantages and disadvantages of business plans

Advantages	Disadvantages
Forces the entrepreneur to think carefully about every aspect of the start-up, which should increase the chances of success	Making a forecast (e.g. of sales) doesn't make it happen; entrepreneurs sometimes confuse the plan with reality; poor sales can come as a terrible shock
May make the entrepreneur realise that he or she lacks the skills needed for part of the plan, and therefore try harder to employ an expert or buy in advice	Problems arise if the plan is too rigid; it is better to make it flexible, so that you are prepared for what to do if sales are poor (or unexpectedly high)
If the plan is well received by investors, they may compete to offer attractive terms for obtaining capital	Plans based on high sales will include lots of staff to meet the demand; risks are lower if the business starts with a low-cost/low-sales expectation
Many entrepreneurs have the whole plan in their head, not on paper; if illness or accident strikes, others will only be able to keep things going if there is a paper plan	Business success is often about people, not paper. An over-focus on a perfect plan may mean too little time is spent visiting suppliers or talking to shoppers

Sources of information and guidance

Government agencies

At the time of writing, the new coalition government has decided to scrap most of the agencies that have supported small businesses. Their view that they were poor value for money was shared by many. The key government agencies for the future are as follows:

1. The Department for Business, Innovation and Skills (BIS, formerly the DTI) runs the Small Firms Loan Guarantee Scheme, which encourages high street banks to lend to high-risk small firms. If the firm collapses, the government guarantees to pick up the bill. Any firm using this approach to borrow capital will have to pay an extra 2 per cent interest per year on the loan. Up to 75 per cent of a loan can be borrowed in this way (i.e. a high street bank has to be willing to put up 25 per cent).
2. Local Enterprise Partnerships, which are a local version of the previous Regional Development Agencies, such as the North-West RDA. The partnerships between local councils and local businesses will be charged with providing advice and help for new firms starting up. It is too early to be sure how effective this structure will be.

Banks

Banks claim to provide great help to new small businesses, but rarely do. The only thing they are all keen to help with is to provide a business plan toolkit. After all, they want you to open your business banking account with them. Just Google 'bank business plan' and you'll be able to choose from at least six options from the various major banks. New firms need a bank account, so banks are essential; it would be wrong to think, though, that small-scale entrepreneurs spend hours talking things through with their bank advisor or manager.

Accountants

For those with no business knowledge it might be helpful to get cash flow and profit forecasts checked by an accountant. For those who have studied Business Studies, this would be an unnecessary

Figure 4.1 An accountant can advise entrepreneurs on tax issues

expense. The only aspect of a business start-up that an accountant would be invaluable for is advice on tax issues. Should the business buy a van or lease it? Should the business start as a limited company or as a sole trader? These are technical questions that an accountant will be able to answer.

Small Business Advisors

Local Enterprise Partnerships should help put entrepreneurs in touch with a local advisor. A mentor is especially invaluable to a young person starting up in business – someone to turn to when the unexpected happens. Say you have opened a phone shop in the high street and a Carphone Warehouse opens next door six weeks later. It would be ideal to talk about what to do with a more experienced businessperson. The problem is that good people will not come cheap.

The Prince's Trust

The Prince's Trust works with unemployed or disadvantaged people up to the age of 30. It can lend up to £4,000 to a new business start-up, but probably more important is that the Trust insists that you regularly attend sessions with a (free) mentor. Due to the royal connections of the Trust, the mentors are often quite high-powered businesspeople, whose advice is invaluable. To find out more, go to www.princes-trust.org.uk.

Issues for analysis

Even if there's no point in having a business plan, it may still be valuable to have done one. For most, the business plan is likely to gather dust after it has served its purpose of raising finance. That may well be right, because the key thing is preparing it, not having it. Putting the plan together forces the entrepreneur to think about every aspect of the business and perhaps start to see a few cracks in their plans. If that is the case, the entrepreneur can put solutions into place now, before the business actually starts up. When the business starts, the figures in the plan will probably soon look silly – too high or way too low.

Business plans – an evaluation

To start a new business requires a great idea based on a strong understanding of potential customers and the competition. The entrepreneur also needs to have the personal qualities to build strong relationships with suppliers, retail buyers and staff. While drawing up a business plan may help in that process, there is a possibility that getting your head buried in paper plans may divert you from the important tasks. Business plans can help attract investment from outsiders and may help a disorganised entrepreneur make fewer mistakes, but it is no substitute for having strong enterprise skills.

Key terms

Competitive advantage: features of your product/service that make it stronger in the marketplace than your competitors.

Executive summary: brief highlights of a report, placed at the front, so that top executives can glance at the main points without having to read the whole report.

Revision questions (30 marks; 30 minutes)

1 Explain in your own words the meaning of the term 'business plan'. (3)

2 Why might young entrepreneurs need a business plan more than middle-aged ones? Briefly explain your answer. (3)

3 Some people think that a business plan aimed at 'dragon' investors should be different from one aimed at bankers. Outline two ways in which a plan aimed at investors might be different from one aimed at a banker. (4)

4 Why might an entrepreneur find it easier to write a business plan for a second business start-up than for his/her first? (4)

5 Re-read the list of advantages and disadvantages of business plans shown in Table 4.1 and decide whether the following entrepreneurs should take time to write out a full business plan. Explain your reasons.

   a) A 30-year-old, previously a teacher, who needs to borrow a small sum to help finance the launch of a night club. (3)

   b) A 50-year-old, previously an accountant, who can personally finance the start-up of a business producing digital radios. (3)

6 How might an accountant help someone draw up a good business plan? (3)

7 If you were to start your own business after completing your A-levels, do you think you would complete a business plan? Explain your answer with reference to your own strengths and weaknesses. (7)

Revision exercises

Data response

Extract from business plan for opening a Thai restaurant in Swindon

Figure 4.2 shows the cash flow forecast for the Thai restaurant in the first 12 months.

Financing requirement

The business will need £80,000 of start-up capital. The directors are investing £40,000 of their own funds, so we wish to borrow £40,000. As shown in the cash flow table, we will be able to repay the sum in full by the end of the first year of trading.

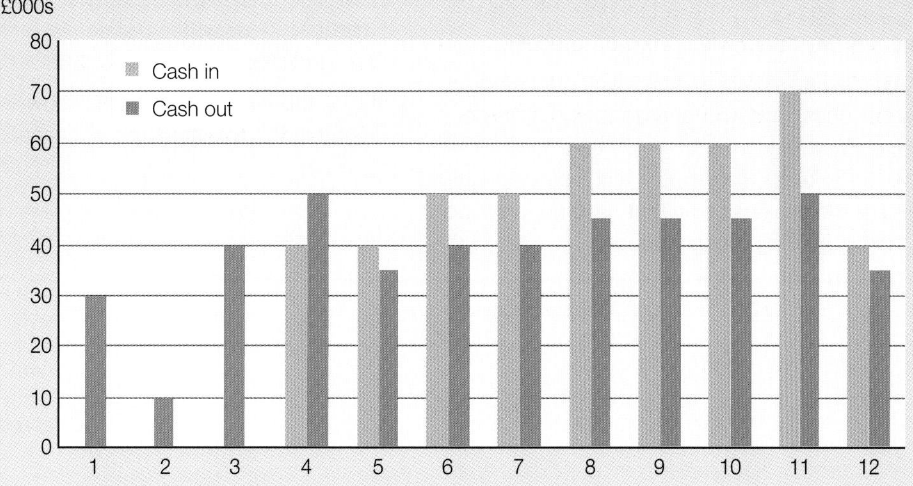

Figure 4.2 Cash in and cash out in first 12 months

Questions (20 marks; 20 minutes)

1 Look carefully at the graph for the first four months of the life of the business. Are the directors borrowing the right sum of money? Explain your answer. (4)

2 If the cash flow forecast proves correct, are the directors right to say that the £40,000 can be repaid by the end of the first year? Explain your answer. (4)

3 Discuss why a banker might be concerned to read 'As shown in the cash flow table, we will be able to repay the sum in full . . .'? (7)

4 Explain why the directors might be wise to borrow rather more capital than they believe they will need to finance the first year of the business. (5)

Data response

It's an almost irresistible combination: relaxation, pampering and calorie-free chocolate. That's what is being offered to customers of a brand new business aimed at smoothing away the stresses of everyday life for the women of the Black Country.

The chocolate therapy is the signature treatment offered by Judith Morgan, who recently launched her holistic therapy business, Bodessa, inside Petra's Hair and Beauty Salon at Hayley Green in Halesowen. After a hitch in supplies of the manufactured gel-based facial mask disrupted the business's first few weeks, Judith set about manufacturing her own Bodessa version.

Opening Bodessa is the culmination of 18 months of planning after Judith made a bold career change after 25 years in the catering industry. She has been encouraged by her husband, Brett, a graphic designer, who has produced some of her literature and designed her logo, and by Business Link West Midlands, who led her through the start-up process.

Judith's adviser acted as a sounding board for the new business and offered impartial advice, support and guidance to help Judith and Brett develop Bodessa. The adviser also helped Judith prepare the business plan that gave her a sound footing in starting the venture.

Judith added: 'The business plan advice was great. It allowed my husband and I to put together a plan that was very realistic, not just for the bank manager to be impressed with.'

Business Link West Midlands adviser, Bob Howard, said: 'As long as a company requires help they can come back to us. They know there's someone here for them who can keep giving them relevant information, perhaps guidance on training and maybe advice on gaining access to new finance to help them progress the business.'

(Source: *Express & Star*, Wolverhampton, 13 August 2007)

Questions (20 marks; 20 minutes)

1 Explain how Judith's start-up might have been helped by the business plan. (5)

2 Outline one feature of the start-up that raises questions about the effectiveness of this business plan. (3)

3 Examine two features of the start-up that might have been less effective without the help of Business Link West Midlands. (6)

4 From the evidence available, how likely is it that Judith's business will succeed? (6)

5 Key concepts in business start-up

Definition

Opportunity cost is the cost of missing out on the next best alternative; transforming inputs into outputs is the process of turning resources into finished products; risk is the chance of a misfortune occurring.

Opportunity cost

This concept will be useful throughout the A-level Business course and is at the heart of every business decision, from small to multinational companies. Opportunity cost can best be explained with reference to football club management: a new Premier League manager might be given a budget of £25 million to buy new players. The money could be spent on Carlos Tevez, or on five £5 million players such as Matthew Upson and Bobby Zamora. If the decision is made to buy the five good players, the opportunity cost is missing out on Tevez. The £25 million can only be spent once, so a judgement must be made about what is in the team's best interests.

Every business faces similar issues. Limited resources mean that hiring a marketing manager leaves less money to spend on a marketing campaign. For a start-up business, lots of money spent on a high profile opening party means less money to pay for staff training.

Figure 5.1 Buying an expensive player such as Carlos Tevez might be in the team's best interests

For a new business, the two most important resources are money and time and both of these have an opportunity cost. Time spent by an entrepreneur creating an attractive website might mean too little time recruiting and training staff, or too little time reflecting on priorities. The same issue arises with money: it can only be spent once.

It therefore follows that every business decision has an opportunity cost, measured in time, money and often both. The same is true in other walks of life. A Prime Minister focused on foreign policy may lose sight of the key issues affecting people at home. A Chancellor who spends an extra £10 billion on education may have to cut back on spending on the NHS.

For a new business start-up, the most important opportunity cost issues are as follows:

- Don't tie up too much capital in stock, as this cash could be used more productively elsewhere in the business.
- Don't overstretch yourself – good decisions take time, so make sure you are not doing too much yourself.
- Take care over every decision that uses up cash; at the start of a business it is hard to get more of it, but more is always needed.

Transforming inputs into outputs

Within every economy there are three sectors: primary, secondary and tertiary.

1 **Primary sector**: growing, fishing, farming, extracting or mining raw materials, such as wheat, cocoa, copper or gold. In less developed economies such as Sierra Leone or Malaysia, primary industries remain crucial. In Britain they represent fewer than 2 per cent of the jobs available. Nevertheless, everything we eat or wear starts with raw materials from the primary sector – some from the UK plus many that are imported from overseas.
2 **Secondary sector**: turning raw materials into finished, processed, probably packaged products. This sector includes all manufacturing, engineering, construction and the oil industry. Traditionally it is where value is added in the process of turning sheets of steel into cars, bundles of wheat into Weetabix or small pieces of plastic and metal into iPods.
3 **Tertiary sector**: the service sector, dominated by wholesaling and retailing, plus financial services, tourism and all the business services you can see in every High Street or in the Yellow Pages.

The importance of this distinction can be seen below. The primary producer only receives 5p for what is sold in a British supermarket for £1.75. The big winner in this case is the 'roaster' – the manufacturer such as Nestlé, who turns raw coffee into the branded product Nescafe. The journey from producer to Starbucks is even more stark, with the beans in a £2 latte yielding no more than 1p to the Kenyan farmer.

Table 5.1 The value chain in a jar of coffee

Producer sells for:	£0.05
World coffee price	£0.35
Roaster (e.g. Nestlé)	£1.20
Tesco store price	£1.75

(Source: Adapted from *Observer*, 25 February 2007)

In exams, it is important to highlight the differences between primary, secondary and tertiary producers (see Table 5.2).

Table 5.2 Primary, secondary and tertiary producers

Primary	Secondary	Tertiary
Rely largely on big buyers, such as manufacturers or big supermarket chains. May find that buyers force them to keep prices low	No direct contact with customers, so brand names are crucial for image and repeat purchase	Direct contact with customers, so well motivated, well trained staff are crucial for image and customer loyalty
Hard to make their products seem different from others, e.g. a kilo of wheat = same as anyone else's kilo of wheat	Can make products seem very different from rivals, e.g. the design and manufacturing quality in a BMW compared with a Ford	Making a service stand out can be done by clever planning or by effective marketing (e.g. 'Tesco: every little helps')
Location is rarely of importance, though the issue of **food miles** may start to make consumers prefer local suppliers	Factory location can be anywhere in the world, as long as the transport links are good and the right staff skills are available	Most service businesses have direct customer contact (plumber, retailer, café, pub, etc.) so location must be close to where customers live

Dealing with risk

Starting a business carries huge risks, both financial and emotional. The fear of failure is very off-putting as it can not only be embarrassing but also stressful. Academics at the American university MIT suggest that there are 14 key characteristics of successful entrepreneurs:

- Drive and energy
- Self-confidence
- High initial and personal responsibility
- Internal locus of control
- Tolerance of ambiguity
- Low fear of failure

- Moderate risk-taking
- Long-term involvement
- Money as a measure, not merely an end
- Use of feedback
- Continuous pragmatic problem solving
- Good use of resources
- Self-imposed standards
- Clear goal-setting

(Source: Jeffery Timmons and colleagues, MIT, quoted on the Open University website: www.open2.net)

Several of the above characteristics relate to risk, such as 'low fear of failure' and 'tolerance of ambiguity (uncertainty)'. Quite simply, individuals who fear the unknown will not start their own business.

Real entrepreneurs, though, have to deal with risk on a day-to-day basis. Every business decision is about the future, so every decision carries a risk that it will be wrong, or that circumstances will change to make it wrong.

Examples of business risk include:

- Stoner Builders wins its £26,000 quote for turning a derelict garage into an office. After four weeks' work, John Stoner realises that the problems of damp in the building are far more serious than expected. He ends up spending £31,000 in costs for £26,000 of revenue.
- Hiring a bright, lively young person with a track record of job-hopping, instead of an older, duller but safer person.
- Umbro, producers of the England kit, were left with huge stocks of unsold shirts when England crashed out of the 2010 World Cup.

To succeed, risks such as these should not cause the entrepreneur concern or sleepless nights. A builder should know that some contracts will go wrong and just make sure that enough profits are made overall to make up for the occasional dog. Every job selection decision is difficult, but it will rarely turn out right to always make the safe choice.

The general lesson is that risk is not something to be feared, it is simply part of business life. A good entrepreneur will be able to make risky decisions quickly, without dithering or getting stressed, and will have sufficiently good judgement to usually manage to get them right.

Figure 5.2 A good entrepreneur can deal with risk and still sleep at night

Key terms

Food miles: how far food has travelled before it reaches your plate (e.g. cherries available in winter – flown 8,000 miles from southern Africa, trucked 200 miles from airport to Tesco warehouse, then trucked 50 miles to the retail store. Food miles = 8,250, plus your five-mile journey to Tesco by car.

Goal-setting: setting targets that are challenging yet realistic.

Primary sector: companies and people working to extract raw materials from the earth or sea (e.g. fishing, farming and mining).

Secondary sector: businesses that transform raw materials into finished goods (e.g. car manufacturing or food processing).

Tertiary sector: companies and people who provide services, either to the public (e.g. retailing or dry cleaning) or to businesses (e.g. accountancy, solicitors).

Revision questions *(25 marks; 25 minutes)*

1 Explain in your own words why time is an important aspect of opportunity cost. (3)

2 Give two ways of measuring the opportunity cost to you of doing this homework. (2)

3 Outline one opportunity cost to a restaurant chef/owner of opening a second restaurant. (3)

4 State whether the following are P(rimary), S(econdary) or T(ertiary):
   a) Cadbury's chocolate
   b) Sainsbury's
   c) A pick-your-own strawberry business
   d) Ryanair (4)

5 If an exam question is about the location of a business, why is it important to know if the business is in the primary, secondary or tertiary sector? (3)

6 Why may a successful entrepreneur be good at 'moderate risk taking' rather than 'high risk taking'? (3)

7 Identify one risk from each of the following business decisions. Briefly explain what you think the risk is.
   a) Doubling the advertising budget when a firm's sales haven't increased compared with last year. (2)
   b) A bakery switching to a new supplier of flour. (2)
   c) An entrepreneur borrowing £80,000 secured against his house, when interest rates are low at 3.25%. (3)

Data exercises

Data response

James Sutton had a job as a Marketing Manager, paying £55,000 a year. His career prospects looked very good, yet he handed in his notice to start up his own online business. He knew that it would take him away from 9–5 work and towards the dedication of 8am until 9pm. If he took on a member of staff, the wage bill would rise by £16,000.

Questions *(10 marks; 15 minutes)*

1 Outline three opportunity cost issues within this short passage. (6)

2 Outline the possible impact on James of the increase in the workload. (4)

Data response

Taking risks

Bored with a dull psychology student conference she'd attended, teacher Sara Cardwell decided to run one of her own. She tracked down one of the country's leading marketing psychologists and built a programme around the parts of the subject A-level students enjoy most. Having set a budget for speakers (£2,000 per day), she contacted London's Westminster Central Hall. This would cost £6,000 for one day and could seat 2,000 delegates. Costs so far totalled £8,000 and she hadn't yet budgeted a penny for marketing. Mailing out to 3,000 schools in the southern half of the country would cost £1,400.

Sara started to get cold feet when she realised the huge costs involved. But she was driven on by a passion to provide a top-class conference. And, after all, if she charged £15 she would make a gross profit of at least £12 per person. Even if the hall was half full she should be able to make a profit. Her boyfriend believed that the risks were too great to be worth taking, but

Sara was convinced that her knowledge of the market would put her in a great position.

Questions (20 marks; 20 minutes)

1 Look back at the 14 characteristics of successful entrepreneurs and identify five of these shown by Sara. (5)

2 Sara suspects that, with just one advertising mail-out, she will only get 1,000 students. Should she risk another £1,400 by sending out another mailing? (7)

3 Discuss whether Sara's business idea was an example of moderate risk-taking. (8)

B3 Revision exercises

In 2002 a cooperative agreement between coffee farmers in 250 Ugandan villages broke down. It had taken years to put together, but disagreements made it collapse. The prize for a successful cooperative was to produce organic coffee beans grown to Fairtrade standards for partners such as Café Direct. This would ensure getting significantly higher prices for the raw coffee beans and also much better credit terms (i.e. being paid quickly to help with cash flow).

Over the next two years, countless hours of work were put into forming a new cooperative. In early 2004 the new 'Gumutindo'* coffee cooperative was Fairtrade certified. Over 3,000 farmers are now part of Gumutindo. They receive a guaranteed price of $1.26 per pound of coffee beans, whereas the world price has often been under $0.80 during the last 10 years. The extra (and stable) income should help the farmers, of whom only 25 per cent have running water and 79 per cent live in mud huts with iron sheet roofing. In future, the Fairtrade organisation will support the cooperative in starting up their own production plant – converting the raw coffee into packs of coffee ready for sale.

*Gumutindo means 'excellent coffee'

(Source: www.fairtrade.org.uk)

Questions (20 marks; 25 minutes)

1 Is the work of the Ugandan villagers in the primary, secondary or tertiary sector? (1)

2 What would be the opportunity cost of the farmers who put 'countless hours of work into forming a new cooperative'? (3)

3 Outline one risk for the farmers and one risk for the Fairtrade organisation in forming a new cooperative with guaranteed high prices for the coffee beans. (6)

4 a) Into which of the three sectors will the Gumutindo cooperative move if they start their own production plant? (1)

b) Discuss whether producing coffee ready for sale would definitely increase the income levels of the 3,000 members of the cooperative. (9)

Legal structure for business

Definition

The legal structure of a business is crucial in determining how serious the financial impact is on the owners, if things go wrong. It also has an impact on the taxation levels to be paid by the business and its owners.

Businesses with unlimited liability

Unlimited liability means that the finances of the business are treated as inseparable from the finances of the business owner(s). So, if the business loses £1 million, the people owed money (the creditors) can get the courts to force the individual owners to pay up, even if that means selling their houses, cars, etc. If the owner(s) cannot pay, they can be made personally bankrupt. Two types of business organisation have unlimited liability: sole traders and partnerships.

Sole traders

A **sole trader** is an individual who owns and operates his or her own business. Although there may be one or two employees, this person makes the final decisions about the running of the business. A sole trader is the only one who benefits financially from success, but must face the burden of any failure. In the eyes of the law the individual and the business are the same. This means that the owner has **unlimited liability** for any debts that result from running the firm. If a sole trader cannot pay his or her bills, the courts can allow personal assets to be seized by **creditors** in order to meet outstanding debts. If insufficient funds can be raised in this way the person will be declared **bankrupt**.

Despite the financial dangers involved, the sole trader is the most common form of legal structure adopted by UK business. In some areas of the economy this kind of business dominates, particularly where little finance is required to set up and run the business and customers demand a personal service. Examples include trades such as builders and plumbers, and many independent shopkeepers.

Figure 6.1 Forming a business partnership means skills and responsibilities can be shared but there are also disadvantages to consider

There are no formal rules to follow when establishing as a sole trader, or administrative costs to pay. Complete confidentiality can be maintained because accounts are not published. As a result many business start-ups adopt this structure.

The main disadvantages facing a sole trader are the limited sources of finance available, long hours of work involved (including the difficulty of taking a holiday) and concern with respect to running the business during periods of ill health.

Partnerships

Partnerships exist when two or more people start a business without forming a company. Like a sole trader, the individuals have unlimited liability for any debts run up by the business. Because people are working together but are unlimitedly liable for any debts, it is vital that the partners trust each other. As a result this legal structure is often found in the professions, such as medicine and law. If the partners fail to draw up a formal document, the 1890 Partnership Act sets out a series of rules which govern issues such as the distribution of profits.

The main difference between a sole trader and a partnership is the number of owners. The key advantages and disadvantages in forming a partnership are described below.

Advantages

- **Additional skills**: A new partner may have abilities which the sole trader does not possess. These can help to strengthen the business, perhaps allowing new products or services to be offered, or improving the quality of existing provision.
- **More capital**: A number of people together can inject more finance into the business than one person alone. This, plus the extra skills, makes expansion easier.
- **Shared strain**: The new partner will help to share the worry of running the business, as well as taking on a share of the workload. This should help to reduce stress and allow holidays to be taken.

Disadvantages

- **Sharing profit**: The financial benefits derived from running the business will have to be divided up between the partners according to the partnership agreement made on formation. This can easily lead to disagreements about 'fair' distribution of workload and profits.
- **Loss of control**: Multiple ownership means that no individual can force an action on the business; decision making must be shared.
- **Unlimited liability**: It is one thing to be unlimitedly liable for your own mistakes (a sole trader); far more worrying, surely, to have unlimited liability for the mistakes of your partners. This problem hit many investors in the Lloyds insurance market in the 1990s. Certain partnerships (called syndicates) lost millions of pounds from huge insurance claims and some investors lost their life savings.

Businesses with limited liability

Limited liability means that the legal duty to pay debts run up by a business stays with the business itself, not its owner/shareholders. If a company has £1 million of debts that it lacks the cash to repay, the courts can force the business to sell all its assets (cars, computers, etc.). If there is still not enough money, the company is closed down, but the owner/shareholders have no personal liability for the remaining debts.

To gain the benefits of limited liability, the business must go through a legal process to become a company. The process of **incorporation** creates a separate legal identity for the organisation. In the eyes of the law the owners of the business and the company itself are now two different things. The business can take legal action against others and have legal action taken against it. Each owner is protected by limited liability and their investment in the business is represented by the size of their shareholding. Limited liability sounds unfairly weighted towards the shareholders, but it encourages individuals to put forward capital because the financial risk is limited to the amount they invest.

In order to gain separate legal status a company must be registered with the **Registrar of Companies**. Two key documents must be completed:

1. **Memorandum of Association**: this governs the relationship between the company and the outside world. It includes the company name, the purpose of the company (often recorded simply as 'as the owners see fit'), limitation of liability and the size of the authorised share capital.
2. **Articles of Association**: these outline the internal management of the company, including the rights of shareholders, the role of directors and frequency of shareholder meetings.

The key advantages and disadvantages which result from forming a limited company are as follows:

Advantages

- Shareholders experience the benefits of limited liability, including the confidence to expand.
- A limited company is able to gain access to a wider range of borrowing opportunities than a sole trader or partnership. This makes funding the growth of the business potentially easier.

Disadvantages

- Limited companies must make financial information available publicly at Companies House. Small firms are not required to make full disclosure of their company accounts, but they have to reveal more than would be the case for a sole trader or partnership
- Limited companies have to follow more expensive rules than unlimited liability businesses (e.g. audited accounts and holding an annual general meeting of shareholders); these things add several thousands to annual overhead costs.

A-grade application

In 2003, Duncan Goose quit his job and founded One Water. He wanted to finance water projects in Africa from profits made selling bottled water in Britain. The particular water project was 'Playpumps': children's roundabouts plumbed into freshly dug water wells. As the children play, each rotation of the roundabout brings up a litre of fresh, clean water.

Duncan thought of forming a charity, but felt that the regulations governing charities might force it to be inefficient. So, for £125 he founded a limited company, Global Ethics Ltd. This enabled him to set the rules, for instance, that the shareholders receive no dividends and the directors receive no fees. But, of course, it also ensured that he and other volunteers who put time into One Water are protected, should something go wrong and big debts build up. Today, One Water is a major business trading internationally. It has funded more than 600 Playpumps, giving clean water to 1 million people, permanently.

Private limited companies

A small business can be started up as a sole trader, a partnership or as a private limited company. For a private limited company, the start-up capital will often be £100, which can be wholly owned by the entrepreneur, or other people can be brought in as investors. The shares of a private limited company cannot be bought and sold without the agreement of the other directors. This means the company cannot be listed on the stock market. As a result, it is possible to maintain close control over the way the business is run. This form of business is often run by a family or small group of friends. It may be very profit focused or, like Global Ethics Ltd, have wholly different objectives than maximising profit.

A legal requirement for private companies is that they must state 'Ltd' after the company name. This warns those dealing with the business that the firm is relatively small and has limited liability. Remember, limited liability protects shareholders from business debts, so there is a risk that 'cowboy' businesspeople might start a company, run it into the ground, then walk away from the company's debts. Therefore, cheques issued by a Ltd company are not as secure as cheques from an unlimited liability business. This is why, for example, many petrol stations have notices saying 'No company cheques allowed.'

Table 6.1 When should a business start up as a sole trader and when as a private limited company?

Sole trader	Private limited company
When the entrepreneur has no intention of expanding (e.g. just wants to run own restaurant in Warwick)	When the entrepreneur has ambitions to expand quickly and therefore needs it to be easier to raise extra finance
When there is no need for substantial bank borrowing (i.e. start-up costs are low)	When large borrowings mean a significant chance of large losses if things go wrong
When the business will be small enough to mean that one person can make all the big decisions	When the business may require others to make decisions (e.g. when the entrepreneur is on holiday or unwell)

Public limited companies

When a private limited company expands to the point of having share capital of more than £50,000 it can convert to a public limited company. The company can then be floated on the stock market which allows any member of the general public to buy shares in it. This increases the company's access to share capital, which enables it to expand considerably. The term 'plc' will appear after the company name (e.g. Marks and Spencer plc or Tesco plc).

The principal differences between private and public limited companies are:

- a public company can raise capital from the general public, while a private limited company is prohibited from doing so
- the minimum capital requirement of a public company is £50,000; there is no minimum for a private limited company
- public companies must publish far more detailed accounts than private limited companies.

Almost every large business is a plc, yet the process of converting from a private to a public company can be difficult. Usually, successful small firms grow steadily, perhaps at a rate of 10 or 15 per cent a year. Even that pace of growth can cause problems, but good managers can cope. The problem of floating on the stock market is that it provides a sudden, huge injection of cash. This sounds great, but it forces the firm to try to grow more quickly, otherwise the new shareholders will say: 'What are you doing with our cash?' (see the Application on Sports Direct).

Other problems with public limited companies

- When a firm becomes a plc, it becomes hard to hold on to any objective other than profit. This is because City analysts and business journalists criticise heavily any business that is not making more money this year than last. This pressure may have been the underlying problem that led BP to underspend on safety measures in America, leading to disaster in Texas in 2005 and in the Gulf of Mexico in 2010.
- The extent to which any one individual, or group, can maintain control of an organisation is severely limited by the sale of its shares on the stock exchange. For example, a family may find their influence on a business diminished when a listing is obtained. In turn, this means that publicly quoted companies are always vulnerable to a takeover bid. In 2009 the one-time family business Cadbury was swallowed up by a multi-billion pound takeover bid from the US giant Kraft.
- Shareholders are the owners of public limited companies, but they do not make decisions on a day-to-day basis. Many have little detailed knowledge of the firm's operations. Nor can they know the directors who, theoretically, they vote onto and off the Board. In fact it is usually the Chairman and Chief Executive who run the show. They have control, though the shareholders supposedly have the power. This situation is known as the **divorce of ownership and control**, and it may lead the directors to

A-grade application

Sports Direct

On 28 February 2007 Mike Ashley made over £900 million when he floated Sports Direct on the London stock market. Ashley had owned 100 per cent of Sports Direct, and sold 43 per cent of his shares at 300p a share. Within a few months, City analysts were troubled by the way Ashley was spending his money. He bought 3 per cent of the shares in Adidas, then made a takeover bid for Newcastle United. He also seemed desperate to spend Sports Direct's money, as it went on a shopping spree including Blacks Leisure, Field & Trek and the Everlast boxing equipment company. With so much going on, it seemed that no one was paying enough attention to the company's trading position. Revenues and profits dropped back and within six months of the float the shares had halved in value. By July 2010, three-and-a-half years after floating, the shares were 110p, giving shareholders a 63 per cent loss. By coincidence, Ocado was being floated on the stock market at the same time. Having never made a profit, this business was being valued at £800 million. Some analysts noted that this 'might be another Sports Direct'.

pursue the interests of their own careers and bank balances rather than the best interests of the business and its staff.

- A separate problem that may be caused by the divorce of ownership and control is **short-termism**. In private companies, where shareholders and directors are usually family members, the desire is to build a successful business to hand over to the next generation. This is how the great retail firms such as Sainsbury's and Marks and Spencer built themselves up. In plcs, the lack of concern about the long-term future of the shareholders may lead directors to focus too much on the short term. Much research has shown that British managers are more likely than others to focus upon short-term issues, possibly to the neglect of long-term investment in research and development (R&D) or staff training.

Other forms of business organisation

Cooperatives

These can be worker-owned, such as John Lewis/ Waitrose, or customer-owned, such as the retail Coop. Cooperatives have the potential to offer a more united cause for the workforce than the profit of shareholders. Workers at John Lewis can enjoy annual bonuses of 20 per cent of their salary as their share of the company's profits. The Coop has been less successful, though its focus on ethical trading has made it more relevant to today's shoppers.

Not-for-profit organisations

Mutual businesses

Mutual businesses, including many building societies and mutual life assurance businesses, have no shareholders and no owners. They exist solely for the best interests of members (i.e. customers). In the 1980s and 1990s, traditional mutual societies such as Abbey National and the Halifax were turned into private companies. Not one of these businesses survived the 2007–2009 Credit Crunch without being bailed out or taken over. Nationwide now says it is 'proud to be different', as it is still a true building society – it has no shareholders pressuring for profits.

Charities

Many important organisations have charitable status. These include pressure groups such as Greenpeace and Friends of the Earth, as well as conventional charities such as Oxfam and Save the Children Fund. Charitable status ensures that those who fund the charity are not liable for any debts. It also provides significant tax benefits.

Issues for analysis

When analysing which type of organisation is the most suitable for a business, consider the following factors:

- The financial risks involved: manufacturing businesses require heavy investment in plant and equipment before anything is available for sale and therefore a great deal of capital is put at risk. This suggests limited liability is essential. Some service businesses such as tax advisors or dry cleaners require relatively little capital outlay. If the owner intends to finance the start-up without any borrowings, there is no need to seek limited liability
- The image you wish to portray. Although cautious businesses may refuse company cheques, most people think *M. Staton Ltd* sounds more established and professional than *Mervin Staton*. In the same vein, a small software production company called TIB Ltd changed its name to TIB plc. They rightly thought it sounds bigger and more impressive. What's in a name? Ask Coca-Cola.
- An organisation considering a move to public company status and a stock market listing has far bigger issues to consider. It must weigh the benefits to be gained, particularly in terms of raising additional finance, against the costs incurred and the loss of control. Many business questions can be analysed fruitfully by considering the short versus the long term. Private (family) versus public (stock market investor) ownership is a classic case in point.

Choosing the right legal structure – an evaluation

Business organisation is a dry, technical subject. It does contain some important business themes, however, and three of these are particularly valuable sources of evaluative comment:

1. The existence of limited liability has had huge effects on business. Some have been unarguably beneficial. How could firms become really big if the owners felt threatened by equally big debts? Limited liability helps firms take reasonable business risks. It also, however, gives scope for dubious business practices – start a firm, live a great lifestyle, then go into liquidation leaving the customers/creditors out of pocket. Then start again. All too often this is the story told by programmes such as the BBC's *Watchdog*. Companies Acts try to make this harder to do, but it still happens. Such unethical behaviour is why government intervention to protect the consumer can always be justified.
2. Bill Gates and Richard Branson are worth billions of dollars. How can such wealth be justified for people who do not save lives (doctors) or help build them (teachers)? The answer lies in the risks involved in business. For every Richard Branson there are hundreds of thousands of small entrepreneurs who have sunk their life savings into a business and seen the savings disappear. Sadly, there are thousands every year who end up personally bankrupt. In other words, in a business world in which risk is ever-present, rewards for success should be accepted.
3. Short-termism is a curse for effective business decision making. There is no proof that a stock exchange listing leads to short termism, only the suspicion that in many cases it does. Of course, massive companies such as Unilever, Nestlé and Shell are likely to be above the pressures for short-term performance. In many other cases, though, it seems that British company directors focus too much on the short-term share price. Could this be because their huge bonuses depend on how high the share price is? Worries about shareholder pressures or takeover bids may distract managers from building a long-term business in the way that companies such as BMW and Toyota have done.

Key terms

Bankrupt: when an individual is unable to meet personal liabilities, some or all of which can be as a consequence of business activities.

Creditors: those owed money by a business (e.g. suppliers and bankers).

Incorporation: establishing a business as a separate legal entity from its owners, and therefore giving the owners limited liability.

Limited liability: owners are not liable for the debts of the business; they can lose no more than the sum they invested.

Registrar of Companies: the government department which can allow firms to become incorporated. Located at Companies House, where Articles of Association, Memorandums of Association and the annual accounts of limited companies are available for public scrutiny.

Sole trader: a one-person business with unlimited liability.

Unlimited liability: owners are liable for any debts incurred by the business, even if it requires them to sell all their assets and possessions and become personally bankrupt.

Revision questions (25 marks; 25 minutes)

1 Explain two differences between a sole trader and a partnership. (4)

2 In your own words, explain the importance of establishing a separate legal entity to separate the business from the individual owner. (4)

3 You can start a business today. All you have to do is tell HM Revenue & Customs (the 'taxman'). Outline two risks of starting in this way. (4)

4 Briefly discuss whether each of the following businesses should start as a sole trader, a partnership or a private limited company.

a) A clothes shop started by Claire Wells, with £40,000 of her own money plus £10,000 from the bank. It is located close to her home in Wrexham. (3)

b) A building firm started by Jim Barton and Lee Clark, who plan to become the number one for loft extensions in Sheffield. They've each invested £15,000 and are borrowing £30,000 from the bank. (3)

5 Explain the possible risks to a growing business of making the jump from a private limited company to 'going public', then floating its shares on the stock market. (5)

6 In what way may the type of business organisation affect the image of the business? (2)

Revision exercises

Data response

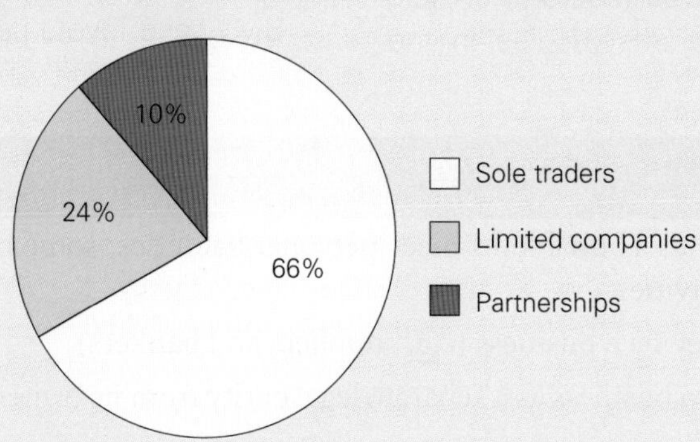

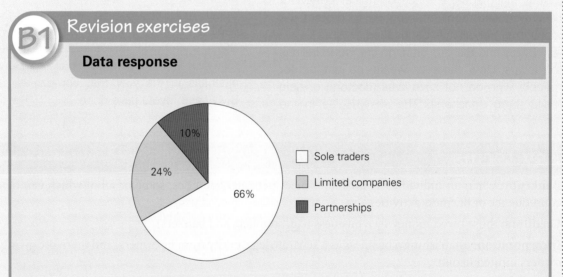

Figure 6.2 UK business organisations (total = 3,600,000)

(Source: Fraser, S. (2005). *Finance for Small and Medium Sized Enterprises: The United Kingdom Survey of SME Finances, 2004*, Warwick Business School)

Questions *(20 marks; 20 minutes)*

1 a) Using the information in the diagram, calculate the number of sole traders and the number of limited companies in the UK. (3)

b) Explain two possible reasons why there are so many more sole traders than companies. (6)

2 What proportion of British businesses operate with unlimited liability? (1)

3 Dr Fraser's research also shows that one in five businesses is principally owned by a woman and that 93 per cent are owned by white and 7 per cent by non-white ethnicity.

a) Examine two possible reasons why women are so much less likely to own a business than men. (6)

b) The percentage figures for non-white business ownership are slightly below the number of non-whites in the population (between 8 and 9 per cent). Outline two reasons that might explain this. (4)

Data response

In April 2007 Bernice Armstrong opened Devoted 2 Vintage in Hemel Hempstead, just north of London. She believed there was a gap locally for an independent shop buying and selling vintage clothes. Her own love of vintage clothes made her keen to start and gave her an insight both into sources of supply and in distinguishing desirable clothes from ones that should go to charity shops.

In 2007 celebrity magazines were full of swirly 1960s clothes, so Bernice made every effort to focus on 1960s originals, for example by Mary Quant, inventor of the mini-skirt. Her prices ranged from £10–£100, making the clothes affordable for most people. Over the following years Bernice focused her efforts on developing an online vintage clothing store. By 2010 the online store was pulling in an important slice of sales.

To follow up this story, go to www.devoted2vintage.co.uk

Questions *(20 marks; 25 minutes)*

1 a) The name of the business is Devoted 2 Vintage. Does that suggest it is a sole trader or a private limited company? (1)

b) Bearing in mind your answer to 1a), outline two factors Bernice should remember about the legal structure of the business she is running. (6)

2 As Bernice expands the business to develop online, should she consider changing the legal structure of the business? If so, why and how? (6)

3 Discuss how well Bernice has done so far in setting up her first business. (7)

7 Market research

Definition

Market research gathers information about consumers, competitors and distributors within a firm's target market. It is a way of identifying consumers' buying habits and attitudes to current and future products. Market research data can be numerical (e.g. 'What proportion of 16–24 year olds buy *The Sun* every day?') or psychological (e.g. 'Why do they buy *The Sun*?').

Conducting start-up market research

Where do you start? What do you need to know first? And how do you find it out?

The starting point is to discover the marketing fundamentals: how big is the market you are thinking about (market size), what is its future potential and what are the market shares of the existing companies and brands?

Market size means the value of the sales made annually by all the firms within a market. For example, in 2009 the UK market for yogurts and pot desserts was worth £1,974 million. Market potential can be measured by the annual rate of growth. In the case of yogurt, this has been at a rate of 4.5 per cent per year, by value. This implies that, by the year 2015, the potential market size will be over £2,550 million.

When looking at a completely new market, these statistics will not be available, so research may be needed into other indicators. For example, the producer of an innovative new fishing rod would find out the number of people who go fishing regularly.

Market shares are also of crucial importance when investigating a market, as they indicate the relative strength of the firms within the market. In 2009, 27 per cent of the yogurt market was held by Müller, making it the leading brand by far. A benefit it received for its strong market share was a distribution level of almost 100 per cent – nearly every grocery store stocked Müller. If one firm dominates, it may be very difficult to break into the market.

So how can firms find out this type of information? The starting point is **secondary research**: unearthing data which already exists.

Methods of secondary research

The internet

These days most people start by 'Googling' the topic. This can provide invaluable information, though online providers of market research information will want to charge for the service. With luck, Google will identify a relevant article that can provide useful information.

Trade press

All the above data about the yogurt market came from an article in *The Grocer* magazine. Every major market is served by one or more magazines written for people who work within that trade. Spending £2.40 on an issue of *The Grocer* provides lots of statistical and other information. Many trade magazines are available for reference in bigger public libraries.

Government-produced data

The government-funded National Statistics produces valuable reports such as the *Annual Abstract of*

Statistics and *Labour Market Trends*. These provide data on population trends and forecasts (e.g. for someone starting a hair and beauty salon, to find how many 16–20-year-old women there will be in the year 2015).

Having obtained background data, further research is likely to be tailored specifically to the company's needs, such as carrying out a survey among 16–20-year-old women about their favourite hair care brands. This type of first-hand research gathers primary data.

Methods of primary research

The process of gathering information directly from people within your target market is known as **primary research** (or field research). When carried out by market research companies it is expensive, but there is much that firms can do for themselves.

For a company that is up and running, a regular survey of customer satisfaction is an important way of measuring the quality of customer service. When investigating a new market, there are various measures that can be taken by a small firm with a limited budget:

- *Retailer research*: the people closest to a market are those who serve customers directly – the retailers. They are likely to know the up-and-coming brands, the degree of brand loyalty, the importance of price and packaging – all crucial information.
- *Observation*: when starting up a service business for which location is an all-important factor, it is invaluable to measure the rate of pedestrian (and possibly traffic) flow past your potential site compared with that of rivals. A sweet shop or a

Table 7.1 Pros and cons of primary and secondary research

	Primary research	Secondary research
Pros	● can aim questions directly at your research objectives ● latest information from the marketplace ● can assess the psychology of the customer	● often obtained without cost ● good overview of a market ● usually based on actual sales figures or research on large samples
Cons	● expensive: £10,000+ per survey ● risk of questionnaire and interviewer bias ● research findings may only be usable if comparable **backdata** exists	● data may not be updated regularly ● not tailored to your own needs ● expensive to buy reports on many different marketplaces

Table 7.2 Development stages for launch of Orange Chocolate Buttons

Development stage	Primary research
1 The product idea (probably one of several)	1 Group discussions among regular chocolate buyers – some young, some old
2 Product test (testing different recipes – different sweetness, 'orangeyness', etc.)	2 A taste test on 200+ chocolate buyers (on street corners or in a hall)
3 Brand name research (testing several different names and perhaps logos)	3 Quantitative research using a questionnaire on a sample of 200+
4 Packaging research	4 As 3
5 Advertising research	5 Group discussions run by psychologists to discover which advertisement has the strongest effect on product image and recall
6 Total proposition test: testing the level of purchase interest, to help make sales forecasts	6 Quantitative research using a questionnaire and product samples on at least 200+ consumers

dry cleaners near a busy bus stop may generate twice the sales of a rival 50 yards down the road.

For a large company, **primary research** will be used extensively in new product development. For example, if we consider the possibility of launching Orange Chocolate Buttons, the development stages plus research would probably be as shown in Table 7.2.

A-grade application

The Toyota MR2

When Toyota launched the MR2 sports car, sales were higher than expected. The only exception was France, where they were very poor. The Japanese Head Office asked the executives of Toyota France to look into this. Why had it been such a flop? Eventually the executives admitted that they should have carried out market research into the brand name MR2 prior to the launch. Pronounced 'Em–Er-Deux' in France, the car sounded like the French swear word 'merde' (crap).

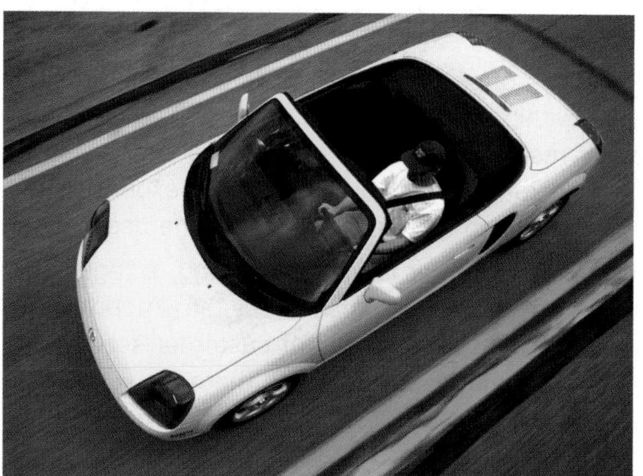

Figure 7.1 The unfortunately named Toyota MR2

Qualitative research

Qualitative research is in-depth research into the motivations behind the attitudes and buying habits of consumers. It does not produce statistics such as '52 per cent of chocolate buyers like orange chocolate'; instead it gives clues as to *why* they like it (e.g. is it really because it's orange, or because it's different/a change?). Qualitative research is usually conducted by psychologists, who learn to interpret the way people say things as well as what they say.

Qualitative research takes two main forms:

1 *Group discussions (also known as focus groups)*: free-ranging discussions led by psychologists among groups of 6–8 consumers. The group leader will have a list of topics to be discussed, but will be free to follow up any point made by a group member. Among the advantages of group discussions are: it may reveal a problem or opportunity the company had not anticipated; it reveals consumer psychology, such as the importance of image and peer pressure.
2 *Depth interviews*: informal, in-depth interviews between a psychologist and a consumer. They have the same function as group discussions, but avoid the risk that the group opinion will be swayed by one influential person.

A-grade application

Researching Morrisons

Following its successful re-launch in 2007, Morrisons was holding group discussions among its customers. One mentioned Tesco's 'Computers for Schools' initiative – and discussion turned towards 'Seeds for Schools', encouraging primary schools to have vegetable patches. Morrisons turned this idea into a nationwide 'Let's Grow' campaign, which 85 per cent of primary schools joined in with. 39 million vouchers were redeemed and Morrisons ended up generating £21 of sales for every £1 spent on the promotion. The whole marketing approach won Morrisons a gold medal at the 2009 IPA Effectiveness Awards (an advertising awards competition).

Table 7.3 Typical research questions to be answered by qualitative research and quantitative research

Qualitative research	Quantitative research
● Why do people *really* buy Nikes?	● Which pack design do you prefer?
● Who in the household *really* decides which brand of shampoo is bought?	● Have you heard of any of the following brands? (Ariel, Daz, Persil, etc.)
● What mood makes you feel like buying Häagen-Dazs ice cream?	● How likely are you to buy this product regularly?
● When you buy your children Frosties, how do you feel?	● How many newspapers have you bought in the past seven days?

Quantitative research

Quantitative research asks pre-set questions on a large enough sample of people to provide statistically valid data. Questionnaires can answer factual questions such as 'How many 16–20 year olds have heard of Chanel No 5?' There are three key aspects to quantitative research:

1 Sampling (i.e. ensuring that the research results are typical of the whole population, though only a sample of the population has been interviewed).
2 Writing a questionnaire that is unbiased and meets the research objectives.
3 Assessing the validity of the results.

Sampling

The two main concerns in sampling are how to choose the right people for interview (**sampling method**) and deciding how large a number to interview (**sample size**). There are three main sampling methods: random, quota and stratified sample.

Random sample

This involves selecting respondents to ensure that everyone in the population has an equal chance of being interviewed. This sounds easy, but is not. If an interviewer goes to a street corner one morning and asks passers-by for an interview, the resulting sample will be biased towards those who are not in work, who do not own a car and have time on their hands (the busy ones will refuse to be interviewed). As a result the sample will not be representative. So achieving a truly random sample requires careful thought.

Research companies use the following method:

- Pick names at random from the electoral register (e.g. every 50th name).
- Send an interviewer to the address given in the register.
- If the person is out, visit up to twice more before giving up (this is to maximise the chances of catching those who lead busy social lives and are therefore rarely at home).

This method is effective, but slow and expensive.

Quota sample

This method involves selecting interviewees in proportion to the consumer profile within your target market. Table 7.4 gives an example.

This method allows interviewers to head for busy street corners, interviewing whoever comes along. As long as they end up achieving the correct quota, they can interview when and where they want to. As this is a relatively cheap and effective way of sampling, it is the one used most commonly by market research companies.

Stratified sample

This approach involves only interviewing those with a key characteristic required for the sample. For example, the producers of Oil of Olay might decide only to interview women aged 30–45 (i.e. the potential buyers of the future). Within this stratum/section of the population, individuals could be found at random (hence *stratified random* sample) or by setting quotas based on factors such as social class and region.

Sample size

Having decided which sampling method should be used, the next consideration is how many interviews should be conducted: 10, 100, 1,000? The most high-profile surveys conducted in Britain are the opinion polls (e.g. asking people how they will vote in a general election). These quota samples

Table 7.4 An example of quota sampling

	Chocolate buyers	Adults Respondent quota (sample: 200)
Men	40%	80
Women	60%	120
Ages 16–24	38%	76
Ages 25–34	21%	42
Ages 35–44	16%	32
Ages 45+	25%	50

of between 1,000 and 1,500 respondents are considered large enough to reflect the opinions of the electorate of 45 million. How is this possible?

Of course, if you only interviewed ten people, the chances are slim that the views of this sample will match those of the whole population. Of these ten, seven may say they would definitely buy Chocolate Orange Buttons. If you asked another ten, however, only three may say the same. A sample of ten is so small that chance variations make the results meaningless. In other words, a researcher can have no statistical confidence in the findings from a sample of ten.

A sample of 100 is far more meaningful. It is not enough to feel confident about marginal decisions (e.g. 53 per cent of people like the red pack design, and 47 per cent like the blue one), but is quite enough if the result is clear cut (e.g. 65 per cent like the name 'Spark'; 35 per cent prefer 'Valencia'). Many major product launches have proceeded following research on as low a sample as 100.

With a sample of 1,000 a high level of confidence is possible. Even small differences would be statistically significant with such a large sample. So why doesn't everyone use samples of 1,000? The answer is money. Hiring a market research agency to undertake a survey on 100 people would cost approximately £10,000. A sample of 1,000 people would cost three times that amount – good value if you can afford it, but not everyone can. As shown in the earlier example of launching Orange Chocolate Buttons, a company might require six surveys before launching a new product. So the spending on research alone might reach £180,000, if samples of 1,000 were used.

Writing a questionnaire

Quantitative research is expensive and its results may influence major decisions such as whether to launch a new product. So a mistake in writing the questionnaire may prove very costly. For instance, the wording may influence respondents to sound more positive about a new product than they really feel. What are the key features of a good questionnaire?

- Clearly defined research objectives. What exactly do you need to find out?
- Ensure that questions do not point towards a particular answer.
- Ensure that the meaning of each question is clear, perhaps by testing (piloting) questions before putting them into fieldwork.
- Mainly use closed questions (i.e. questions with a limited number of pre-set answers that the respondent must tick); only in this way can you ensure quantifiable results.
- It is useful, though, to include a few open questions, to allow respondents to write a sentence or two, providing more depth of understanding.
- Ensure that the questionnaire finishes by asking full demographic and user details, i.e. the respondent's sex, age, occupation – and therefore social class – and buying habits. This allows more detailed analysis of sub-groups within the sample.

Other important considerations in primary research

Response rate

If a company sends out 2,000 questionnaires and only 200 people send back a response, the question must be asked: are those who respond typical of those who do not respond? Or is there a bias built into the findings as a consequence of the low response rate?

Face-to-face versus self-completion

In the past, most surveys were conducted by interviewers who asked the questions face-to-face. This had drawbacks such as cost and the risk of bias (e.g. a bubbly young interviewer may generate more positive responses). Clear benefits, however, included a high response rate and the assurance that the interviewer could help to explain an unclear question. Today, self-completion questionnaires, probably online, are increasingly common.

Market research today

Market research is increasingly influenced by technology. Instead of standing on windy street corners, interviewers are more likely to be sitting in a telephone booth in an office. There are also more and more internet opinion polls, in which a pop-up questionnaire appears on the screen. For instance, someone looking at the Amazon shopping site might be asked to answer questions about book-buying.

An even stronger trend is towards database-driven research. Instead of finding the right people by trial and error, client firms supply research companies with database information on current or ex-customers. Retailers such as Tesco and Sainsbury have millions of customer names on their databases, gained from customers' membership of 'loyalty card' schemes such as Tesco Clubcard. Shoppers are grouped into categories such as regular/irregular shoppers, petrol buyers, disposable nappy buyers and so on. If Tesco wants to survey customer satisfaction with their baby products section, they know exactly who should be contacted.

The future of market research is clearly bound up in technology. The basics will remain crucial, however: the avoidance of bias in the wording of questions, large enough sample sizes to provide valid data, and intelligent analysis of the research findings.

Issues for analysis

When developing an argument in answer to an exam question, market research offers the following main lines of analysis:

- the key role of market research in market orientation (i.e. basing decisions upon the consumer, rather than the producer's needs or opinions)
- the need for a questioning approach to data – when presented with a research finding one needs to know: was the sample size large enough? Who paid for the research? Businesspeople learn to ask questions about every 'fact' shown by research
- the importance of market knowledge: large, established firms have a huge advantage over newer, smaller firms because of their knowledge of consumer attitudes and behaviour, built up from years of market research surveys.

Market research – an evaluation

In large firms, it is rare for any significant marketing decision to be made without market research. Even an apparently minor change to a pack design will only be carried out after testing in research. Is this overkill? Surely marketing executives are employed to make judgements, not merely do what surveys tell them?

The first issue here is the strong desire to make sure that business decisions are as scientific as possible. In other words, to act on evidence, not on feelings. Quantitative research, especially, fits in with the desire to act on science not hunch. Yet this can be criticised, such as by John Scully, former head of Apple Computers, who once said 'No great marketing decision has ever been made on the basis of quantitative data'. He was pointing out that true innovations such as the Apple iPad were the product of creativity and hunch, not science.

The second issue concerns the management culture. In some firms, mistakes lead to inquests, blame and even dismissal. This makes managers keen to find a let-out. When the new product flops, the manager can point an accusing finger at the positive research results: 'It wasn't my fault. We need a new research agency.' In other firms, mistakes are seen as an inevitable part of learning. For every Sinclair C5 (unresearched flop) there may be an iPod (unresearched moneyspinner). In firms with a positive, risk-taking approach to business, qualitative insights are likely to be preferred to quantitative data.

Key terms

Bias: a factor that causes research findings to be unrepresentative of the whole population (e.g. bubbly interviewers or misleading survey questions).

Primary research: finding out information first-hand (e.g. Coca-Cola designing a questionnaire to obtain information from people who regularly buy diet products).

Sampling method: the approach chosen to select the right people to be part of the research sample (e.g. random, quota or stratified).

Sample size: the number of people interviewed; this should be large enough to give confidence that the findings are representative of the whole population.

Secondary research: finding out information that has already been gathered, e.g. the government's estimates of the number of 14–16 year olds in Wales.

A Revision questions *(35 marks, 35 minutes)*

1. State three ways in which a cosmetics firm could use market research. (3)
2. Outline three reasons why market research information may prove inaccurate. (6)
3. Distinguish between primary and secondary research. (3)
4. What advantages are there in using secondary research rather than primary? (3)
5. Which is the most commonly used sampling method and why? (3)
6. List three key factors to take into account when writing a questionnaire. (3)
7. Explain two aspects of marketing in which consumer psychology is important. (4)
8. Outline the pros and cons of using a large sample size. (4)
9. Identify three possible sources of bias in primary market research. (3)
10. Why may street interviewing become less common in the future? (3)

Revision exercises

Market research assignment

Hampton is a medium-sized producer of health foods. Its new company strategy is to break into the £400 million market for breakfast cereals. It has thought up three new product ideas that it wishes to test in research before further development takes place. They are:

1 *Cracker*: an extra-crunchy mix of oats and almonds
2 *Fizzz*: crunchy oats which fizz in milk
3 *St James*: a luxury mix of oats, cashews and pecan nuts.

The research objectives are to identify the most popular of the three, in terms of product trial *and* regular usage; to identify price expectations for each; to find what people like and dislike about each idea and each brand name; and to be able to analyse the findings in relation to consumers' demographic profile and current usage patterns.

Questions *(30 marks; 30 minutes)*

1 Write a questionnaire using the above details, bearing in mind the advice given in Section 7.5. (12)
2 Explain which sampling method you would use and why. (6)
3 Interview six to eight people using your questionnaire, and then write a 200-word commentary on its strengths and weaknesses. (12)

Data response

Each year more than £1,000 million is spent on pet food in the UK. All the growth within the market has been for luxury pet foods and for healthier products. Seeing these trends, in early 2008 Town & Country Pet Foods launched 'HiLife Just Desserts', a range of pudding treats for dogs. They contain Omega-3 but no added sugar and therefore have no more than 100 calories per tin.

Sales began well, especially of the Apple & Cranberry version. Now sales have flattened out at around £1 million a year and the company thinks it is time to launch some new flavours. Three weeks ago they commissioned some primary research that was carried out using an online survey linked to pet care websites. The sample size was 150.

The main findings were as follows.

1 Have you ever bought your dog a petfood pudding?

Never	Just once	Yes in past, but no longer	Yes, still do
61%	13%	12%	14%

2 Which of these flavours might you buy for your dog?

	Never	Might try	Might buy monthly	Might buy once a week
Muesli yogurt	61%	19%	15%	5%
Rhubarb crumble	43%	33%	22%	2%
Apples and custard	52%	34%	12%	2%

The marketing director is a bit disappointed that none of the new product ideas has done brilliantly, but happy that there is one clear winner. She plans a short qualitative research exercise among existing HiLife customers, and hopes to launch two new flavours in time for the annual Crufts' Dog Show in three months' time.

Questions *(20 marks; 30 minutes)*

1 Outline whether the sample size of 150 was appropriate in this case. (4)

2 Examine the marketing director's conclusion that 'none of the new product ideas has done brilliantly, but happy that there's one clear winner'. (7)

3 a) Explain one method of qualitative research that could be used in this case. (3)

b) Analyse two ways in which qualitative research might help the marketing director. (6)

C Essay questions *(40 marks each)*

1 'Market research is like an insurance policy. You pay a premium to reduce your marketing risks.' To what extent do you believe this statement to be true?

2 After ten years of rising sales, demand for Shredded Wheat has been slipping. Discuss how the marketing manager might make use of market research to analyse why this has happened and help decide the strategy needed to return Shredded Wheat to sales growth.

3 Steve Jobs, boss of Apple, once said that he ignored market research in the early stages of the iPod. He believes that research is useful in relation to existing products, but does not work with innovative new products.

a) Why may this be?

b) How could research be used to best effect for assessing new innovations?

8 Understanding markets

Definition

A market is where buyers meet sellers; examples include eBay or Smithfield meat market. The key elements within every market are its size (i.e. how much is spent by customers in a year), the extent to which it can be subdivided (e.g. the confectionery market into chocolate, sugar-based sweets and chewing gum), and the extent to which the market is dominated by one or two companies or brands.

Types of market

Local vs national

Most new small firms know and care little about the size of the national market. If you have just bought an ice cream van that you intend to operate in Chichester, it doesn't matter whether the size of the UK market for ice cream is £500 million or £600 million a year. Your concern is the level of demand and the level of competition locally. And you will probably be delighted if you achieve annual sales of £0.1 million (£100,000).

In the case of the market for ice cream in Chichester, there are several things to consider:

- How do locals buy ice cream at the moment? (Multipacks from supermarkets? Individual cones from ice cream stalls or vans?)
- How many tourists come to the city? Do they come all year round? What type of ice cream do they buy? Where do they buy it?
- How much competition is there? What do competitors offer and charge at the moment? Are there gaps in the market that you can move into?

Other firms are focused more on the national market. For example, Klein Caporn is a small food company that started in 2005. It produces high quality, high priced ready-to-eat meals. It started by targeting small grocers, but soon found that the sales volumes were too low to cover its costs. A sales breakthrough in Waitrose supermarkets was followed in 2007 by acceptance by Sainsbury's. This enables the company to deliver to just two warehouses, cutting business costs dramatically; then Waitrose and Sainsbury distribute to their local shops. So Klein Caporn has a national presence, even though sales remain well below 1 per cent of the market for ready meals.

To operate at national level, Klein Caporn has to deal professionally with the supermarket buyers and produce eye-catching packaging that can compete effectively with national and multinational competitors.

Physical and electronic (virtual)

In the past, all markets used to be physical. The London Stock Exchange was a place where buyers met sellers and face-to-face agreements took place. Similarly, auctions were physical, with bidders having to catch the eye of the auctioneer.

Today an increasing number of markets are electronic. The stock market exists only on computer screens, and the likes of eBay are transforming auction and other markets worldwide.

From a business point of view, the key factors about electronic markets (e.g. for finding hotel rooms or flights) is that:

- they are fiercely price competitive, so the companies supplying services have huge pressure to keep their costs as low as possible
- they do not rely on physical location (e.g. a business can easily be run from a bedroom, such as selling Wii computer games)
- the market is easy and quite cheap to enter, so new competitors can arrive at any time

- they provide a 'long tail' of competitive, profitable small businesses, able to carve their own little niche in markets; this is very difficult to achieve in the high street, where rents are so high that only big firms can afford them.

Factors determining demand

Demand is the desire of consumers to buy a product or service, when backed by the ability to pay. It is also known as 'effective demand' (i.e. only when the customer has the money is demand effective). Several factors determine the demand for a specific product/service.

Price

Price affects demand in three ways:

1. You may want an £80,000 Mercedes convertible, but you cannot afford it (i.e. the price puts it beyond your income level); the higher the price, the more people there are who cannot afford to buy.
2. The higher the price, the less good value the item will seem compared with other ways of spending the money (e.g. a Chelsea home ticket costing £48 is the equivalent of going to the movies six to eight times: is it worth it?). The higher the price of an item, the more there will be people who say 'it's not worth it'.
3. It should be remembered that the price tag put on an item gives a message about its 'value' (i.e. a ring priced at 99p will inevitably be seen as 'cheap', whether or not it is value for money), so although lower prices should boost sales, firms must beware of ruining their image for quality.

Income

The British economy grows at about 2.5 per cent a year. This means that average income levels double every 30 years. Broadly, when your children are aged about 16–18, you are likely to be twice as well off as your parents are today. Economic growth means we all get richer over time (and lazier, and fatter, and spend more time in traffic jams).

The demand for most products and services grows as the economy grows. Goods like cars and cinema tickets are '**normal goods**', for which demand rises broadly in line with incomes. In some cases it grows even faster, for example, if the economy grows by 3 per cent in a year, the amount spent on foreign holidays can easily rise by 6 per cent. This type of product is known as a **luxury good**.

Other goods behave differently, with sales falling when people are better off. These products are known as **inferior goods**. In their case, rising incomes mean falling sales. For example, the richer we get, the more Tropicana we buy and the less Tesco orange squash. As orange squash is an inferior good, a couple of years of economic struggle (and perhaps more people out of work) would mean sales would increase as people switch from expensive Tropicana to cheap squash.

Actions of competitors

Demand for British Airways' Heathrow–New York flights does not only depend on their price and the incomes of consumers. It also depends on the actions of their rivals. If Virgin Atlantic is running a brilliant advertising campaign, demand for BA flights might fall as customers switch to Virgin. Or if American Airlines pushes its prices up, people might switch to BA.

The firm's own marketing activities

Following the same logic, if British Airways is running a new advertising campaign, perhaps based on improved customer service, it may enjoy increased sales. In effect its sales will rise if it can persuade customers to switch from Virgin and American

Figure 8.1 Some markets boom at Christmas – such as toy sales

Airlines to BA. One firm's sales increase usually means reduced sales elsewhere.

Seasonal factors

Most firms experience significant variations in sales through the year. Some markets boom in the summer and slump in the winter, such as ice cream, soft drinks, lager and seaside hotels. Others boom at Christmas, such as sales of perfume, liqueurs, greetings cards and toys. Other products that have less obvious reasons for seasonal variations in demand include cars, cat food, carpets, furniture, TVs and newspapers. The variation is caused by patterns of customer behaviour; nothing can be done about that – a well-run business makes sure it understands and can predict the seasonal variations in demand, and then has a plan for coping.

Market size and trends

Market size is the measurement of all the sales by all the companies within a marketplace. It can be measured in two ways: by volume and by value. Volume measures the quantity of goods purchased, perhaps in tons, in packs or in units. Market size by value is the amount spent by customers on the volume sold. So the difference between volume and value is the price paid per unit.

Table 8.1 gives an example of some figures for the UK market for butter and spreads.

Table 8.1 UK butter and spreads market

2009/10 market by value	£1,093 million
2009/10 market by volume	415 million kilos
Average price per kilo	263.3 pence (£1093 /415)

(Reproduced from *The Grocer*, 3 July 2010. © William Reed Business Media Ltd.)

Market size matters because it is the basis for calculating market share (i.e. the proportion of the total market held by one company or brand). This, in turn, is essential for evaluating the success or failure of a firm's marketing activities. Market size is also the reference point for calculating trends. Is the market size growing or declining? A growth market is far more likely to provide the opportunities for new products to be launched or new distribution initiatives to be successful.

Recent figures and forecasts for the car market in China help show the importance of market trends. In 2001 the UK car market was four times bigger than China's. In 2005 China accelerated past Britain. Table 8.2 shows the forecasts for the coming years.

In 2009 China became the world's biggest car market. Clearly these figures show that success in China will be far more important to car firms than success in Britain.

Table 8.2 Sales of new passenger cars (actual and forecast)

Year	China	Britain
2007	6,000,000	2,400,000
2008	6,700,000	2,100,000
2009	10,300,000	2,000,000
2012 (forecast)	15,000,000	2,100,000
2020 (forecast)	25,000,000	2,400,000

(Source: Forecasts by industry experts)

Market share

Market share is the proportion of the total market held by one company or product. It can be measured by volume, but is more often looked at by value. Market share is taken by most firms as the key test of the success of the year's marketing activities. Total sales are affected by factors such as economic growth, but market share only measures a firm's ability to win or lose against its competitors. As

Table 8.3 Brands with the highest UK market share

Leading brand in its market	Sales of leading brand	Market size (by value)	Market share	Share of nearest competitor
Walkers Crisps*	£497 million	£2,171 million	22.9%	6.2%
Cadbury's Dairy Milk	£371 million	£3,069 million	12.1%	6.2%
Pampers	£277 million	£467 million	59.3%	21.5%
Actimel	£114 million	£248 million	45.9%	15.8%
Magnum Ice Cream	£88 million	£437 million	20.1%	7.4%

*Not including Sensations, Potato Heads or other Walkers brands

(Source: *The Grocer*, 19 December 2009, quoting from Nielsen)

shown in Table 8.3, rising market share can also lead to the producer's ideal of market leadership or market dominance. Cadbury's Dairy Milk has market leadership among confectionery brands. Pampers has market dominance in the UK market for disposable nappies. The five different brands in the table show the different levels of competition in different sectors.

There are many advantages to a business in having the top selling brand (the brand leader). Obviously, sales are higher than anyone else's, but also:

- the brand leader gets the highest distribution level, often without needing to make much effort to achieve it. Even a tiny corner shop stocks Whiskas as well as a 'Happy Shopper' own-label cat food. Success breeds success
- brand leaders are able to offer lower discount terms to retailers than the number two or three brands in a market. This means higher revenues and profit margins per unit sold
- the strength of a brand-leading name such as Wall's Magnum makes it much easier to obtain distribution and consumer trials for new products based on that brand name.

Market segmentation

Most markets can be subdivided in several different ways. If you go to WHSmith and look at the magazine racks, you will see the process in action. There are magazines for men and (many more) for women. Within the women's section, there are magazines for children, teens, young adults, the middle aged and elderly. Then there are magazines that target different interests and hobbies, from football to computer consoles to gardening.

Market segmentation is the acknowledgement by companies that customers are not all the same. 'The market' can be broken down into smaller sections in which customers share common characteristics, from the same age group to a shared love of Manchester United. Successful segmentation can increase customer satisfaction (if you love shopping and celebs, how wonderful that 'Look' magazine is for you!) and provide scope for increasing company profits. After all, customers may be willing to pay a higher price for a magazine focused purely on the subjects they love, instead of buying a general magazine in which most of the articles stay unread.

The keys to successful market segmentation are:

- research into the different types of customer within a marketplace (e.g. different age groups, gender, region, personality types)
- find out if customers have common tastes or habits (e.g. younger readers may be more focused on fashion and celebrities than older ones)
- devise a product designed not for the whole market, but for a particular segment; this might only achieve a 1 per cent market share, but if the total market is big enough, that might be highly profitable.

Issues for analysis

The key to analysis is precision. Terms such as inferior goods and normal goods have to be understood so well that you spot where they are relevant and are able to use them to develop your answer. Every student would recognise that a Mercedes sports car is a luxury product, but not all could continue by saying that its sales will therefore grow especially fast when times are good, but may slump when the economy is struggling.

To analyse the market that a business is operating in, be sure to consider the market size, trends and share, the degree of segmentation, the factors determining demand and the type of market (e.g. local versus national). This is a powerful combination of concepts that should provide a lot of scope for analytic answers.

Understanding markets – an evaluation

Almost every large business carries out detailed market analysis on a regular basis by buying 'retail audits' to find out how retail sales are doing. It can be said, though, that some managers suffer from 'paralysis by analysis'. In other words, they gather so much data (some of it conflicting) that they end up unable to make a decision. Contrast this approach with that of Apple boss, Steve Jobs, who focuses on understanding customers, not analysing the market as it stands at present. He believes that Apple can always stay one step ahead, by thinking about what customers will want in future. Given Apple's success, it is hard to argue with him.

Key terms

Inferior goods: products that people turn to when they are less well off, and turn away from when they are better off (e.g. Tesco Value baked beans instead of Heinz).

Luxury goods: Products that people buy *much* more of when they are better off (e.g. jewellery, sports cars and holidays at luxury hotels).

Normal goods: Products or services for which sales change broadly in line with the economy (i.e. if the economy grows by 3 per cent, sales of say travel and fast food rise by 3 per cent).

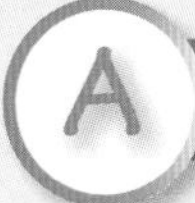

Revision questions *(35 marks, 35 minutes)*

1 Outline three features of the market for fast food near to where you live. (6)

2 Pages 59–60 list five factors determining the demand for a product: price, income, actions of competitors, marketing activities and seasonality. Identify which two of these would most heavily affect sales of:

a) Strawberries

b) EasyJet tickets to Barcelona

c) Tickets to see Newcastle United

d) DFS Furniture (8)

3 Explain in your own words the difference between market size by volume and market size by value. (2)

4 a) Toyota's share of the UK car market is about 6 per cent. If it continues with that share, how many UK car sales would that amount to in 2020; and how many Toyota cars would be sold in China in 2020, assuming the same market share? (4)

b) Outline two ways Toyota might respond to that sales difference. (4)

5 Why might a shoe shop focusing on 'Little Feat' be able to charge higher prices per pair than a general shoe shop? (2)

6 Explain in your own words how the market for shoes could be segmented. (3)

7 Look at Table 8.3. Discuss which business should be happier with its market position: Walkers or Pampers. (6)

Revision exercises

Data response

In late August 2007 entertainment retailer ChoicesUK called in the receivers. It was unable to continue trading after losing money consistently during 2007. As many as 1,700 jobs were threatened at ChoicesUK's 200 branches.

This came on top of the collapse of Fopp music retailers earlier in the year. At the same time, industry giant HMV suffered a halving of its profits. The reason was the same – the collapse in the total market for CDs and DVDs, compounded by a switch to buying online or downloading. The UK CD market, for example, fell by 10 per cent in the first half of 2007.

Questions *(15 marks; 15 minutes)*

1 Outline two reasons why a whole market may shrink in size, as happened to CD sales in the first half of 2007. (4)

2 ChoicesUK collapsed as the market declined. Explain two ways in which it might have set about boosting its market share (to combat the decline in the market as a whole). (6)

3 In the past, more than half the annual sales of ChoicesUK have taken place in the three months before Christmas. Should the directors have kept the business going a few months more? (5)

Data response

Lidl and Aldi winning grocery wars

Discount grocers are the big winners in 2007, TNS Worldpanel figures show. The grocery market grew by 4% year-on-year in the 12 weeks to 16 July 2007. Tesco, Sainsbury's and Asda all grew slightly faster than the total market, while Somerfield sales actually fell by 6%. Lidl and Aldi bucked the trend with sales growth of 13% and 11% respectively. Iceland also performed well, growing by 12%. Perhaps these three low-cost grocers benefited from the collapse of Kwik-Save.

The changes leave Tesco as the market leader with 31.5% (unchanged on 2006), while Asda's share grew from 16.6% to 16.7% and Sainsbury's from 16% to 16.2%. Morrisons suffered a fall in market share, from 11.3% to 11.1%. A decline of 0.2% may seem trivial, but as the value of the UK grocery market is £128.2 billion a year, 0.2% market share represents sales of £256.4 million!

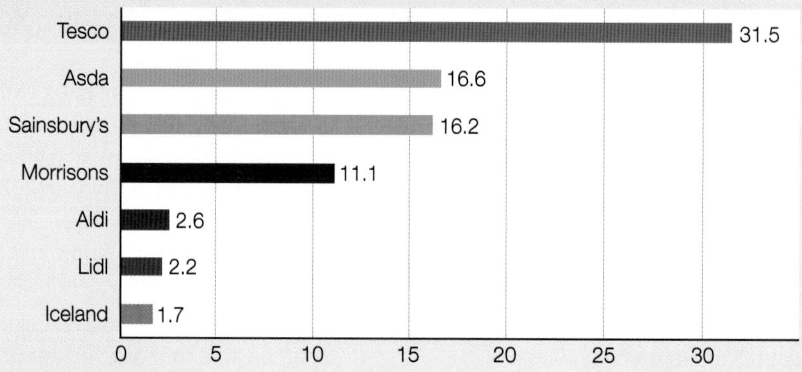

Figure 8.2 UK grocery market share, 2007

(Source: TNS Worldpanel and Nielsen, quoted in *The Grocer*, 28 July 2007)

Table 8.4 Percentage change in sales (2007 compared to 2006)

	Percentage change
Tesco	+5
Sainsbury's	+6
Asda	+6
Morrisons	+2
Somerfield	−6
Aldi	+11
Lid	+13
Iceland	+12

(Source: TNS Worldpanel and Nielsen, quoted in *The Grocer*, 28 July 2007)

Questions *(30 marks; 30 minutes)*

1 a) What was the grocery market size and market growth in 2007? (2)

b) Identify three possible reasons why sales at Somerfield actually fell in 2007. (3)

2 a) Show your workings to calculate that a 0.2% share of the UK Grocery market equals £256.4 million. (3)

b) Use the figures and the bar chart to work out the value of the UK 2007 sales of Lidl. (2)

c) Examine two *possible* reasons why Lidl enjoyed the biggest sales growth within the grocery market in 2007. (6)

3 a) Outline **two** ways in which Tesco may benefit from being the grocery market leader. (4)

b) Ten years ago, Sainsbury's was the UK grocery market leader. Discuss whether it could return to that position within the next 10 years. (10)

Sources of finance

Definition

All businesses need money. Where the money comes from is known as 'sources of finance'.

The need for finance

Starting up

New businesses starting up need money to invest in long-term assets such as buildings and equipment. They also need cash to purchase materials, pay wages and to pay the day-to-day bills such as water and electricity. Inexperienced entrepreneurs often underestimate the capital needed for the day-to-day running of the business. Generally, for every £1,000 required to establish the business, another £1,000 is needed for the day-to-day needs.

Growing

Once the business is established there will be income from sales. If this is greater than the operating costs, the business will be making a profit. This should be kept in the business and used to help the business to grow. Later on, the owners can draw money out of the business, but at this stage as much as possible should be left in. Even so, there may not be enough to allow the business to grow as fast as it would like to. It may need to find additional finance and this will probably be from external sources.

Other situations

Businesses may also need finance in other circumstances. They may have a cash flow problem caused by changes in market conditions. A major customer may refuse to pay for the goods, causing a huge gap in cash inflows. Or there may be a large order, requiring the purchase of additional raw materials. In all these cases, businesses will need to find additional funding.

Internal and external sources of finance

Finance for business comes from two main sources: inside the business (known as 'internal sources of finance' and outside the business (known as 'external sources of finance').

Internal sources

- Existing capital can be made to stretch further. The business may be able to negotiate to pay its bills later or work at getting cash in earlier from customers; the average small firm waits 75 days to be paid (i.e. two and a half months); if that period of time could be halved, it would provide a huge boost to cash flow.
- Nothing soothes a difficult cash situation better than profit. It is also the best (and most common) way to finance investment into a firm's future. Research shows that over 60 per cent of business investment comes from reinvested profit.

External sources

If the business is unable to generate sufficient funds from internal sources then it may need to look to external sources. There are two sources of external capital: loan capital and share capital.

Loan capital

- The most usual way of obtaining loan capital is through borrowing from a bank, either in the form of a bank loan or an overdraft. A loan is usually for a set period of time. It may be short term (one or two years), medium term (three to five years) or long term (more than five years). The loan can either be repaid in instalments over time or at the end of the loan period. The bank will charge interest on the loan. This can be fixed or variable. The bank will demand **collateral** to provide security in case the loan cannot be repaid.

- An overdraft is a very short-term loan. It is a facility that allows the business to be 'overdrawn'. This means that the account is allowed to go 'into the red'. The length of time that this runs for will have to be negotiated. The interest charges on overdrafts are usually much higher than on loans.

Share capital

- Alternatively, if the business is a limited company it may look for additional share capital. This could come from private investors or **venture capital** funds. Venture capital providers are interested in investing in businesses with dynamic growth prospects. They are willing to take a risk on a business that may fail, or may do spectacularly well. They believe that if they make ten investments, five can flop and four can do reasonably well, as long as one does fantastically. Peter Theil, the original investor in Facebook, probably turned his $0.5 million investment into $200 million or more (i.e. made a profit of 39,900%!)
- Once it has become a public limited company (plc), the business may consider floating on the stock exchange. For smaller businesses this will usually be on the Alternative Investment Market (AIM).

A-grade application

Financing growth

How do rapidly growing small firms finance their growth? By venture capital? By loans? To find an answer to this question, Hamish Stevenson from Templeton College, Oxford, looked at 100 of the fastest growing UK firms. One of these is R Frazier, a firm which recycles computers. Its sales grew from £294,000 to £7,400,000 in just three years. In common with the majority of the firms, R Frazier's early growth was self-funded, in other words from reinvested profits and trade credit. 'These are the real entrepreneurs,' says Stevenson. 'They grab money where they can. It is fly-by-the-seat-of-their-pants finance.' The 54 firms which used this method were doing so 'through default not by design', according to the research. In other words they had no alternative.

Twenty-one of the firms received external finance from share capital: 15 from venture capital houses and six from business angels. Just ten used long-term bank debt. Having survived, even thrived, through these hectic early years, as many as 40 of the firms are looking at, or in the process of, floating their firms on the London **stock market**. This would secure the finance for the next stage of growth.

How much finance can the business obtain?

The type and amount of finance that is available will depend on several factors. These are as follows.

- *The type of business*: a sole trader will be limited to the capital the owner can put into the business plus any money he or she is able to borrow. A limited company will be able to raise share capital. In order to become a plc it will need to have share capital of £50,000+ and have a track record of success. This will make borrowing easier.
- *The stage of development of the business*: a new business will find it much harder to raise finance than an established firm. As the business develops it is easier to persuade outsiders to invest in the business. It is also easier to obtain loans as the firm has assets to offer as security.
- *The state of the economy*: when the economy is booming, business confidence will be high. It will be easy to raise finance, both from borrowing and from investors. It will be more difficult for businesses to find investors when interest rates are high. They will invest their money in more secure accounts such as building societies. Higher interest rates will also put up the cost of borrowing. This will make it more expensive for the business to borrow.

Advantages and disadvantages of sources of finance

Internal sources

Reinvested profit

The profit generated by the business will provide a return for the investors in the business and can be ploughed back into the business to help it to grow. The advantage of reinvested profit is that it does not have an associated cost. Unlike loans it does not have to be repaid and there are no interest charges. The disadvantage is that it may be limited so will constrain the rate of business expansion.

Cash squeezed out of day-to-day finances

By cutting stocks, chasing up customers or delaying payments to suppliers, cash can be generated. This has the advantage of reducing the amount that needs to be borrowed. However, this is a very short-term solution and if the cash is taken from working capital for a purpose such as buying fixed assets, the firm may find itself short of day-to-day finance.

Sale of assets

An established business has assets and these can be sold to raise cash. The business loses the asset but has the use of the cash. It makes good business sense for businesses to dispose of underused assets as they can finance development without extra borrowing. If the asset is needed, it may be possible to sell it, but immediately lease it back. In this way, the business has use of the money and the asset. This is known as sale and leaseback.

External sources

Bank overdrafts

This is the commonest form of borrowing for small businesses. The bank allows the firm to overdraw up to an agreed level. This has the advantage that the firm only needs to borrow when and as much as it needs. It is, however, an expensive way of borrowing, and the bank can insist on being repaid within 24 hours.

Trade credit

This is the simplest form of external financing. The business obtains goods or services from another business but does not pay for these immediately. The average credit period is two months. It is a good way of boosting day-to-day working capital. A disadvantage might be that other businesses may be reluctant to trade with the business if they do not get paid in good time.

Venture capital

This is a way of obtaining outside investment for businesses that are unable to raise finance through

A-grade application

Council's *Dragons' Den*-style backing creates 405 jobs

Many small businesses complain that the knock-on effect of the banking crisis is that it is much harder to get loans from banks. Cardiff City Council has come up with an innovative way of helping some of those businesses in its area. It has set up a 'Dragons' Den'-style investment scheme working alongside its other business initiatives.

Deputy leader Neil McEvoy presented the results of the first year of the Capital Cardiff Fund. 32 companies have been assisted with a total of £655,143 through grants, loans and, in the case of two companies, MedaPhor and Q Chip, direct investment through buying an equity stake.

It is anticipated that the cash will create 405 jobs.

Mr McEvoy said he wanted to move the council away from giving money to businesses through grants and hoped to buy more equity stakes to ensure there was a direct return to the taxpayer. He said: 'There has been a change in culture. This is a complete reversal of what we used to do. Going forward, I want to use loans and equity instead of grants to fund businesses. We should get something back for the public purse.'

Describing the current use of non-repayable grants to encourage investment as a 'dependency culture', he said: 'We need to move away from that and get something back for our money.'

The cash the city has doled out to businesses so far has gone to 32 firms involved in sectors from creative industries to bioscience, IT, manufacturing, food, training and financial services.

(Source: From an article by David James, *South Wales Echo*, 11 June 2010)

the stock markets or loans. Venture capitalists invest in smaller, riskier companies. To compensate for the risks, venture capital providers usually require a substantial part of the ownership of the company. They are also likely to want to contribute to the running of the business. This dilutes the owner's control but brings in new experience and knowledge. The term 'dragon' became a well known term for a venture capital provider thanks to the BBC TV series *Dragons' Den*.

Finance should be adequate and appropriate

Having adequate funding means ensuring the business has sufficient access to finance to meet its current and future needs. This is a major issue for new firms and for those that are expanding rapidly. When a business expands without sufficient finance, it is known as **overtrading**.

Appropriate financing means matching the type of finance to its use. A distinction is made in company financing between short- and long-term finance (see Figure 9.1). Short-term finance is usually considered to be for less than one year; medium-term is three to five years; long-term finance is longer than five years.

Short-term finance should not be used to finance long-term projects. Using short-term finance such as overdrafts puts continual pressure on the company's cash position. An overdraft should only be used to cope with ups and downs in cash flows. By its very nature, growth is a long-term activity, so appropriate long-term finance should be sought to fund it.

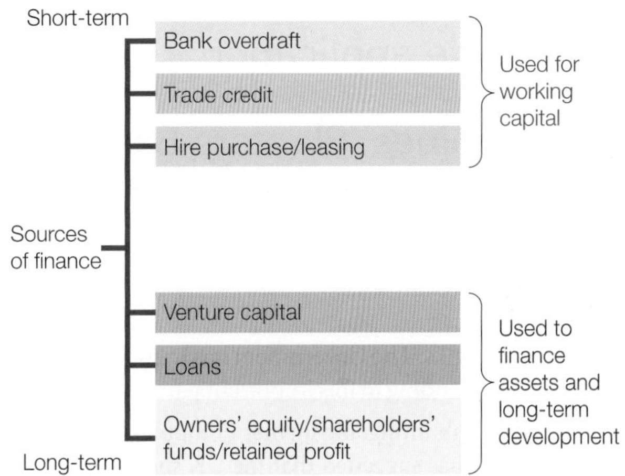

Figure 9.1 Short- and long-term sources of finance

A-grade application

Northern Rock

The effects of the banking crisis in 2007/2008 are still being felt in 2010 and will continue to affect many economies for many years. Banks have long been seen as organisations that give financial advice to business and private customers. It was ironic that not only had they made rash decisions regarding investments but that they proved in some cases to be incapable of managing their own affairs. Northern Rock was a prime example. In September 2007 it became the first British bank in 150 years to suffer a 'run on the bank', as savers feared for the bank's solvency. Northern Rock had expanded rapidly, financing its long-term growth with short-term finance; when the finance dried up, the bank collapsed. The business proved to have neither adequate nor appropriate finance. The crisis was averted only when the Bank of England guaranteed that no customer would lose their money.

Figure 9.2 Queues outside Northern Rock

Issues for analysis

When analysing or suggesting appropriate sources of finance, ask yourself the following questions.

- Why is the business seeking finance? The key here is to ensure that the finance is suitable for the business in its particular circumstances. A new business will have very different needs to a growing business. Remember the finance should be adequate and appropriate.
- Is the business stable or risky? If risky, the form of financing should be as safe as possible. Remember that financial institutions are unlikely to lend to risky or unproven enterprises.
- What is the owner's attitude to sharing the business? If the owners are reluctant to lose control of the business, it is not a good idea to suggest raising finance by selling more shares. Financing growth by borrowings may be more appropriate.

A-grade application

Philippines' Planters Bank a model for small business banking

There has been much talk following the 'credit crunch' of the difficulties that small businesses face in getting loans from the banks. The Government has tried to force banks to increase lending to this important part of the economy.

Jesus Tambunting, the former Philippines ambassador to the UK, has suggested that the UK should look to the Philippines for a banking model that lends effectively to small businesses. Mr Tambunting is the chairman of Planters Bank, which lends to the owners of small- and medium-sized businesses (SMEs) in the Philippines.

He said that banks had to get back to 'basic banking' and that more dedicated small business banks should emerge so that customers could be better served. 'It's not viewed as commercially viable by the banks,' he said. 'You need an institution like us that's totally focused on SMEs. If you have a regular bank it is not going to work.'

'Admittedly it is not easy to lend to SMEs. We charge a higher rate but it's to compensate for a lot of the work. We are doing a lot of hand-holding. They may be first-time borrowers. We try to educate them about what you need in a bank to approve a loan.'

Planters' loans typically range in size from $10,000 to $1m. Where businesses do not have collateral, Planters makes use of loan guarantee schemes run by the Philippines Government, which are similar to the UK's Enterprise Finance Guarantee.

(Source: www.Telegraph.co.uk, 10 June 2010)

Sources of finance – an evaluation

Finding finance may involve balancing conflicting interests. Internal sources of finance may be too limited to provide opportunities for business development. Obtaining external finance increases the money available, but has its downsides. Borrowing too much can be risky. Raising extra share capital dilutes the control held by existing shareholders.

Having adequate and appropriate finance at each stage in the business's development will ensure it stays healthy. Decisions about where to obtain the finance will be a matter of considering the business objectives, the stage of development of the business and the reasons for the funding requirement.

Key terms

Collateral: an asset used as security for a loan. It can be sold by a lender if the borrower fails to pay back a loan.

Overtrading: when a firm expands without adequate and appropriate funding.

Public limited company (plc): a company with limited liability and shares which are available to the public. Its shares can be quoted on the stock market.

Share capital: business finance that has no guarantee of repayment or of annual income, but gains a share of the control of the business and its potential profits.

Stock market: a market for buying and selling company shares. It supervises the issuing of shares by companies. It is also a second-hand market for stocks and shares.

Venture capital: high-risk capital invested in a combination of loans and shares, usually in a small, dynamic business.

Revision questions *(20 marks; 30 minutes)*

1 Describe the problem caused to a company if a major customer refuses to pay a big bill. (3)

2 Why do banks demand collateral before they agree to provide a bank loan? (2)

3 Outline two ways in which businesses can raise money from internal sources. (4)

4 What information might a bank manager want when considering a loan to a business? (4)

5 Read the Application report on Northern Rock. Explain the two mistakes made by the bank. (4)

6 Outline two sources of finance that can be used for long-term business development. (4)

7 Explain why a new business might find it difficult to get external funding for its development. (5)

8 Outline one advantage and one disadvantage of using an overdraft. (4)

Revision exercises

Data response

Odd Jobs Ltd

Jeff Hale was made redundant from his job in the printing industry at the age of 51. Having worked with the firm since he was 15, he received a small pension that would be paid straightaway and a lump sum redundancy payment of £30,000.

He decided to set up a business called Odd Jobs Ltd. The idea was to fill the gap in the market between the DIY enthusiast and general builders. He knew from experience that it was often very difficult to get a builder to come and do the smaller jobs.

He set up the business as a limited company with a friend, Malcolm Baines, who had also been made redundant. They each invested £20,000 of their redundancy money. The remainder they used to reduce their mortgages to take some financial pressure off them while the business was becoming established. They rented a small office and a van and bought tools and office equipment. After making their purchases they were confident that they had sufficient working capital to finance the business until it became profitable.

Their policy was to charge a reasonable rate for the job. They had a fixed scale of charges for run-of-the-mill jobs and gave a detailed estimate for any more complicated work.

They soon got a reputation for good quality work and after six months they found that they no longer needed to advertise. They resisted the temptation to do larger jobs, preferring to keep to their original idea. Most jobs took less than half a day to complete.

Seven years later they now employ two office staff and a team of four other workers. They have bought three vans with the help of a £40,000 bank loan. Each van is equipped with a full set of tools. The business is prospering and they can look back with satisfaction. Even during a period of recession they were mostly unaffected.

Jeff and Malcolm feel that there is no more room for expansion in their hometown. They have been looking at setting up a branch in another town 35 km away. They feel that this is near enough to keep control of both businesses and to gain some advantage from the good reputation of the business.

They have prepared a business plan and feel that to make the venture work they will need to get a loan or some other external funding. They estimate that they will need around £40,000, of which £10,000 will be spent on office equipment and tools and £15,000 on the purchase of a new van. The remainder will be used as working capital to fund office rental and wages.

Questions *(25 marks; 25 minutes)*

1 Assuming the role of bank manager, make a list of questions that you would want to ask Jeff and Malcolm before considering their loan. Explain why you want the information. (8)

2 If the bank will not provide the loan, explain how else the business could obtain the £40,000 needed for the expansion. (6)

3 Assuming that they can get the funding, do you consider that Jeff and Malcolm should go ahead with the expansion? Explain your decision. (11)

Data response

Bobelle

In early 2008 Claire Watt-Smith launched a fair-trade fashion business called Bobelle. Its main product line is a series of handbags and purses made from super-smooth eel-skin leather. The skins used to be thrown away when eels (a delicacy in the Far East) were cooked. Now the skins are, in effect, recycled by turning them into soft leather.

Claire started the business with just £6,000. Most was from her student loan, but there was also a small investment by her mother. At the time, she reflects: 'We were at the start of a recession. Banks didn't want to lend.'

In 2009/2010, the second year of trading, Bobelle had a turnover of £65,000. It also had a small bank overdraft facility, which Claire rarely used. With distribution expanding to include 60 stores and a thriving e-commerce website, future growth looks likely. Claire is not sure that she can continue to finance growth through reinvested profits; she may need some outside capital investment. If so, she will turn her sole trader business into a private limited company.

Questions *(20 marks; 20 minutes)*

1 How much external finance did Claire raise to start up Bobelle? (3)

2 Explain the difference between an overdraft and an overdraft facility. (4)

3 Outline two reasons why a small business that's growing rapidly might need 'outside capital investment'. (6)

4 Explain how Claire might be able to raise fresh capital after turning the business into a private limited company. (7)

Location factors for a business start-up

Definition
Location decisions are about where to site the company's buildings (e.g. its factory, its head office and/or its shops).

Where to locate?

A business cliché in the hotel and catering industries is: 'What are the three most important factors for success? Location, location, location.' Many shop owners would say the same thing. The problem is that because everybody knows the importance of location, good locations are incredibly expensive and very hard to come by. The location a small business start-up would most like will already have been taken by Starbucks, Topshop, O², etc.

The high cost of a good location is true throughout the world, but especially in Britain.

This is a question which a new business will have to consider carefully as location could influence its chance of success. There are several factors that will influence a firm's choice of location. The quantitative ones take into account the financially related factors, whereas the qualitative ones are concerned with the non-financial influences, such as the family links that may attract the owner to a particular area.

This unit will focus on the different factors and show how the importance of these will vary according to the type of business involved.

Figure 10.1 Starbucks and other high-profile businesses occupy prime locations

Quantitative factors

Cost of land

If a firm chooses a high-cost location it may find that the prices it has to charge to help cover the costs may increase and this may make the firm less price competitive. This is why firms for which a competitive selling price is vital in achieving sales will search for the **least-cost site**.

Space

Although a new firm will not be concerned with expansion in the early years, if it is successful it may need to increase the scale of its operations in the long term and this will be cheaper and less disruptive if the firm has the opportunity to extend its existing premises rather than relocating to larger premises.

Accessibility of supplies

Whether a firm needs to be close to its suppliers will depend upon whether it is using large materials that are costly to transport. A firm that uses bulky materials, often to produce smaller end products, will be better situated near its suppliers as it will be more cost effective. These firms are referred to as

bulk decreasing. A firm that also relies on regular deliveries or employs a **just-in-time** system will also benefit from being close to its suppliers. On the other hand, firms like soft drinks companies would be described as **bulk increasing** as their products gain weight throughout the production process through the addition of water, so they would be more likely to locate nearer the market. Today, the bulk decreasing theory applies less because of two reasons: first, better transport links has meant that the costs of transportation have fallen, meaning that firms are not under as much pressure to locate near their suppliers; second: the growth of the service sector has meant that firms locate nearer the consumer.

Labour

The skills and size of workforce required will be dependent upon the nature of the business. If a firm needs a large workforce it will have to ensure that it locates in an area which is accessible or close to populated areas that can supply the required labour. Locating in an area with high employment may create recruitment difficulties, which may constrain a firm's chance of success, especially as it grows.

Market

For service industries such as retailers, locating close to their market is the most important factor. Customers do not expect to travel miles for hairdressers, restaurants or shops. However, there are an increasing number of service industries that sell via the internet and these firms will be able to operate from a cheap out-of-town location that customers will not visit.

Infrastructure

Infrastructure describes the provision of all services in an area, including transport links, telecommunication systems, health services and educational institutions. For many firms, however, it is the transport links that represent a key influence on their choice of location. In order for a firm to organise its operations smoothly, it must be able to access its suppliers and its market quickly and cost effectively. This is not always possible if transport links are poor. But remember that even when an area has high quality infrastructure, it may be so popular with businesses that the resulting congestion may reduce accessibility.

Government intervention

Financial incentives offered by government in an attempt to help areas with high unemployment may affect a firm's choice of location. However, there are restrictions on the types of firms that can attract this funding and it is unlikely that a new firm will meet the criteria that are necessary to attract such funding.

Qualitative factors

In addition to the quantitative factors, some owners of businesses may choose their location for purely personal reasons. Anita Roddick, founder of the Body Shop, set up her firm in Brighton because this is where she and her family lived. Other firms locate in areas due to the high quality of life and beauty that the area provides.

Which factor is the most important?

This will depend on the nature of the business: the factor that may attract one firm may not attract another. Some new businesses may select their location purely on the grounds of personal preference, whereas others may select the least-cost location. Table 10.1 shows that different factors will be important to different types of firms.

Figure 10.2 Anita Roddick set up the Body Shop in her home town of Brighton

Table 10.1 Which location factor is the most important?

Nature of the business	Factors that will be most important	Examples
Service businesses	If the customer needs to visit the business to purchase the product, then proximity to the market will be crucial. In addition, the image of a location and its surroundings will also play a role	Gap Lush Costa Coffee
Manufacturing businesses	Most manufacturers will be concerned with proximity to suppliers or the size of land required for its operations. This means that many manufacturing firms may locate in out-of-town sites that provide the opportunity for expansion in the future	Bath Ales Brewery
Method of distribution	As previously highlighted, many firms do not come into direct contact with their customers as they sell via the internet and use distribution firms to deliver their products. This will mean that such firms will not need to consider the proximity of their market or the image and appearance of their premises. However, high quality transport links will be extremely important to such firms	ASOS Amazon
Labour-intensive business	If the firm relies heavily on labour in the production of its products, then its labour costs will represent a high proportion of its costs. This may lead the firm to locate in areas where the cost of living is cheaper and there is a plentiful supply of labour as this will help to reduce its labour costs	In 2010 Kraft moved production of Cadbury's chocolate from Keynsham (near Bristol) to Poland

Changes in the location factors

As a business becomes established, the factors that influence its location may change. For example, a newly formed business may select a location near to the owner's residence, but as a firm becomes established and starts to grow, it may find that it needs to extend and requires larger premises. In the long term a successful firm may encounter increasing competition and this may mean that it needs to lower its prices, which may result in it looking for the least-cost location.

Technology and choice of location

The role of technology has had a major influence on a firm's choice of location. Technology and the ease of communication that this facilitates has enabled some firms to become more 'footloose'. This means that they are not tied to any particular location and can operate anywhere without considering any of the influences previously discussed. However, the ability to be footloose will always be determined by the nature of the business.

Issues for analysis

You demonstrate the skill of analysis every time you use theory or business logic to develop a solution to a business problem. Good analysis acknowledges that short-term solutions may have long-term implications. For example, if a firm chooses a location because it attracts government finance, this may be a good decision in the short term, but it may not be the best location in the long term if the firm needs to expand its premises or access a wider geographical market.

Location factors for a business start-up – an evaluation

You demonstrate the skill of evaluation when you make judgements based on assessing and weighing up different evidence. Good evaluation is also demonstrated when you assess the quality, reliability and relevance of the evidence. For example, it is important to remember that new start-ups do not have access to the same financial resources as well established businesses and they are also more likely to focus on a smaller and more local market. Therefore, influences such as national transport links may not be as important in their choice of location as the cost of rent.

It is critical that you demonstrate your evaluation skills in relation to location by recognising that the factors that sway new entrepreneurs in the real world are not always the factors that influence well established firms. Many new businesses start out in spare rooms, garages and garden sheds until success enables them to expand their operations and locate to another place. Furthermore, it is important to distinguish between theory and practice. For example, in theory we assume that all service businesses want to locate near to their market, whereas in practice, proximity to the market may be important, but it may not be vital. This is because an increasing number of firms' contact with the market place is made via the internet and telephone call centres.

Key terms

Bulk reducing/bulk increasing: a firm that uses large bulky materials to produce smaller end products/a firm that uses small materials to produce larger end products.

Footloose: a business that is not tied to a particular location as it relies on technology and communication links.

Infrastructure: the network of utilities such as transport links, telecommunications systems, health and education services.

Just-in-time: a manufacturing system that aims to minimise costs of holding stocks of raw materials, components and work in progress by producing goods in response to a definite order. It requires efficient ordering and delivery systems.

Labour intensive/capital intensive: a process in which labour costs represent a high proportion of the total costs. Small businesses and businesses in the service sectors are likely to be labour intensive. By contrast, a capital intensive process relies more on machinery in the production of its products.

Least-cost site: a business location that allows a business to minimise its costs.

Revision questions *(30 marks, 30 minutes)*

1. Explain what is meant by the 'quantitative' factors that may influence a firm's choice of location. (3)
2. Describe one factor that would be important to a manufacturing firm but not a retail firm when choosing a location. (2)
3. Explain why a firm relying on mail order may not locate in a high rent area. (2)
4. How might the use of just-in-time production influence the location of a business? (3)
5. State two factors that would influence the location of a firm that employs a labour intensive process. (2)
6. How may selecting the least-cost location improve a firm's competitive ability? (4)
7. Explain two reasons why a firm may decide to choose a location near to its supplier. (4)
8. Identify two qualitative factors that may influence a firm's choice of location. (2)
9. Explain how a cheap location for a new service industry may represent a 'false economy'. (4)
10. What is meant by the term 'footloose'? Identify two factors that may prevent a business from being footloose. (4)

Revision exercises

Data response

Choosing the right location for a pizza takeaway

Leona and Seun want to open a Domino's pizza franchise outlet in a medium-sized town in Bedfordshire. It will make pizza for takeaway or delivery. After some weeks of research, they have narrowed their choice down to two locations. Which should they go for?

Profiles of two locations

	Martin Way	Dame Alice Street
Road details	Busy main road from town to M1; near big housing estate	Busy high street near station; next to Primark
Accommodation	3-bed flat above premises in good order; access from back of shop; rental value up to £100 per week	Two flats, each with 2 beds; separate access from street; rental value £200 per week each
Leasehold details	Lease 15 years; price £55,000	Lease 12 years; price £220,000
Rent per year	£12,500 per annum	£68,000 per annum
Parking	Plenty at the back of premises	NCP car park 200 m away

Questions *(30 marks; 35 minutes)*

1 Discuss the pros and cons of each location, bearing in mind the type of business. (14)

2 Write a three-slide presentation on:

- strengths of Martin Way location
- strengths of Dame Alice Street location
- which you recommend and why. (16)

Data response

John Michaels set up a business producing wind-up radios 14 months ago. He produces the radios in his garage and sells them via an onlne retail business specialising in organic, 'green' products. Since starting up his business, the sales of his radios have increased by 18 per cent. He is now considering renting a small industrial unit which would enable him to increase the number of radios he could produce.

Questions *(20 marks; 20 minutes)*

1 What factors should John take into account before moving his production into the industrial unit? (6)

2 Explain how John's profits could be affected by his decision to move to the industrial unit. (4)

3 What are the benefits of selling the radios via an online retail business? (5)

4 What qualitative factors may be behind John's decision to relocate production from the garage to the industrial unit? (5)

Data response

Metro's banking revolution

July 29th 2010 was the opening day for the first brand new bank on the British high street for more than 100 years. US-owned Metro Bank planned a new customer-focused experience, with longer opening hours and seven-days-a-week counter service. The first branch opened in Holborn, London. The location was brilliant, at an extremely busy junction at the entrance of Holborn tube station. It not only has a vast number of commuters and tourists passing by, there are also lots of people who live nearby.

Most new banks would tend to locate in the City of London, to establish their good name. The decision to go to Holborn shows the owner's focus on the customer, e.g. making it easy for busy commuters to go to their bank in the early evening.

It seems that Metro is targeting small businesses which often have to pay fees for everyday banking facilities such as depositing coins. 'The location is interesting as there are lots of small businesses in the locality and the opening hours – till 8pm – and the ability to deposit coins in large quantities easily and without charge will really appeal to these customers,' said David Black, a banking analyst.

The tradition in service businesses has been to say that location is critical. In these days of online banking, has Metro made a mistake in setting itself up in a very expensive Central London location?

Questions *(25 marks; 30 minutes)*

1 Examine one strength and one weakness of Metro Bank's start-up location. (8)

2 Explain why location might be especially critical for a business start-up in the service sector. (5)

3 Discuss whether location still matters in a sector such as banking, where online banking is taking a rising market share. (12)

11 Employing people

Definition
An employee is someone who works for an organisation under a contract of employment in return for a salary or wage.

Introduction: taking on new staff

Many entrepreneurs are obliged to carry out a number of different tasks and roles when they start out in business. Not only are they responsible for decision making and creative input, they are also required to carry out all the day-to-day activities needed to keep the business going. However, as the business expands, this approach may act as an obstacle to further growth. Most entrepreneurs will have an area of expertise that led them into business in the first place, but it is highly unlikely that they will have all of the skills needed to run a business successfully. In addition, working around the clock may be necessary initially but, in the long term, can lead to stress and poor decision making. Eventually, any ambitious entrepreneur will have to employ new staff.

Factors to consider

Recruitment can be an expensive process, and has to be considered in relation to the wider objectives of the firm. Therefore, before spending time and money hiring staff, there are a number of factors to think about.

The business should start by identifying the skills, qualities and experience that are needed to continue to operate successfully. This requires a clear understanding of the exact nature of the firm's product and the market in which it operates. A detailed analysis of the marketplace usually forms a major part of a firm's business plan (see Unit 4).

The next step would be to pinpoint current skill strengths and weaknesses, so that gaps in expertise can be filled. For example, trying to get the books to balance without the financial skills required to do so can use up a great deal of time. This could be spent more profitably promoting products, dealing with customers and managing suppliers.

Another factor to consider is the length of time that workers are likely to be needed. For instance, additional staff may be taken on in order to respond to an increasing workload. Is this increase likely to be temporary or permanent? How many extra hours of work will be needed each week? Once a business has developed a clear understanding of its workforce needs, it will be in a position to choose from a number of employment options.

Employment options

The firm may wish to consider a number of possible options before deciding on the best way of taking on additional workers (see Figure 11.1). This should help to ensure that the extra help can be acquired without creating unaffordable labour costs.

Part-time vs full-time employees

Employer surveys generally classify jobs as being part-time if the contracted period of work is equal to or less than 30 hours per week. Approximately 7.63 million, or just over 25 per cent, of employees were employed on a part-time basis within the UK

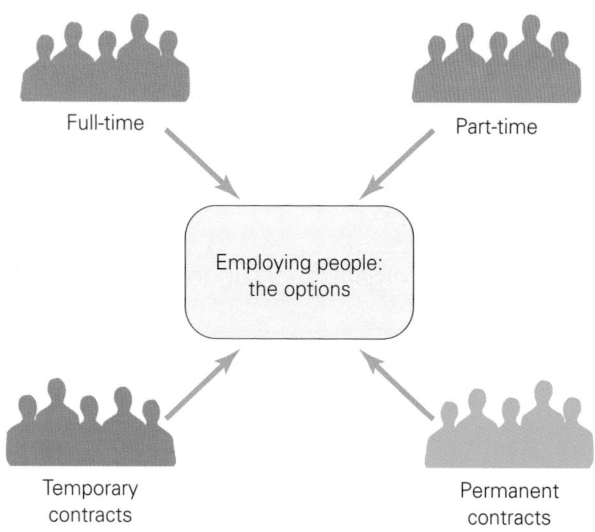

Figure 11.1 Employment options

in 2010. Employing part-time rather than **full-time employees** can offer a business a number of benefits.

- It can be a more efficient way of meeting labour requirements, especially for small businesses, by keeping costs down when there is no need for full-time cover.
- Employing part-timers can also help to increase the degree of workforce flexibility, allowing firms to cater for predicable fluctuations in demand.
- Offering part-time contracts to staff may also help to improve the quality and productivity of the workforce. It may attract more applicants for job vacancies, including women with young children. The option of working part-time may also lead to a more motivated workforce, reduced absenteeism and labour turnover.

However, relying too heavily on **part-time employees** may mean additional induction, training and administration costs for a firm. It may also lead to a deterioration in communication, if staff see very little of each other, making it difficult to coordinate activities.

Temporary vs permanent employees

A **temporary employee** is employed for a limited period of time by a business. Such workers are often hired on fixed-term contracts (i.e. a **contract of employment** based on a definite period of time, such as three months). Employment is terminated once the contract expires and no notice is required from the employer, although the contract can be ended sooner if either side does give notice. The advantages of employing staff on a temporary basis include the following.

- A more flexible workforce can be created to cope with changes in demand over certain periods of time. For example, a retailer might choose to recruit sales assistants on a temporary basis to help deal with increased demand and maintain customer service standards over the Christmas sales period.
- Temporary workers can be used to cover for **permanent employees** – for instance, during maternity/paternity leave or secondment to another area of the business.
- Employing workers on fixed-term contracts allows even small businesses to gain access to highly specialised skills, such as IT or marketing, without having to bear the costs of having to permanently hire what are likely to be expensive employees.

The level of commitment of temporary employees to the business is, however, likely to be much lower than that of workers on permanent contracts. Lack of job security may mean that workers move to permanent jobs elsewhere as and when such positions arise, resulting in increased labour turnover. This, in turn, could lead to higher recruitment costs and lower productivity while new workers familiarise themselves with their duties.

Using employment agency staff

One possibility for businesses looking to hire staff on a temporary basis is to use an **employment agency**. Although the workers supplied carry out duties within the business, they are paid by the agency. This means that the business has a contract with the agency, rather than individual workers, and pays a fee for its services.

Agency staff are often used to cover for short-term holiday or sickness absence, or in situations where there is a high labour turnover, such as in the hotel and catering industries. The main advantage to a business of using agency workers is that the agency is the employer; this makes the agency responsible for the recruitment and administration functions involved in employing staff. This is very useful if the job is something like a security guard or an office cleaner. Topshop wants to be good at selling attractive, fashionable clothes; it does not want its store managers worrying about recruiting new cleaners.

Figure 11.2 Security guards may be employed by an agency

External advisers, consultants and contractors

A business in need of expert skills over a specific period of time may decide to use a business adviser, consultant or contractor. These individuals or organisations provide agreed services, such as accountancy or human resources functions, for a set time and fee.

Advisers, consultants and contractors can provide a cost-effective means of completing one-off projects or accessing skills and expertise to improve the performance of the business. They avoid the need for the potentially costly recruitment and training of permanent workers who may be under-utilised, especially in small firms. However, consultants and advisers can be very expensive, and their frequent or lengthy use may actually end up costing the business more than taking on permanent employees. These 'outsiders' may also fail to understand the special character of an individual business, and may lack commitment to its long-term success.

Legal responsibilities

Regardless of whether workers are employed on a full- or part-time, temporary or permanent basis, firms must be aware of the responsibilities involved in taking on additional staff. Employers have a number of obligations, including the need to provide a safe and secure environment, to treat workers fairly and avoid discrimination. All workers must be given a written statement of the terms and conditions of their contract of employment, and have a number of legal entitlements, including:

- the right to receive the **National Minimum Wage**
- minimum levels of rest breaks
- paid holidays and statutory sick pay.

Employers are required to register with HM Revenue & Customs (HMRC) and establish a payroll in order to deduct income tax and National Insurance contributions from employees' pay.

Part-time and fixed-term employees have the same employment rights as their full-time colleagues. This means that, by law, employers must treat staff in the same way, regardless of the basis for their employment. Therefore, part-time staff should receive, pro rata, the same terms and conditions, including rates of pay, holidays and access to training, promotion and redundancy. Failure to treat staff fairly could result in an employee making a complaint to an **employment tribunal**, potentially leading to the firm having to pay compensation.

A-grade application

Small firms fear changes to the law

Changes to UK employment law in recent years could be discouraging small businesses from hiring new staff, according to some commentators. New regulations designed to provide agency workers with greater protection and bring UK employment law in line with the European Union's Agency Workers Directive, were laid before Parliament in January 2010 and are due to be implemented across the country by October 2011.

However, Russell Lawson of the Federation of Small Businesses in Wales claimed that this legislation, together with recently increased provision for maternity leave and the extension of flexible working rights to adult carers, had all added to small business fears about employing workers. A poll conducted by the FSB in 2009 indicated that 99% of its members were less likely to recruit temporary workers once the agency workers' legislation was implemented.

(Source: www.walesonline.co.uk)

Issues for analysis

Opportunities for analysis using this topic are likely to focus on the following areas:

- the reasons for and against a small business expanding its workforce
- the advantages and/or disadvantages to a firm of employing staff on a part-time or full-time basis
- the benefits and drawbacks of employing staff on a temporary or full-time basis
- the suitability of using consultants or contractors to a firm in given circumstances
- the difficulty for a new business of knowing whether strong sales will persist long enough to justify hiring permanent, full-time staff.

Employing people – an evaluation

Taking on extra workers is one of the hardest decisions that an entrepreneur is likely to face. This is the point in the firm's development where the individual is forced to admit that she or he cannot do everything. There may also be a reluctance to hand over some control to others – people who may have different opinions and challenge the way the business is run. Employing someone with strongly opposing views is likely to lead to conflict and, unless everyone is heading in the same direction, the business will not move forward. However, a successful firm requires a range of skills and experience. Refusing to bring in additional support and expertise can seriously damage the potential of the business to continue to survive and thrive.

Key terms

Contract of employment: a legal document setting out the terms and conditions of an individual's job. These include the responsibilities of the employee, rates of pay, working hours, holiday entitlement, etc.

Employment agency: an organisation that supplies workers with particular skills, on a short- or long-term basis, to other businesses, in return for a fee.

Employment tribunal: an informal courtroom where legal disputes between employees and employers are settled.

Full-time employees: staff who are under contract to work the normal basic full time hours of a business.

National Minimum Wage: the lowest hourly wage rate that an employer can legally pay to an employee.

Part-time employees: staff who are contracted to work for anything less than what is considered the normal basic full-time hours of a business.

Permanent employees: workers with a contract of employment with a business that is open-ended (i.e. there is no time given at which the contract is due to end).

Temporary employees: employees on fixed-term contracts of employment, either for a predetermined time, or until a specific task or set of tasks is completed.

Revision questions *(40 marks; 40 minutes)*

1 Outline three reasons why a small business may need to take on additional staff. (6)

2 Suggest two reasons why the owner of a small business might be reluctant to employ more staff. (2)

3 Explain why a business might consider plans to expand the workforce in relation to its wider objectives. (4)

4 Examine two advantages of employing part-time staff to a small, expanding business. (6)

5 Suggest two reasons why an over-reliance on part-time staff could, in fact, increase the costs of a business. (4)

6 Briefly explain what is meant by a fixed-term contract. (2)

7 Analyse the main advantages and disadvantages of using temporary workers for a domestic cleaning business. (6)

8 Suggest one suitable method of dealing with the following staff shortages:

a) providing cover for a receptionist on two weeks' holiday (1)

b) providing extra sales assistance at a delicatessen on Saturdays (1)

c) providing additional waiters and kitchen staff at a restaurant over the busy Christmas period. (1)

9 Suggest one benefit and one drawback to a small business of using consultants to provide specialist skills. (4)

10 Briefly explain the main risks for a small business from failing to stick to legislation regarding the employment of workers. (3)

Revision exercises

Data response

Flexible working at City Sightseeing Glasgow

City Sightseeing is a company set up to provide visitors to Glasgow with guided sightseeing tours. Its double-decker buses operate 362 days a year between 8am and 6pm, with tour guide services available for almost 24 hours a day. The nature of the business means that the company is required to adopt a flexible approach to its workforce. The company employs 70 people in the summer, falling to around 20 people in the winter. The business deliberately targets those who are not interested in working a full '9 to 5' week, including students, workers over the age of 40 and women returning to the labour market. At the beginning of both the summer and winter, each employee is required to indicate the number of hours they would like to work in the forthcoming season. Staff typically work between two and six days a week and job sharing is common.

Making sure that all shifts are covered and standards of service are maintained requires careful management and staff are encouraged to give as much notice as possible about changes in their work schedule. However, adopting a flexible approach to the workforce has also led to a number of benefits. The company does not need to advertise job vacancies, absenteeism is low and the staff retention is over 90%.

(Source: British Chamber of Commerce)

Questions *(15 marks; 20 minutes)*

1 Explain two reasons why the nature of City Sightseeing's business requires it to employ a large percentage of part-time and temporary workers. (6)

2 Analyse the main implications for City Sightseeing of employing part-time and temporary staff, rather than full-time, permanent staff. (9)

B2 Data response

The Gourmet Chocolate Pizza Company

Helen Ellis took the decision to set up her own business in 2006. Her job as a part-time administrator had come to an end after the company employing her had closed down. Supported by her family, and keen to continue to work from her Nottingham home, Helen surfed the internet, looking for inspiration. She came across the concept of chocolate pizzas from an American website and was confident that, by putting her own twist on the idea, she had a successful venture on her hands. The result was the Gourmet Chocolate Pizza Co – a business producing and selling chocolate-based pizzas, covered with a selection of mouth-watering toppings, to order online and over the telephone.

Working from home for 18 months had proved to Helen that she had many of the skills and qualities required to run her own business: hard working and dedicated, with good organisational skills and an ability to deal with suppliers and the general public. Helen decided to pay a professional designer in order to get the business's website up and running quickly, and carried out her own research to see how other similar businesses marketed themselves.

The business start-up required Helen to put in a lot of hours, including evenings and weekends. However, despite doing this and receiving a great deal of unpaid help from her mother, the increasing workload made it difficult to run the business effectively. Although Helen was managing to meet the growing number of orders, she was unable to cope with all the other jobs involved in expanding the business. In particular, the need for additional production staff to help box up the pizzas persuaded Helen to hire an extra worker.

Her search focused on finding someone who was flexible and reliable, could show initiative and shared a similar approach to the business. After taking advice on employment terms and conditions, the new employee was hired on a six-month temporary contract initially, before being appointed on a permanent basis.

According to Helen, 'employing another member of staff was the best thing I did ... a bit daunting, but one of those things you need to do to push the business forward, so really you take a deep breath and do it.' By 2010, the company's workforce had increased to five, consisting of three production workers, one dispatch worker and an assistant manager. Only one worker is employed on a part-time basis. This expansion means that Helen is no longer directly involved with production, allowing her to focus on growing the business.

Figure 11.3 The Gourmet Chocolate Pizza

(Source: Gourmet Chocolate Pizza Company)

Questions *(35 marks; 40 minutes)*

1 a) Identify two qualities possessed by Helen Ellis that helped her establish her business. (2)

b) What is meant by the term 'temporary contract'? (2)

c) What is meant by the term 'part-time basis'? (2)

2 Explain one advantage and one disadvantage to Helen's business of employing new staff. (6)

3 Examine the benefits of appointing a new member of staff on a temporary contract initially. (9)

4 Assess the possible consequences for the Gourmet Chocolate Pizza Co from Helen's decision to no longer be directly involved in the production process. (14)

12 Calculating revenue, costs and profit

Definition

Revenue is the value of total sales made by a business within a period, usually one year. Costs are the expenses incurred by a firm in producing and selling its products; this is likely to include expenditure upon wages and raw materials. Profit is the difference which arises when a firm's sales revenue exceeds its total costs.

Business revenues

The revenue or income received by a firm as a result of trading activities is a critical factor in its success. When starting up, businesses may expect relatively low revenues for several reasons:

- their product is not well known
- they are unlikely to be able to produce large quantities of output
- it is difficult to charge a high price for a product which is not established on the market.

Entrepreneurs start their financial planning by assessing the income or revenue that they are likely to receive during the coming financial year. Businesses calculate their revenue through use of the following formula:

Sales revenue = volume of goods sold × average selling price

You can see that there are two key elements which comprise sales revenue: the quantity of goods that are sold and the prices at which they are sold. A firm seeking to increase its revenue can plan to sell more goods or aim to sell at a higher price. Some firms may maintain high prices even though this policy depresses sales. Such companies, often selling fashion and high-technology products, believe that this approach results in higher revenue and ultimately higher profits.

To sustain high revenues from relatively few sales, a business has to be confident that consumers will be willing to pay a high price for the product, and that direct competition will not appear – at least in the short term. This is only possible if the start-up business has a product or service that is really special and different, unique even. An additional advantage of a low output strategy is that it keeps down the cost of producing the goods or services. This is important in the early stages of running an enterprise.

The other way to boost revenue is to charge a low price in an attempt to sell as many products as possible. In some markets this may lead to high revenues and profits. Firms following this approach are likely to be operating in markets where the goods are fairly similar and consumers do not exhibit strong preferences for any brand. This is true of the market for young holidaymakers in Ibiza or Benidorm. Price competition is fierce as businesses seek to maximise their sales and revenue (see Figure 12.1).

Some businesses adopt a revenue-orientated approach for different reasons. If the company experiences circumstances where few of its costs vary with the level of its output then it will seek to maximise revenue. Because its costs are not sensitive to the level of its sales, then maximising sales will result in maximum profits. This is the position for the operators of both theme parks and football clubs. Whereas making and selling a Mercedes creates revenue but also a lot of costs, the theme park's costs are largely **fixed costs**. Attracting extra customers on a day adds few costs. Similarly, football clubs have the same costs whether their stadium is full or half empty. So when playing a less attractive team, many Premier League teams set children's ticket prices as low as £5.

A-grade application

Farmers operate low-cost system

Trials at Harper Adams University College have established new lower cost methods of looking after cattle over the winter months. The trials revealed that leaving young cattle in the field over the winter months (out-wintering) feeding on root crops such as turnips can cut costs by almost 50 per cent compared with keeping them indoors. Cattle kept indoors only gained the same amount of weight as those kept outdoors but cost more in feed and labour.

Harper Adams researcher, Simon Marsh, said that fixed and variable costs were cut by 48 per cent using the out-wintering system.

Looking after cattle during the winter months is expensive partly due to the high cost of animal feed. Any system that can reduce costs by such a figure (and thereby boost profits) is likely to be of interest to farmers at a time of rising costs.

(Source: Adapted from *Farmers Guardian*, April 2009, www.farmersguardian.com)

You will have realised from the analysis so far that price, cost and volume are all important elements of a firm's planning and success. Each of these factors affects the others and all of them together determine the profitability of a business.

Alternative ways to maximise revenue

Maximum price	Maximum sales
24-carat gold ring A Mercedes car A wedding dress	Theme parks Football clubs Railway companies

Figure 12.1 Alternative ways to maximise revenue

The new venture

Paul Merrills has achieved his lifetime ambition of opening a restaurant specialising in French cuisine in south London. Paul is a highly regarded and experienced restaurateur and wants to create a unique atmosphere in his new venture. How would you advise him to maximise his revenue in these circumstances?

If a business cannot control its costs then it will be unable to sell its products at a low price and this in turn will mean a low sales volume. This will mean that overhead costs such as the rent of a factory will be spread over a low output, causing further pressure on costs of production. It is to the costs of production that we now turn our attention.

The costs of production

Costs are a critical element of the information necessary to manage a business successfully. Managers need to be aware of the costs of all aspects of their business for a number of reasons.

- They need to know the cost of production to assess whether it is profitable to supply the market at the current price.
- They need to know actual costs to allow comparisons with their forecasted (or budgeted) costs of production. This will allow them to make judgements concerning the cost-efficiency of various parts of the business.

Fixed and variable costs

This is an important classification of the costs encountered by businesses. This classification has a number of uses, for example, it is the basis of calculating break-even which is covered in a later unit.

Fixed costs

Fixed costs are any costs which do not vary directly with the level of output. These costs are linked to time rather than to level of business activity. Fixed costs exist even if a business is not producing any goods or services. An example of a fixed cost is rent, which can be calculated monthly or annually, but will not vary whether the office or factory is used intensively to produce goods or services or is hardly utilised at all.

If a manufacturer can double output from within the same factory, the amount of rent will not alter – thus it is a fixed cost. In the same way, a seaside hotel has mortgage and salary costs during the winter, even though it may have very few guests. Given that fixed costs are inevitable, it is vital that managers work hard at bringing in customers to keep the fixed costs covered.

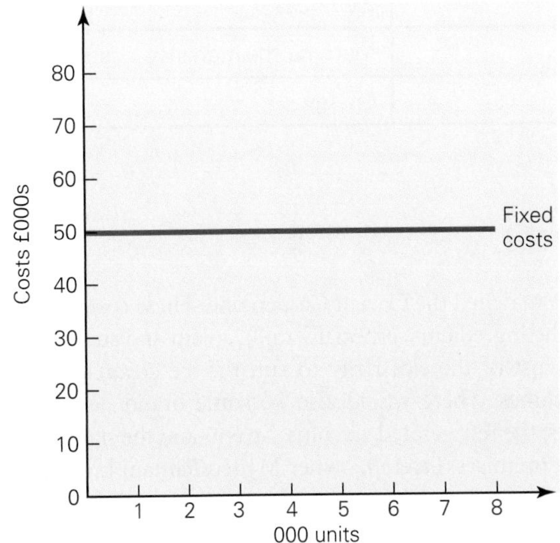

Figure 12.2 Fixed costs

In Figure 12.2, you can see that the firm faces fixed costs of £50,000 irrespective of the level of output. How much would the fixed costs per unit of production be if production were a) 1,000 units a year and b) 8,000 units a year? What might be the implications of this distinction for the managers of the business?

Other examples of fixed costs include the uniform business rate, management salaries, interest charges and depreciation.

In the long term fixed costs can alter. The manufacturer referred to earlier may decide to increase output significantly. This may require renting additional factory space and negotiating loans for additional capital equipment. Thus rent will rise, as may interest payments. We can see that in the long term fixed costs may alter, but that in the short term they are – as their name suggests – fixed!

Variable costs

Variable costs are those costs which vary directly with the level of output. They represent payments made for the use of inputs such as labour, fuel and raw materials. If our manufacturer doubled output then these costs would double. A doubling of the sales of Innocent Strawberry Smoothies would require twice the purchasing of strawberries and bananas. There would also be extra costs for the packaging, the wage bill and the energy required to fuel the production line.

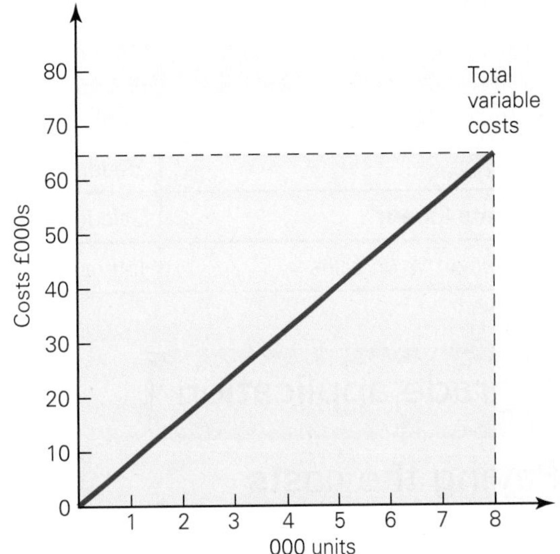

Figure 12.3 Variable costs

The graph in Figure 12.3 shows a firm with variable costs of £8 per unit of production. This means that variable costs rise steadily with, and proportionately to, the level of output. Thus, a 10 per cent rise in output will increase **total variable costs** by the same percentage.

However, it is not always the case that variable costs rise in proportion to output. Many small businesses discover that as they expand, variable costs do not rise as quickly as output. A key reason for this is that as the business becomes larger it is able to negotiate better prices with suppliers. Its suppliers are likely to agree to sell at lower unit prices when the business places larger orders.

Table 12.1 shows some examples of costs; some of these are easy to classify as either variable or fixed costs. Other costs, though, are more difficult to classify.

Total costs

When added together, fixed and variable costs give the **total costs** for a business. This is, of course, a very important element in the calculation of the profits earned by a business.

The relationship between fixed, variable and total costs is straightforward to calculate but has some important implications for a business. If a business has relatively high fixed costs as a proportion of total costs, then it is likely to seek to maximise its sales to ensure that the fixed costs are spread across as many units of output as possible. In this way the impact of high fixed costs is lessened. For small businesses, it is often variable costs that are high,

Table 12.1 Classifying costs

Variable costs	Fixed costs	Difficult to classify
Raw materials	Rent	Delivery costs
Packaging	Heating and lighting	Electricity
Piece-rate labour	Salaries	Machine maintenance costs
Commission % on sales	Interest charges	Energy

A-grade application

Paying the costs

In 2010 Scoop opened its second London ice cream parlour. All the ice cream would carry on being made at the original Covent Garden store, but delivered daily to the new branch near Piccadilly Circus (one mile away). This meant that all the fixed production costs would remain unchanged (e.g. rent of the floor space, the machinery and the professional ice cream maker's salary). Variable costs would double, as long as the new parlour's sales matched the Covent Garden one. These costs would be the ingredients, especially milk, cream and sugar, plus the cost of the electricity to run the ice cream-making machines. There would also be some brand new fixed costs: the refrigerated van plus the rent and the staff at the new premises. Overall, owner Matteo Pantani knew that he could increase his revenue by 100 per cent while total costs would increase by 75–80 per cent, enabling him to boost profit considerably.

for example high food costs at a restaurant. This may make them push their prices up to a level that makes customers reluctant to come regularly. This can be the start of a slippery downwards slope for the business.

Profit

Having considered revenues and costs it is now appropriate to focus upon a prime motive for businesses: profit. Profit is a comparison of revenues and costs. This comparison determines whether or not an enterprise makes any profit. As we saw at the beginning of this unit, the key formula is:

Profit = total revenue − total costs

However, it is worth remembering that some businesses are not established with the objective of making profits. Not-for-profit businesses, also known as social enterprises, operate with other objectives. For example, Katie Alcott from Bristol received an entrepreneurship award in 2007 for her social enterprise 'Frank Water'. Katie's business sells bottled spring water in the UK, and uses the proceeds to provide clean, safe water for villages in India and Africa. Her aim is to support others, not to make a profit.

Calculating profit

Although the profit formula is simple (revenue – costs), it is easy to make mistakes when calculating the figures. The problems rarely come from calculating revenue; the hard part is getting total costs right. The example on the next page may help.

Figure 12.4 Katie's business aim is to provide clean, safe water

Gwen and John's pasta restaurant charges £10 for three courses and has an average of 800 customers per week. The variable costs are £4 per customer and the restaurant has fixed costs of £3,400 per week. To calculate profit:

1 Calculate revenue: price × number of customers
£10 × 800 = £8,000
2 Calculate total costs: fixed costs + total variable costs (number of customers × variable costs per meal)
£3,400 + (800 × £4 = £3,200)
3 Calculate profit: total revenue − total costs
£8,000 − (£3,400 + £3,200) = £1,400 per week

See the Workbook section for exercises that will enable you to practise this very important skill.

Types of profit

Although profit is always revenue minus costs, there are different profit figures which are used. Managers frequently refer to operating profit. This is the amount remaining once all fixed and variable costs have been deducted from total revenue, but before tax has been paid.

Perhaps a more important measure is profit after tax, since this is the profit which the business can decide how to allocate. The most important uses to which these profits can be put are:

- payments to the owners of the business, to partners or to shareholders in the form of dividends
- reinvestment into the business to purchase capital items such as property and machinery.

A-grade application

Shopfitting company to cut costs

Employees at the shopfitting firm Havelock Europa have been warned that the company will have to cut costs due to a 'dire' trading year in 2009. The company, which employs 800 people mainly in Scotland, recorded a £5.9 million loss in 2009 compared with a profit of £7 million in 2008.

David Hurcomb, Havelock Europa's acting chief executive, said that the plan was to increase sales (and therefore revenue) as well as cutting costs and that success in finding new business will shape the extent of cost cutting. The company has not said how many jobs are at risk and David Hurcomb commented 'The focus is on every cost in the business, including warehousing, transport and suppliers.'

(Source: adapted from BBC News, June 2010)

The importance of profit

Undeniably profits are important to the majority of businesses. Profits are usually assessed in relation to some yardstick, for example the amount invested or sales revenue. We will consider how to measure profits in relation to other variables in Unit 19.

Profits are important for the following reasons:

- they provide a measure of the success of a business (especially important for a new business)
- they are the best source of capital for investment in the growth of the business, (e.g. to finance new store openings or to pay for new product development)
- they act as a magnet to attract further funds from investors, enticed by the possibility of high returns on their investment.

However, it is not uncommon for a new business to fail to make profits in the first months – or even years – of trading. The need to generate profits becomes more important as time passes. A business ultimately needs to make profits to reward its owners for putting money into the enterprise.

Issues for analysis

Forecasting costs and revenues can be tricky for an entrepreneur starting a new business. It is not possible to look back at trading records for guidance and therefore the likelihood of inaccuracy is greater. At this stage of a business's history all cost and revenue figures are forecasts and therefore not necessarily correct. It is possible that entrepreneurs will underestimate fixed and variable costs and overestimate revenues, thereby suggesting higher profits (or lower losses) than proves to be the case.

A key element with respect to the revenues earned by a business is the relationship between the price charged and the volume of sales achieved. Choosing the right price is an exercise requiring considerable judgement on the part of the entrepreneur. Simply raising price will not necessarily provide more revenue for a business. If a 10% price rise causes customer numbers to fall by 15%, the business will have lower revenues than it started with. Factors influencing consumers' decisions will include the quality of the products in question and how strong the competition is.

You might like to consider circumstances in which firms might earn higher revenue by raising prices, and when the opposite could be true. Do you think a firm could earn more revenue by *lowering* its price?

Calculating revenue, costs and profit – an evaluation

One important issue for evaluation in relation to costs, revenues and profits for a new enterprise is to judge the likely accuracy of the forecast figures and the degree of reliance that can be placed upon them. This is an important judgement for a number of stakeholders who may have an interest in the new business. Investors will obviously look closely at any forecast figures before committing money to the enterprise and suppliers will want to be assured of payment before agreeing to supply any raw materials.

It is also worth thinking whether profits are the best measure of success for a new business. A successful first year of trading may see an enterprise gain a customer base and repeat orders by supplying at competitive costs. This may result in small profits initially while the business builds a reputation. Profits may become a more important measure of success in the longer term.

An assessment of the true worth of a business's performance as measured by its profits would also take account of the general state of the economy: are businesses in general prospering, or is it a time of recession? They would also take into account any unusual circumstances such as, for example, the business being subject to the emergence of a new competitor.

Key terms

Fixed costs: do not vary as output (or sales) vary.

Piece-rate labour: paying workers per item they make (i.e. with no regular pay).

Total costs: all the costs of producing a specific output level (i.e. fixed costs + total variable costs).

Total variable costs: all the variable costs of producing a specific output level (i.e. variable costs per unit × the number of units sold).

Variable costs: the costs of producing one unit (also known as unit variable costs).

Revision questions (30 marks; 30 minutes)

1 Why might a business initially receive relatively low revenues from a product newly introduced to the market? (3)

2 State two circumstances in which a company may be able to charge high prices for a new product. (2)

3 For what reasons might a firm seek to maximise its sales revenue? (4)

4 If a business sells 4,000 units of Brand X at £4 each and 2,000 units of Brand Y at £3 each, what is its total revenue? (4)

5 State **two** reasons why firms have to know the costs they incur in production. (2)

6 Distinguish, with the aid of examples, between fixed and variable costs. (4)

7 Explain why fixed costs can only alter in the long-term. (3)

8 Give **two** reasons why profits are important to businesses. (2)

9 State **one** advantage and **one** disadvantage that may result from a business deciding to lower the proportion of profits it distributes to its owners. (4)

10 State two purposes for which a business's profits might be used. (2)

Revision exercises

Calculation practice questions (30 marks; 30 minutes)

1 During the summer weeks Devon Ice Cream has average sales of 4,000 units a week. Each ice cream sells for £1 and has variable costs of 25p. Fixed costs are £800.

a) Calculate the total costs for the business in the summer weeks. (3)

b) Calculate Devon Ice Cream's weekly profit in the summer. (3)

2 a) If a firm sells 200 Widgets at £3.20 and 40 Squidgets at £4, what is its total revenue? (3)

b) Each Widget costs £1.20 to make, while each Squidget costs £1.50. What are the total variable costs? (3)

c) If fixed costs are £300, what profit is the business making? (3)

3 'Last week our sales revenue was £12,000 which was great. Our price is £2 a unit, which I think is a bit too cheap.'

a) How many unit sales were made last week? (2)

b) If a price rise to £2.25 cuts sales to 5,600 units, calculate the change in the firm's revenue. (4)

4 BYQ Co has sales of 4,000 units a month, a price of £4, fixed costs of £9,000 and variable costs of £1. Calculate its profit. (4)

5 At full capacity output of 24,000 units, a firm's costs are as follows:

managers' salaries	£48,000
materials	£12,000
rent and rates	£24,000
piece-rate labour	£36,000

a) What are the firm's total costs at 20,000 units? (4)

b) What profit will be made at 20,000 units if the selling price is £6? (1)

Data response

Cleaning up

Mary Ruffett saw the building of a large new housing estate across the road from her home as an opportunity, not an eyesore. The estate contained 500 new homes and was nearing completion with only a few houses left to sell. Most were large detached houses and Mary had noticed that there were no window cleaners offering their services on the estate. Although she had no experience as an entrepreneur or a window cleaner, Mary was interested.

Mary did some sums and researched local window cleaners in Yellow Pages – there was only one listed. She could take out a loan to purchase a van, a ladder and the other equipment needed. She estimated that this would cost her £350 each month to repay. Her variable costs per house cleaned would be minimal – she estimated 50 pence per house. The tricky bit was the price to charge but eventually she estimated £4 per household. Limited research amongst the new occupants of the estate suggested that she might be able to clean the windows of 125 houses each month. At a price of £5 per household she forecast that she would have 100 customers monthly.

Questions *(25 marks; 30 minutes)*

1 Which of Mary's two prices would provide her with the higher monthly revenue? (3)

2 Calculate Mary's monthly profits (or losses) in each case. (6)

3 Analyse two possible reasons why Mary's financial forecasts might not prove to be accurate. (7)

4 Analyse the case for and against Mary charging £5 per household for her window cleaning service. (9)

Data response

Chalfont Computer Services Ltd

Robert has decided to give up his job with BT and to work for himself offering computer services to local people. He has paid off his mortgage and owns his house outright, so feels this is the time to take a risk. Robert has no experience of running a business, but is skilled in repairing computers and solving software problems. In the past Robert has repaired computers belonging to friends and family and is aware of the costs involved in providing this service. He believes that with the increase in internet usage, there will be plenty of demand for his services. Robert has spoken to a few people in his local pub and this has confirmed his opinion. Robert needs to raise £10,000 to purchase equipment for his business and to pay for a new vehicle. He intends to ask his bank for a loan.

The work Robert has already done allows him to forecast that the average revenue from each customer will be £40, while the variable costs will be £15. His monthly fixed costs will be £1,000. Robert estimates that he will have the following number of customers.

Month	Number of customers
January	40
February	50
March	60
April	82

Questions *(25 marks; 30 minutes)*

1 What is meant by the term 'variable costs'? (2)

2 Calculate Robert's forecast profits for his first three months' trading. (5)

3 Robert estimates that if he cut his prices by 10 per cent he would have 20 per cent more customers each month. Calculate the outcome of these changes and whether this would benefit Robert. (8)

4 Examine the case for and against a bank lending Robert £10,000 on the basis of his forecast profits. (10)

Essay questions *(40 marks)*

1 Discuss whether a new ethnic restaurant, trading in a very competitive market, should aim to maximise its revenue, rather than its profits, during its first year of trading.

2 For all new enterprises it is vital to sell at the right price – this is the most important determinant of profits. Discuss whether this view is always correct.

Break-even analysis

Definition
Break-even analysis compares a firm's revenue with its fixed and variable costs to identify the minimum level of sales needed to cover costs. This can be shown on a graph known as a break-even chart.

Introduction

The starting point for financial management is to know how much goods or services cost to produce. This was covered in detail in Unit 12. Businesses also benefit from knowing how many products they have to produce and sell in order to cover all of their costs. This is particularly important for new businesses with limited experience of their markets. It is also of value for established businesses that plan to produce a new product.

Table 13.1 shows the forecast revenue and cost figures for Burns and Morris Ltd – a business that is planning to start manufacturing silk ties.

You can easily identify that 400 is the number of sales Burns and Morris Ltd must achieve each week to break-even. Note what happens to its profits if sales are lower or higher than this figure.

To calculate the break-even point we need information on both costs and prices. A change in costs or in the firm's pricing will change the level of output at which the firm breaks-even.

Break-even can be calculated and shown on a graph. The calculation of break-even is simpler and quicker than drawing break-even charts.

Table 13.1 Forecast revenue and cost figures for Burns and Morris Ltd

Output of ties (per week)	Sales income (£ per week)	Total costs (£ per week)
0	0	10,000
100	4,000	11,500
200	8,000	13,000
300	12,000	14,500
400	16,000	16,000
500	20,000	17,500
600	24,000	19,000

Calculating break-even

Calculating the break-even point for a product requires the following information:

- the selling price of the product
- its **fixed costs**
- its variable costs per unit.

Fixed costs are expenses which do not change in response to changing demand or output. Fixed costs have to be paid whether or not the business is trading; examples include rent, business rates and interest charges. On the other hand, variable costs will alter as demand and output adjust. An increase in output will require greater supplies of fuel and labour, for example, and the costs of these items will rise. A doubling of demand will double variable costs.

The break-even output level can be calculated by the formula:

$$\text{Break-even output} = \frac{\text{Fixed costs}}{(\text{selling price per unit} - \text{variable cost per unit})}$$

The example below shows how to use this formula to calculate break-even as part of the planning for a new enterprise.

Example: Sue's guided tours

Sue Pittman is planning to offer an open-top bus tour in London during the summer months to take tourists on sightseeing tours of the capital. The bus will conduct four trips each day and Sue estimates that the cost of each trip will be £400 in fuel, food and wage costs for the driver and courier. The trip will include a snack and soft drinks for all the passengers, as well as a London guidebook. She estimates that these items will cost £10 for each passenger on the bus. The maximum number of passengers Sue is allowed to take on each trip is forty. Sue intends to price the day trips at £30 per passenger.

The first thing we should note is that the fixed cost of each tour is forecast to be £400. Sue will have to pay for the fuel for the bus and the wages of her employees, as well as depreciation on the vehicle irrespective of how many passengers she has. So it is easy to fill in the top of the formula we set out above. Fixed costs per tour are £400.

Calculating the bottom half of the formula is only a little more difficult. We know that she will charge each passenger £30 per tour and that the variable costs associated with each passenger will be £10. This is to pay for the snacks and drinks and the guidebook given to each passenger. The amount left (the **contribution**) will be £20 for each customer. So the formula will look like this:

$$\text{Sue's break-even output} = \frac{\text{Fixed costs}}{(\text{selling price per unit} - \text{variable cost per unit})}$$

$$= \frac{£400}{(£30 - £10)}$$

$$= \frac{£400}{£20}$$

$$= 20 \text{ passengers}$$

In other words, Sue will need 20 passengers on each of her tours if she is to break-even.

As we have seen, break-even level of output can be calculated using the simple equation above, but more understanding of the sensitivity of the relationships between costs, sales revenue and production can be achieved through the use of break-even charts.

Break-even charts

A break-even chart is a graph showing a business's revenues and costs at all possible levels of demand or output. The break-even chart is constructed on a graph by first drawing the horizontal axis to represent the output of goods or services for the business in question. The vertical axis should represent costs and sales values in pounds. The horizontal axis shows output per time period: usually output per month or year.

Example: Berry & Hall Ltd

Berry & Hall Ltd are manufacturers of confectionery. The company is planning to launch a new line called Aromatics – a distinctive sweet with a very strong fragrance. The company intends to sell these sweets for £1 a kilogram. The variable cost of production per kilogram is forecast at 60 pence and the fixed costs associated with this product are estimated to be £50,000 a year. The company's maximum output of Aromatics will be 250,000 kilograms per year.

First, put scales on the axes. The output scale has a range from zero to the company's maximum output – this will be 250,000 kilograms. The vertical axis records values of costs and revenues. Since revenue is usually the higher figure we simply multiply the maximum output by the selling price and then place values on the axis up to this figure. In this case it will have a maximum value on the axis of £250,000 (£1 × 250,000).

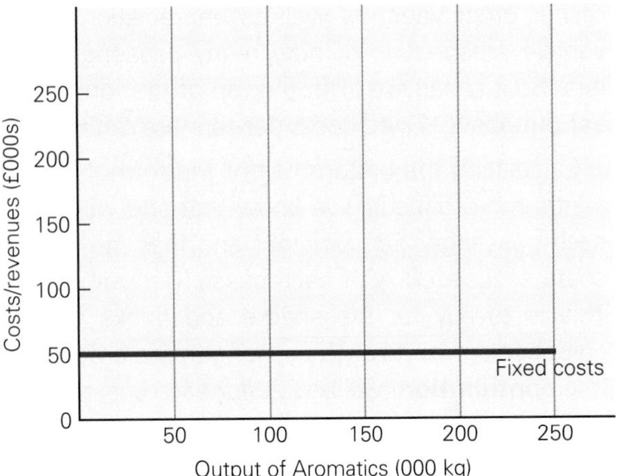

Figure 13.1 Fixed costs for Aromatics

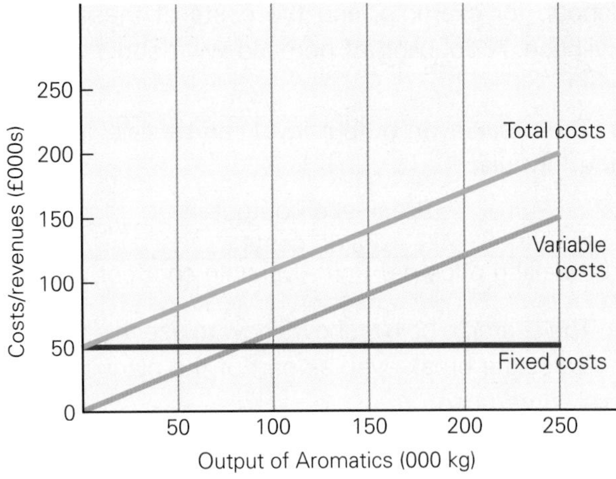

Figure 13.2 Fixed, variable and total costs for Aromatics

Having drawn the axes and placed scales upon them, the first line we enter is fixed costs. Since this value does not change with output, it is simply a horizontal line drawn at £50,000 (see Figure 13.1).

These costs cover rent and rates for the factory that will be used to produce Aromatics and also interest paid on loans taken out by Berry & Hall Ltd to establish production of the new sweet.

Next, add on variable costs to arrive at total costs. The difference between total costs and fixed costs is variable costs. Total costs start from the left hand of the fixed costs line and rise diagonally. To see where they rise to, calculate the total cost at the maximum output level. In the case of Aromatics, this is 250,000 kilograms per year. The total cost is fixed costs (£50,000) plus variable costs of producing 250,000 kilograms (£0.60 × 250,000 = £150,000). The total cost at this level of output is £50,000 + £150,000 = £200,000.

This point can now be marked on the chart (i.e. £200,000 at an output level of 250,000 kilograms). This can be joined by a straight line to total costs at zero output: £50,000. This is illustrated in Figure 13.2.

Finally, sales revenue must be added. For the maximum level of output, calculate the sales revenue and mark this on the chart. In the case of Aromatics the maximum output per year is 250,000 kilograms; multiplied by the selling price, this gives £250,000 each year. If Berry & Hall does not produce and sell any Aromatics it will not have any sales revenue. Thus zero output results in zero income. A straight diagonal line from zero to £250,000 represents the sales revenue for Aromatics (see Figure 13.3).

This brings together costs and revenues for Aromatics. A line drawn down from the point where total costs and sales revenue cross shows the break-even output. For Aromatics, it is 125,000 kilograms per year. This can be checked using the formula method explained earlier.

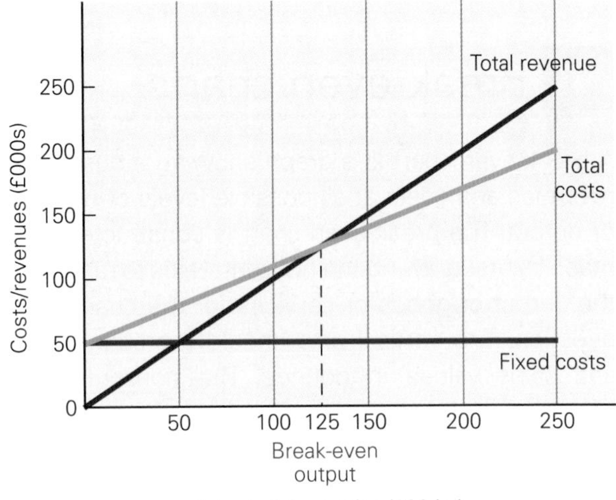

Figure 13.3 Break-even output for Aromatics

Using break-even charts

Various pieces of information can be taken from break-even charts such as that shown in Figure 13.3. As well as the level of break-even output, it also shows the level of profits or losses at every possible level of output. Many conclusions can be reached, such as those noted below.

- Any level of output lower than 125,000 kilograms per year will mean the product is making a loss. The amount of the loss is indicated by the vertical distance between the total cost and the total revenue line. For example, at an output level of 90,000 units per year, Aromatics would make a loss of £14,000 for Berry & Hall Ltd. This is because sales are worth £90,000 but costs are £104,000 (£54,000 + £50,000).
- Sales in excess of 125,000 kilograms of Aromatics per year will earn the company a profit. If the company produces and sells 150,000 kilograms of Aromatics annually, it will earn a profit of £20,000. At this level of output total revenue is £150,000 and total costs are £130,000. This is shown on the chart by the vertical distance between the total revenue line (which is now the higher) and the total cost line.
- One feature of a break-even chart is that it can show the **margin of safety**. This is the amount by which demand can fall before the firm starts making losses. It is the difference between current sales and the break-even point. If annual sales of Aromatics were 175,000 kilograms, with a break-even output of 125,000 kilograms, then the margin of safety would be 50,000 kilograms:

  margin of safety = 175,000 − 125,000 = 50,000 kilograms
- That is, output could fall by 50,000 units before Berry & Hall incurred a loss from its new product. The higher the margin of safety the less likely it is that a loss-making situation will develop. The margin of safety is illustrated in Figure 13.4.

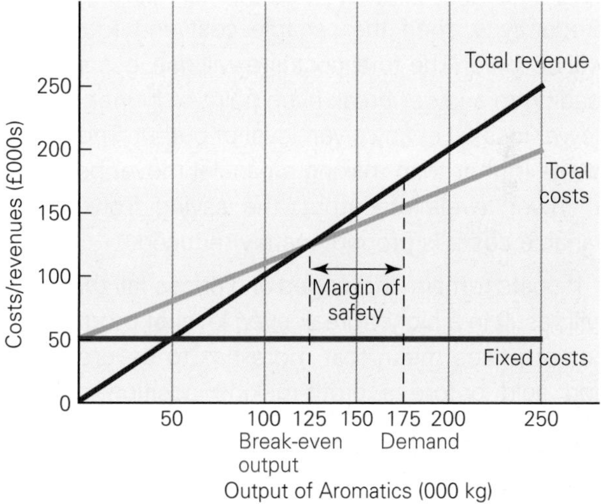

Figure 13.4 Margin of safety

Break-even analysis in a changing environment

The application of break-even analysis to the planned production of Aromatics shows how the technique operates. But it assumed a very stable (and therefore unrealistic) business environment. Competitors might have reacted to the introduction of Aromatics by producing similar products if it was a genuinely new idea, or was generating high profits. This competition may have forced Berry & Hall to reduce the price of Aromatics even before they entered onto the market. Alternatively, competitors' actions may have generated the need for more advertising, raising Berry & Hall's costs. In either case the break-even point and the break-even chart would change.

Suppose that Berry and Hall did have to carry out additional advertising for the launch of Aromatics and that this advertising cost £25,000 over the first

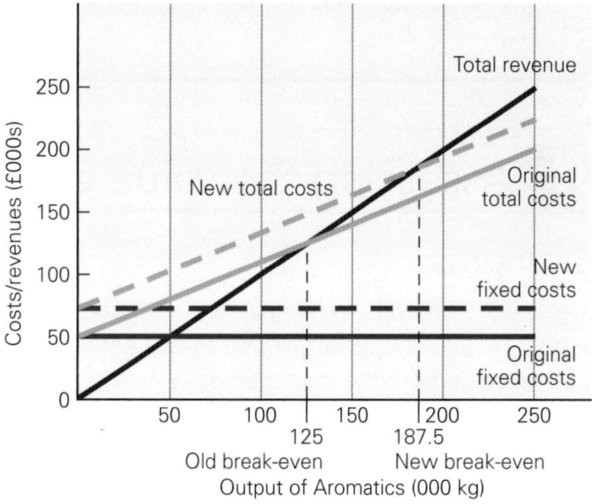

Figure 13.5 A rise in fixed costs

year. What impact would this have upon the break-even point and the break-even chart? The extra costs would require a higher output (and income) to break-even. The rise in marketing costs can be regarded as a fixed cost because this cost must be borne whatever the level of output. This is shown in Figure 13.5.

The break-even chart shows the increased fixed cost and total cost lines which create a higher break-even output. This also has the effect of reducing the level of profit (or increasing the loss) made at any level of output. Any factor leading to a fall in fixed costs will have the opposite effect.

Other external factors can impact upon the break-even level of output and associated profits. If the cost of labour declines, due perhaps to improving productivity, then the variable cost and total cost will be lower. The total cost line will rise less steeply leading to a lower break-even point of higher profits (lower losses) at any given level of output. The curve pivots (rather than making a parallel move) because at lower levels of output, the saving from lower variable costs is proportionately reduced.

If costs remain unchanged and prices fall then this will result in a higher break-even level of production. Lower prices mean that more has to be produced and sold before a profit-making position can be reached. Conversely, a rise in price will result in a lower level of production necessary for break-even to be attained. Figure 13.6 illustrates the impact of a fall in the market price of a product. When using break-even analysis, a business may draw several charts using different prices to assess the impact of various prices for a new product. This approach is particularly useful in markets where prices may be volatile.

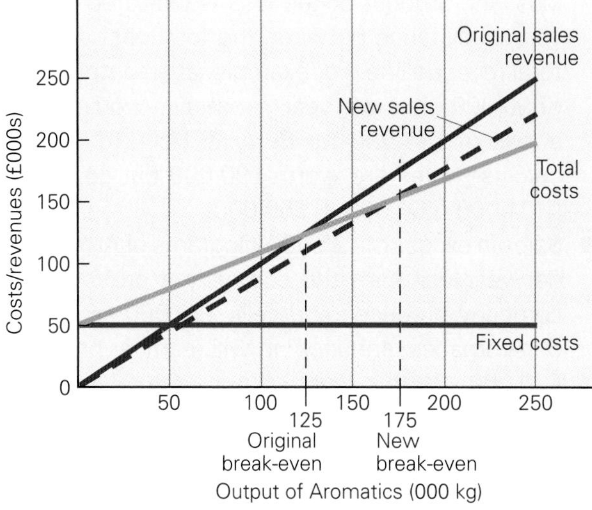

Figure 13.6 Effects of a fall in market price

Summary of possible changes to the break-even chart that may occur in the exam:

1. Prices can go up or down. If a price is increased, the revenue line starts in the same place but rises more steeply.
2. Fixed costs can rise or fall, so you might have to draw a new horizontal line. But remember that a change to fixed costs will also affect the total cost line.
3. Variable costs can rise or fall. An increase will make the variable cost line rise more steeply, though it will still start at the same point: at the fixed cost line. A change in variable costs will change the total costs line as well.

Note that each of these three changes will alter the break-even point.

Assessing the value of break-even analysis

Strengths

Break-even analysis is simple to understand and useful, particularly for small and newly established businesses where the managers may not be able to employ more sophisticated techniques. Businesses can use break-even to:

- estimate the future level of output they will need to produce and sell in order to meet given objectives in terms of profits
- assess the impact of planned price changes upon profit and the level of output needed to break-even
- assess how changes in fixed and/or **variable costs** may affect profits and the level of output necessary to break-even
- take decisions on whether to produce their own products or components or whether to purchase from external sources

- support applications for loans from banks and other financial institutions: use of the technique may indicate good business sense as well as forecast profitability.

Weaknesses

- The model assumes that costs increase constantly and that firms do not benefit from bulk buying. If, for example, a firm negotiates lower prices for purchasing larger quantities of raw materials then its total cost line will no longer be straight. It will in fact level out at higher outputs.
- Similarly, break-even analysis assumes the firm sells all its output at a single price. In reality firms frequently offer discounts for bulk purchases.
- A major flaw in the technique is that it assumes that all output is sold. This may well not be true and, if so, would result in an inaccurate break-even estimate. In times of low demand, a firm may have difficulty in selling all that it produces.
- Break-even analysis is only as good as the data on which it is based: poor quality data can result in inaccurate conclusions being drawn.

A-grade application

English football clubs fail to break-even

An annual review of football finance has shown that recent seasons have been challenging in financial terms for English football clubs.

The editor of the 2010 report, Dan Jones, argues that football faces a number of financial issues including rising wage bills for players. 'It is a real game of two halves with Premier League finances', he says, referring to the season 2008/09 which the report covers.

'On the revenue side, things are still very successful and continuing to grow, and getting closer to that £2 billion revenue target across the Premier League. But it is the cost control side of things where the problem is.'

Portsmouth Football Club failed to break-even in 2010 because it failed to control its costs and a high level of spending on players' wages was one factor which took the club into administration. However, unexpected declines in revenues can also contribute to failure to reach break-even. Relegation or failure to qualify for European competitions are obvious examples.

Football clubs are preparing for a future where revenue growth is likely to be lower and controlling costs will become more important. Even wealthy and high-spending clubs such as Chelsea are moving towards '... a break-even model' says Dan Jones. 'Although they are not there yet their losses have slimmed considerably.'

(Source: adapted from BBC News, June 2010)

Table 13.2 How changes in business circumstances affect the break-even chart

	Cause	Effect
Internal factors	• Extra launch advertising	• Fixed costs rise, so total costs rise and break-even point rises
	• Planned price increase	• Revenue rises more steeply; break-even point falls
	• Using more machinery (and less labour) in production	• Fixed costs rise while variable costs fall; uncertain effect on break-even point
External factors	• Fall in demand	• Break-even point is not affected, though margin of safety is reduced
	• Competitors' actions force price cut	• Revenue rises less steeply; break-even point rises
	• Fuel costs rise	• Variable and total cost lines rise more steeply; break-even point rises

Issues for analysis

Analytical issues in relation to break-even centre upon the effective use of break-even charts. It is important to appreciate how changes in the business environment might affect the break-even position of a business. Any analysis of break-even should recognise that changes in revenues or costs will impact upon the level of break-even output.

As an example, you should be able to state whether, in the following circumstances, break-even output will rise or fall:

- wage negotiations result in a 4 per cent pay rise
- the business rate levied upon a firm's premises is increased
- the market price for the business's product increases
- a change in the price of oil means that fuel prices fall by 5 per cent.

A break-even chart shows the level of profit or loss at any level of output. If the business's circumstances change, it is important to be able to quantify the extent to which profitability changes at any level of output.

Break-even analysis – an evaluation

There is a risk in exams of assuming that break-even charts tell you 'facts'. Break-even analysis seems simple to conduct and understand and it appears to be cheap and quick to carry out. That assumes, of course, that the business knows all its costs and can break them down into variable and fixed. Tesco certainly can, but not every business is as well managed. Football clubs such as Sheffield Wednesday, Portsmouth and Darlington have hit financial problems, partly because of ignorance of their financial circumstances. Similarly, few NHS hospitals could say with confidence how much it costs to provide a heart transplant.

Break-even analysis is of particular value when a business is first established. Having to work out the fixed and variable costs will help the managers make better decisions, for example on pricing. It also shows profit and loss at various levels of output, particularly when presented in the form of a chart. Indeed it may be that financial institutions will require this sort of financial information before lending any money to someone aspiring to run a business.

As long as the figures are accurate, break-even becomes especially useful when changes occur, such as rising raw material costs. The technique can allow for changing revenues and costs and gives a valuable guide to potential profitability.

Key terms

Break-even chart: a line graph showing total revenues and total costs at all possible levels of output or demand from zero to maximum capacity.

Contribution: total revenue less variable costs. The calculation of contribution is useful for businesses which are responsible for a range of products.

Fixed costs: fixed costs are any costs which do not vary directly with the level of output, for example, rent and rates.

Margin of safety: the amount by which current output exceeds the level of output necessary to break-even.

Variable costs: those costs which vary directly with the level of output. They represent payments made for the use of inputs such as labour, fuel and raw materials.

Key formulae

Break-even output: $\frac{\text{fixed costs}}{\text{contribution per unit}}$

Contribution per unit: selling price – variable costs per unit

Margin of safety: sales volume – break-even output

Total contribution: contribution per unit × unit sales

Revision questions (25 marks; 25 minutes)

1 What is meant by the term 'break-even point'? (2)

2 State **three** reasons why a business might conduct a break-even analysis. (3)

3 List the information necessary to construct a break-even chart. (4)

4 How would you calculate the contribution made by each unit of production which is sold? (2)

5 A business sells its products for £10 each and the variable cost of producing a single unit is £6. If its monthly fixed costs are £18,000 how many units must it sell to break-even each month? (3)

6 Explain why the variable cost and total revenue lines commence at the origin of a break-even chart. (3)

7 What point on a break-even chart actually illustrates break-even output? (2)

8 Explain how, using a break-even chart, you would illustrate the amount of profit or loss made at any given level of output. (2)

9 Why might a business wish to calculate its margin of safety? (2)

10 A business is currently producing 200,000 units of output annually and its break-even output is 120,000 units. What is its margin of safety? (2)

Revision exercises

Data response

Paul Jarvis is an entrepreneur and about to open his first hotel. He has forecast the following costs and revenues:

- maximum number of customers per month: 800
- monthly fixed costs: £10,000
- average revenue per customer: £110
- typical variable costs per customer: £90

Some secondary market research has suggested that Paul's prices may be too low. He is considering charging higher prices, though he is nervous about the impact this might have on his forecast sales. Paul has found his break-even chart useful during the planning of his new business, but is concerned that it might be misleading too.

Questions (45 marks; 50 minutes)

1 a) Construct the break-even chart for Paul's planned business. (9)

b) State, and show on the graph, the profit or loss made at a monthly sales level of 600 customers. (4)

c) State, and show on the graph, the margin of safety at that level of output. (4)

2 Paul's market research shows that in his first month of trading he can expect 450 customers at his hotel.

a) If Paul's research is correct, calculate the level of profit or loss he will make. (5)

b) Illustrate this level of output on your graph and show the profit or loss. (3)

3 Paul has decided to increase his prices to give an average revenue per customer of £120.

a) Draw the new total revenue line on your break-even chart to show the effect of this change. (3)

b) Mark on your diagram the new break-even point. (1)

c) Calculate Paul's new break-even number of customers to confirm the result shown on your chart. (6)

4 Paul is worried that his break-even chart may be 'misleading'. Do you agree with him? Justify your view. (10)

Data response

The Successful T-Shirt Company

Shelley has recently launched the Successful T-Shirt Company. It sells a small range of fashion T-shirts. The shirts are available in a range of colours and all contain the company's logo which is becoming increasingly desirable for young fashion-conscious people.

The shirts are sold to retailers for £35 each. They cost £16.50 to manufacture and the salesperson receives £2.50 commission for each item sold to retailers. The distribution cost for each shirt is £1.00 and current sales are 1,000 per month. The fixed costs of production are £11,250 per month.

The company is considering expanding its range of T-shirts and has approached its bank for a loan. The bank has requested the company draw up a business plan including a cashflow forecast and break-even chart.

Questions (30 marks; 40 minutes)

1 What is a break-even chart? (4)

2 Calculate the following:

a) The variable cost of producing 1,000 T-shirts.

b) The contribution earned through the sale of one T-shirt. (6)

3 Shelley has decided to manufacture the shirts in Poland. As a result the variable cost per T-shirt (*including* commission and distribution costs) will fall to £15 per T-shirt. However, fixed costs will rise to £12,000.

a) Calculate the new level of break-even for Shelley's T-shirts.

b) Calculate the margin of safety if sales are 1,000 T-shirts per month. (10)

4 Should Shelley rely on break-even analysis when taking business decisions? Justify your view. (10)

Data response

US: Saab lowering break-even point

Newly reorganised car-maker Saab is steadily reducing its break-even point and has more than enough cash to survive as it begins to rebuild sales, its chief executive officer has said. After near-liquidation by former owner General Motors, Saab must rebuild its sales from the start, CEO Jan Ake Jonsson told news agency AFP.

'We had been closed down for seven weeks,' Jonsson told reporters in Detroit. 'We couldn't order any material or do any advertising because we were in liquidation,' he said. 'Now we have about 4,500 cars in stock. We're completely focused on getting our products out as quickly as possible.'

The company is currently living on reserves, including loans from the European banks and a US $200m technology deal with Beijing Auto, according to AFP, though Jonsson said Saab should be able to break even in the second half of 2011. He hopes to reduce operating costs to the point where Saab can break even with annual sales of 80,000 to 85,000 vehicles though potential sales are significantly higher. Jonsson is confident Saab could sell as many as 125,000 units annually 'at which point we would be quite profitable.' 'These are very conservative estimates,' he told AFP, noting that Saab had sold 98,000 cars in 2008 when it was still owned by GM.

(Source: www.just-auto.com, 13 May 2010)

Questions (25 marks; 30 minutes)

1 Explain why Saab's management might have wanted to 'steadily reduce its break-even point'. (6)

2 a) If Jonsson achieves his sales expectations for Saab, what would be the company's margin of safety? (4)

b) Explain the possible importance of that safety margin to a business like Saab. (6)

3 In May 2010 Jonsson said Saab 'should be able to break-even in the second half of 2011'. Discuss the threats to Saab's survival in the period up until it reaches its break-even point. (9)

Essay questions *(40 marks each)*

1 'Break-even is the most vital part of a business plan for a new enterprise.' Do you agree with this statement? Justify your view.

2 'Break-even analysis is of limited value to a start-up business because it ignores the market.' To what extent do you agree with this statement?

14 Cash flow management and forecasting

Definition

Cash flow is the flow of money into and out of a business in a given time period. Cash flow forecasting is estimating the flow of cash in the future.

The importance of cash flow management

Managing cash flow is one of the most important aspects of financial management. Without adequate availability of cash from day to day, even a company with high sales could fail. As bills become due there has to be the cash available to pay. If a company cannot pay its bills, suppliers will refuse to deliver and staff will start looking for other jobs. Cash flow problems are the most common reason for business failure. This is particularly true for new businesses: it is estimated that 70 per cent of businesses that collapse in their first year fail because of cash flow problems.

Businesses need to continually review their current and future cash position. In order to be prepared and to understand future cash needs, businesses construct a **cash flow forecast**. This sets out the expected flows of cash into and out of the business for each month. In textbooks cash flows are normally shown for six months but they can be done for any period of time. Most firms want to look 12 months ahead, so the cash flow forecast is constantly updated.

A-grade application

In 2010 Portsmouth Football Club became the first Premier League club to go bust. In spite of getting into the FA Cup Final, the club was unable to pay its debts. The Administrator, Andrew Andronikou, estimated that the club owed around £119 million. There has been much discussion about how this level of debt had built up but it seems that the size of the wages bill was a major problem. It was estimated that the wages bill over the previous three years was at least 10 per cent higher than the revenue coming into the club. The administrator pointed out that over a five-year period, the wages bill was £247 million and total revenue was £221 million.

Who needs to use a cash flow forecast?

All businesses can benefit from using cash flow forecasts, but they are particularly useful for business start-ups. A carefully planned cash flow forecast will help ensure that the business has enough finance to keep afloat during the early months. This is the most difficult period for a business as sales may be slow. There will be little income but bills still need to be paid.

Existing businesses also need to be aware of their cash position. In many cases there are seasonal factors that make cash hard to manage. Every year a seaside hotel has to cope with winter months when cash flow will almost certainly be negative; in other words, cash out will be higher than cash in. A cash flow forecast will help to ensure that the business plans for future cash needs and will cope if unexpected events happen. If a business is growing, cash flow forecasts can be particularly useful. They enable the business to ensure that any growth is backed by sufficient funding.

Preparing a cash flow forecast

To prepare a cash flow forecast, businesses need to estimate all the money coming into and out of the business, month by month. These flows of money are then set onto a grid showing the cash movements in each month.

Cash in

In the example in Table 14.1 the business, Visible Engineering Ltd, is a new start-up. The business will receive an injection of capital of £30,000. This will be received in March. The business will start production in April and will only receive cash when sales start in May. Cash inflows are expected to increase each month until reaching a maximum of £15,000 in August.

It is important that the income from sales is shown when the cash is received not when the sale is made.

Outflow

Table 14.2 shows the cash outflow for Visible Engineering Ltd. In March the firm will buy machinery for £23,000. Materials will cost £6,000 each month. The first delivery in April must be paid for on delivery. After that the supplier will give the firm two months' credit so the next payments do not need to be made until July. Rent for the building costs £2,000 per month but the owner requires two months' rent in advance. Wages are estimated to be £2,000 per month and there are other expenses of £1,000 per month.

When these figures have been entered onto the grid, the total expenditure can be calculated.

Table 14.1 Cash inflow for Visible Engineering Ltd

Month (cash inflow, £s)	March	April	May	June	July	August
Capital	30,000					
Sales			7,000	10,000	13,000	15,000
Total inflow	**30,000**	**0**	**7,000**	**10,000**	**13,000**	**15,000**

Table 14.2 Cash outflow for Visible Engineering Ltd

Month (cash outflow £s)	March	April	May	June	July	August
Equipment	23,000					
Materials	0	6,000			6,000	6,000
Rent	4,000	2,000	2,000	2,000	2,000	2,000
Wages		2,000	2,000	2,000	2,000	2,000
Other expenses		1,000	1,000	1,000	1,000	1,000
Total outflow	**27,000**	**11,000**	**5,000**	**5,000**	**11,000**	**11,000**

The cash flow forecast can now be completed by calculating the following:

- *Monthly balance*: this is cash inflow for the month minus cash outflow. It shows each month if there is a positive or a negative movement of cash. In this case inflow is greater than outflow except in April. When outflow is greater than inflow, the monthly balance will be negative. This is shown in brackets to indicate that it is a minus figure.
- *Opening and closing balance*: this is like a bank statement. It shows what cash the business has at the beginning of the month (opening balance) and what the cash position is at the end of the month (closing balance). The closing balance is the opening balance plus the monthly balance (e.g. for August, the month starts with £1,000 in the bank, another £4,000 flows in during the month, so the month closes with a bank balance of £5,000). The closing balance shows

the business its expected net cash position each month.

Table 14.3 shows the completed cash flow forecast. This shows that there is a negative cash balance for the months of April, May and June. Only in July does the business start having a positive cash flow.

As there is no such thing as negative money, this cash flow forecast shows the business that it must take action if it is to avoid problems in the early months. The easiest remedy for a cash flow problem such as this is a bank overdraft.

Table 14.3 Cash flow forecast for Visible Engineering Ltd

Month (£s)	March	April	May	June	July	August
Cash inflow						
Capital	30,000					
Sales			7,000	10,000	13,000	15,000
Total inflow	**30,000**	**0**	**7,000**	**10,000**	**13,000**	**15,000**
Outflow						
Equipment	23,000					
Materials	0	6,000			6,000	6,000
Rent	4,000	2,000	2,000	2,000	2,000	2,000
Wages		2,000	2,000	2,000	2,000	2,000
Other expenses		1,000	1,000	1,000	1,000	1,000
Total outflow	**27,000**	**11,000**	**5,000**	**5,000**	**11,000**	**11,000**
Monthly balance	3,000	(11,000)	2,000	5,000	2,000	4,000
Opening balance	0	3,000	(8,000)	(6,000)	(1,000)	1,000
Closing balance	**3,000**	**(8,000)**	**(6,000)**	**(1,000)**	**1,000**	**5,000**

Benefits of cash flow forecasts

A cash flow forecast will enable a business to do the following things.

- Anticipate the timing and amounts of any cash shortages. In the example above, the business can see from the cash flow forecast if it has sufficient cash. In fact this business does not have enough cash for three months (April, May and June). There is no such thing as negative money so the business will not be able to make some of its payments: it will not be able to pay wages or the rent. This would mean that although the business looks cash rich in the longer term – by July they have a positive cash flow – they might not survive.
- Arrange financial cover for any anticipated shortages of cash. Having information about when the business will have a cash shortage means that the business can take measures to ensure that it has cash available. In the example above, the business needs to find additional finance for the three months when it has a cash shortage.
- Review the timings and amounts of receipts and payments.
- Obtain loans (if the problems are long term) or overdrafts (if the problems are short term).

If a firm wants to take out a loan, the bank will always request a cash flow forecast. Banks do this in order to ensure that the business:

- has enough cash to enable it to survive
- is able to pay the interest on the loan
- will be able to repay the loan
- is aware of the need for cash flow management.

A-grade application

Blockbuster warns that it is in danger of bankruptcy

The DVD rental chain Blockbuster warned early in 2010 that it was facing the possibility of going bankrupt. The US-based company is facing a double squeeze on its cash flow. High interest payments on its huge debt are one burden but it is also generating lower revenue because of a change in the way its customers view films. The market has changed from store-based rentals to more online operations. The new technology that allows films to be downloaded or streamed directly has also affected the revenue of the business. In the UK the company is trying to reduce costs by renegotiating the leases on its 630 stores.

How reliable are cash flow forecasts?

In order to prepare a cash flow forecast, businesses need to make assumptions about the future, although they may be able to make some use of actual figures, such as the monthly rent agreed with the landlord.

When looking at cash flow forecasts, it is useful for the firm to be aware that the figures are estimates and to build in some safety margins. Companies should ask themselves what would happen if:

- sales are lower than expected
- the customer does not pay up on time
- prices of materials are higher than expected.

Example

Treasured Memories produces commemorative pottery. The company has been approached by a London store to supply a limited edition of 1,000 plates for the 60th anniversary of the Queen's accession to the Throne on 8 February 2012. The plates will sell to the store for £35 each. The cost of materials is £9 per plate and labour costs are £8 each. Additional variable costs will be £3 per plate.

Figure 14.1 Commemorative pottery products

The store wants to have the plates available for sale from June 2011. The store will pay for the goods in August 2011. The plates will take four months to produce, so production needs to start in February 2011. Production would then be evenly spread over four months. The suppliers of the materials have agreed to give them one month's credit. The order seems too good to refuse, but the finance manager is worried. He has produced the cash flow forecast shown in Table 14.4.

Using spreadsheets enables companies to look at some of these possibilities. With the use of spreadsheets it is possible to adjust both the timings and amounts. This enables a business to evaluate the most likely and the worst-case situations. The business also needs to be aware that the figures are based on current assumptions about the market and the economic climate. If changes are detected look at how these will affect the cash flow position.

The cash flow forecast shows that the order could cause serious cash flow problems for the company. The company has decided to accept the order, but it needs to ensure that it has sufficient cash to finance production until March. The management has done this by negotiating an overdraft facility of up to £20,000. They have also negotiated to pay for supplies after two months rather than one month. Finally, they have negotiated with the store to receive payment in July 2011. All of these measures mean they now feel confident to accept the order and although they have an overdraft facility, this will be used for a minimum length of time and the cost will be kept to a minimum.

Table 14.4 Treasured Memories cash flow forecast

Month (£s)	February	March	April	May	June	July	August
Income							35,000
Expenditure							
Wages	2,000	2,000	2,000	2,000			
Materials		2,250	2,250	2,250	2,250		
Other costs	750	750	750	750			
Total expenditure	2,750	5,000	5,000	5,000	2,250		
Opening balance	0	(2,750)	(7,750)	(12,750)	(17,750)	(20,000)	(20,000)
Closing balance	(2,750)	(7,750)	(12,750)	(17,750)	(20,000)	(20,000)	15,000

Issues for analysis

When answering an exam question on cash flow management and forecasting, it is important to understand that the figures are only the starting point for analysis and decision making. Consideration needs to be given to the following points.

- The validity of the figures: who constructed the forecast? Are the figures reliable and unbiased?
- What the figures show (i.e. a careful analysis of the position month by month).
- The need to take full account of the circumstances of the business. If sales are to a foreign country, payment may not be certain and even if it arrives, changes in currency values may make cash inflows worth fewer pounds than forecast.
- The differences between cash flow and profitability.

Cash flow management – an evaluation

There is no doubt that cash flow management is a vital ingredient in the success of any small business. For a new business, cash flow forecasting helps to answer key questions:

- Is the venture viable?
- How much capital is needed?
- Which are the most dangerous months?

For an existing business, the cash flow forecast identifies the amount and timing of any cash flow problems in the future. It is also useful for evaluating new orders or ventures.

Nevertheless, completing a cash flow forecast does not ensure survival and consideration needs to be given to its usefulness and limitations. It must be remembered that cash flow forecasts are based on estimates. These estimates are not just amounts but also timings. The firm must be aware that actual figures can differ wildly from estimates – especially for a new, inexperienced firm. When preparing cash flow forecasts, managers need to ask themselves 'what if?' A huge mistake is to only look at one forecast. It is far better to look at **best case** and **worst case** possibilities. Spreadsheets allow for easy manipulation of data, making it easy to see the impact of single and multiple changes to the forecast figures. This should help to reduce the risks but it does not guarantee results. Having completed a cash flow forecast and taken the necessary steps to ensure financing also does not guarantee success. The firm needs to be continually aware of the economic and market climate and its current cash position.

Key terms

Best case: an optimistic estimate of the best possible outcome (e.g. if sales prove much higher than expected).

Cash flow forecast: estimating future monthly cash inflows and outflows, to find out the net cash flow.

Negative cash flow: when cash outflows are greater than cash inflows.

Overdraft: short-term borrowing from a bank. The business only borrows as much as it needs to cover its daily cash shortfall.

Worst case: a pessimistic estimate assuming the worst possible outcome (e.g. sales are very disappointing).

Revision questions (25 marks; 25 minutes)

1 What is meant by 'cash flow'? (2)

2 Why is it important to manage cash flow? (4)

3 What is a cash flow forecast? (3)

4 Explain two limitations of cash flow forecasts. (4)

5 Give two reasons why a bank manager might want to see a cash flow forecast before giving a loan to a new business. (2)

6 How might a firm benefit from delaying its cash outflows? (3)

7 What problems might a firm face if its cash flow forecast proved unreliable? (3)

8 How might a firm benefit from constructing its cash flow forecasts on a computer spreadsheet? (4)

Revision exercises

Cash flow activity

A business is to be started up on 1 January next year with £40,000 of share capital. It will be opening a designer clothes shop. During January it plans to spend £45,000 on start-up costs (buying a lease, buying equipment, decorating, etc.). On 1 February it will open its doors and gain sales over the next five months of: £12,000, £16,000, £20,000, £25,000 and £24,000 respectively. Each month it must pay £10,000 in fixed overheads (salaries, heat, light, telephone, etc.) and its variable costs will amount to half the revenue.

Complete the cash flow table to find out:

1 The company's forecast cash position at the end of June.

2 The maximum level of overdraft the owners will need to negotiate with the bank before starting up.

Cash flow table (all figures in £000s)

	Jan	Feb	Mar	Apr	May	June
Cash at start						
Cash in						
Cash out						
Net cash flow						
Opening balance						
Closing balance						

Data response

Merlin Construction

Merlin Construction has planning permission to convert an old office block into four flats. The directors managed to borrow £130,000 from the bank in January. They used £100,000 to buy the building that month. The work will start in January and take nine months to complete. The plan is to build and sell the two upstairs flats in June and then complete the ground floor flats. These will be sold in September. The flats should sell for £60,000 each. Materials are estimated to cost about £10,000 a month with one month's credit. Wages and salaries will be £4,000 a month. Interest charges will be £1,000 a month. Other expenses will be £1,000 a month.

Questions *(30 marks; 35 minutes)*

1. Construct a cash flow forecast for the business for January to September. (10)
2. Outline two significant features of this cash flow forecast. (6)
3. Discuss two possible courses of action. (8)
4. Examine two ways in which the cash flow forecast might be unreliable. (6)

Data response

D&S Jewellers

Danielle and Sujugan chose to open a jewellery shop because she loves the products and he knows how to get them – cheaply from India. They opened their first shop in May and in the period until August managed to break even. That was fine because they knew that jewellery shops make 50 per cent of the year's takings in the run-up to Christmas, so both were confident that the first year was going well. Despite help from an uncle who has been in the jewellery business for 35 years, Sujugan has not quite finished this cash flow forecast for the next six months.

Cash flow forecast for D&S Jewellers

Month (£s)	Sept	Oct	Nov	Dec	Jan	Feb
Cash inflow						
From cash sales	12,000	16,000	20,000	80,000	6,000	5,000
From credit sales	5,000	6,000	10,000	14,000	50,000	2,000
Total cash in	**17,000**	**22,000**	**a**	**b**	**c**	**d**
Cash outflow						
Security costs	3,000	3,000	3,000	4,000	3,000	3,000
Buying jewellery stocks	10,000	25,000	55,000	5,000	0	2,000
Rent	9,000	0	0	9,000	0	0
Wages	8,000	8,000	8,000	8,000	8,000	8,000
Other expenses	1,000	1,000	1,000	1,000	1,000	1,000
Total outflow						
Monthly balance	(14,000)	**e**	**f**	**g**	**h**	**i**
Opening balance	8,000	**j**	**k**	**l**	**m**	**n**
Closing balance	**o**	**p**	**q**	**r**	**s**	**t**

Questions (25 marks; 25 minutes)

1 Explain two problems Sujugan may have had in drawing up this cash flow forecast for D&S Jewellers. (6)

2 Complete the job for Sujugan by working out all missing figures a–t. (10)

3 What would you recommend that Danielle and Sujugan do about this forecast? Explain the reasons behind your answer. (9)

Data response

From Cocoa to Cash

Joe Callery and David O'Doherty started Celtic Chocolates in 1990 in a converted cottage in County Meath, Ireland. It cost about £50,000 to get the chocolate business started.

'It took about two years to get a marketable product together', says Joe Callery. 'For the first two years, we were really selling nothing'. Only in 1995 did the business start to generate a positive cash flow. Now annual turnover is above €1.5m and the business has 20 full-time staff. A factory built behind the cottage has since been extended. 'In food manufacturing, you have to invest constantly to stay ahead.'

The product portfolio is based on three product ranges: purely seasonal products such as Easter Eggs; seasonal luxury after-dinner mints and truffles; and a range of 'free-from' chocolates, including diabetic and dairy-free chocolates. They are all at the luxury end of the market, though they can be bought at supermarkets such as Tesco as well as at specialty food stores.

'This whole business revolves around Christmas and Easter. We have just finished Easter production and will close for two weeks. Then from May to September we will be preparing for Christmas. Single days, such as St Valentine's Day or Mother's Day, are not significant.'

For this reason, Celtic Chocolates has worked hard to build up its specialist lines. 'The real difficulty is cash flow during down times. Specialist lines will sell all year round. In Ireland, we have 700–800 retail customers all buying at Christmas and Easter. About 200 customers buy all year round. That's what keeps us going.'

A long time ago, the company learnt about the risks of relying on one big customer. In 1999, Boots was its main client, accounting for about 40 per cent of turnover. Then Boots decided to cut back all products that were not central to its business and Celtic Chocolates was dropped. The sales slump forced the firm to make redundancies.

Starting a business is about surviving the first five years, according to Callery. 'We had borrowed money to finance investment, then rates went through the roof', he said. 'At the end of the first year, interest rates were so high that we owed more money to the bank than we had at the beginning – even though we had paid back 20 per cent of the amount borrowed.'

'We just kept going, that's all you can do. Sometimes you just have to wait it out.'

In 2008 Celtic Chocolates celebrated winning a coveted Gold Award at Britain's 'Great Taste Awards' for its new Organic Fairtrade mint products. In 2010 further awards came the company's way for its 'Free From' range. Twenty years after its start-up, Celtic Chocolates is a perfect example of how a small business can find a profitable niche in a big marketplace.

Questions (30 marks; 35 minutes)

1 Analyse why a new business such as Celtic Chocolates might struggle with cash flow in the early stages of its start-up. (8)

2 Explain why it's risky for cash flow for a business such as Celtic Chocolates to 'rely on one big customer'. (6)

3 a) Explain the seasonal cash flow problem faced by Celtic Chocolates. (6)

b) Discuss whether Celtic Chocolates should decide to put an end to its seasonal cash flow problems by scrapping the production of lines such as Easter Eggs. (10)

Setting budgets

Definition

A budget is a target for costs or revenue that a firm or department must aim to reach over a given period of time.

Introduction

Budgeting is the process of setting targets covering all aspects of costs and revenues. It is a method for turning a firm's strategy into reality. Nothing can be done in business without money; budgets tell individual managers how much they can spend to achieve their objectives. For instance, a football manager might be given a transfer **expenditure budget** of £20 million to buy players. With the budget in place, the transfer dealing can get underway.

A budgeting system shows how much can be spent, and gives managers a way to check whether they are on track. Most firms use a system of budgetary control as a means of supervision. The process is as follows:

1. Make a judgement of the likely sales revenues for the coming year.
2. Set a cost ceiling that allows for an acceptable level of profit.
3. This budget for the whole company's costs is then broken down by division, department or by cost centre.
4. The budget may then be broken down further so that each manager has a budget and therefore some spending power.

In a business start-up, the budget should provide enough spending power to finance vital needs such as building work, decoration, recruiting and paying staff and marketing. If a manager overspends in one area, she or he knows that it is essential to cut back elsewhere. A good manager gets the best possible value from the budgeted sum.

What is budgeting for?

- To ensure that no department or individual spends more than the company expects, thereby preventing unpleasant surprises.
- To provide a yardstick against which a manager's success or failure can be measured (and rewarded). For example, a store manager may have to meet a monthly sales budget of £25,000 at a maximum operating cost of £18,000. As long as the budget holder believes this target is possible, the attempt to achieve it will be motivating. The company can then provide bonuses for achieving or beating the profit target.
- To enable spending power to be delegated to local managers who are in a better position to know how best to use the firm's money. This should improve and speed up the decision-making process – and help motivate the local budget holders. The management expert Peter Drucker refers to 'management by self-control'. He regards this as the ideal approach. Managers should have clear targets, clear budgets and the power to decide how to achieve them. Then they will try everything they can to succeed.
- Budgeting can motivate the staff in a department. If budget figures are used as a clear basis for assessing their performance, it becomes clear to staff what they must achieve to be considered successful.

Types of budget

Income budget

The **income budget** sets a minimum target for the desired revenue level to be achieved over a period of time. If a manager knows, half way through the year, that sales figures have not been strong enough to achieve the target, he might decide to run a price promotion or a 'buy one get one free' (BOGOF). When buying a new car it is clever to wait for the last day of the month, as showroom managers are often trying desperately to achieve their monthly sales target. Their incentive may be a salary bonus or a monthly prize such as a trip to the Caribbean for the month's top-performing sales manager. Your incentive is a cheaper car!

Expenditure budget

The **expenditure budget** sets a maximum target for costs (e.g. the manager of McDonald's in Derby may have a staff budget of £2,100 for the month of November). Spending beyond an expenditure budget occasionally will be tolerated, but a manager who persistently overspends is likely to get a stern talking to. An intelligent boss will also question expenditure underspending (e.g. not spending the budget for safety training, as this may cause huge problems later on).

Profit budget

The **profit budget** is a function of the previous two budgets: the higher the income budget and the lower the expenditure, the higher the profit. Senior managers should look with care at how a profit budget has been met or beaten. For example, the profit achievement may have been a result of cost-cutting that threatens health and safety. Of course, managers are supposed to meet their profit targets, but there is more to running a business successfully than simply getting the numbers right.

A-grade application

The BP disaster

On 23 March 2005 a huge explosion at BP's Texas oil refinery killed 15 people and injured more than 180, most of whom were BP's own staff. The refinery, America's third biggest, had suffered safety problems before. In 2004 two workers died when scalded by super-heated water that escaped from a high-pressure pipe and, in a separate incident, BP was fined $63,000 for safety breaches at the plant.

After an enquiry, the Chairwoman of the US Chemical Safety Board reported that 'BP implemented a 25% cut on fixed costs from 1998 to 2000 that adversely impacted maintenance expenditures at the refinery'. The report stated that 'BP's global management' (i.e. British Head Office) 'was aware of problems with maintenance spending and infrastructure well before March 2005'. Yet they did nothing about it. The Chairwoman delivered the final critique: 'Every successful corporation must contain its costs. But at an ageing facility like Texas City, it is not responsible to cut budgets related to safety and maintenance without thoroughly examining the impact on the risk of a catastrophic accident'. BP confirmed that its own internal investigation had findings 'generally consistent with those of the CSB'.

In 2010, there was an echo of this disaster when an explosion on a BP well in the Gulf of Mexico killed 11 people and caused the biggest oil spill in American history.

(Source: Adapted from Topical Cases, www.a-zbusinesstraining.com)

Setting budgets

Setting budgets is not an easy job. How do you decide exactly what level of sales are likely next year, especially for new businesses with no previous trading to rely on? Furthermore, how can you plan for costs if the cost of your raw materials tends to fluctuate? Most firms treat last year's budget figures as the main determinant of this year's budget, with minor adjustments made for inflation and other foreseeable changes. Given the firm's past experience, budget-setting should be quite quick and quite accurate.

For start-ups, setting budgets will be a much tougher job. The entrepreneur will need to rely on:

- a 'guesstimate' of likely sales in the early months of the start-up
- the entrepreneur's expertise and experience, which will be better if the entrepreneur has worked in the industry before
- the entrepreneur's instinct, based on market understanding
- a significant level of market research.

An alternative approach is zero budgeting. This approach sets each department's budget at zero and demands that budget holders, in setting their budget, justify every pound they ask for. This helps to avoid the common phenomenon of budgets creeping upwards each year.

The best criteria for setting budgets are:

- to relate the budget directly to the business objective. If a company wants to increase sales and market share, the best method might be to increase the advertising budget and thereby boost demand
- to involve as many people as possible in the process. People will be more committed to reaching the targets if they have had a say in how the budget was set.

A-grade application

Budgeting helps but is not easy for start-ups

Stanford University research into 78 business start-ups showed that firms with budgeting systems were more likely to survive and experience significant growth rates. They reported that budgeting systems allowed senior staff access to the information needed when making decisions. However, they acknowledged the difficulties in setting budgets for new start-ups. They point out that for a new company, predicting the future is hugely unpredictable and setting 12-month budgets is likely to be unrealistic.

Simple budget statements

A simple example of a budget statement is shown in Table 15.1.

This information is only of value if it proves possible for a manager to believe that these figures are achievable. Only then will he or she be motivated to try to turn the budgets into reality.

Table 15.1 Example of a budget statement

(£s)	January	February	March
Income	25,000	28,000	30,000
Variable costs	10,000	12,000	13,000
Fixed costs	10,000	10,000	11,000
Total expenditure	20,000	22,000	24,000
Profit	5,000	6,000	6,000

Problems in setting budgets

The main problem is that individual managers want as much spending power as possible (a high budget). This will help them do their job successfully and more enjoyably (e.g. a big expense account). The bosses, though, want to keep costs as low as possible among junior managers (i.e. to set low budgets). A senior Cadbury's manager might feel sure that an advertising budget of £2 million will be enough for Creme Eggs this year. Yet the brand manager for Creme Eggs may have a convincing argument for why £3.5 million is needed. (And no-one knows the 'right' figure.)

The main problems in setting budgets occur when:

- a new firm or new manager lacks experience in knowing what things really cost
- a senior manager is too arrogant to listen to his/her staff, and just sets a budget without discussion (successful budgets should be agreed, not set)
- the type of business makes it hard to set budgets in a meaningful way (meaning that managers struggle to take them seriously); see the Application box below.

A-grade application

Chessington World of Adventures

In April 2010 Chessington World of Adventures opened up for its summer season. The newly appointed Merchandise Manager (in charge of all non-food sales) was given his sales budget for the year, which had been set 6 per cent higher than for 2009. He thought the budget was quite ambitious, especially when a cold April and May meant that crowds were down. Then the period June–August saw hot, dry weather and the turnstiles were buzzing again. As a hot day at Chessington can boost crowds by 50 per cent, he didn't need to make any effort to meet his budget. Do budgets have a purpose in a business such as this?

Figure 15.1 Plenty of thirsty customers

Issues for analysis

Especially relevant to a small business owner will be deciding whether designing and implementing a budgeting system will cost more in terms of time and money than it might save. In other words, he or she must decide on the opportunity costs involved. In the often chaotic world of a small business start-up, it is easy to see how time spent talking to customers and suppliers would be more valuable. It is harder to appreciate how time spent in front of a computer spreadsheet estimating revenues and costs will help to enhance profit and the chances of survival.

Setting budgets – an evaluation

The sophistication of budgeting systems is usually directly linked to the size of a business. Huge multinationals have incredibly complex budgeting systems. For a small business start-up, any budgeting system is likely to be far more simplistic. Most will rely on a rough breakdown of how the start-up budget is to be divided between the competing demands. There is, however, no doubt that budgeting provides a more effective system of controlling a business's finances than no system at all.

Key terms

Expenditure budget: setting a maximum figure on what a department or manager can spend over a period of time; this is to control costs.

Income budget: setting a minimum figure for the revenue to be generated by a product, a department or a manager.

Profit budget: setting a minimum figure for the profit to be achieved over a period of time.

Revision questions *(30 marks; 30 minutes)*

1 Explain the meaning of the term 'budgeting'. (2)

2 List three advantages that a budgeting system brings to a company. (3)

3 Why is it valuable to have a yardstick against which performance can be measured? (3)

4 What are the disadvantages of a zero-based budgeting system? (3)

5 Briefly explain how most companies actually set next year's budgets. (3)

6 Why should budget holders have a say in the setting of their budgets? (4)

7 Complete the following budget statement by filling in the gaps: (8)

	January	February	March	April
Income	4,200	4,500	4,000	
Variable costs	1,800		2,000	1,800
Fixed costs	1,200	1,600		1,600
Total costs		3,600	4,100	
Profit				600

8 Amend the budget statement completed in Question 7 to show the income levels needed to generate a profit of £1,000 per month, assuming there is no change in costs. (4)

Revision exercises

Data response

The partnership began in the Atlantic Ocean. Kurt and Brian were both windsurfing fanatics and got to know each other one winter in the Canary Isles. Looking for a way to fund ever more expensive winter water sports trips, they pooled their savings to buy the lease on a flooded former gravel pit back in the UK. The location, just outside London, gave them access to a large market of affluent water sports enthusiasts. 'KB Wetsports' could provide this market with their fix of windsurfing, dinghy sailing or kayaking. In addition to the fees for use of the lake and tuition fees for beginners, a shop would also feature at the centre, selling specialist water sport supplies that were hard to find inland. Both Kurt and Brian had studied management at university and knew that budgeting would be important. They could use it to control expenses and to motivate their small team of staff. They drew up the budget statement below:

	Jan–Mar	Apr–Jun	Jul–Sep	Oct–Dec
Shop sales	200	3,000	5,000	2,000
Lake fees	0	22,000	25,000	2,800
Stock	2,500	1,000	2,500	1,000
Wages	1,000	5,000	5,000	1,000
Overheads	1,000	4,000	6,000	4,000
Profit				

Questions (30 marks; 30 minutes)

1 Complete the budget statement by filling in the gaps. (4)

2 Adjust the budget to show the effect of a 50 per cent increase in shop sales in the third quarter and a 25 per cent increase in wages in quarter 4. (4)

3 Explain why a budgeting system might help KB Wetsports to:

a) control expenses (6)

b) motivate staff (6)

4 To what extent is budget-setting crucial to the success of a small business start-up such as KB Wetsports? (10)

Data response

Cutting work trip hotel costs

According to new research, UK organisations are over spending by £1.3 billion every year on unnecessarily extravagant business trips. Nearly half of all organisations fail to produce an official business travel policy. Therefore, many employees admit to booking what they want and 88% claim not to be influenced by cost.

Stephen Alambritis, Chief Spokesman, Federation of Small Businesses, commented: 'Business owners understand the importance of face-to-face meetings and consider personal contact with customers an essential part of generating new sales. But well-run firms control the cost of business travel, setting budgets for both transport and accommodation. Controlling costs across the business underpins future growth and success.'

The findings were alarming – UK businesses simply don't maintain financial control over employee business trips.

The wastage facts:

- Nearly half (48%) of all organisations never set a business trip budget. This figure rises to 59% when relating to small to medium businesses.
- Over 40% of employees make their own individual business trip arrangements and claim that they can spend what they like on trips.
- An overwhelming 88% say they aren't influenced by cost.
- Almost a third (30%) of 18–29 year olds exploit business trips as perks.
- Only 12% of employees believe their organisations are interested in cost-cutting.

This clear lack of control has left employees free to squander up to £1.3 billion of their employer's money every year.

(Source: Adapted from 'Cutting work trip hotel costs', www.workingbalance.co.uk)

Questions (20 marks; 25 minutes)

1 Identify and explain three pieces of evidence from the text that demonstrates the problems for firms that operate without a budget. (9)

2 Explain how a small business might benefit from setting expenditure budgets for its business travel. (5)

3 Outline two problems a business might have in setting a travel budget. (6)

Assessing business start-ups

Definition

Assessing means weighing up (i.e. making a judgement). This assessment should mirror the ways in which entrepreneurs need to decide: should I go ahead or not?

Introduction

Social entrepreneur Duncan Goose had, by mid-2010, established One Water as a £2 million brand. It was funding the building of a new water pump in Africa every eight days, and he was able to focus the six staff on his primary objective: one new water pump built every day.

Yet he was already looking towards a new project, One Toilet Tissue. The profits from selling the tissue would fund hygienic toilet blocks in schools in Africa. But launching a new idea takes time and money – and he was short of both. If One Toilet Tissue drained Duncan's energies and those of his staff, what might be the effect on One Water? Duncan had to make a careful assessment of whether or not to start up his next project.

Although he could see the reasons against, Duncan decided to go ahead. His objective in giving up a comfortable job and salary to start One was to make a difference. How could he stop now? The opportunity was there for building on One Water's success, so it would seem wrong to stop. The risks of failure only made it more of a challenge. Duncan made an assessment of the risks, costs and benefits of starting One Toilet Tissue, but was motivated mainly by his personality: he wanted the challenge.

How should one assess whether or not a business start-up is worthwhile? There are four issues to consider:

- the business objectives
- the business plan
- the risks involved
- the possible causes and consequences of failure.

Start-up objectives

There are three main types of objective when starting a business: financial, personal and social.

Financial

Some entrepreneurs are consciously setting out to get rich. They may be hoping to make enough money to retire by the age of 45 or even 25. For them, the ideal is to start up and build a business so that it can be sold or **floated** on the stock market. Either way, they will turn hard work into capital – lots of it. Mike Ashley started Sports Direct as a teenager and – aged 42 – floated it on the stock market. He sold 43 per cent of the business for more than £900 million, keeping the remaining 57 per cent of the shares. He then used his personal cash to buy Newcastle United FC.

The other financial goal is not to get rich, but simply to make a living. People who open a small grocery or sweetshop want to earn enough for the family, but may not be especially ambitious. Their financial goals may be no more than to make £25,000–£40,000 a year from the business.

Personal

Many people start up their own business because they want to prove that they can succeed. Perhaps they are disappointed with their own career and feel: 'this will show them'. Or they are trying to prove something to themselves.

Among the key personal goals are to:

- be my own boss
- show what I can do
- get out of a boring career
- be able to build something
- avoid later regrets (if failing to take advantage of a business opportunity)
- build something for my family.

Social

As in the case of Duncan Goose, some people are true **social entrepreneurs**. The way they achieve their personal goals is through an enterprise that has a purpose other than profit-making. Yet it would be wise to be sceptical. For every one person who is a true social entrepreneur, there are probably ten who cover their financial ambitions in green or charitable clothing. If 'carbon neutral' is a message that sells, many will adopt the slogan as a way to boost profit. Despite this, the fact that true social entrepreneurs exist means that it would be simplistic to suggest that all business start-ups are about making money.

Assessing start-up objectives

The success of a new organisation can only be measured in relation to the objectives of its founder. A London pizza business called Pizza Euforia started eight years ago with the ambition of creating a chain of 20 restaurants within three years. Today there are two outlets, one of which is barely breaking even. Clearly this is no success. Yet government statistics show that restaurant start-ups have one of the lowest survival rates of all businesses: 40 per cent fail within three years. So Pizza Euforia failed in relation to the founders' objectives, but not compared with national data.

The reason for setting an objective is to give a target to strive for (i.e. to provide motivation). The clearer the objective the better, such as the One Water objective of building one water pump per day. Some new firms start with no clear objective. The entrepreneur may just be looking for survival in year 1 'and then let's see where we get to'. Woolly objectives such as this may interfere with the firm's progress. The problem will be most acute if the business employs several staff. Ideally, every staff member would treat every customer as precious – the future of the business. This would be easier to establish if everyone had a clear sense of purpose and direction.

Assessing the strengths and weaknesses of a business plan

There are two issues to consider here. A business plan is a detailed look at why and how a business idea could become successful. To raise capital from investors, there is an earlier stage that must be mastered: the **business model**. Investors want the business idea summed up briefly, so that they can try to picture how the business can succeed. Examples include the following:

- 'Chocolate': a chain of High Street outlets offering varieties of hot chocolate, chocolate shakes, chocolate ice creams and chocolate bars; mainly takeaway but with bar stools for eating in; start with one outlet, build to four or five then use franchising for further growth.
- 'Eggxactly': patent-protected waterless cookers for the perfect 'boiled' egg selling for around £30. Start by manufacturing in Britain and selling direct on the internet; once the business has built up, distribute more product to retailers, moving production to China when sales volumes are high enough.

A good business model must have the potential to become profitable and – for venture capital investors – have significant growth prospects.

The business plan should develop the business model into a working document. It should show what needs to be done, by when and at what cost. A strong business plan will not necessarily be very long, but it will cover all the key aspects of the specific business being looked at. For example, a

Figure 16.1 The business plan for 'Chocolate' needs to be more detailed than the business model

business plan for Eggxactly will need to set out the following.

- The track record of the manufacturer chosen to supply the products and whether there is a back-up company in case of supply problems.
- The relationship between internet orders and supply. Will there be a big warehouse of stock or will each item be produced, packed and posted per order?
- The supply cost per machine. What gross profit will that generate compared with the £30 selling price?
- The method used to attract customers to the website. If a marketing campaign is needed, how big is the budget and how will it be spent?
- How a Chinese supplier will be selected and monitored. Will there be a permanent Eggxactly employee in China to carry out quality checks?

These and many other issues must be tackled fully. If an important aspect of the business seems poorly thought through, investors may look elsewhere.

Why start-ups can be risky

The future is uncertain, therefore every business decision is risky. Latest research shows that only one in seven new products is a success, and these products are the high-profile ones from companies such as L'Oreal or Cadbury – launched in a blaze of publicity. Table 16.1 shows how old the Cadbury product portfolio is. Between these years of success have come countless new product flops – most forgotten by now. So, if big companies with big market research and advertising budgets struggle, how can a small business start-up be anything other than risky?

The risks come from all directions; all are based on uncertainty. A small business cannot know how high or low sales will be, nor can it know for certain what all its costs will be. Hiring staff may prove far

Table 16.1 Cadbury brands – successes and flops

Cadbury's big-sellers		Cadbury's flops	
Brand	**Launch date**	**Brand**	**Launch date**
Cadbury's Dairy Milk	1905	Cadbury Strollers	1995
Cadbury's Milk Tray	1915	Fuse Bar	1996
Cadbury's Flake	1920	Cadbury's Marble	1998
Crunchie Bar	1929	Cadbury's Spira	1999
Cadbury's Fudge	1949	Cadbury's Brunchbar	2001
Cadbury's Creme Egg	1971	Dream with Strawberries	2004
Double Decker	1976	Double Decker with Nuts	2005
Cadbury's Heroes	1999	Melts	2006
Cadbury's Wispa (relaunch)	2009		

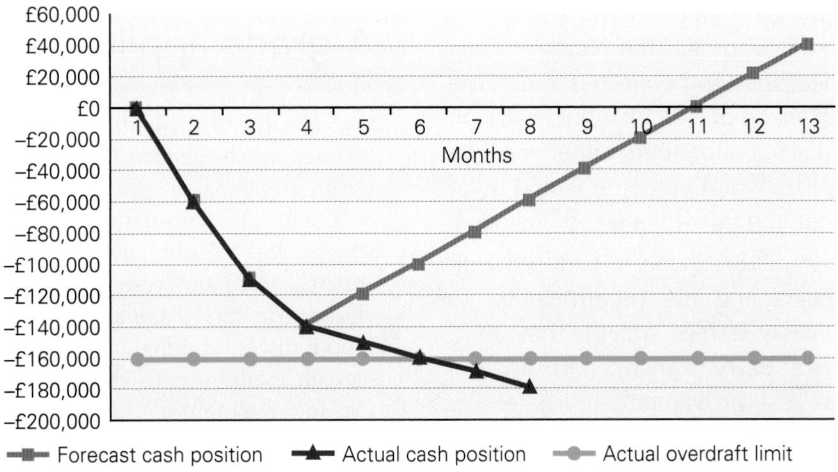

Figure 16.2 Cash flow crisis

harder than expected, and keeping good staff may be the hardest thing of all. The big risk at the start is that teething troubles may hit the cash position of the business, forcing it to close. Figure 16.2 shows what might happen to a restaurant with a set-up cost of £140,000 that has fewer customers than forecast in its first year. Instead of making profits in the months after opening, it is losing money. Its bank could close it down at any time after month six.

Why start-ups may fail

There are three main types of reason for start-up failure:

- poor analysis of the market (i.e. the opportunity did not exist)
- right idea, but poor execution of the plan (i.e. put into practice badly)
- right idea, but bad luck (e.g. fierce competitor opens nearby or something unexpected happens).

Poor market analysis

China Fang opened in Cheshire in 2009. Its location was on a busy main road in a beautiful corner building. There was a side-road for parking and enough room for a kitchen and a restaurant seating 40 people. It opened to good customer numbers as local residents were curious to try it. There were no other restaurants nearby, just a pizza takeaway. Early customers were very pleased with the quality of the food and service, though they found the prices 'a little high'. All seemed well set, but after a month or two customer numbers steadily fell away. The problem was that locals preferred to go into the town centre, where there was a bit of a buzz in the evenings. A visit to China Fang was too low-key and quiet. It was a good restaurant in the wrong location. The restaurant closed in early 2011.

Right idea, wrong execution

A good business idea might be poorly carried out. There are an enormous number of mistakes that can be made, including the following:

- Poor staff recruitment and/or training and/or supervision: staff may enjoy joking with each other in a way that irritates or insults customers.
- Faulty purchasing: a young entrepreneur may set up a stylish clothes shop but prove poor at selecting and buying stock from suppliers such as the fashion houses (i.e. right shop but wrong stock).
- Too desperate: any business needs to establish itself and the process is hard to rush; over-hasty 'buy-one-drink-get-one-free' offers can make a bar busy without building brand loyalty; when another bar makes a better promotional offer, the customers desert the first one.
- Failure to control cash flow: the business operation may be going well, but if the finances are poorly managed, the bank may close down a business with a great future.

Right idea, bad luck

You might come up with a well-considered plan for a new cinema in a town that does not have one. You spend £15,000 on the research into whether this would be a worthwhile project and you're sure it's a winner. Then, just as you sign the papers to buy a good site, you hear that someone has the same idea, but is a month ahead of you. You could carry on and fight it out, or pull out altogether; either way you have been unlucky. The worst outcome would be to carry on the fight but end up with a failed business.

An entrepreneur should respond to bad luck with undimmed confidence and the determination to try again. Unfortunately it may not be that easy. Established hoteliers Barry Hancox and Andrew Riley opened Russell's – a restaurant and hotel – in Worcestershire having borrowed 80 per cent of the £1.5 million set-up costs from the bank. An entrepreneur with a business start-up failure to his/her name would have no chance of borrowing so much. Worse still, losses made from one failure – however unlucky – make it harder to find the personal capital to start again.

A-grade application

Chef David Everitt-Matthias opened Le Champignon Sauvage in Cheltenham in 1987. The year after the business opened, interest rates in Britain hit 15 per cent and the restaurant takings slumped. Quite simply, 'lots of our customers went bust'. David suffered nearly two years with the business close to closure. He survived, and has since faced foot and mouth disease and flooding, but the business is well enough established to cope. It is now a Michelin two-star restaurant (i.e. more highly rated than many of Gordon Ramsay's restaurants), but bad luck nearly stopped it in its tracks.

Issues for analysis

When tackling the issue of business start-up in an exam, bear in mind the following points.

- Awareness of risk and potential failure is a thoroughly good thing; fear of failure could easily become a serious problem; the good entrepreneur tries to anticipate possible problems and allow for them in the cash flow forecast – but doesn't treat possible problems as impossible hurdles.
- Therefore a good business plan will be based on realistic objectives and will allow for real life proving tougher than expected; every new business should press for a generous overdraft limit from the bank – to give a satisfactory cushion if things get tough.
- Despite the risks, the personal and financial rewards from entrepreneurship can be massive. How else would a fan on the terraces be able to end up buying Newcastle United? A Saturday Lottery win would hardly buy a player!

Assessing business start-ups – an evaluation

Every new business is unique, as each one depends upon the personality, character and motives of the founder, plus the specific market, competitive and economic context. Timing is another vital factor, in which luck plays a particularly important part. An ice cream parlour opening in May one year may be blessed with a hot summer; opening the following year may be cursed with rain and gloom.

It is because of these factors that it is hard to be sure whether a business plan will succeed or not. Whenever assessing a business start-up, it is very unwise to sound too certain about whether it will succeed or fail.

Key terms

Business model: the precise way in which profit will be generated from a specific business idea.

Floated: making a public company's shares widely available for purchase on the stock market.

Social entrepreneurs: strictly speaking, this should mean people who start up an organisation in pursuit of purely social objectives; but some profit-seekers dress themselves in social or environmental clothing.

Revision questions *(20 marks; 20 minutes)*

1 Identify two entrepreneurial qualities shown by Duncan Goose. (2)

2 Explain in your own words why it is wise to have doubts about some of the businesses that call themselves 'social enterprises'. (4)

3 Outline two ways to assess whether a business start-up has been a success. (4)

4 Explain why potential investors would want to hear about the business model before reading a business plan. (4)

5 Outline two possible reasons why an established firm such as Cadbury can achieve no better than a one in seven success rate when launching new products. (4)

6 Look again at Figure 16.2. If the entrepreneur had thought hard about the risks of starting a new restaurant, how might he have done things differently? Identify two points. (2)

Revision exercises

Data response

In 2005 Michael Birch started up a social networking site, Bebo, that became the British rival to Facebook. In 2008 he sold Bebo to AOL for an astonishing $850 million. Still in his 30s, he never had to work again. Yet far from making him relax, within nine months he was undergoing open heart surgery. After recovering, he began to look for new online enterprises to start up or to invest in.

In 2005 Birch had seen the opportunity for a broad social networking site, but now the space has been taken entirely by Facebook. So he is looking at a niche market: 'Jolitics' – a sophisticated social networking site for people interested in or active in politics. This is planned to open in early 2011.

A June 2010 *Financial Times* article reported him as saying: 'I don't understand why you wouldn't want to set up a new start-up. Not many entrepreneurs really want to retire. You don't start up a company to sell it and make money. There is a great satisfaction in achieving something.'

Birch is open about the importance of risk-taking and of making mistakes. He says that his own success rate has been 50-50, with three start-up flops and three successes. He agrees with the widespread view that Britain is tougher on 'failures' than America. There, a start-up failure is a badge of honour. In Britain people see a business failure as a personal failure. Birch believes that real entrepreneurs see a business flop as something to be learnt from.

Questions *(30 marks; 30 minutes)*

1 Explain why an entrepreneur might benefit from involvement in a failed start-up. (6)

2 Facebook is the mass-market social networking site.

a) Outline the case for and the case against a niche site such as 'Jolitics'. (6)

b) Do you think 'Jolitics' could be a business success? Justify your view. (8)

3 Discuss whether entrepreneurs are looking for 'satisfaction in achieving something' or planning to become very rich. (10)

Data response

Glasses Direct

In 2004 22-year-old Jamie Murray-Wells used the last of his student loan to start a business: Glasses Direct. Puzzled that two pieces of glass and some plastic frames could cost £250 in a high street optician, Jamie researched into the industry with care. When he approached manufacturers, he was greeted with suspicion; they worried that he might jeopardise their profits. But eventually he persuaded them to supply him. In September 2004 he started selling pairs of glasses over the internet for £15 a pair. Although he had no money for advertising, journalists were keen to write about his story, so he had terrific free PR (public relations). In the first year he sold 22,000 pairs, generating revenues of more than £300,000. By 2006 sales were heading towards £3 million, helped by a growing reputation for great customer service from the 17 staff.

From the start Jamie made it clear that he wanted to 'Get very big, very fast'. He realised that this would require outside finance. Since 2004 his family had helped provide the capital to grow; now it was time for serious investment by a venture capital fund. It took until July 2007 to achieve the right package. Two venture capital companies invested £2.9 million with the intention of using the capital on marketing – to make Glasses Direct a household name. It is not clear what percentage of the shares has been retained by Jamie and his family, but it is believed to be around 50 per cent. In 2009 Jamie suggested that his aim was to make the business a £1 billion company.

Questions *(25 marks; 25 minutes)*

1 a) Identify the business objective at Glasses Direct. (1)

b) Explain why this objective may have helped encourage staff to provide 'great customer service'. (5)

2 Look at the three personal objectives on pages 131–2. Outline which one of them you believe was most important for Jamie when starting Glasses Direct. (5)

3 Glasses Direct seems to have enjoyed a relatively untroubled start up. Outline two risks that the company faced, even though things turned out well. (6)

4 As Glasses Direct was growing satisfactorily, discuss whether Jamie was right to sell around 50 per cent of the shares in exchange for the £2.9 million of fresh capital. (8)

17 Using budgets

Definition
A budget is a target for costs or revenue that a firm or department must aim to reach over a given period of time.

Introduction

We examined the benefits and problems of budgeting in Unit 15. This unit examines how budgets are *used* in managing a business. There are two main reasons that budgets are used when managing a business:

- as a means of delegating spending power
- as a method of monitoring business performance.

Budgets as a means of delegating spending power

Once a business grows beyond a simple, one-person operation, there will be times that the boss is not around to authorise spending money – even small amounts like ordering a little extra stock or paying the window cleaner. To make sure the business can run smoothly, the boss needs to find a way to give staff the power to make spending decisions themselves. However, the boss will want to ensure that these decisions are not going to bankrupt the firm. Budgets can be used to allow employees to decide what money to spend within the limits specified by the budget.

If an entrepreneur who has successfully opened a beauty salon wants to open a second branch, they will need to appoint a manager of the second branch. The entrepreneur can then agree budget targets for the income and expenditure of the second branch, knowing that the manager will be working hard to hit these targets.

The budgets for costs should help to avoid any unexpected financial surprises – since the manager would be expected to discuss any budget overspend with the entrepreneur before it is incurred. The manager can run the shop on a day-to-day basis, spending whatever money needs to be spent, without checking with the boss all the time.

This principle applies to huge multinational companies as well as businesses that have just started growing. In a huge firm, there will be many more budget holders and many more separate budgets; however, the concept is the same as shown in the example in Figure 17.1.

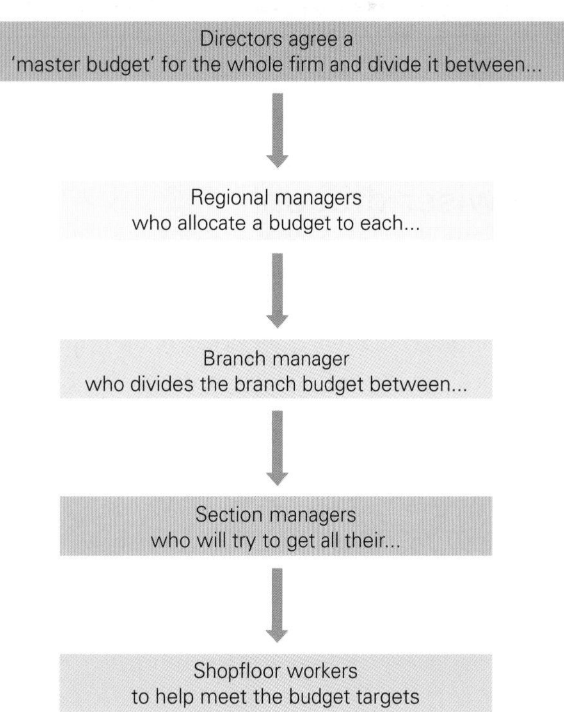

Directors agree a
'master budget' for the whole firm and divide it between...
Regional managers
who allocate a budget to each...
Branch manager
who divides the branch budget between...
Section managers
who will try to get all their...
Shopfloor workers
to help meet the budget targets

Figure 17.1 Budget holders

Budgets as a method of monitoring business performance

With budgets in place for each department, the management has **criteria** against which success can be measured. Budget-holders will try to exceed revenue budgets or stay under cost targets. The implication, of course, is that budgeted figures will be compared with what actually happens to make a judgement on performance. It is this process of comparison that allows budgets to be used as a method of monitoring business performance.

Budgetary variances

Variance is the amount by which the actual result differs from the budgeted figure. It is usually measured each month, by comparing the actual outcome with the budgeted one. It is important to note that variances are referred to as adverse or favourable – not positive and negative. A **favourable variance** is one which leads to higher than expected profit (revenue up or costs down). An **adverse variance** is one which reduces profit, such as costs being higher than the budgeted level.

Table 17.1 shows when variances are adverse or favourable.

The value of regular variance statements is that they provide an early warning. If a product's sales are slipping below budget, managers can respond by increasing marketing support, or by cutting back on production plans. In an ideal world, slippage could be noted in March, a new strategy put into place by May and a recovery in sales achieved by September. Clearly, no firm wishes to wait until the end-of-year profit and loss account to find out that things went badly. An early warning can lead to an early solution.

Table 17.1 Adverse or favourable variances

Variable	Budget	Actual	Variance	
Sales of X	150	160	10	Favourable
Sales of Y	150	145	5	Adverse
Material costs	100	90	10	Favourable
Labour costs	100	105	5	Adverse

A-grade application

A wiser dragon

Rachel Elnough was one of the original dragons on the BBC programme *Dragon's Den*. As founder of the gift company, Red Letter Days, she was making a £1m profit on a turnover of £10m at the height of the firm's success.

Once she stepped back from day-to-day control of the company, things started to go wrong. Although budgets were set, they were poorly monitored. Therefore, problems in reaching targets only became clear to her once the firm was in too much trouble to save. She ended up losing her business to two of the other dragons – Peter Jones and Theo Paphitis (and she was dropped from the BBC series).

Figure 17.2

Management by exception

In a large company, with many separate cost centres, senior managers will have hundreds of budget statements to review each month. In order to avoid information overload, most budgeting systems work on the basis of management by exception. Senior managers will only concern themselves with departmental budgets which show large variances (probably adverse). In large companies, management authority is usually **delegated** down through the organisation. Senior managers only get involved with problem areas or areas of great success.

Issues for analysis

- Variances are the key to analysing budgets. Once a variance between budgeted and actual figures has been identified, the analysis can begin. The important step is to ask why that variance occurred. Does the person responsible know the reason? Is it a one-off, or does this same person offer a different excuse each month for poor performance?
- Variance analysis is a means of identifying symptoms. It is down to the user of the variance figures to make a diagnosis as to the exact nature of any problem, and then to suggest the most appropriate cure.
- Although budgets and variances sound very focused upon numbers, they are rooted in everyday actions by people. Sales budgets will only be achieved if the sales force is enthusiastic and well managed. Production costs will only be kept down if wastage is low and commitment is high. When analysing budgetary problems, therefore, managers soon find themselves looking at the quality of management in departments such as marketing and production.

Using budgets – an evaluation

Budgets are a management tool. The way in which they are used can tell you a lot about a firm's culture. Firms with a culture of bossy management will tend to use a tightly controlled budgetary system. Managers will have budgets imposed upon them and variances will be watched closely by supervisors. Organisations with a more open culture will use budgeting as an aid to discussion and empowerment.

Whatever the culture, if a manager is to be held accountable for meeting a budget, he or she must be given influence over setting it and control over reaching it. Although budgets are set for future time periods, analysis of actual against budgeted performance can only take place after the event. This is true of all financial monitoring and this leads to doubts as to its effectiveness as a planning tool. Other measures may be far more reliable in predicting future performance – market research indicating growing levels of customer complaints may well be more useful in predicting future performance.

From an even broader perspective, it could be argued that budgets and other financial measures are unhelpful in some circumstances. Perhaps firms should look at their objectives before deciding on the most useful measure of performance. Financial measures are fine for firms attempting to maximise their profits, but sales figures will be more relevant for firms pursuing an objective of growth, while customer complaint levels will be particularly relevant to firms aiming for excellence in their levels of service.

Key terms

Adverse variance: a difference between budgeted and actual figures that is damaging to the firm's profit (e.g. costs up or revenue down).

Criteria: yardsticks against which success (or the lack of it) can be measured.

Delegated: passing authority down the hierarchy.

Favourable variance: a difference between budgeted and actual figures that boosts a firm's profit (e.g. revenue up or costs down).

Revision questions (40 marks; 40 minutes)

1 Explain the meaning of the term 'budgeting'. (3)

2 What are the two main advantages that using a budgeting system brings to a company? (2)

3 Why is it valuable to have a yardstick against which performance can be measured? (3)

4 How might a firm respond to an increasingly adverse variance in labour costs? (4)

5 Explain what is meant by a 'favourable cost variance'. (2)

6 Why is management by exception a useful time-saving measure for management? (4)

7 Explain two drawbacks of budgeting. (4)

8 Briefly explain why a shop with a favourable income variance might expect some cost variances to be adverse. (4)

9 Look at the table below and then answer the questions that follow.

a) Calculate the budgeted and actual profit figures for May and June. (4)

b) Identify the following:

i) a month with a favourable revenue variance

ii) a month with an adverse fixed cost variance

iii) a month with an adverse variable cost variance

iv) a month with a favourable fixed cost variance

v) a month with an adverse total cost variance

vi) a month with an adverse revenue variance

vii) a month with a favourable total cost variance

viii) a month with an adverse variable cost variance

ix) a month with an adverse profit variance

x) a month with a favourable profit variance (10)

	May		June	
	Budgeted	Actual	Budgeted	Actual
Revenue	3,500	3,200	4,000	4,200
Variable costs	1,000	900	1,200	1,500
Fixed costs	1,200	1,200	1,300	1,100
Total costs	2,200	2,100	2,500	2,600
Profit				

Revision exercises

Data analysis

£000s	January			February		
	B	A	V	B	A	V
Sales revenue	140	150	10	180	175	?
Materials	70	80	(10)	90	95	?
Other direct costs	30	35	(5)	40	40	0
Overheads	20	20	0	25	22	?
Profit	20	15	(5)	?	18	?

Questions *(20 marks; 20 minutes)*

1 What are the five missing numbers from the variance analysis above? (5)

2 Examine one financial strength and two weaknesses in this data, from the company's viewpoint. (9)

3 How might a manager set about improving the accuracy of a sales budget? (6)

B2 Data response

Clinton and Collins Ltd

Budget data for Clinton and Collins Ltd (£000s)

	January		February		March		April	
	B	A	B	A	B	A	B	A
Sales revenue	160	144	180	156	208	168	240	188
Materials	40	38	48	44	52	48	58	54
Labour	52	48	60	54	66	62	72	68
Overheads	76	76	76	78	76	80	76	80
Profit	(8)	(18)	(4)	(20)	14	(22)	34	(14)

Questions *(25 marks; 25 minutes)*

1 Use the data to explain why February's profits were worse than expected. (5)

2 Why might Clinton and Collins Ltd have chosen to set monthly budgets? (5)

3 Explain how the firm might have set these budgets. (4)

4 The directors of Clinton and Collins Ltd knew that the recession was causing problems for the firm but were unsure as to whether things were improving or worsening. To what extent does the data suggest an improvement? (11)

18 Improving cash flow

Definition
Cash flow is the flow of money into and out of a business in a given time period.

Managing day-to-day finances

Even when the high set-up costs have been completed, new businesses can be shocked by the amount of capital needed to run the business day by day. To operate, the business needs money to buy stock, to pay wages and the day-to-day bills such as electricity and telephone bills. If the bills cannot be paid on time, there are serious consequences and in the worst situation the business may fail.

The cash cycle

Managing the day-to-day finances is a continuous process. When a business starts up it takes time to generate income. Money to pay for stock and the running costs will need to be found from the initial capital invested in the business. As the cash cycle gets going, income from customers will be available to pay for expenditure. The firm needs to ensure that there is always enough cash to meet daily requirements. If the business is expanding, extra care needs to be taken (see Figure 18.1). Each business will have its own distinct cycle. Businesses may also suffer unexpected shocks and need cash to be able to cope with these.

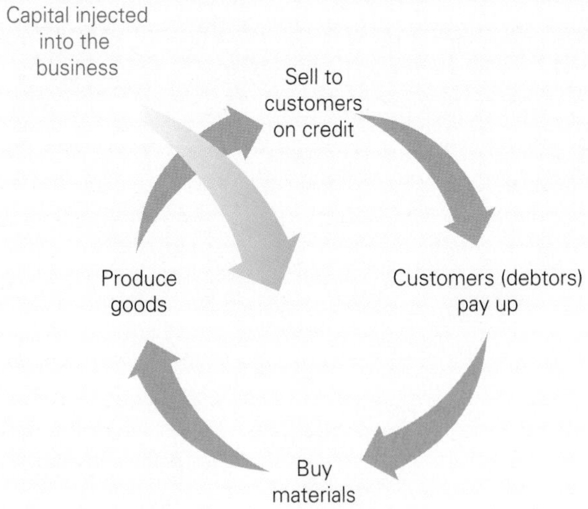

Figure 18.1 The cash cycle

Problems caused by insufficient cash flow

- *With suppliers*: a firm with too little cash will struggle to pay its bills on time and may resort to delaying payments. Unpaid suppliers may refuse credit for a future order.
- *Banks are quick to sense a cash flow crisis*: banks are equally quick to reduce the bank's risk by calling in any overdrafts. As they can insist on being repaid within 24 hours, the speed of repayment can put firms in terrible difficulties.
- *Opportunities may be missed*: the business may not be able to buy supplies in bulk, removing the advantage of lower prices. Even more importantly, it may have to refuse a large order because it cannot finance the extra cash requirement.

In the longer term, shortage of cash means insufficient funds are available for development. The business will not be able to grow as rapidly as rivals and this may make it hard to stay competitive.

Managing cash flow

Good management of cash flow starts with good forecasting. Cash flow forecasts will help to predict any cash shortfalls, enabling the business to take steps to avoid any cash flow problems. It is helpful to have a generous overdraft limit, which can be drawn upon when needed, as this can act as a safety net for the business. Good cash flow management also involves improving the cash position at all times. This can be done by speeding up the cash inflows into the business and delaying or reducing cash outflows.

A-grade application

Late payments woes

A survey from RBS and NatWest, published in April 2010, found that 71 per cent of SMEs (small and medium enterprises) had been affected by late payments in the past year. The study estimates that in the last year a total of £62 billion was owed to businesses in bills paid beyond agreed deadlines. Around £15 billion was more than 120 days overdue. Another survey, from the Forum of Private Business, found that small businesses currently have an average of £47,000 tied up by late payments. This is around 35 per cent of turnover.

Stephen Alambritis, head of public affairs at the Federation of Small Businesses, said: 'Poor payment practices can drastically affect cash flow for small firms at a time when business owners are doing their best to hold on to precious funds.'

(Source: www.smallbusiness.co.uk, 15 April 2010)

Improving cash flow into the business

The business can improve the flow of cash into the business in several ways, as described below.

- *Getting goods to the market in the shortest possible time*: the sooner goods reach the customer, the sooner payment is received. Production and distribution should be as efficient as possible.
- *Getting paid as quickly as possible*: the ideal arrangement is to be paid cash on delivery. Most business, though, works on credit. Even worse, it's interest-free credit, so the customer has little incentive to pay up quickly. Early payment should be encouraged by offering incentives such as discounts for early payment.
- *Controlling debtors*: confusingly this is known as credit control. If customers do not pay on time, this will obviously mean that the cash does not come into the business when expected. Businesses can reduce the likelihood of non- or late payment by ensuring the debtor is credit-worthy before granting credit (by getting a bank reference).
- *Factoring*: it may be possible to speed up payments by factoring money owed to the business. The company is able to receive 80 per cent of the amount due within 24 hours of an invoice being presented. The factor then collects the money from the customer when the credit period is over and pays the seller the remaining 20 per cent less the factoring fees. These depend on the length of time before the payment is due, the credit rating of the creditor and current rates of interest. The fees are usually no more than 5 per cent of the total value of the sale.

Reducing cash outflows from the business

The other way of improving cash flow is to manage the outflow of cash from the business. This can be done by:

- *Obtaining maximum possible credit for purchases*: delaying payment of bills will keep cash in the business for longer.
- *Controlling costs*: this can be done by keeping administrative and production costs to a minimum. Efficient production reduces costs and savings may be possible by upgrading machinery to replace labour. This will benefit the firm's profit as well as its cash flow.
- *Keeping stocks of raw materials to a minimum*: good stock management such as a just-in-time system means that the business is not paying for stocks before it needs them for production. Controlling stock losses means that less is spent on replacements for lost or damaged stock.

Keeping cash in the business

Cash flow can also be improved by keeping cash in the business. Minimising short-term spending on new equipment keeps cash in the business. Things that the business can do include the following.

- *Lease rather than buy equipment*: this increases expenses but conserves capital.
- *Renting rather than buying buildings*: this also allows capital to remain in the business.
- *Postponing expenditure*: for example, on new company cars.

Finding additional funding to cover cash shortages

If the business is unable to keep a healthy cash flow by internal management, it may need to look outside to cover cash shortages. This can be done by the following means:

- *Using an overdraft*: an overdraft is arranged with a bank. It allows the business to overdraw up to an agreed limit negotiated in advance. Overdrafts usually incur interest rates as high as 6 per cent over base rate. However, an overdraft ensures the firm only borrows money on the days it really needs it, making it a very flexible form of borrowing. This makes it suitable for small or short-term shortages of cash. Although it should only be used to fund short-term problems, a recent study of firms in Bristol found that 70 per cent of small firms had a permanent overdraft. A risky aspect of an overdraft is that the bank can withdraw the facility at any time and demand instant repayment. So, when a firm needs it most, such as in a recession, it may not be available.

Figure 18.2 Looking for a way to cover a cash shortage

- *Taking out a short-term loan*: this incurs a lower rate of interest than an overdraft. Although less flexible than an overdraft, short-term loans offer more security and may have fixed interest charges (whereas on an overdraft they are variable).
- *Sale and leaseback of assets*: if a business has fixed assets it may be possible to negotiate a sale and leaseback arrangement. This will release capital and give an immediate inflow of cash. The equipment will be paid for through a leasing arrangement. This will be a regular and ongoing cost that must be budgeted for.

A-grade application

Tesco's sale and leaseback deals

In April 2010 Tesco announced plans to continue its expansion plans. Included in this were 2.4 million sq ft (the equivalent of 80 superstores) in Britain and 8.5 million sq ft overseas, not including ambitious plans to open nine large shopping centres in China. How is it funding this? Of course its huge annual revenue gives it cash to invest, but for many years it has been following a policy of releasing capital from its massive property portfolio. It has done this by organising sale and leaseback deals. As an example, in 2009 it carried out a deal worth £514 million which involved 15 stores and two distribution centres. By doing this it continues to have use of the property but also has use of the capital raised to help fund its expansion plans.

Table 18.1 Ways to improve cash flow

Measure	Result	Drawbacks
Discounting prices	● Increases sales ● Reduces stock ● Generates cash	● May undermine pricing structure ● May leave low stocks for future activity
Reduce purchases	Cuts down expenditure	May leave business without means to continue
Negotiate more credit	Allows time to pay	May tarnish credit reputation
Delay payment of bills	Retains cash	Will tarnish credit reputation
Credit control – chase debtors	Gets payments in and sooner	May upset customers
Negotiate additional finance	Provides cash	● Interest payments add to expenditure ● Has to be repaid
Factor debts	● Generates cash ● A proportion of the income is guaranteed	● Reduces income from sales ● Costs can be high
Selling assets	Releases cash	Assets are no longer available
Sale and leaseback	● Releases cash ● Asset is still available	● Increases costs – lease has to be paid ● Company no longer owns asset

Issues for analysis

Especially for small firms, cash flow is the equivalent of blood circulating round the body. If the cash dries up, the firm dies. When looking at how the firm can improve its cash flow, consideration must be given to the type of firm and its market situation. There is no point suggesting that the firm should demand cash payment if it is supplying large businesses in a highly competitive market.

Consideration could also be given to how much cash the business needs. It would be nice if there were a perfect, 'right' level of cash, but there is not. Tesco has operated successfully for decades with an apparently very tight cash position.

When looking at solutions to cash flow problems, it is important to consider what is causing the problem and how long the problem might go on for. There is a lot of difference between a problem caused by poor payment and one that is caused by poor sales.

Improving cash flow – an evaluation

Managing cash flow is very important for every business. Too much cash is wasteful – too little can be disastrous. Businesses need to consider their cash requirements right from the outset. Most new businesses underestimate their operating cash needs. New firms often only allow £20 of day-to-day capital for every £100 of spending on long-term assets. Accountants usually advise a £50:£50 ratio.

Improving cash flow will often uncover problems elsewhere in the business. Perhaps the reason there is poor stock control is that the person in charge is demotivated. In this respect, managing cash flow is an integrated activity, involving each aspect of the company. Efficient production keeps costs to a minimum and turns raw inputs into finished goods in the shortest possible time. Effective management of stock can have considerable impact on cash needs. Effective marketing ensures that the goods are sold and that demand is correctly estimated, thereby avoiding wasted production. Cash then flows in from sales. A business with plenty of cash flowing in and out is a healthy business.

Key terms

Bad debts: payments that are long overdue and cannot be expected to be received.

Credit period: the length of time allowed for payment.

Factoring: obtaining part-payment of the amount owed from a factoring company. The factoring company will then collect the debt and pass over the balance of the payment.

Sale and leaseback: a contract that, at the same time, sells the freehold to a piece of property and buys back the leasehold.

Revision questions *(40 marks; 40 minutes)*

1 Why is cash flow an especially important topic for small firms rather than large ones? (4)

2 Outline the probable cash cycle for a small sandwich shop. (4)

3 Explain why 'good management of cash flow starts with good forecasting'. (3)

4 Outline two problems that might arise if a firm is operating with very poor cash flow. (4)

5 Why might a business be unable to get a loan or overdraft if it has cash flow difficulties? (4)

6 What impact does the length of the business process have on cash flow? (4)

7 Getting money in from customers is a vital part of cash flow management. List two things a firm can do to ensure that cash is collected efficiently. (4)

8 How might a small producer of shelf fittings benefit from factoring? (4)

9 Outline three ways in which a business can improve its cash flow situation. (6)

10 What internal factors could affect a firm's cash flow? (3)

Revision exercises

Data response

Credit crunch 'hits small firms'

Small UK firms are struggling in the face of the credit crisis to secure the loans they need to expand or even survive, a business group has warned. Those who could get loans now face paying interest rates in excess of 10%, according to the Federation of Small Business (FSB). 'The issue is that the banks are being more choosy over who they lend money to until they ride out the storm,' said FSB spokesman Matthew Knowles. 'There's a bit of a "Computer Says No" mentality. Banks often see small businesses as more of a risk – and because they aren't able to tick all the boxes which the banks set out, they struggle to borrow.'

The FSB said that some of its members were borrowing at between 10% and 11% – more than two percentage points above the rates they had previously been able to get. It added that there was a broader concern that small businesses would not be able to afford to expand. 'This is a big worry,' Mr Knowles said. 'A large majority of start-ups are not going on to employ one or two people, which is what we need to see to bring about a reduction in unemployment.'

The credit crunch has followed woes in the US sub-prime mortgage sector, which specialises in loans to people with poor credit histories or on low incomes.

Rising interest rates have led to record levels of loan defaults and home repossessions – and that has sparked fears about which lenders might be exposed to the bad debts.

Questions *(30 marks; 30 minutes)*

1 What is meant by the term 'credit crunch'? (2)

2 Why are banks less willing to lend to small businesses? (6)

3 What is the rate of interest that small businesses are likely to be paying? (2)

4 On a £10,000 loan with an interest rate of 12%, how much will the interest charges be for the first year of the loan? (4)

5 Why will a lack of available credit stop small businesses from expanding? (8)

6 Explain how a lack of easy credit for larger firms may affect smaller businesses. (8)

Data response

Dell in late payment Hall of Shame

Direct computer seller Dell has been entered into a late payments Hall of Shame for (without negotiation) adding an extra 15 days to the time it aims to settle invoices.

Dell wrote to suppliers telling them it was changing its terms and conditions from 10 July 2010 because of 'current economic conditions'. It will now settle invoices in 65 days rather than 50. The computer giant has been awarded the dishonour by the Forum of Private Business.

A spokesman for the Forum said smaller companies had no choice but to put up and shut up when a big customer decides to change payment terms. He said it was time the government acted to stop the bully-boy tactics of big firms.

Late payments by large organisations has been a campaigning issue for small business for some time – they tend to struggle with cash flow at the best of times, and most small companies have to settle their own bills within 30 days.

One in five Forum members said problems with late payments had become worse in recent months. On average, members said 36 per cent of turnover was tied up in late payments at any given time.

(Source: www.theregister.co.uk/business/small_biz, 28 June 2010)

Questions *(25 marks; 30 minutes)*

1 Explain why Dell may have decided to extend its payment period in this way. (5)

2 GX Ltd is a small business supplying £40,000 of computer parts to Dell each month. Dell is GX's biggest customer, taking 50 per cent of all GX's output.

a) Explain the impact of Dell's decision on GX Ltd's cash flow. (6)

b) Outline three actions GX could take to rebuild its cash flow position. (6)

c) Which of the three actions do you think would be the best? Justify your view. (8)

Case study

Hatta Lighting

Hatta Lighting plc makes component parts for the car industry. It started out making bulbs but now also supplies a range of electrical and electronic components. The company started as a family-run business but expansion has meant that five years ago it became a public limited company. During the last two years its performance has been mediocre and dividends paid to shareholders have been falling. The share price has also fallen. One of the largest shareholders has decided that change is necessary and has managed to exert enough pressure to replace the established chairman. The new chairman has a strong financial background but has been involved in the retail industry for many years. He has asked the management team to produce some information and the team has come up with the data in Table 18.2.

After examining these figures, the new chairman is very concerned about the cash flow situation of the company. Several large debts totalling £500,000 are due to be paid shortly and the firm does not have sufficient cash available to pay these. He sees this as being the most urgent issue facing the company and he has arranged an urgent meeting of all the managers. He has asked each of the three department heads (marketing, finance and production) to come up with ideas to solve the problem.

Questions *(45 marks; 50 minutes)*

1 What might be the reasons for the increase in the stock of finished goods and materials? (6)

2 Consider what suggestions the production director might make and explain your reasoning. (10)

3 The finance director sees slow payment as his major problem. Examine the ways in which the firm might tackle this problem. (10)

4 Outline the contribution the marketing department might make to help improve the cash flow situation. (9)

5 Apart from tackling the issue of slow payment, consider what other short-term measures the firm might take to overcome the immediate cash crisis. (10)

C Essay questions *(40 marks each)*

1 Managing cash flow is vital for the future of any business. Discuss.

2 In periods of economic downturn, it is even more important to control cash flow. Do you agree with this statement?

3 'Managing cash flow is not just the business of the finance department. It is the responsibility of everyone in the business.' To what extent do you agree with this statement?

Table 18.2

	Last year	This year	Industry average
Stock turnover materials (days)	44	48	40
Stock of finished goods (£000)	780	910	700
Average days before payment	38	54	42
Working capital at year end (£000)	560	380	Unknown

Measuring and increasing profits

Definition

Net profit is the profit left after all the operating costs have been deducted from revenue. Net profit margins look at the percentage profit compared with the sales revenue of the business.

Measuring performance

The performance of organisations may be measured in many ways, such as:

- sales or sales growth
- market share
- the job satisfaction of its employees
- its track record on environmental issues
- the quality of its relationships with suppliers
- customer satisfaction.

The most appropriate measure(s) will depend on the nature of the organisation; a hospital may look at the number of successful operations, a university may measure the number and class of the degrees of its students, and a sports club may measure the number of matches played and won. Organisations will often have several different measures to assess their performance in different areas. However, one of the most common measures of success for organisations is net profit.

Figure 19.1 Woolworths closed in 2009

Net profit measures the profit left after all the operating costs of the business have been deducted. These costs may include the costs of producing and marketing the products, as well as fixed costs (such as rent). Net profit is the lifeblood of the organisation, because unless the business makes a profit, it cannot finance growth. In a growing economy, with new opportunities arising all the time, a business that cannot grow is condemned to a slow death. A perfect example of this is Woolworths. In its 2007 financial year it made a net profit that was less than 1 per cent of its sales. In other words, of every £1 taken through a Woolworths till, less than 1p was the company's net profit. Not surprisingly, the company ultimately failed and its stores closed in January 2009.

Net profit and net profit margin

The net profit of a business is an absolute number that is measured in value terms. For example, a business might earn a net profit of £10,000. Is this a good level of profit or not? To find out, the profit is measured in relation to the total value of sales. This is known as the net profit margin:

$$\text{Net profit margin} = \frac{\text{net profit} \times 100}{\text{sales}}$$

For example, if the net profit is £10,000 and the sales are £50,000 the net profit margin is:

$$\frac{10{,}000 \times 100 = 20\%}{£50{,}000}$$

This means that 20 per cent of the firm's revenue is actually profit (i.e. of every £1 of sales, 20p is net profit). Notice that the net profit margin is a percentage.

What is a good net profit margin?

The typical net profit margin in an industry will vary from one sector to another. The food retail market, for example, is a very competitive market and the profit per sale (i.e. the profit margin) is likely to be quite low (e.g. 5 per cent). However, provided you can sell a high volume of items, your overall net profits can still be high. You may make relatively little profit per can of beans, but provided you sell a lot of beans your overall profits may still be high.

In the case of luxury items such as Ted Baker clothes or Rolex watches, the profit margin is likely to be much higher. However, although the profit per sale is relatively high this does not automatically mean the profits are high – that depends on how many items you sell.

A-grade application

Dell

In 2010 Dell, the world's largest computer maker, reported a 6 per cent fall in overall profits despite an increase in sales, due to its falling profit margins. The company saw sales of its personal computers rise by 29 per cent over the first three months of 2010, but consumers were choosing to buy the less profitable, cheapest models. Influenced by the recession and a lack of demand generally in the economy, customers looked for better deals and bargains, leading to lower profit margins on sales. Even though more computers were sold by Dell, its total profits fell.

Table 19.1 Net profit margins from selected 2009 company accounts

	Net profit	Sales	% net profit margin
Tesco	£2,954 million	£354,327 million	5.44%
Sainsbury's	£466 million	£18,911 million	2.46%
Ted Baker	£17.7 million	£152 million	11.4%

The return on capital

Profitability measures profit in relation to some other variable. As we have seen, the net profit margin measures profit in relation to sales. We might also want to measure the net profit in relation to the amount invested in a project. The money invested is often called 'capital'.

If, for example, a business invests £20,000 into a project and this generates a profit of £5,000, then the return on the capital invested (known as **return on capital**) is 25 per cent:

$$\text{Return on capital} = \frac{\text{net profit}}{\text{capital invested}} \times 100$$

$$= \frac{£5000}{£20{,}000} \times 100 = 25\%$$

The return on capital is an important indicator of the success of a project or business. Imagine a business proposal is expected to earn a return on capital of 25 per cent: this is very good compared to the return you are likely to get if you invest your money into a bank. The opportunity cost (i.e. the return you could get elsewhere) is probably lower than 25 per cent, which makes the project attractive.

If, however, you expected to invest £20,000 and you generated profits of only £500:

$$\text{Return on capital} = \frac{\text{net profit}}{\text{capital invested}} \times 100$$

$$= \frac{£500}{£20{,}000} \times 100 = 2.5\%$$

In this case, the return on capital is only 2.5% and you would probably expect to earn more if you saved your money in a bank instead.

Return on capital and the net profit margin

Obviously the return on capital is linked to the net profit margin. The overall returns will depend on how many units are sold and on the profit per sale (the net profit margin).

If the firm can sell the same amount of products but with a higher profit margin, the overall return on capital will increase. Alternatively, if the net profit margin remains the same but more units are sold, this will also boost the overall return on capital.

Methods of improving profits

To increase profits a business must:

1. increase revenue
2. decrease costs
3. do a combination of 1 and 2.

To increase revenue a business may want to consider its marketing mix. Changes to the product may mean that it becomes more appealing to customers. Better distribution may make it more available. Changes to promotion may make customers more aware of its benefits. However, the business needs to be careful that rising costs do not swallow up the rise in sales revenues.

To reduce costs a business may examine many of the functional areas (such as marketing, operations, people and finance) by asking the following questions:

- Could the firm continue with fewer staff?
- Could money be saved by switching suppliers?
- Do the firm's sales really benefit from sponsoring the opera?
- Are there ways of reducing wastage?

Essentially, a business should look for ways of making the product more efficiently (e.g. with better technology) by using fewer inputs or paying less for the inputs being used. However, a business must be careful that when it reduces costs, the quality of service is not reduced. After all, this might lead to a fall in sales and revenue. Cutting staff in your coffee shop may cut costs but if long queues form, it may also reduce the number of customers and your income. Managers must weigh up the consequences of any decision to reduce costs.

A-grade application

Average wages in Vietnam are lower than those of its neighbours such as Thailand and China. Vietnamese factory workers earn just two-thirds of what their colleagues in China take home.

Companies such as Foxconn, which assembles consumer electronics and phones for big brand companies such as Apple and Sony, operate on very low profit margins and so try to find the lowest cost location they can. This makes Vietnam very attractive as a production base. The toy industry is another low-cost, high-volume industry which is why you will find many well known brands now being produced there rather than China. Wages in China's coastal manufacturing areas have risen between 15 and 20 per cent a year recently; this has significantly reduced producers' profit margins so they have decided to relocate to Vietnam.

Methods of increasing profit margins

To increase net profits in relation to sales, a business could do the following:

- *Increase its price:* this would boost the profit per sale, but the danger is that the sales overall may fall so much that the overall profits of the business are reduced. (Notice the important difference again between the net profit margin and the overall level of profits – you could make a high level of profit on one can of beans relative to its price but if you only sell one can, your total profits are not that impressive!) The impact of any price increase will depend on the price elasticity of demand; the more price elastic demand is, the greater the fall in demand will be, and the less likely it is that a firm will want to put up its prices. On the other hand, a price-elastic demand may mean it is worth cutting price. Although less profit may be made per item (there is a lower profit margin), the overall profits may increase due to the boost in sales.

- *Cut costs:* if this can be done without damaging the quality in any significant way, then this clearly makes sense. Better bargaining to get the supply prices down or better ways of producing may lead to higher profits per sale. However, as we saw above, the business needs to be careful that reducing costs does not lead to a deterioration of the service or quality of the product, as this may damage sales.

Profits and the functions of business

As we can see, the profits and the profitability of a business depend on all the different functions of the business. The operations management may determine how much can be produced and sold. Human resources management may affect how many people need to be employed and the costs of staff. Marketing decisions will affect the sales and revenue earned. To boost profits you may consider each and every one of these functions to look for ways of increasing revenue and/or cutting costs.

A-grade application

In 2010 energy firms in the UK were being criticised for their high profit margins by the government body that regulates the energy industry (called Ofgem). Because the energy companies offer such a vital product and have such power, the government monitors them to see how they behave in relation to customers. Even though the price at which these companies buy the energy themselves (the wholesale price) has fallen, these savings have not led to lower prices for households. This means the energy companies have been benefitting from increasing profit margins.

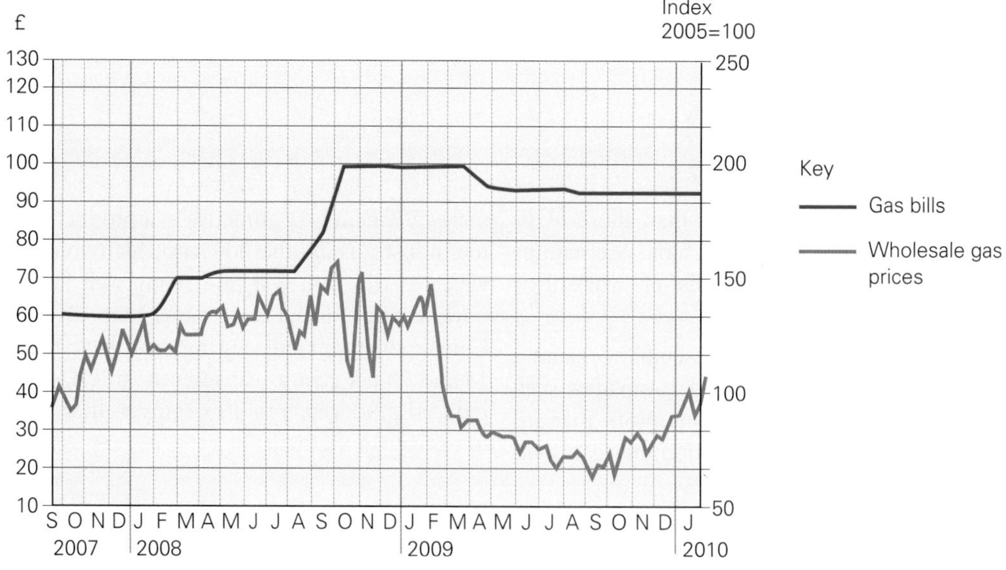

Figure 19.2 Wholesale gas prices and level of gas bills
(Source: Office for National Statistics/Bloomberg)

Issues for analysis

Many organisations survive without profit, but largely because of government or private charity. This unit is largely about business organisations that need profit to survive and, especially, to grow. If a business is as unprofitable as Woolworths, it cannot be expected to survive for long.

In exams there are various questions to ask yourself about a loss-making firm:

- What has caused the losses: **internal reasons** or external ones? Internal ones would include poor decision making.
- What may be the downsides to any new approach? Will staff cutbacks cost more from damaged morale than they provide from lower wage costs?
- Finally, what is the timescale of the decision making? Is the business forced to take action immediately to boost profit, or can it wait to see if the current poor circumstances will ease off?

Measuring and increasing profit – an evaluation

A difficulty with questions about poor profits is that many suggestions made in exams are too obvious. As shown in Table 19.1, Sainsbury's has only half the profit margin of Tesco. But is it worth pointing out to Sainsbury's that it could look for bulk-buying discounts on its supplies? Of course not. A good exam answer will show the maturity to see that Sainsbury's managers will already be doing all they can to tackle the problem.

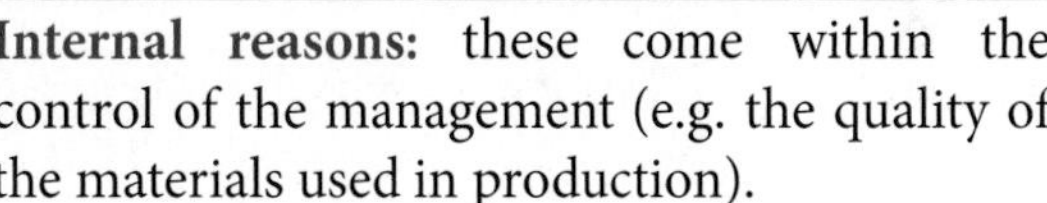

Key terms

Internal reasons: these come within the control of the management (e.g. the quality of the materials used in production).

Return on capital: profit as a percentage of the capital a firm invests in a project.

Revision questions (25 marks, 25 minutes)

1 What is meant by 'revenue'? (2)

2 What is meant by 'net profit'? (2)

3 Does an increase in price necessarily increase revenue? Explain your answer. (3)

4 How can revenue increase without an increase in cash inflows? (2)

5 Is profitability measured in pounds or percentages? (1)

6 What is the equation for the net profit margin? (2)

7 How can the net profit margin increase and yet the return on capital fall? (2)

8 Explain two ways of increasing profits. (4)

9 Why might cutting costs end up reducing profits? (3)

10 In what ways do the different functions of a business affect its profits? (4)

Revision exercises

Data response

SOFA-SOGOOD Ltd is a retailer of sofas. It had been experiencing a very slow summer. Revenues had been falling but costs had been pushed up by pay increases, higher rent costs and higher interest payments on debts. As a result, net profits had fallen by 20 per cent on last year. Renis, the managing director, was very disappointed that revenue had fallen because he had cut prices by 5 per cent and had expected customer numbers to increase sharply. Once it became clear that this discounting policy was not working, he imposed a pay freeze on everyone in the company and a policy of non-recruitment: if any staff member left, he or she would not be replaced.

Questions *(30 marks; 30 minutes)*

1 Distinguish between revenue, costs and net profit. (3)

2 Explain why a fall in price might not have led to an increase in revenue. (5)

3 Apart from the methods mentioned in the text, analyse two other actions SOFA-SOGOOD Ltd might take to improve its profitability. (8)

4 Discuss the advantages and disadvantages to the business of the staffing cost-saving actions taken by Renis. (14)

Data response

Farmoor College

Farmoor College is a private sixth form based in London that charges students to study for their A-levels. The fees are £15,000 a year. The college is proud of its small classes (average size five students) and its excellent examination results. This year it has 200 students studying with it, which is about its present capacity in terms of the number of classrooms available. The college has a core of key staff but employs other teachers and support staff depending on the levels of demand in any year. The college's net profit margin is 12 per cent and the capital invested in the business is £15 million.

Questions *(40 marks; 40 minutes)*

1 Calculate the likely net profits for the college this year. (3)

2 Calculate the college's likely return on capital this year. Comment on your findings. (4)

3 Outline two costs the college is likely to have. (4)

4 Explain one factor that might cause a change in demand for the college. (4)

5 Explain how the net profit of the college might be used. (5)

6 Analyse how you might measure the performance of the college apart from looking at its financial results. (8)

7 Discuss the ways in which the college might increase its profits. (12)

Cash flow vs profit

Definition

Cash flow is the movement of cash into and out of a firm's bank account.
Profit is when revenue is greater than total costs.

Introduction

A year ago a busy bar in Wimbledon closed down. Regulars were surprised, shocked even, that such a successful business had failed. The business *was* operating profitably, but the owners had become too excited by their success. Their investment into two new bars elsewhere in London had drained too much cash from the business, and the bank had panicked over the mounting debts. It forced the business to close. A profitable business had run out of cash.

To understand how cash differs from profit, the key is to master profit. On the face of it, profit is easy: total revenue *minus* total costs. Common sense tells you that revenue = money in and costs = money out. Unfortunately, that's far too much of a simplification.

Distinguishing revenue from cash inflow

Revenue is *not* the same as money in. Revenue is the value of sales made over a specified period: a day, a month or a year. For example, the takings at a clothing outlet last Saturday were as follows: £450 of cash sales, £2,450 on credit cards and £600 on the outlet's store card (i.e. £3,500 in total) (see Figure 20.1). Note that the cash inflow for the day is just £450 (i.e. that revenue is not the same as 'cash in').

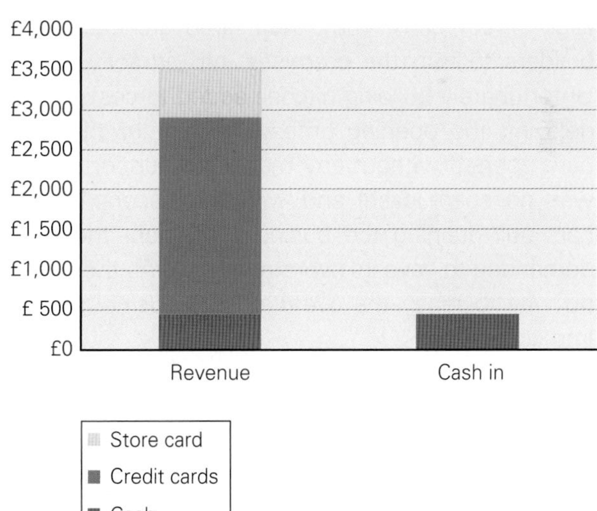

Figure 20.1 Saturday takings at a clothing outlet

Whereas revenue comes from just one source (customers), cash inflow can come from many sources. It is not limited to trading. Selling an old warehouse for £600,000 does not generate revenue, but it does bring in cash. Similarly, taking out a bank loan could not be classed as revenue, but it does put cash into your bank current account.

So cash inflows *can* be part of the revenue, but they do not have to be. Therefore cash and revenue are not the same. Table 20.1 illustrates the differences between cash inflows and revenue.

Table 20.1 Differences between cash inflows and revenue

Financial item	Cash inflow	Revenue
Cash sales made to customers	✓	✓
Credit sales made to customers	✗	✓
Capital raised from share sales	✓	✗
Charge rent on flat upstairs	✓	✓
Take out a £20,000 bank loan	✓	✗
Carry out a sale and leaseback	✓	✗

Distinguishing costs from cash outflow

The same distinction applies to costs and cash outflows. There are many reasons why a firm might pay out cash and paying the business costs is only one of them. For example, the firm may pay out **dividends** to its shareholders, or it may repay a bank loan, or it may buy a piece of land as an investment.

In the case of the Wimbledon bar, the £200,000 annual profit gave the owners the confidence to buy leases on two new premises. They put together a business plan for expansion and received a £90,000 bank loan plus a £80,000 overdraft facility from a High Street bank. They then hired architects and builders to turn the premises into attractive bars. Unfortunately building hitches added to costs while delaying the opening times. The first of the new bars opened without any marketing support (there was no spare cash) and with the second of the bars still draining the business of cash, the bank demanded to have its overdraft repaid. As there was no way to repay the overdraft, the business went into liquidation.

So, a profitable business may run out of cash, simply because it expands too ambitiously, perhaps unluckily. There are other reasons why a profitable business might run into **negative cash flow**, as outlined below.

Seasonal factors

A firm that is generating sufficient revenue to cover its costs over a twelve-month period might still hit short-term cash flow problems. This is a particularly difficult problem for new small firms. A new bicycle shop opens in the spring and may enjoy an excellent first six months' trading. The owners may get quite excited at the good profit level, buy a new van and have a much-needed holiday. They would have expected the winter half year to be pretty poor for bike sales, but may be shocked by the level of decline. By February they may run out of cash and be unable to pay their staff. If only they had known the pattern of demand, the owners could have saved money in the first half of the year, but a

Table 20.2 Differences between cash outflows and costs

Financial item	Cash outflow	Costs
Cash payments to suppliers	✓	✓
Purchases from suppliers on credit	✗	✓
Paying out wages	✓	✓
Repayment of bank loans	✓	✗
Tax bill received but not yet paid	✗	✓
Buying freehold property*	✓	✗
Paying the electricity bill	✓	✓

*Because a £500,000 property is worth £500,000, an accountant would not treat it as a cost.

Figure 20.2 Bicycle sales may be seasonal

fundamentally profitable business may close down due to a cash flow crisis.

Problems with credit periods

If a firm gives credit periods to its customers, there is risk from a serious delay to a credit payment. For example, a builder who has put a great deal of money into renovating a large house finds that the client keeps delaying the final payment. The more serious the builder's cash flow problems become, the stronger the position of the client. So a profitable business may be thrown into a cash crisis that could threaten its survival.

Cash-rich firms can be unprofitable

It is also possible for a cash-rich business to be unprofitable and this has given rise to several business scandals in the past. A classic situation is as follows. A new insurance company is started up and builds up a customer base through extensive TV advertising. New customers pay in their insurance premiums, which helps to pay for the advertising and a rapid build-up of staff. As extra customers join, the business finds itself awash with cash. In fact, because there are few if any insurance pay-outs yet, the business may be barely profitable (i.e. it may be operating at no more than its true break-even point). Yet because the cash inflows arrive before the cash outflows, the business is cash-rich. An honest and well-run business will be aware of this, and make sure to save the cash rather than spend it. There have been many cases, though, where the proprietors have paid out large sums (to themselves, perhaps) and later been unable to pay out to the policy holders. The legal protection provided by limited liability can ensure that the owners enjoy pay-outs from 'profits' that prove an illusion.

A-grade application

On 28 June 2009 there were cheers as Bernie Madoff was sentenced to 150 years in prison. The 71-year-old was convicted for running a $65 billion 'Ponzi scheme' – defrauding tens of thousands of people out of their life savings. Those looking to retirement gave it to Madoff to invest, as he promised high, stable dividends and had the credibility of a former Chairman of the New York NASDAQ stock exchange.

In fact Madoff invested little of the money that savers gave him. He used new cash to pay dividends to older investors – and to fund a lavish lifestyle. The Ponzi scheme collapsed in December 2008 when recession-hit investors tried to withdraw their savings. Madoff had been cash-rich, but there were no underlying profits to provide a fall-back position.

What does all this imply for managers?

The key is to appreciate that cash flow and profit are different aspects of the same thing. Cash flow and profit are linked, but not the same. Good financial planning requires an estimate of the likely profitability of a course of action. It then requires a careful forecast of the flows of cash in and out of the business. Profitability shows the long-term value of a financial decision; cash flow shows the short-term impact of that decision on the firm's bank balance.

Cash vs profit: an example

Trish decides to open a beauty salon. She estimates that annual fixed overheads will be £120,000 and annual revenues £300,000 offset by variable costs at 20% of revenue (i.e. £60,000).

In other words, annual profit should be: £300,000 – (£160,000 + £60,000) = £80,000

The start-up costs of opening the salon are expected to be £60,000, so the business will be profitable from year 1.

However, there are some important cash flow issues to consider: first, how long will it take before the salon opens its doors (and cash starts flowing in)? Second, will the business *really* start at a revenue level equivalent to £300,000 per year (£25,000 per month), or will it take many months before sales rise to a satisfactory level?

Table 20.3 shows the cash flow position of the business, assuming that it takes three months to prepare the beauty salon (building work, decoration and so on) and that it will take four months before regular custom has built up fully. The forecast is for the first eight months.

As you can see, even after eight months the business still has a serious cash flow problem. If the figures remain the same, it will be another six months before cumulative cash flow (the bank account) becomes positive. So the 'profitable' first year (and any accountant would confirm that the year is profitable) ends in the red.

The reason is simple. The cash investment to set up the business all takes place at the start, before the salon can generate a penny of cash inflow. The cash flow problem is because the cash outflow occurs before the cash inflows arrive. Therefore, the bank must be kept informed so that it is willing to keep the business afloat. Unless the overdraft requirements are clear and predicted, the bank manager may lose faith and demand all loans to be repaid.

Table 20.3 Cash flow forecast for a new beauty salon

All figures in £000s	1	2	3	4	5	6	7	8
Cash at start	0	(20)	(40)	(60)	(64)	(64)	(59)	(51)
Cash in	0	0	0	10	15	20	25	25
Cash out	20	20	20	14	15	15	17	17
Net cash	(20)	(20)	(20)	(4)	(0)	5	8	8
Cumulative cash*	(20)	(40)	(60)	(64)	(64)	(59)	(51)	(43)

*This is the firm's bank balance at the end of each month.

Issues for analysis

A key difference between cash flow and profit is *time*. Starting a vineyard may prove hugely profitable – eventually. But experts warn that it takes 10 years to recover the initial costs of starting up (i.e. cash flow will be negative for 10 years). Cash flow measures today's money in and money out; profit is a more long-term calculation.

The other key factor is the type of business. Most new business start-ups are vulnerable to cash flow problems, but which are in the toughest position? It is hardest by far for manufacturers, especially if they have an innovative new product. They have to spend months, perhaps years, developing the product, then building, equipping and staffing a factory. Only then (after all that cash outflow) can they start producing a product and start to sell it to retailers. Even when they have made a sale and delivered the goods, many retailers take 60 days to pay their bills. The impact on cash flow is awful, even for a product that later proves to be highly profitable.

Cash flow vs profit – an evaluation

Especially for small firms, every significant decision needs to be assessed in terms of cash flow as well as profit. The cash flow forecast predicts the impact on the bank balance and may show the need for extra overdraft facilities to be negotiated. Or, if the firm's cash position is already weak, it may be safer to postpone the proposal.

Yet cash flow is no substitute for calculating profit. A cash-rich business idea (such as insurance) may inevitably lead to **insolvency**, if the business is not profitable. Getting cash inflows at the start seems great, but will turn into a nightmare if the cash outflows eventually start flooding in.

Remember, then, that cash flow and profit are not the same. Cash flow measures the short term and profit shows the longer term financial result of a decision. Clever managers look at both before they proceed.

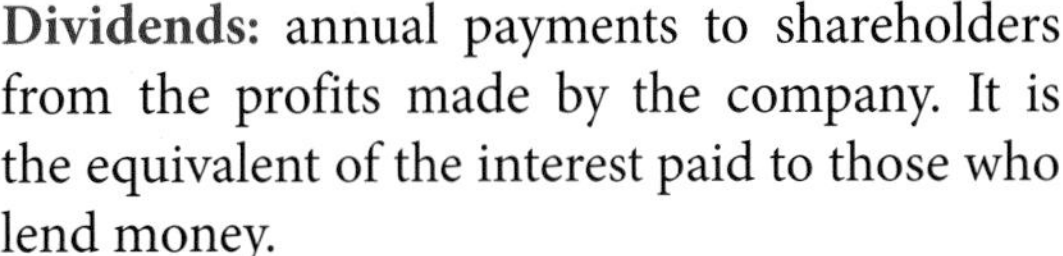

Key terms

Dividends: annual payments to shareholders from the profits made by the company. It is the equivalent of the interest paid to those who lend money.

Insolvency: inability to pay the bills, forcing closure.

Negative cash flow: when cash outflows outweigh cash inflows.

Sale and leaseback: selling the freehold to a piece of property then simultaneously leasing it back, perhaps for a period of 20 years. The owner gives up tomorrow's valuable asset in exchange for cash today.

A Revision questions *(20 marks; 25 minutes)*

1 Explain in your own words why cash inflow is not the same thing as revenue. (3)

2 Look again at Table 20.1. Explain why taking out a £20,000 bank loan generates cash inflow but not revenue. (3)

3 Give two reasons why a profitable business might run out of cash when it expands too rapidly. (2)

4 Look again at Table 20.2. Explain why 'purchases from suppliers on credit' is treated as a cost, yet not as a cash outflow. (3)

5 Identify whether each of these business start-ups would be cash-rich or cash-poor in the early years of the business.

- a) A pension fund, in which people save money in return for later pay-outs. (1)
- b) Building a hotel. (1)
- c) Starting a vineyard (grapes only harvestable after 3–5 years) (1)

6 Look again at Table 20.3 and the accompanying text and explain why the cash flow of the beauty salon is different from its profit. (4)

7 Why is it important for a small business to look both at profit and cash flow? (2)

B1 Revision exercises

Data response

On 23 August 2007 the former boss of a £1 billion insurance company broke down in tears at Southwark Crown Court. Michael Bright led the stock market flotation of Independent Insurance in 1986. Rapidly expanding the business, the company's market value soared to £1 billion in 2000. It had 500,000 personal policy holders and 40,000 business customers. A year later the business was bust, after underestimating the cost of claims and overseas expansion. About 1,000 employees were out of work. Serious Fraud Office investigators were called in to examine the collapse. It was six years, though, before the case against three leading executives was brought to trial. Eventually Bright was sentenced to seven years in jail and, in February 2009, Bright and other leading executives each had £1 million confiscated by the courts.

Questions (15 marks; 20 minutes)

1 Outline three groups of people (stakeholders) who would have lost out in the collapse of Independent Insurance. (6)

2 Explain how a fast-growing insurance business could be cash-rich, yet unprofitable. (9)

B2 Data response

Investment Dragon Peter Jones on cash and profit

Managing your cash in a focused manner is fundamental to survival, let alone success. Businesses are more likely to fail because they run out of cash – not because they're unable to generate a profit. You can have a lorry load of orders with the promise of untold profits in the pipeline, but if you don't have the cash to make and sell your products in the first place, and you are unable to pay your immediate bills, your business will fold.

Cash flow is a common hurdle for small and start-up enterprises. For that reason, it is important to **strengthen cash flow** from the outset.

- **Monitor profit** and **avoid over-commitment**. One common mistake entrepreneurs make is that they see a run-rate of business and immediately start to incur costs. They'll rent an office, take on new lease commitments, buy a new car. These monthly payments can result in losing sight of the real cash that's generated through the business.
- **Grow the business organically** and **keep costs down**, especially if you can't access bank finance. Focus on keeping costs to a bare minimum. Forget the office; work from home. Forget the car; use public transport. Grow the business, grow a pot of cash and then invest in the business. Using that money to reinvest is vital.
- **Reinvest profits wisely**
  - Understand what your start-up and ongoing costs are. Be realistic. It is better to overestimate expenditure and time and underestimate revenue than fall short of revenue and overspend.
  - Evaluate and monitor profit continually.
  - Reinvest your profit. That way, you'll scale the business far quicker than if you use the profit to rent another office building or buy a car. It's how you spend the profit that's important. Entrepreneurs always spend profit on the business. Successful entrepreneurs invest that profit on the right areas to maximise growth and enhance existing offerings.

(Source: www.peterjones.tv)

Questions (20 marks; 25 minutes)

1 Explain why, in the first paragraph, Peter Jones seems to be suggesting that cash flow is more important than profit for a small business (4)

2 By 'run-rate' Peter Jones means the revenue generated by the business once it is up and running. Why does he think an entrepreneur should wait before spending at this rate? (5)

3 Growing 'organically' means from within (i.e. not rushing to buy up other businesses). Organic growth is usually at a slow enough pace to cope with cash flow pressures. Examine why rapid growth can cause big cash flow problems. (6)

4 Explain why it is 'better to overestimate expenditure and time and underestimate revenue'. (5)

21 Integrated finance

Introduction

The great thing about a finance question is that if you get it right you get full marks. With most written questions a right answer might score only three or four out of six, or five or six out of ten. So revision on finance can be uniquely helpful at producing high grades.

Calculations in themselves, however, are only a means to an end. Businesses do financial calculations to help them to manage the business. In examinations you should treat the figures the same way. Do not just revise *how* to calculate variances, but also think about *why* a business would do this.

When answering questions on finance, and even when revising, ask yourself the following questions.

- What do they show?
- What do they not show?
- What other information would help to explain the situation?

Even if you get a calculation wrong, you can still gain marks by showing your workings and by your written interpretation of your wrong result. Examiners use the term 'the own-figure-rule'. This means that, even if you say a firm has a negative variance of £50,000 instead of the correct answer of a £500,000 positive variance, you can get full marks for a written analysis of your wrong answer.

Another factor to consider is that the finance answer is only part of the information needed to make an assessment of the situation. Remember that, in business, finance does not stand alone. It is always connected to other aspects of the business, such as marketing or production. Controlling costs is not just important for profit – it also contributes to the marketing effort by enabling the company to charge lower, more competitive prices. Raising finance is linked to a firm's need to expand or invest in new facilities or equipment. This means that what may seem like a 'finance' question is in fact linked to many other aspects of the business, and therefore gives you plenty of opportunities to explore these lines of argument, as well as just ploughing through calculations (see below for more on this).

So, don't be scared of finance. There are some calculations to be done (not that many at AS), but if you practise how to do these using the methods outlined in this book, it will get easier. Studying finance is much more than just calculating things; it also involves interpreting findings and placing finance in the context of the rest of the business.

Why study finance?

All organisations (even charities, hospitals and schools) have to raise finance in some way, decide how it should be spent, and monitor and control its usage. Even if the overall performance of an organisation is not measured in financial terms (although it often is in the form of profit), the effective management of its finances is extremely important. Whether you are a university, manufacturer, farmer, government department or retailer, you need to know about budgets, costs, cash flow and managing money. Studying and understanding finance is therefore very important, and the financial function plays a critical role in the success of a business.

When studying finance at AS, we consider the following aspects.

- The best way of raising money. What options are open to a business (e.g. getting a loan or selling shares) and which is the best option. This may depend on factors such as costs and the desire to retain control of the business.

- How many units a business has to sell to break-even and what profit or loss would be made at other levels of output. We also consider the impact on break-even of a change in costs or price. An understanding of break-even is very important when it comes to assessing the viability of a business idea.
- How to set financial targets, such as how much different departments can spend; this is called budgeting and we are interested in what budgets to set, how to set them and what to do if they are not achieved.
- How to forecast the money likely to come into and out of the business: cash flow forecasting is needed to help anticipate whether the business is going to be short of funds at any time, or if the business is going to have too much money sitting idle (in which case we should look to use it more productively).

Who is concerned about finance?

Finance is important to many groups inside and outside of the business. Here are some examples.

- Employees will want to see if the business continues to be viable because they will want to ensure that their jobs continue and that their wages remain competitive. They may also want to see if the rewards they are receiving seem fair compared to the profits of the business.
- Customers will look to the business to provide products that are good value for money. This means the business must control costs so that it can charge a reasonable price and still be profitable.
- Investors will be looking for a return on their capital and will want to know that the business is being financially well managed.
- The government will want the business to succeed, both as a source of employment and as a tax payer.

So a well-managed business will have a wide impact. Finance as a tool for good management will play its part. Financial decisions will impact on other aspects of the business and therefore are indirectly a part of the relationship with the customers and other external groups.

Finance and other business functions

No single department in a business can stand alone. This is especially true of finance. Key links with other business functions include the following.

- The amount that can be spent on marketing is likely to influence its effectiveness; the launch of a new perfume, for example, usually requires more than £1 million to be spent on promotion – this may simply not be affordable for some businesses. At the same time, the success of marketing influences the revenue the firm earns and the funds it has for other areas of the business.
- Efforts to control costs may impact on the operations of a business; they may affect which suppliers are chosen, and the nature of the materials and equipment used. Under-investment in facilities may limit the quality of a firm's output. However, controlling costs may be part of a low-price marketing strategy such as that which Ryanair and Primark have pursued.
- Decisions regarding the rewards paid to employees will obviously affect costs but may also affect motivation and performance. Lower rewards may cut costs in the short term but damage the quality of the products and long-term

Figure 21.1 Controlling costs is part of Ryanair's low-price marketing strategy

sales. On the other hand, higher levels of productivity by employees will reduce unit costs.

As you can see, financial decisions must be closely integrated with the other functions – a change in one area will inevitably affect the other functions.

A-grade application

The supermarket group Sainsbury announced an increase in both sales and profits in 2010. The UK's third-biggest supermarket chain opened 51 new convenience stores over the year. Chairman David Tyler said sales growth was beating rivals'.

'We have delivered sales growth ahead of the market and good profit growth,' he said. Some 127,000 of Sainsbury's staff will share a record bonus pot of £80m. As well as the convenience stores, the chain added 38 new supermarkets and has almost 900 outlets across the country. It is also expanding its online grocery business; sales here were up by 20%.

A/A*-grade finance

Getting the calculations right is obviously one element of the A/A*-grade finance answer. Remember, though, that Unit 2 consists of Marketing, People and Operations as well as Finance, so your knowledge of finance will generate A-grade marks only if you are able to place finance in a wider business context. For example, a successful marketing mix requires a large enough budget to be effective. Even a huge firm such as Cadbury would struggle to justify spending the £20+ million that it would cost to establish an effective rival to the Mars brand Maltesers. No less important is that brilliant new products (e.g. iPod, iPad or Wii) are often expensive to develop. So a finance team that is too tight with budgets must be sure that it isn't stifling the company's growth.

Another important consideration is understanding what is included in the figures and what is not. The figures may not tell the whole story. An A/A*-grade student will know that the figures may be only part of the picture, and will look for other information. Two businesses may have identical sales this year, but what about future prospects? One may be facing fierce competition from a new rival or experiencing problems with its staff; the other may have no threats and so faces a healthier outlook. A/A*-grade students apply their answers to the circumstances of the specific business.

Figure 21.2 Brilliant new products are expensive to develop

An A/A*-grade student will also be able to make recommendations and support them. Studying finance topics requires understanding the current situation in order to see how to improve it (e.g. improving cash flow). A D-grade candidate might do little more than outline the possible solutions: take out an overdraft or loan, use factoring or sell assets. To decide which of these options is the right one, an A/A*-grade student will consider factors such as the following:

- What options are open in this specific case? A brand new firm would not have spare assets to sell, whereas a retailer would not be able to use factoring easily (as this only applies when businesses sell on credit to other businesses).
- What are the consequences of the different choices? If you decide to sell assets, will you still be able to function? And if an entrepreneur takes out an overdraft, will the bank insist that she gives a personal guarantee to repay it if the business cannot do so? (This is quite likely.)

A good answer will be well supported and in context. A decision to cut prices to boost profits may work if demand is price elastic, but not if it is price inelastic. A decision to cut costs may work provided it can be done without much impact on quality, but may be risky if it involves a major reduction in the features offered by a product.

Issues for analysis

There are several recurrent themes in finance. Being able to discuss these will often help to give a deeper, more evaluative, answer to a finance question.

- *Issue 1 – The importance of profit:* profit is clearly important to a business; it is necessary for the business to continue and an essential requirement for growth. However, it does not have to be the overriding consideration and many businesses balance other objectives with the profit motive. For example, some small businesses may fulfil a personal need to survive financially with other personal needs such as enjoying work. Larger businesses may balance the profit made with the requirement to maintain good public relations or acting in a socially responsible manner. Businesses may also forego immediate profit in order to put in place strategies for growth or survival or increased profit in the future.
- *Issue 2 – Profit vs profitability:* it is very important to understand the difference between profit and profitability. Profit is an absolute number. We might say that a particular business project earned a profit of £10,000 last year. Is this good or bad? We would need to relate this in some way to another number such as the amount invested in it. If you invested £20,000 and earned a £10,000 profit, this is a 50 per cent return on your investment, which is good. If you invested £100,000 and earned £10,000 profit this is a 10 per cent return, which is not so impressive. Profitability measures profit in relation to some other figure and is measured in percentages. The need to understand the difference between profitability and profit should be clear: a £10,000 profit may be a return on capital of either 50 per cent or 10 per cent, depending on how much has been invested. Terms such as 'profit margin' and 'profit' cannot be used interchangeably – you need to understand exactly what they mean and use them carefully.
- *Issue 3 – The ethics of profitability:* the media contain a great deal of discussion about the ethics of profitability (i.e. the moral dimension). Businesses need profit, but how much, and at what cost?
  - What balance should be struck between profit and issues such as protecting the environment, exploiting workers or exploiting customers? Should producers of 'natural fruit smoothies' act as if they are the customer's friend if they are charging very high prices and making very high profits? Is this hypocrisy?
  - What about firms that produce or buy their products from developing countries where employees are paid very low wages? Is this acceptable? Or is it better that people in developing countries have some income rather than none?

  Answering these questions will require a balancing of the various interests involved. When answering a question involving ethics, it is important to look at all sides of the issue and to avoid becoming emotionally involved with one point of view. This may be very difficult if you have strong beliefs about an issue such as animal welfare or the treatment of staff in developing countries compared to the UK. By all means express your views, but remember to balance them with the other side of the case. When considering the rights and wrongs of profits, many people will be involved and it becomes important to look at issues from a variety of perspectives.
- *Issue 4 – The importance of cash:* understanding this issue requires an understanding of the difference between cash flow and profit. A business must have enough cash on a day-to-day basis to meet the business's commitments. Even if the cash is not available within the business, all is not lost if it is able to generate the required cash from external sources. A common mistake students make in exams is to use the words 'profit' and 'cash' interchangeably. If you still find it hard to separate the two, re-read Unit 20.
- *Issue 5 – Is financial management only for*

large businesses? While larger companies have the resources to employ financial experts, good financial management is essential for all businesses. Many new businesses fail because of poor financial management; in fact, it is one of the most common causes of early business failure. If anything, small businesses may need even tighter financial management than larger businesses. They will not have the resources to buffer the business if mistakes are made. They are also less likely to have access to outside funding to bail them out in difficult times. Small firms may also have just one or two products, which means financial risks are more concentrated. However, as the business grows there will be a widening gap between ownership and control. The shareholders may not take an active role in the day-to-day affairs of the business; in this situation, financial management systems will be necessary to keep control of the business and to ensure that the managers are pursuing the interests of the investors.

Revision questions *(50 marks; 40 minutes)*

1 List three ways in which decisions by the finance department can affect other functions of the business, such as marketing, people or operations. (3)

2 What is meant by profit? (2)

3 Why is profit important to a business? (2)

4 What is the difference between profit and cash flow? (2)

5 How is the concept of 'contribution' used in break-even analysis? (2)

6 Explain what is meant by budgeting. (2)

7 Why do firms produce cash flow forecasts? (4)

8 What is the difference between profits and profitability? (2)

9 List the two most likely sources of finance for a new business. (2)

10 Explain two possible benefits of budgeting. (4)

11 What is meant by a return on capital? (2)

12 What is meant by an increase in the profit margin? Why might profits fall as a result? (4)

13 Explain two ways a firm might improve its cash flow. (4)

14 Distinguish between fixed and variable costs. (3)

15 What is the effect of an increase in the variable cost per unit on the break-even output? (2)

16 Why might introducing budgets motivate some staff? (3)

17 How can variance analysis help a manager to make decisions? (3)

18 A few years ago customers queued to get their money out of Northern Rock bank. They feared that the bank's poor cash flow would make the bank unable to allow customers to withdraw their cash. Outline two possible effects of this upon the bank. (4)

Data exercises

Data response

DeDeLicious Ltd

DeDeLicious Ltd produces luxury chocolates that are sold mainly through independent stores and delicatessens. The business was set up in 2007 and its head office is in the centre of Oxford. The company's turnover this year is expected to be £400,000. Its net profit margins have generally been around 20 per cent, until recent increases in the cost of milk and pay increases for staff squeezed them to 12 per cent. JoJo Salter, the managing director, is also concerned about the cash flow difficulties that the firm has experienced recently. Its main customers have been slow to pay for the company's products despite DeDeLicious reminding them that payment was due on several occasions. JoJo has talked to a bank that provides a factoring service, but dropped the idea when she realised that its charges would amount to 6 per cent of the revenues of the business. As she told her finance manager: 'That will halve our profit margins!' JoJo is having sleepless nights about the financial situation because the company already has a big overdraft.

Questions *(30 marks; 30 minutes)*

1 What is meant by an overdraft? (2)

2 Excluding the possibility of factoring, calculate the company's expected profits for this year. (3)

3 Explain one way in which the company might increase its profits. (4)

4 Analyse two ways in which DeDeLicious might improve its cash flow. (7)

5 Should improving its cash flow be more important for DeDeDelicious than improving its profit margin? Justify your answer. (14)

Data response

Tescopoly power

With the credit crunch underway, many manufacturers were already concerned about their cash flow. Then came a big shock. Tesco announced that it would be changing its payment terms to suppliers of non-food items such as TVs, books, clothing and gardening supplies. Starting in Autumn 2008, Tesco would be switching from paying within 30 days to paying within 60 days. So, with hardly any warning, the cash flow forecasts of hundreds (Tesco says 300) of manufacturers will have to be torn up and redone.

The attraction for Tesco is clear. As it spends more than £3,000 million a month (!) on supplies, a one-month delay in paying could boost the firm's cash position by hundreds, even thousands, of millions of pounds. With the world economy entering recession, what could be cleverer than that? For a small manufacturer supplying Tesco, though, this would be especially infuriating. It would pretty much mean the mighty Tesco raiding the small firm's bank account to boost its own.

Despite their anger, no small supplier came out in public to complain about the change in terms. The *Financial Times* newspaper suggested this was because they feared 'retribution from the retailer'. On 30 October 2008, though, they found a surprising defender in the form of the chief executive of the huge Reckitt Benckiser company (Nurofen, Airwick, Cillit Bang and many other brands). Bart Becht warned that it could 'push some smaller players out of business'. Smaller suppliers will certainly have been outraged to hear that Reckitt had *not* been approached by Tesco to make any changes to its credit terms.

Tesco's defence is that it is only asking for 60 days' credit from suppliers of slower-moving stock such as books and kettles. Even if there is justification for doubling the credit period, three reasons make it especially hard to forgive Tesco's action:

1 The threat to small producers posed by the banks' current difficulties.

2 The fact that Tesco has such a hugely strong financial position itself.

3 The very short notice given; suppliers needed plenty of warning so that they could plan for the vicious hit to their cash flow represented by this move. Did Tesco's executives simply not understand the implications for its suppliers? Or did it not care?

In tough times like these, Tesco appears to be showing the worst side of big business. We can all understand a business being tough on its competitors. But these are not competitors, they are suppliers. In the past, Tesco has often boasted of its pride in working with suppliers and forming strong long-term relationships. It is showing how hollow these warm words can be.

(Source: Topical Cases, A–Z Business Training)

Questions *(40 marks; 45 minutes)*

1 Explain the impact of Tesco's action on a small supplier, assuming that 75 per cent of its output is being sold to Tesco. (6)

2 a) Assume that this same small supplier has the cash flow forecast shown below. Re-work the cash flow assuming that Tesco's new payment rules begin on 1 November and use Table 2 for your answer. (12)

Table 1

	October	November	December	January
Cash in	£200,000	£260,000	£270,000	£140,000
Cash out	£180,000	£220,000	£230,000	£170,000
Net cash	£20,000	£40,000	£40,000	(£30,000)
Cumulative cash	(£10,000)	£30,000	£70,000	£40,000

Table 2

	October	November	December	January
Cash in	£200,000			
Cash out	£180,000			
Net cash	£20,000			
Cumulative cash	(£10,000)			

b) Discuss the best way for a small firm to overcome this cash flow problem. (10)

3 Discuss whether large firms such as Tesco should be forced by law to pay their bills within 30 days. (12)

Data response

Cleaning up

Maria Gari came to the UK to work in 2005. She began working as a cleaner for a hotel in London but soon realised there was a huge demand for cleaners in the area. Combining her savings and a loan from the bank, she began her own business cleaning other people's houses and doing their ironing. Her initial investment to buy a car, design a logo, get the supplies and materials she needed and promote the business added up to £30,000.

In the first year she earned a net profit of £1,000 after she had paid herself a reasonable salary. It was hard work but the business grew very fast and she soon took on other staff to help her. To distinguish her business from many of the competitors, her staff wore uniforms and she insisted on an extremely high level of customer service. 'The customer always comes first, even when they are wrong' was one of her mottos. 'When they come back to their houses I want them to walk in and be amazed by what you have done' was another of her favourite sayings, along with 'We don't just clean, we transform.' By the fifth year, the turnover of the business was in six figures and she had surprised herself at how well it was going. She was now employing over 50 cleaners and had to appoint five supervisors to help manage them.

Maria's financial adviser, Vicky, was pleased with the sales growth of the business but said that, with more overheads and other cost increases, the net profit margin had fallen by 5 per cent in the last year. Maria thought this could easily be improved by increasing her prices: 'I am sure that this will boost our profit margins and our profits and that can't be bad.' Vicky seemed less convinced but knew that it was sometimes not worth arguing with Maria.

Going through last year's figures in relation to the budgeted figures, Vicky highlighted that the fall in the net profit margin had occurred despite the fact that revenue had a positive variance of 10 per cent. Vicky decided to look at the variances for the different types of costs in more detail.

Questions *(50 marks; 50 minutes)*

1 What was the return on capital in Maria's first year of trading? Comment on your finding. (5)

2 Explain two possible reasons why Maria's budgets proved inaccurate. (6)

3 Analyse the possible benefits to the business of examining the costs and revenue variances. (9)

4 Do you think that increasing prices will increase the net profit margin and the net profits of the business? (15)

5 Instead of increasing prices, do you think it would be better for Maria to cut costs in the following year, in order to boost the company's profits? (15)

Productivity and performance

Definition

Productivity is a measure of efficiency; it measures the output of a firm in relation to its inputs.

What is productivity?

Productivity is a measurement of a firm's efficiency. It measures output in relation to inputs. A firm can increase its efficiency by producing more with the same inputs (an increase in **capacity**) or producing the same amount with fewer inputs.

The most common measure is **labour productivity**. This measures the amount a worker produces over a given time. For example, an employee might make ten pairs of jeans in an hour. Measuring productivity is relatively easy in manufacturing where the number of goods can be counted. In the service sector it is not always possible to measure anything tangible. Productivity in services can be measured in some cases: the number of customers served, number of patients seen, the sales per employee. But how can the productivity of a receptionist be measured?

When considering a firm's efficiency, it is important to distinguish between productivity and total output. By hiring more employees, the firm may increase the total output but this does necessarily mean that the output *per* employee has gone up. Similarly, it is possible to have less total output with higher productivity because of a fall in the number of workers. Imagine, for example, 20 employees producing 40 tables a week in a furniture company. Their productivity on average is two tables per week. If five employees make 15 tables, the overall output has fallen, but the output *per worker* has risen. This situation of falling output but rising productivity happened in many manufacturing companies in the UK in the 2008–2009 recession. Faced with falling demand, many companies were forced to rationalise their organisation. This led to high levels of redundancies and extra work for those who still had a job. The result was that there were fewer people working but at the same time there was often higher output per person.

Figure 22.1 What is the output per worker at the furniture company?

A-grade application

Each year the Harbour Report provides feedback on the productivity of the US car industry. Published in 2009, the figures in Table 22.1 show the production of mid-size cars in 2007. Productivity is shown not as output of cars per person, but in terms of the time taken to produce each car (the lower the figure the better).

In its report, Harbour says that 'Toyota is the best in the industry. It is not a matter of spending more than competitors, but of effective *kaizen* improvement activities and the flexibility that comes with well-coordinated engineering.' The report also suggests that the highest productivity factories are increasingly the highest quality plants as well. It seems that well managed staff will succeed at both together.

Table 22.1 US car industry productivity in 2007

Producer and location	Actual production 2007	Production hours per vehicle	Percent over benchmark
Toyota, Georgetown	358,077	18.69	Benchmark
General Motors, Fairfax	188,432	19.34	3.5%
Ford, Hermosillo	213,458	20.78	11.2%
Chrysler, Sterling Heights	238,106	22.29	19.3%
General Motors, Orion	153,416	26.74	43.1%

Why does productivity matter?

The output per employee is a very important measure of a firm's performance. It has a direct impact on the cost of producing a unit. If productivity increases then, assuming wages are unchanged, the labour cost per unit will fall. Imagine that in one factory employees make five pairs of shoes a day but in another one they make ten pairs a day. Assuming the wage rate is the same, this means the labour cost of a pair of shoes will be halved in the second factory (see Table 22.2). With lower labour costs, this firm is likely to be in a better competitive position.

By increasing productivity, a firm can improve its competitiveness. It can either sell its products at a lower price or keep the price as it was and enjoy a higher profit margin. This is why firms continually monitor their productivity relative to their competitors and, where possible, try to increase it. However, they need to make sure that quality does not suffer in the rush to produce more. It may be necessary to set both productivity and quality targets.

Table 22.2 Shoe factory productivity and wage costs

	Daily wage rate	Productivity rate (per day)	Wage cost per pair
Factory 1	£50	5	£10
Factory 2	£50	10	£5

How to increase productivity

Increase investment in modern equipment

With modern, sophisticated machines and better production processes, output per worker should improve. Many modern factories are '**capital intensive**' as they have very few production workers; mechanisation and automation are everywhere. However, firms face financial constraints and should be cautious about assuming that mechanisation guarantees higher profits.

Many managers call for new technology when in fact more output can be squeezed out of the existing equipment. It may prove more efficient to run the machines for longer, spend more on careful maintenance to prevent breakdowns and discuss how to improve working practices. Firms can often achieve significant productivity gains without new equipment. This is the reason for the success of the ***kaizen*** (continuous improvement) approach taken by many firms. Important benefits can be achieved from what seem like relatively small changes to the way the firm operates rather than large scale investment in technology.

Improve the ability level of those at work

To increase productivity, a firm may need to introduce more training for its employees. A skilled and well trained workforce is likely to produce more and make fewer mistakes. Employees should be able to complete the task more quickly and will not need as much supervision or advice. They will be able to solve their own work-related problems and may be in a better position to contribute ideas on how to increase productivity further. This is especially important for businesses that are **labour intensive**.

However, firms are often reluctant to invest in training because employees may leave and work for another firm once they have gained more skills. Training also involves higher costs in the short run, which the business may not be able to afford, and the actual training period may cause disruptions to the normal flow of work. There is also a danger that the training will not provide sufficient gains to justify the initial investment and so any spending in this area needs to be properly costed and researched.

Simply training people for the sake of it is obviously of limited value. However, in general, UK firms do not have a particularly good record in training and more investment here could probably have a significant effect on the UK's productivity levels.

It should also be remembered that elaborate training may not be necessary for a firm which recruits the right people. Great care must be taken in the selection process to find staff with the right skills and attitudes. A firm with a good reputation locally will find it much easier to pick the best people. This is why many firms take great care over their relations with the local community.

Improve employee motivation

Professor Herzberg once said that most people's idea of a fair day's work was less than half what they could give if they wanted to. The key to success, he felt, was to create the circumstances in which people wanted to give all they could to the job. His suggestions on how to provide job enrichment are detailed in Unit 26.

There is no doubt that motivation matters. A motivated sales force may achieve twice the sales level of an unmotivated one. A motivated computer technician may correct twice the computer faults of an unmotivated one. And, in both cases, overall business performance will be affected.

The role of management

The management's style and ability can have a significant impact on motivation and on how effectively resources are used. Good managers can bring about substantial productivity gains through well organised work, the effective management of people and the coordination of resources. Bad managers can lead to wastage, inefficiency and low productivity.

Perhaps the key management role is to identify increasing productivity as a permanent objective. For example, the Japanese bulldozer company Komatsu set a target of a 10 per cent productivity increase every year, until the world-leading American producer Caterpillar had been overtaken. In many firms, productivity is not a direct target. The focus, day by day, is on production, not productivity. After all, it is production which ensures customer orders are fulfilled. An operations manager, faced with a 10 per cent increase in orders, may simply ask the workforce to do overtime. The work gets done; the workforce is happy to earn extra money; and it's all rather easy to do. Harder by far to reorganise the workplace to make production more effective. Managers whose main focus is on the short term, therefore, think of production not productivity.

A-grade application

Motivation on the pitch

When Fulham Football Club appointed a new groundsman, few people even noticed. The fans had always been proud of the pitch, but newly appointed Frank Boahene was not impressed. He thought it needed a dramatic improvement before the August start to the new season. With no time to re-seed the pitch, he decided the best way to strengthen the grass was to cut it three times a day! First thing in the morning and last thing in the afternoon was not a problem. But he also chose to 'pop back' from his home in Reading (an hour's drive) to do the third cut at 11.00 at night. Every day! That's motivation.

Issues for analysis

When answering a case study or essay it might be useful to consider the following points.

- Productivity is an important determinant of a firm's ability to compete in this country or overseas because it can have a significant impact on unit costs.
- High productivity does not in itself guarantee that a firm is competitive; it also depends on

other factors such as the cost of materials, product quality, product design, good marketing and external factors such as the exchange rate.

- The productivity within an industry will depend on a combination of factors such as training, capital equipment and production techniques; the main single factor is the quality of management.

Productivity and performance – an evaluation

Greater labour productivity can lead to greater efficiency and higher profitability. This is because, other things being equal, it lowers the labour cost per unit. However, productivity is only one factor which contributes to a firm's success. A firm must also ensure it produces a good quality product, that it is marketed effectively and that costs are controlled. There is little point increasing productivity by 20 per cent if at the same time you pay your staff 30 per cent more. Similarly, there is no point producing more if there is no actual demand. Higher productivity, therefore, contributes to better performance but needs to be accompanied by effective decision making throughout the firm.

The importance of productivity to a firm depends primarily on the level of value added involved. Top price perfumes such as Chanel have huge profit margins. Production costs are a tiny proportion of the selling price. Therefore a 10 per cent productivity increase might have only a marginal effect on profit and virtually none on the competitiveness of the brand. For mass market products in competitive markets, high productivity is likely to be essential for survival. A 5 per cent cost advantage might make all the difference. Therefore, when deciding on an appropriate recommendation for solving a business problem, a judgement is required as to whether boosting productivity is a top priority for the business concerned.

Key terms

Capacity: total output which could be produced with existing resources.

Capital intensive: high level of capital equipment compared to labour.

***Kaizen*:** a Japanese term meaning continuous improvement. Regular, small increases in productivity may achieve more (and be less disruptive) than major changes to working methods.

Labour intensive: high level of labour input compared to the amount of capital equipment.

Labour productivity: output per worker.

Revision questions *(40 marks, 45 minutes)*

1. What is meant by the term 'productivity'? (3)
2. Why might it be hard to measure the productivity of staff who work in service industries? (4)
3. How does productivity relate to labour costs per unit? (4)
4. Explain how a firm might be able to increase its employees' productivity. (4)
5. How can increased investment in machinery help to boost productivity? (3)
6. Identify two factors which help and two which limit your productivity as a student. (4)
7. Outline the likely effect of increased motivation on the productivity of a teacher. (5)
8. Look at the table below and calculate the change in productivity at BDQ Co since last year. (4)
9. Explain how motivation and productivity might be linked. (4)
10. Explain how productivity can be linked to unit labour costs. (5)

BDQ Co	Output	Number of staff
Last year	32,000	50
This year	30,000	40

Revision exercises

Data response

Productivity in recession

When the recession hit in 2008, businesses were surprisingly reluctant to make people redundant. So the fall in output affected the efficiency of production (i.e. productivity). As output per worker fell, unit wage costs rose, even though wage increases were modest. Look carefully at Figure 22.2 before answering the questions below.

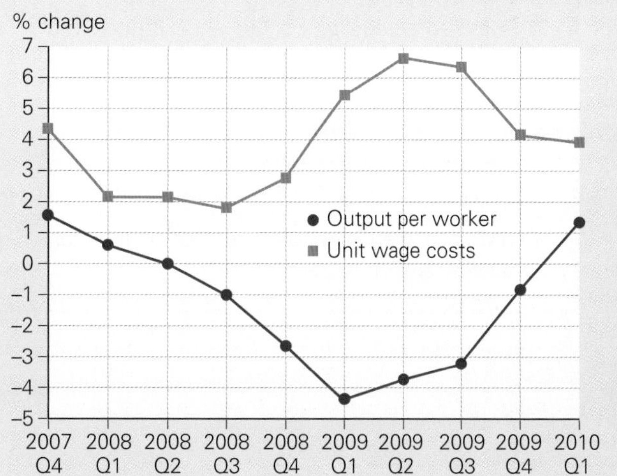

Figure 22.2 Productivity in recession (year-on-year % figures)
(Source: ONS)

Questions *(30 marks; 35 minutes)*

1 Explain how a fall in the productivity of UK firms might affect UK exports. (6)

2 Briefly explain why unit wage costs were stable in the first quarter (Jan–March) 2010. (6)

3 Spartax Ltd produces widgets for washing machines. It chose to cut its workforce by 20 per cent in autumn 2008 in response to a 10 per cent fall in its sales. Explain how its productivity would be affected by this staff cut. (6)

4 Discuss the possible reasons why most UK firms were willing to allow productivity to fall during the recession instead of cutting back sharply on staff numbers. (12)

Data response

Going potty

Farah Stewart was trying to explain the need to boost productivity to the employees at her ceramics factory, FS Ltd. Relations between Farah and her staff had not been good in recent years. The company was not doing well and she blamed the workers. 'On average you work eight hours a day at £8 an hour and produce around 160 pots each. Meanwhile, at Frandon I am told they produce 280 pots a day. Can't you see that this makes it cheaper for them and if things go on like this, we'll be out of business? You need to work much harder to get our unit costs down! I know you are expecting to get a pay rise this year but I cannot afford it until you produce more; then we'll think about it.'

Jeff Battersby, the spokesperson for the employees, was clearly annoyed by Farah's tone. 'First Ms Stewart, have you ever considered that if you paid us more we might produce more for you? I'm not surprised productivity is higher at Frandon – they get about £80 a day. There's no point demanding more work from us if you are not willing to pay for it – we're not slaves you know. If you paid us £10 an hour like Frandon, I reckon we could increase productivity by 50 per cent. However, that's not the only issue: they've got better equipment. It's not our fault if the kilns don't work half the time and take an age to heat up. Sort out the equipment and our pay and you'll soon see productivity improve. Why not *ask* us next time instead of jumping to conclusions?'

Questions *(60 marks; 60 minutes)*

1 FS Ltd employs 50 pot makers while Frandon Ltd employs 30 people in production. Calculate the total output for each of the two companies. (4)

2 With reference to FS Ltd and Frandon Ltd explain the difference between 'total output' and 'productivity'. (6)

3 Calculate the average labour cost per pot at FS Ltd if employees are paid £8 an hour and their daily output is 160 pots each. (4)

4 What is the wage cost per pot at Frandon (assume an 8-hour day)? (3)

5 Analyse the short- and long-term benefits to Frandon of its lower labour costs per unit. (12)

6 Jeff Battersby claims that if the employees at FS Ltd were paid £10 an hour their productivity would increase by 50 per cent. What would the unit wage cost be then? (5)

7 Would you recommend Farah increases the pay of her employees to £10 an hour? Justify your answer. (12)

8 Discuss the possible gains from involving employees in discussions about how to improve productivity. (14)

23 Organisational structure

Definition

Organisational structure is the formal and systematic way the management of a business is organised. When presented as a diagram, it shows the departmental functions and who is answerable to whom.

Introduction

As organisations became larger and more complex, early management thinkers such as F W Taylor and H Fayol considered how to structure an organisation. Both saw the function of organisations as converting inputs, such as money, materials, machines and people, into output. Therefore, designing an organisation was like designing a machine, the objective being to maximise efficiency. Early managers wanted to be told the best way to manage and the organisational structure which would work best.

Taylor and Fayol based their thoughts largely on the way an army is organised. The key features of the hierarchy would be as follows.

- To break the organisation up into divisions with a common purpose; in business, this was usually the business functions: marketing, finance and so on.
- Every individual would answer to one person – their **line manager**.
- No manager would be overloaded with too many subordinates, so the **span of control** was kept low.
- To achieve low spans of control, it was necessary to have many management layers, as shown in Table 23.1.

Table 23.1 Management layers

Military	Business
• Captain	• Senior Manager
• Lieutenant	• Manager
• Sergeant	• Team Leader
• Corporal	• Supervisor
• Foot soldier	• Shopfloor worker

The growing business

In the early stages of a new business, there are often only one or two people involved. When the business is so small, the day-to-day tasks are carried out by the owner(s). It is not necessary to have a formal organisation structure as communication and coordination will be carried out on an informal, face-to-face basis. However, as the business grows and more people become involved, the firm will need to develop a more formal organisational structure. This will show the roles, responsibilities and relationships of each member of the firm. This is often illustrated through an organisational chart: a diagram that shows the links between people and departments within the firm. It also shows communication flows/channels, lines of authority and layers of hierarchy. Each of these terms will be explained later in the unit.

When Matteo Pantani founded Scoop ice cream in Covent Garden in 2007, he only employed part-time staff at the counter (i.e. to serve the ice cream and take the money). Matteo made the ice cream and ran the business. Although he didn't need to think about a hierarchy or a structure, Figure 23.1 shows what it initially looked like.

As the business grew, Matteo opened a second outlet in 2010, in Brewer Street, Soho. This meant

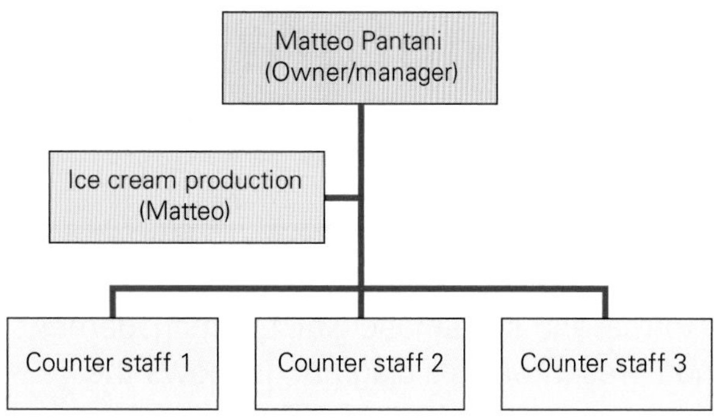

Figure 23.1 Scoop: 2007 hierarchy

he needed a manager to run the Soho outlet, while Matteo was largely at Covent Garden (he also needed time to look for the third Scoop). By mid-2010, then, the organisational hierarchy was as shown in Figure 23.2.

The point, of course, is to appreciate how much more complex a hierarchy becomes as the business grows.

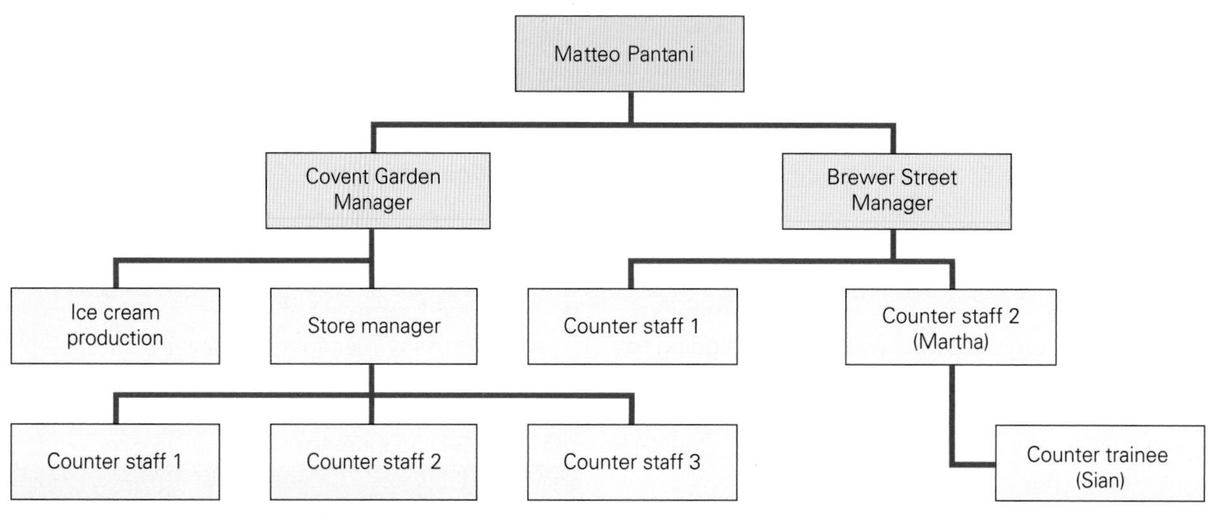

Figure 23.2 Scoop: 2010 hierarchy

Roles and relationships

We will now look at the different roles and relationship within organisations. This is illustrated in Figure 23.2.

Roles

Roles describe the different tasks that individuals are responsible for. At this point it is important to define responsibility, authority and accountability. Responsibility means carrying the burden of blame, even if an error is made by a subordinate. After all, if Alex Ferguson plays his reserve goalkeeper in a football match, it is Ferguson who will be blamed if the keeper lets in a soft goal. Authority means having the power to make a decision or carry out a task. However, if Matteo delegated authority to the Covent Garden Manager to carry out a particular task, Matteo would still retain the overall responsibility for that task. This shows how important it is for a manager to consider carefully who they delegate tasks to. Accountability is the extent to which an individual is held responsible for his or her decisions and actions.

Directors

Directors are members of 'the Board' (i.e. the board of directors who handle the most senior appointments and set out the main aims and objectives of the business). There are two types of director:

1. Executive directors, who are appointed to the Board because they head up important divisions or departments (e.g. the Marketing Director).
2. Non-executive directors: part-time directors from outside the business; their job is to take an independent view of the shareholders' best interests.

Manager

A manager is a person responsible for organising others to carry out tasks. A line manager is the person immediately above someone in the organisational chart. For example, Sian's line manager is Martha.

Team leader

This role will usually arise in firms that organise themselves in a **matrix management** structure. This is where the firm allocates its workers into project teams rather than departments and a team leader will manage the workers involved in a particular project. Project teams will be made up of people with different skills, for example, in a typical team there will be financial, marketing and operations specialists. This will enable them to make integrated decisions for the project. Building and engineering firms usually adopt this matrix approach in which the team leader is responsible for the management of the tasks and people involved.

Other key terms

Levels of hierarchy

These show the number of different supervisory and management levels between the bottom of the chart and the top of the hierarchy. In Scoop in 2010 there are four levels of hierarchy.

Span of control

This describes the number of people directly under the supervision of a manager. If managers have very wide spans of control, they are directly responsible for many staff. In such cases, they may find that there are communication problems or the workers may feel that they are not being given enough guidance. The ideal span of control will depend upon the nature of the tasks and the skills and attitude of the workforce and manager. Table 23.2 shows the advantages and disadvantages of a narrow span of control.

Chain of command

This shows the reporting system from the top of the hierarchy to the bottom (i.e. the route through which information travels throughout the organisation). In an organisation with several levels of hierarchy, the chain of command will be longer and this could create a gap between workers at the bottom of the organisation and managers at the top. If information has to travel via several people, there is also a chance that it may become distorted.

Centralisation and decentralisation

This describes the extent to which decision-making power and authority are delegated within an organisation. A centralised structure is one in which decision-making power and control remains in the hands of the top management levels. A decentralised structure delegates decision-making power to workers lower down the organisation. Many organisations will use a combination of these approaches, depending upon the nature of the decision involved. For example, in many schools and colleges, the decisions concerning which resources to use will be decentralised (i.e. taken by teachers as opposed to the senior management team). Other decisions, concerning future changes in subjects being offered, may be centralised, that is taken by senior managers.

Table 23.2 Advantages and disadvantages of a narrow span of control

Advantages	Disadvantages
Allows close management supervision, vital if staff are inexperienced, labour turnover is high or if the task is critical (e.g. manufacturing aircraft engines)	Workers may feel over-supervised and therefore not trusted; this may cause better staff to leave as they are looking for more personal responsibility
Communications may be excellent within the small, immediate team (e.g. the boss and three staff)	Communications may suffer within the business as a whole, as a narrow span means more layers of hierarchy, which makes vertical communications harder
Many layers of hierarchy means many rungs on the career ladder, so promotion chances arise regularly (though each promotion may mean only a slightly different job)	The narrow span usually leads to restricted scope for initiative and experiment; the boss is always looking over your shoulder and this will alienate enterprising staff

Recent changes in organisation structures

In the past, some firms had very tall hierarchical structures which meant many layers of management, often with quite narrow spans of control. This made them expensive to run, because of the management salaries that had to be paid. Tall structures also resulted in longer chains of command which could have a negative impact on communication. More recently, companies have liked to announce that they are becoming flatter, meaning fewer layers of management, with each manager having a wider span of control. Although some managers dislike this increased responsibility, their workers may thrive under the increased independence that is gained. Furthermore, the firm will have reduced overhead costs which should mean greater efficiency.

Why is organisational structure so important?

As a firm grows, more people will become involved, so to ensure that the different tasks are fulfilled, it will be vital that every person is clear about what their role involves and who they are answerable/accountable to and responsible for. Poor organisational structures will lack coordination and the following problems could result:

- poor communication leading to mistakes
- duplication of tasks
- tasks being overlooked
- different departments failing to work together effectively.

In the longer term, these problems will create a sub-standard service and this will have an impact on the firm's sales, revenue and profit. As a firm expands, it must ensure that its organisation structure accommodates the growth.

Issues for analysis

When discussing the topic of organisation structure, it is important to recognise that the structures are not static and they should adapt to the environment in which they operate. If more people enter the firm, then changes should take place and this may have an impact on the roles and relationships of the existing workers.

The key to a high-scoring exam answer is to think about the match between the structure and the type of organisation. When Google started up, it had virtually no structure; brilliant people were hired and told to do brilliant things; the structure was deliberately loose. Today Google is a vast business, needing a tighter structure, but probably not too tight as to strangle innovation.

Organisational structure – an evaluation

There is no 'ideal' organisational structure or span of control. What works for one business may fail in another, even if both are the same size. In exams there will usually be hints about whether the structure is working. A flat hierarchy may be at the heart of an innovative business, or there may be signs that staff lack direction and morale. A tall hierarchy may be at the centre of a focused, career-orientated workforce, or it may be bureaucratic and incapable of a quick decision. The judgement is yours.

Key terms

Line manager: a manager responsible for meeting specific business targets and responsible for specific staff.

Matrix management: where staff work in project teams in addition to their responsibilities within their own department. Therefore, staff can be answerable to more than one boss.

Span of control: the number of staff who are answerable directly to a manager.

Revision questions (30 marks; 30 minutes)

1 What is meant by the term 'chain of command'? (2)

2 Define span of control. (2)

3 Some theorists believe that the ideal span of control is between three and six. To what extent do you agree with this? (5)

4 Explain two implications of a firm having too wide a span of control. (4)

5 Explain what an organisational chart shows. (4)

6 Why is it important for a growing firm to think carefully about its organisational structure? (4)

7 State three possible problems for a business with many levels of hierarchy. (3)

8 What is meant by the term 'accountable'? (2)

9 What do you think would be the right organisational structure for a hospital? Explain your answer. (4)

Revision exercises

Data response

Look again at the Scoop hierarchy charts (Figure 23.1 and Figure 23.2).

Questions (20 marks; 25 minutes)

1 Explain why communication might be harder in the larger Scoop of 2010. (6)

2 Should the Brewer Street counter staff be allowed to contact Ice Cream Production directly, for example, if they see they are running out of vanilla ice cream? Explain your reasoning. (6)

3 Examine two ways in which Matteo may find his management responsibilities more difficult when he opens his third Scoop outlet. (8)

Data response

Chicken Little

Peter (known as 'Paxo') Little set up his free range chicken farm in the early 1990s. At the time it was an unusual move, especially on the grand scale envisaged by 'Paxo'. His farm had the capacity to produce 250,000 chickens every 45 days, making 4 million birds a year. Since then the business has grown enormously, to a turnover of £25 million today.

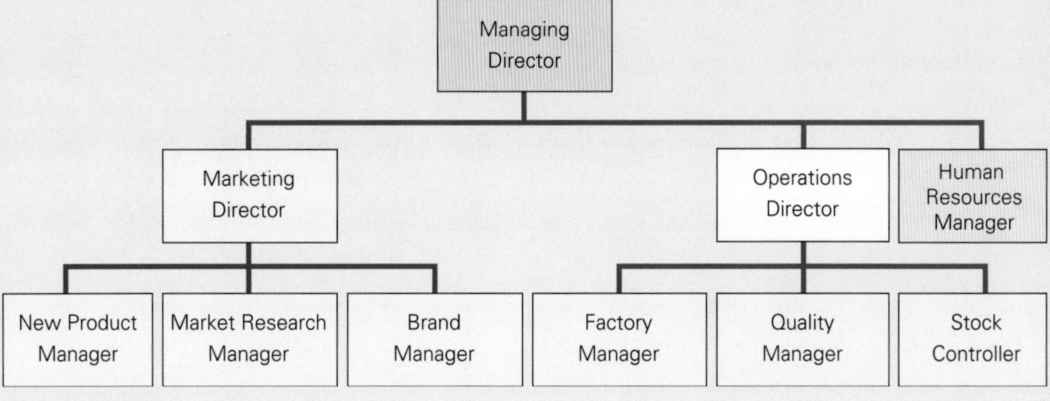

Figure 23.3 Organisational structure of Chicken Little farms

But Paxo is getting concerned that his business is not as efficient as it used to be. As Managing Director, he finds that he rarely hears from junior staff; not even the quality manager's five staff who used to see him regularly. As he said recently to the Operations Director, 'the communication flows seem like treacle today, whereas they used to be like wildfire'.

Fortunately, the boom in demand for free range and organic produce has helped the business. So even though the team spirit seems to have slipped away, profits have never been higher. Unfortunately the Marketing Director keeps talking about rumours that a huge Dutch farming business is about to set up poultry farms in Britain. That might set the cat among the chickens.

Questions *(25 marks; 30 minutes)*

1 a) What is the Managing Director's span of control? (1)

b) Comment on the strength and weaknesses of this organisational structure. (6)

c) How important does Human Resources seem within this business? (3)

2 Explain why vertical communications may not be as effective today as they used to be in the past at Chicken Little. (5)

3 Discuss the ways in which the Factory Manager might benefit or suffer from the organisational structure shown in the diagram. (10)

24 Measuring the effectiveness of the workforce

Definition

Staff costs are usually between 25 per cent and 50 per cent of a firm's total costs. So firms try to measure the performance of their people objectively (i.e. in an unbiased way). Calculations such as staff productivity can be used to measure the success of initiatives such as new methods of working or payment.

The need to measure performance

Managers require an objective, unbiased way to measure the performance of personnel. The firm needs to be able to see whether:

- the workforce is fully motivated
- the workforce is as productive as it could be
- the personnel policies of the business are helping the business to meet its goals.

It is not possible to measure these things directly. How, for example, can the level of motivation of workers be measured accurately? Instead, a series of indicators are used which, when analysed, can show the firm if its personnel policies are contributing as much to the firm as they should.

There are two main performance indicators used to measure the effectiveness of a personnel department:

1 labour productivity
2 labour turnover.

Figure 24.1 How can workers' performance be measured accurately?

Labour productivity

Calculating labour productivity

Labour productivity is often seen as the single most important measure of how well a firm's workers are doing. It compares the number of workers with the output that they are making and is expressed through the formula:

$$\frac{\text{output per period}}{\text{number of employees per period}}$$

For example, if a window cleaner employs 10 people and in a day will normally clean the windows of 150 houses, then the productivity is:

$$\frac{150}{10} = 15 \text{ houses per worker per day}$$

At its simplest, the higher the productivity of the workforce, the better it is performing. Any increase in the productivity figure suggests an improvement in efficiency. The importance of productivity lies in its impact on labour costs per unit. For example, the productivity of AES Cleaning is 15 houses per worker per day; MS Cleaning achieves only 10.

Assuming a daily rate of pay of £45, the labour cost per house is £3 for AES but £4.50 for MS Cleaning. Higher productivity leads to lower labour costs per unit – and therefore greater competitiveness both here and against international rivals.

Productivity

Productivity is covered in more detail in Unit 22. The key thing for this unit is to remember that productivity is just one way to measure staff performance. There are others, including labour turnover.

Labour turnover

Measuring labour turnover

This is a measure of the rate of change of a firm's workforce. It is measured by the ratio:

$$\frac{\text{number of staff leaving the firm per year}}{\text{average number of staff}} \times 100$$

So a firm which has seen five people leave out of its staff of 50 has a labour turnover of:

$$\frac{5}{50} \times 100 = 10\%$$

As with all of these figures, it would be a mistake to take one figure in isolation. Instead it would be better to look at how the figure has changed over a number of years – and to look for the reasons why the turnover rate is as it is.

Causes of labour turnover

If the rate of labour turnover is increasing, it may be a sign of dissatisfaction within the workforce. If so, the possible causes could be either internal to the firm or external.

Internal causes of an increasing rate of labour turnover could include the following:

- A poor recruitment and selection procedure, which may appoint the wrong person to the wrong post. If this happens, then eventually the misplaced workers will wish to leave to find a post more suited to their particular interests or talents.
- Ineffective motivation or leadership, leading to workers lacking commitment to this particular firm. They will feel no sense of loyalty or ownership to the business, and will tend to look outside the firm for promotions or new career opportunities, rather than looking for new ways in which they could contribute to 'their' firm.
- Wage levels that are lower than those being earned by similar workers in other local firms. If wage rates are not competitive, workers will feel dissatisfied by their position and may look elsewhere to find a better reward for doing a similar job.

External causes of an increasing rate of labour turnover could include the following:

- More local vacancies arising, perhaps due to the setting up or expansion of other firms in the area.
- Better transport links, making a wider geographical area accessible for workers. New public transport systems such as Manchester's network of trams or Newcastle's Metro Rail links enable workers to take employment that was previously out of their reach.

Consequences of high labour turnover

A high rate of labour turnover can have both negative and positive effects on a firm. The negative aspects would be:

- the cost of recruitment of replacements
- the cost of retraining replacements
- the time taken for new recruits to settle into the business and adopt the firm's **culture**
- the loss of productivity while the new workers adjust.

On the positive side, labour turnover can benefit the business in several ways:

- new workers can bring new ideas and enthusiasm to the firm
- workers with specific skills can be employed rather than having to train up existing workers from scratch
- new ways of solving problems can be seen by workers with a different perspective, whereas existing workers may rely on tried and trusted techniques that have worked in the past.

On balance, then, there is a need for firms to achieve the *right* level of labour turnover, rather than aiming for the lowest possible level.

A-grade application

Labour turnover at Red Carnation Hotels (RCH)

Liz McGivern joined the RCH luxury hotel chain just after the 2001 terrorist attack on New York. Business was soon down by 20% as American tourists disappeared. Yet she noticed a shocking detail about RCH; its labour turnover was 80%. This would be poor for any hotel, but luxury hotels have to offer good service, which would always be tricky if new, inexperienced staff were dealing with guests. Nothing could be done about nervous flyers, but the high labour turnover was inexcusable.

Liz carried out some internal research which revealed high levels of staff dissatisfaction due to poor management and strained internal relationships. Her solution was to implement a company-wide training programme focusing on improved customer service. The cost per person was in the order of £1,000 so, with a staff of more than 500, this was a substantial investment by the directors. Fortunately it went well, resulting in improved repeat business from guests and a sharp fall in labour turnover. In 2001 it had been far above the industry average, but by 2009 Red Carnation's 24% labour turnover was well below the 31% for the industry as a whole. Even more importantly for the business, the revenue received per room rose by 11% at a time when the market trend was towards falling room rates.

(Source: www.people1st.co.uk)

Evaluating the success of personnel management

Productivity and labour turnover data provides the firm with a commentary on its performance. Poor productivity and high labour turnover might be a commentary on poor management in the workplace. For the most effective comparisons, good managers analyse the figures to identify:

- changes over time (i.e. this year versus last year)
- how the firm is performing compared with other similar firms
- performance against targets, such as a 20 per cent improvement on last year.

Each of these comparisons will tell the firm how it is performing in relation to a yardstick. This will indicate to the firm where it is performing well and where it may have a problem. The firm must then investigate carefully the reasons for its performance before it can judge how well its personnel function is operating.

For example, labour productivity may have fallen since 12 months ago. Closer investigation may show that the fall was due to the time taken to train staff on new machinery installed at the start of the year. Figures may show that productivity in the last six months was actually higher than at any time in the past, and the firm could be confident that future productivity will continue to increase. An apparent problem was actually masking an improvement for the firm.

Issues for analysis

There are several important business issues relating to personnel performance indicators.

- Business success comes from being the best and staying the best. This is always hard but is the only way to be sure of staying at the top. Football managers might say all that counts is what happens on the pitch, but lateness or absence from training is often a good indicator of problems to come. Every manager should be alert to early warning signs, find out the reasons and tackle them straight away.
- Personnel issues are considered 'soft' by some employers. Who cares about labour turnover or health issues, they say, as long as the job gets done and profits are high? This may be true in the short term. For firms pursuing long-term growth, however, the quality and involvement of staff are crucial. So morale matters. As do absence and lateness.

Measuring workforce effectiveness – an evaluation

Performance ratios such as labour turnover raise questions – they do not supply answers. Follow-up staff surveys or discussions may be needed to discover the underlying problems. Figures such as these give the firm an indication of what issues need addressing if the firm is to improve its position in the future, but this must be taken within the context of the business as a whole. A high labour turnover figure may have been the result of a deliberate policy to bring in younger members of staff who may be more adaptable to a changing situation at the factory.

Measures of personnel effectiveness are merely indicators for a firm to see where it may be facing problems. The measures may indicate poor performance, or reflect the short-term effect of a change in business strategy.

It must be remembered that these figures are all looking to the past. They tell the firm what has happened to its workforce. Although this has a strong element of objectivity, it is not as valuable as an indication of how the indicators may look in the future.

Key terms

Culture: the accepted attitudes and behaviours of people within a workplace.

Labour productivity: output per person.

Labour turnover: the rate at which people leave their jobs and need to be replaced.

Revision questions *(20 marks; 20 minutes)*

1 Define the following terms:
   a) Labour productivity
   b) Labour turnover (4)

2 Why might an increase in labour productivity help a firm to reduce its costs per unit? (3)

3 In what ways might a hotel business benefit if labour turnover rose from 2 per cent to 15 per cent per year? (4)

4 Some fast food outlets have labour turnover as high as 100 per cent per year. What might be the effects of this on a firm? (4)

5 How might a firm know if its personnel strategy was working effectively? (5)

Revision exercises

Data response

A firm has the following data on its personnel function:

	Year 1	Year 2
Output	50,000	55,000
Average no. of workers	250	220
No. of staff leaving the firm	12	8
Working days per worker (possible)	230	230
Average no. of staff absent	4	3

Questions *(15 marks; 15 minutes)*

1 Calculate the following ratios for both years:

a) labour productivity

b) labour turnover (5)

2 Explain what questions these figures might raise in the minds of the firm's management. (10)

Data response

Monitoring personnel performance at Best Motors

James West, the new Personnel Officer at Best Motors, manufacturer of the world famous hand-made sports cars of the same name, sat down at his desk and considered the figures in front of him. He would need to report on the existing position of the business to Elizabeth Best, the Chief Executive, on Friday.

James knew the company operated for fifty weeks of the year (only closing down for the annual works holiday), and that all employees worked full time, five days each week. He opened his briefcase and got out a calculator. 'The first thing to do is determine the key human resource indicators,' he thought to himself as he started to work.

	4 years ago	3 years ago	2 years ago	Last year	This year
Number of leavers	3	2	4	6	7
Working days lost due to absence	124	102	145	169	204
Total annual output	780	803	805	790	811
Number of shop floor accidents	5	3	7	2	4
Average number of employees	23	25	25	24	26

Questions *(25 marks; 30 minutes)*

1 Calculate labour turnover and labour productivity at Best Motors for all five years. (10)

2 Using your results, evaluate the effectiveness of Best Motors' personnel management. (8)

3 What additional information would you seek to help James gain a better understanding of how staff have been managed at Best Motors? Explain your reasoning. (7)

Case study

Turner's Butchers

Turner's Butchers is a chain of three shops in a large town in the North of England. The shops are all supplied with prepared and packaged produce from Turner's Farm, owned by the same family.

The management is particularly concerned at present by the differing performance of the three shops. In particular, they feel there may be a problem with the personnel management in the chain. The concerns were highlighted recently in a report looking at various indicators of personnel effectiveness. The key section of the report is shown below:

Workforce performance data per shop			
	Grayton Road	St John's Precinct	Lark Hill
Staff (full-time)	8	6	7
Labour turnover	25%	150%	0
Absence rate	5%	12%	1%
Sales per employee (£000s)	14	15	18

Questions *(30 marks; 45 minutes)*

1. Briefly outline your observations on each of the three shops in terms of their personnel management. (12)
2. Give possible reasons for the factors you described in Question 1. (9)
3. Taking the business as a whole, make justified recommendations as to how any problems could be tackled by the management. (9)

25 Recruitment and training

Definition

Recruitment (and **selection**) is concerned with filling job vacancies that may arise within a business. The process involves a number of activities, including defining the job, attracting suitable candidates and selecting those best suited to fill it. **Training** is a provision of work-related education, where employees learn new skills or develop the skills they already possess.

The need for effective recruitment

Every service business relies on its staff to present the face of the organisation to the customer. It can be a gloomy, perhaps bored face, or it can be lively and smiling. Many factors are involved in this stark difference, but it certainly helps if you recruit bright, enthusiastic staff in the first place.

In 2011, Tesco is recruiting for its Graduate China programme. Staff selected will be on a fast-track route to management, specialising in buying, store management or marketing. Tesco already has 70 stores in China and is planning a huge expansion programme. The lucky graduates will have terrific career prospects.

Despite the expenses involved, businesses like Tesco recognise the importance of committing sufficient resources to recruitment. Hiring the right people with the right skills is vital if company objectives are to be achieved.

A-grade application

The rapid growth of low-cost airlines has forced Ryanair and EasyJet to compete fiercely for the scarcest resource: qualified pilots. To attract them, this is what each airline was offering in summer 2010:

Table 25.1 Employment packages for pilots

	EasyJet	Ryanair
Annual salary	£81,509	'Up to £100,000'
Days off a year	137 days	162 days
Extra remuneration	7% pension contribution	Share option scheme
Extra attraction	Share options	Home every night

Source: www.easyjet.com and www.ryanair.com

The recruitment process

The recruitment process may be triggered by a number of events. For example, an existing employee may have chosen to leave their job, perhaps as a result of retirement or after finding employment elsewhere. At this point, it would be worth analysing the vacant job role – do all of the responsibilities associated with the vacant job still need to be carried out or are some redundant?

Could the remaining duties be reorganised among the existing employees? Alternatively, additional workers may need to be recruited in order to support a firm's expansion strategies, or employees with new skills may be required to help develop new products or new markets.

Once the firm has established its human resources requirements, the next step is to consider the nature of work and workers required in order to draw up a **job description** and a **person specification**.

A job description relates directly to the nature of the position itself, rather than the person required to fill it. Typically, a job description would contain the following information:

- the title of the post
- details of the main duties and tasks involved
- the person to whom the job holder reports and any employees for whom the job holder is responsible.

A person specification identifies the abilities, qualifications and qualities required of the job holder in order to carry out the job successfully. The main features of a person specification include:

- any educational or professional qualifications required
- necessary skills or experience
- suitable personality or character (e.g. ability to work under pressure or as part of a team).

Both documents have an important influence on both recruitment and selection: not only can they be used to draw up job adverts, but also to assess the suitability of candidates' applications and may also form the basis of any interview questions.

Figure 25.1 The person specification identifies the abilities and qualities required of the job holder

A-grade application

Recruitment at Waitrose

Graduates looking for jobs in the retail sector are being targeted by a Waitrose recruitment drive this summer. The retailer is looking to take on eight graduates who will be placed in store-based retail management roles and have the opportunity to become a department manager within 12 to 24 months.

Competition for places is expected to be tough, with Waitrose receiving some 2,500 applications for just 12 spots during its last recruitment campaign, and it has developed a new online system to help it identify the highest quality candidates. Applicants fill out an online form and personality questionnaire before sitting an online test which helps the retailer to filter out less suitable candidates.

The test assesses a graduate's judgment and decision-making abilities based on typical workplace situations. The test will help whittle down the thousands of applicants to some 150 who then attend an assessment at one of Waitrose's selection centres before going forward to interview.

(Source: www.graduate-jobs.com/gco/conews.jsp, 21 July 2010)

Internal recruitment

A business may choose to fill a vacancy internally (i.e. from the existing workforce). This could be done either by redeploying or promoting a worker from elsewhere in the business. Although internal recruitment can have a number of benefits, it also has a number of disadvantages and is obviously of no use when a business needs to expand its workforce in order to respond to an increase in demand.

Table 25.2 Advantages and disadvantages of internal recruitment

Advantages	Disadvantages
● It is likely to be quicker and cheaper than external recruitment ● Greater variety and promotion opportunities may motivate employees ● It avoids the need (and cost) of induction training ● The firm will already be aware of the employee's skills and attitude to work	● Existing workers may not have the skills required, especially if the business wants to develop new products or markets ● Relying on existing employees may lead to a stagnation of ideas and approaches within the business ● It may create a vacancy elsewhere, postponing external recruitment, rather than avoiding it

Recruiting external candidates

Firms can choose from a range of methods to attract external candidates to fill a job vacancy (**external recruitment**). Such methods include the following.

- *Media advertising*: placing job adverts in newspapers or specialist magazines, on the radio, TV or by using dedicated employment websites such as www.jobstoday.co.uk
- *Job centres*: government-run organisations which offer a free service to firms and tend to focus on vacancies for skilled and semi-skilled manual and administrative jobs.
- *Commercial recruitment agencies*: such as Alfred Marks or Reed which will carry a number of human resources functions, including recruitment, on behalf of firms in return for a fee.
- *Executive search consultants*: paid to directly approach individuals – usually those in relatively senior positions (known as poaching or headhunting).

In addition, many businesses have careers pages on their own websites which are used to advertise vacancies.

The choice of recruitment method or methods used by a business will depend on a number of factors, including:

- the cost of the recruitment method
- the size of the recruitment budget
- the location and characteristics of the likely candidates.

Table 25.3 Advantages and disadvantages of external recruitment

Advantages	Disadvantages
● It should result in a wider range of candidates than internal recruitment ● Candidates may already have the skills required to carry out the job in question, avoiding the need for (and cost of) training	● It can be an expensive and time-consuming process, using up valuable resources ● It can have a de-motivating effect on members of the existing workforce, who may have missed out on promotion

Selecting the best candidate

Once a number of suitable candidates have applied for the vacancy, the selection process can begin. This will involve choosing the applicant who most closely matches the criteria set out in the person specification for the job. A number of **selection techniques** exist, including the following.

- *Interviews*: still the most frequently used selection technique; interviews may consist of one interviewer or a panel. Interviews are relatively cheap to conduct and allow a wide variety of information to be obtained by both sides, but are often susceptible to interviewer bias or prejudice and are, therefore, considered to be an unreliable indicator on their own of how well a candidate will carry out the job in question.
- *Testing and profiling*: aptitude tests measure the level of ability of a candidate (e.g. the level of ICT skills), whereas psychometric profiling

examines personality and attitudes (e.g. whether the candidate works well under pressure or is an effective team player). Profiling is commonly used as part of management and sales consultancy recruitment, but it is questionable as to whether recruiting a 'personality type' for a particular job is desirable: recruiting a wider range may lead to a more interesting and creative environment.

- *Assessment centres*: these allow for more in-depth assessment of a candidate's suitability by subjecting them to 'real-life' role plays and simulations, often over a number of days. Although assessment centres are considered to be an effective selection method, they can be expensive and tend, therefore, to be reserved for filling more senior, management positions.

Determine the number and type of employees required
↓
Conduct job analysis for each vacancy to identify the various duties and responsibilities involved
↓
Create a job description and person specification
↓
Advertise the vacancy (internally and/or externally) to attract suitable applicants
↓
Draw up a shortlist of the most suitable applicants for interview
↓
Decide on the most suitable candidate(s) using appropriate selection method(s)
↓
Appoint the successful candidate and inform those who have been unsuccessful

Figure 25.2 The recruitment process

Although a firm can only be certain that the right person has been recruited once he or she starts work, effective recruitment and selection will reduce the risk involved. There are a number of methods that can be used to evaluate the process, including calculating the cost and time involved in filling a vacancy, the percentage of candidates who actually accept job offers and the rate of retention of staff once employed.

A-grade application

Poor recruitment procedures can damage retailers' brand image

A survey of job applicants in the retail sector in 2010 found that almost half (49%) had formed a negative view of the company concerned following an unsuccessful application for a job vacancy, and almost a fifth (18%) had taken their custom elsewhere as a result. The research, carried out by SHL, a leading talent assessment organisation, found that the biggest issue for job seekers was the lack of communication provided by retail firms. According to the survey respondents, the greatest concern was not being told whether their job application had been successful (46%), followed by a lack of feedback about applications (39%), as well as not acknowledging receipt of an application (36%)

Source: SHL

Training

The purpose of training is to help employees to develop existing skills or gain new ones. Types of training include the following.

Induction training

Induction training aims to make newly-appointed workers fully productive as soon as possible by familiarising them with the key aspects of the business. Induction would typically include:

- information on important policies and procedures, such as health and safety
- a tour of the organisation and an introduction to colleagues
- details of employment (e.g. payment arrangements, holiday entitlement) and basic duties.

On-the-job training

On-the-job training is where employees are not required to leave their workplace but actually receive instruction while still carrying out their job. This means that workers can receive training while remaining productive to some extent. Common methods include mentoring, coaching and job rotation.

Off-the-job training

Off-the-job training is where employees leave their workplace in order to receive instruction. This may involve using training facilities within the firm (e.g. seminar rooms) or those provided by another organisation, such as a university, college or private training agency. Although this will inevitably involve a temporary loss of production, it should allow the trainee to concentrate fully on learning and perhaps allow access to more experienced instructors than those available within the workplace.

Labour market failure

Like any market, the labour market is made up of supply (labour services provided by those who wish to work) and demand (firms in need of workers to produce goods or provide services). An efficient labour market would require firms to provide training for their workers in order to improve their skills and knowledge. However, the danger of poaching may create a general disincentive for firms to invest in training, for fear that the short-term costs and disruption of training may not be recouped if newly-trained employees are enticed to work elsewhere (**labour market failure**). In such circumstances, the government may become involved in training provision, in order to ensure the economy remains competitive.

Training and the Government

The UK government uses a number of methods to support and encourage firms to train their workers, including the following.

- *Modern apprenticeships*: structured programmes aimed at improving the level of technical skills within the workforce. Apprentices receive a combination of on-the-job training within a firm participating in the scheme and off-the-job training, usually by day-release to a local college, over a period of at least 12 months.
- *Investors in People*: promotes training by setting out a list of criteria or 'standards' for firms to work towards. Those who do are allowed to display the Investors in People logo and are likely to enjoy a number of benefits, including improved quality, a reduction in costs and enhanced employee motivation.

At the time of writing, it appears the 2010 Coalition government seems more likely to leave training initiatives to the 'free market' rather than to intervene directly.

Table 25.3 Benefits and costs of training

Benefits	Costs
• It increases the level and range of skills available to the business, leading to improvements in productivity and quality • It increases the degree of flexibility within a business, allowing it to respond quickly to changes in technology or demand • It can lead to a more motivated workforce by creating opportunities for development and promotion	• It can be expensive, both in terms of providing the training itself and also the cost of evaluating its effectiveness • Production may be disrupted while training is taking place, leading to lost output • Newly-trained workers may be persuaded to leave and take up new jobs elsewhere (known as **poaching**), meaning that the benefits of training are enjoyed by other businesses

A-grade application

UK firms encouraged to train their way out of recession

Research carried out by Cranfield School of Management has claimed that training existing staff can be more effective than external recruitment. The findings of the research were published in a report entitled 'Nurturing Talent'. Nearly 1,200 firms took part in the study. Three quarters of the respondents felt that training their own staff was more beneficial to their businesses than recruiting people from outside. Half the businesses had discovered that training made staff more likely to stay. One third of the businesses found it increased employee motivation, while almost one half said they saved money by doing so. The research findings have been used by both union leaders and senior business figures, including the chairmen of BT and Marks and Spencer, to encourage firms to maintain their spending on training during the recent recession.

Source: *The Sunday Times*

Recruitment and training: an evaluation

Recruitment and training are key aspects of human resources management (HRM) and the importance of effective HR strategies in helping a firm – however large or small – to achieve its objectives cannot be overstated. 'Having the right person with the right skills in the right job at the right time' will allow a business to maintain or improve its competitiveness – having the wrong person is likely to lead to a deterioration in performance and an increase in costs. Many organisations continue to view training in particular as an avoidable expense, choosing to cut training budgets when under pressure to cut costs, or to poach employees already equipped with the necessary skills from other firms. New employees can bring a number of benefits, including fresh ideas and approaches to work. However, such an approach may fail to weigh up the possible long-term impact on the quality and motivation of the workforce, and the implications of this for productivity and competitiveness.

Issues for analysis

Opportunities for analysis are likely to focus on the following areas:

- the advantages and/or disadvantages of a firm using internal or external recruitment to fill job vacancies
- the suitability of recruitment and/or selection methods used in a given situation
- the costs and benefits involved in training
- the relevance of a particular training programme in terms of meeting the needs of both the employer and the employee.

Key terms

External recruitment: where a job vacancy is filled by appointing a candidate from outside the business.

Induction training: familiarises newly-appointed workers with key aspects of their jobs and their employer, such as health and safety policies, holiday entitlement and payment arrangements. The aim is to make employees fully productive as soon as possible.

Internal recruitment: where a job vacancy is filled by appointing someone from the existing workforce.

Job description: a document that outlines the duties and responsibilities associated with a particular job role.

Labour market failure: in the context of training, this refers to the reluctance of employers to invest in training for fear that staff, once trained, will be poached by other firms attempting to avoid training costs. If sufficient firms are discouraged from training employees, overall skill levels within the workforce will fall, leading to a loss of competitiveness for the economy as a whole.

On-the-job training: where employees acquire or develop skills without leaving their usual workplace, perhaps by being guided through an activity by a more experienced member of staff.

Off-the-job training: where employees leave their normal place of work in order to receive instruction, either within the firm or by using an external organisation such as a college or university.

Person specification: a document that outlines the qualifications, skills and other qualities needed to carry out a particular job successfully.

Selection techniques: the processes used by an organisation to choose the most appropriate candidate for a job, such as interviewing or testing.

Revision questions (40 marks; 40 minutes)

1 State two reasons why a business might need to recruit new employees. (2)

2 Briefly explain the difference between a job description and a person specification. (4)

3 Outline two factors that would influence the method of recruitment used by a business. (4)

4 Suggest two reasons why internal recruitment may not be a suitable means of filling vacancies for a rapidly expanding business. (2)

5 Outline one advantage and one disadvantage of external recruitment. (4)

6 Examine one suitable method for recruiting applicants to the following job roles:
   a) Caretaker for a local school (3)
   b) A temporary sales assistant for a high street retailer over the Christmas period (3)
   c) A marketing director for a multi-national company (3)

7 Examine one advantage and one disadvantage of using interviewing as a method of selecting candidates for a job vacancy. (4)

8 Suggest two methods that a firm could use to evaluate the effectiveness of its recruitment and selection procedure. (2)

9 Outline two reasons why a firm should provide induction training for newly-recruited employees. (4)

10 Briefly explain why market failure might lead to a skills gap in the UK labour market. (5)

Revision exercises

Data response

Recruiting people with a passion at Pret A Manger

According to Pret A Manger, talent management is one of the biggest challenges for firms operating in the fiercely competitive UK hospitality industry. The company has grown steadily since its set up in 1986 but still retains a strong entrepreneurial character, despite employing over 4,000 people. Its workers are chosen from a wide pool of recruitment, in order to reflect its customer base. In 2010, around 70% of vacancies at the company were filled within three days. Pret's employees are encouraged to hand out 'talent spotter' cards to people that they believe would fit in at the company.

Job candidates undergo an initial screening interview and are selected on the basis of their personal qualities and passion for customer service, rather than their hospitality skills. Those candidates that pass successfully through the interview stage complete a 'joiner experience day', where they are paid to work in a Pret store close to where they live. At the end of this, the store team vote on whether or not the candidates should be appointed.

Source: Pret A Manger

Questions (25 marks; 30 minutes)

1 State two 'personal' qualities that a sales assistant at Pret A Manger should possess. (2)

2 Analyse two benefits of Pret A Manger's approach to recruitment. (9)

3 Assess the importance of effective recruitment and selection for a company like Pret A Manger. (14)

Data response

China Graduate Programme: Applications will open early in Jan/Feb 2011

We (Tesco) operate in 14 countries across the globe, employ over 470,000 employees and have over 4,000 stores worldwide. Our International Business is a major element of our future growth. In 2004 we introduced Tesco to China and now trade in more than 70 hypermarkets, employing over 20,000 people. We have grown our number of stores significantly each year, and will continue to do so. What's more, we are committed to recruiting top talent and investing in their development. And that's where you fit in.

Our business in China is growing and developing fast. Which is both great news for us and great news for you. We've got 10 fantastic opportunities split between Store Operations, Commercial Buying and Merchandising, and Marketing. The roles are split between northern, southern and eastern China.

The China Graduate Programme is a 12-month Fast-Track scheme. Once selected, you'll join us in China during August, and then spend approximately seven months on a structured development programme in the UK. This will include time in our UK stores, where it all started and where it all still happens. You'll then develop skills in your chosen business area, before making a permanent move to China to complete your programme.

To drive our business growth internationally and make your mark, you'll be:

- Qualified or expecting at least a 2:1 degree (or equivalent) in any discipline
- Fluent in both English and Mandarin
- Interested in, and with an understanding of, Retail
- Driven and determined to learn and deliver for the customer in a challenging environment
- Confident in your analytical skills
- Able to influence others and have excellent interpersonal skills
- Willing and able to relocate to China
- Mobile according to the needs of the business (although you will initially be based in one location).

Ideally, you'll also have:

- A degree from a UK University
- Work experience in a customer-facing role (retail experience would be a real advantage!).

For the 2010 China Graduate Programme the recruitment process is as follows:

- Website closes for applications: 26th February
- Telephone interviews: Feb–March
- Face-to-face interviews in the UK: March–April
- Psychometric tests: April
- Assessment Centres in the UK: 18–21 May
- Offers made: late May
- Start date in China: 16th August

(Source: Tesco)

Questions *(25 marks; 30 minutes)*

1 Explain why Tesco may want all candidates to have a 'psychometric test'. (6)

2 Consider whether the programme seems likely to attract high-calibre applicants. (6)

3 Does this programme seem attractive to you personally? Explain your views. (13)

Data response

Solving skills shortages at Mulberry

Mulberry is a leading manufacturer of luxury handbags and leather goods, based in the south-west of England. Its reputation depends to a great extent on maintaining a highly skilled workforce, trained to handle valuable materials and use a variety of leatherworking techniques, such as cutting and stitching. These techniques are complicated to teach, requiring lengthy training periods before workers can become productive.

With an ageing workforce and a chronic shortage of workers with the appropriate manufacturing skills across the UK textile industry generally, Mulberry was faced with a dilemma. If it recruited and trained workers in-house it would not qualify for public funding available for employees undertaking recognised qualifications. However, the courses offered by external training providers were too general and, therefore, failed to address the company's specific training needs.

The company's solution was to set up a partnership with Bridgewater College, a further education institution with a reputation for supporting local employers. The collaboration resulted in a new two-year apprenticeship qualification, designed precisely to meet Mulberry's training needs. Apprentices spend the majority of their time at the company's industrial plant in Somerset, training 'on the job' and learning a range of techniques. The apprentices also spend half a day each week at the college learning about the leather industry and developing skills such as teamwork and communication. The scheme allows Mulberry to control the content of the training and, because the scheme is recognised by the relevant awarding bodies, the company receives £2,500 of public funds for each apprentice trained.

(Source: Skillfast UK)

Questions *(25 marks; 30 minutes)*

1 Briefly explain, using examples, the difference between 'on-the-job' and 'off-the-job' training. (4)

2 Analyse one benefit and one drawback to a company such as Mulberry from its new apprenticeship scheme. (9)

3 To what extent do you agree that the reputation and, therefore, success of UK manufacturers like Mulberry depends on maintaining a highly skilled workforce? (12)

Essay questions *(40 marks each)*

1 Stamford Software Solutions, a medium-sized IT company based in the south-east of England, needs to recruit a new sales manager. Consider how the company should go about doing this.

2 According to the Leitch Report, UK employers spend an estimated £33 billion in total each year on training, yet one-third of employers provide no training at all. Evaluate the main consequences for firms who choose not to train their staff.

Motivation in theory

Definition

One key theorist (Professor Herzberg) believes motivation occurs when people do something because they *want* to do it; others think of motivation as the desire to achieve a result. The difference between these two definitions is important and should become clear in this unit.

Introduction

A recent study by the Hay Group found that just 15 per cent of UK workers consider themselves 'highly motivated'. As many as 25 per cent say they're 'coasting' and 8 per cent admit to being 'completely demotivated'. In the same survey, employees felt they could be 45 per cent more productive if they were doing a job they loved, and 28 per cent more productive with better training. Poor management is part of the problem, as 28 per cent say they would be more productive with a better boss.

The Hay Group calculates that if the under-performance was tackled successfully, the value of UK output would rise by more than £350 billion a year. So motivation matters. This is why it merits a unit to itself – and why many consider motivation theory to be the most important topic within Business Studies.

F W Taylor and scientific management

Although there were earlier pioneers, the starting point for the study of motivation is F W Taylor (1856–1917). As with most of the other influential writers on this subject, Taylor was American. His influence over the twentieth-century world has been massive. Much business practice in America, Europe, Japan and the former Communist countries is still rooted in his writing and work.

A recent biography of Taylor is titled *The One Best Way*; this sums up neatly Taylor's approach to management. He saw it as management's task to decide exactly how every task should be completed, then to devise the tools needed to enable the worker to achieve the task as efficiently as possible. This method is evident today in every McDonald's in the world. Fries are cooked at 175 degrees for exactly three minutes, then a buzzer tells employees to take them out and salt them. Throughout every McDonald's is a series of dedicated, purpose-built machines for producing milkshakes, toasting buns, squirting chocolate sauce, and much else. Today, 100 years after his most active period working in industry, F W Taylor would feel very much at home ordering a Big Mac.

So, what was Taylor's view of the underlying motivations of people at work? How did he make sure that the employees worked effectively at following 'the one best way' laid down by managers?

Taylor believed that people work for only one reason: money. He saw it as the task of the manager to devise a system that would maximise efficiency. This would generate the profit to enable the worker to be paid a higher wage. Taylor's view of human nature was that of 'economic man'. In other words, people were motivated only by the economic motive of self-interest. Therefore, a manager could best motivate a worker by offering an incentive (a 'carrot') or a threat (the 'stick'). Taylor can be seen as a manipulator, or even a bully, but he believed his methods were in the best interests of the employees themselves.

Taylor's influence stemmed less from his theories than his activities. He was a trained engineer who acted as a very early management consultant. His methods were as follows:

- observe workers at work, recording and timing what they do, when they do it and how long they take over it (this became known as time and motion study)
- identify the most efficient workers and see how they achieve greater efficiency
- break the task down into small component parts that can be done quickly and repeatedly
- devise equipment specifically to speed up tasks
- set out exactly how the work should be done in future; 'each employee', Taylor wrote, 'should receive every day clear-cut, definite instructions as to what he is to do and how he is to do it, and these instructions should be exactly carried out, whether they are right or wrong'
- devise a pay scheme to reward those who complete or beat tough output targets, but that penalises those who cannot or will not achieve the **productivity** Taylor believed was possible; this pay scheme was called **piece rate** – no work, no pay.

As an engineer, Taylor was interested in practical outcomes, not in psychology. There is no reason to suppose he thought greatly about the issue of motivation. The effect of his ideas was profound, though. Long before the publication of his 1911 book *The Principles of Scientific Management*, Taylor had spread his managerial practices of careful measurement, monitoring and – above all else – control. Before Taylor, skilled workers chose their own ways of working and had varied, demanding jobs. After Taylor, workers were far more likely to have limited, repetitive tasks; and to be forced to work at the pace set by a manager or consultant engineer.

Among those influenced by Taylor was Henry Ford. His Model T was the world's first mass-produced motor car. By 1911 the Ford factory in Detroit, USA, was already applying Taylor's principles of high **division of labour**, purpose-built machinery and rigid management control. When Ford introduced the conveyor belt in 1913, he achieved the ultimate Taylorite idea: men's pace of work dictated by a mechanical conveyor belt, the speed of which was set by management.

Eventually workers rebelled against being treated like machines. **Trades union** membership thrived in factories run on Taylorite lines, as workers wanted to organise against the suffocating lives they were leading at work. Fortunately, in many western countries further developments in motivation theory pointed to new, more people-friendly approaches.

Elton Mayo and the human relations approach

Elton Mayo (1880–1949) was a medical student who became an academic with a particular interest in people in organisations. Although an Australian, he moved to America in 1923. Early in his career, his methods were heavily influenced by F W Taylor. An early investigation of a spinning mill in Pennsylvania identified one department with labour turnover of 250 per cent compared to 6 per cent elsewhere in the factory. His Taylorite solution was to prescribe work breaks. These had the desired effect.

Mayo moved on to work at the Hawthorne plant of the Western Electric Company in Chicago. His investigations there are known as the Hawthorne Experiments. He was called in to Hawthorne to try to explain the findings of a previous test into the effects of lighting upon productivity levels. The lighting conditions for one work group had been varied, while those for another had been held constant. The surprise was that whatever was done to the lighting, production rose in *both* groups. This proved that there was more to motivation and efficiency than purely economic motives.

Between 1927 and 1932 Mayo conducted a series of experiments at Hawthorne. The first is known as the Relay Assembly Test. Six volunteer female assembly staff were separated from their workmates. A series of experiments was carried out. The results were recorded and discussed with the women. Every 12 weeks a new working method was tried. The alternatives included:

- different bonus methods, such as individual versus group bonuses
- different rest periods
- different refreshments
- different work layout.

Before every change, the researchers discussed the new method fully with the operators. Almost without exception productivity increased with every change. At the end, the group returned to the original method (48-hour, 6-day week with no breaks) and output went up to its highest level yet! Not only that, but the women claimed they felt less tired than they had at the start.

The experiments had started rather slowly, with some resistance from the operatives. Progress became much more marked when one member of the group retired. She was replaced by a younger woman who quickly became the unofficial leader of the group.

Mayo's conclusions

- The women gained satisfaction from their freedom and control over their working environment.
- 'What actually happened was that six individuals became a team and the team gave itself wholeheartedly and spontaneously to cooperation in the experiment' (Mayo, 1949).
- Group norms (expectations of one another) are crucial and may be influenced more by informal than official group leaders.
- Communication between workers and managers influences morale and output.
- Workers are affected by the degree of interest shown in them by their managers; the influence of this upon motivation is known as 'the Hawthorne effect'.

The consequences of Mayo's work were enormous. He influenced many researchers and writers, effectively opening up the fields of industrial psychology and industrial sociology. Many academics followed Mayo's approach in what became known as the Human Relations school of management.

Businesses also responded to the implications of Mayo's work for company profitability and success. If teamwork, communications and managerial involvement were that important, firms reasoned that they needed an organisational structure to cope. In Taylor's era, the key person was the engineer. The winners from Mayo's work were personnel departments. They grew throughout America and Britain in the 1930s, 1940s and 1950s as companies tried to achieve the Hawthorne effect.

Maslow and the hierarchy of needs

Abraham Maslow (1908–70) was an American psychologist, whose great contribution to motivation theory was the 'hierarchy of needs'. Maslow believed that everyone has the same needs – all of which can be organised as a hierarchy. At the base of the hierarchy are physical needs such as food, shelter and warmth. When unsatisfied, these are the individual's primary motivations. When employees earn enough to satisfy these needs, however, their motivating power withers away. Maslow said that 'It is quite true that humans live by bread alone – when there is no bread. But what happens to their desires when there *is* bread?' Instead of physical needs, people become motivated to achieve needs such as security and stability, which Maslow called the safety needs. In full, Maslow's hierarchy consisted of the elements listed in Table 26.1.

Table 26.1 Maslow's hierarchy of needs: implications for business

Maslow's levels of human need	Business implications
Physical needs (e.g. food, shelter and warmth)	Pay levels and working conditions
Safety needs (e.g. security, a safe, structured environment, stability, freedom from anxiety)	Job security, a clear job role/description, clear lines of accountability (only one boss)
Social needs (e.g. belonging, friendship, contact)	Team working, communications, social facilities
Esteem needs (e.g. strength, self-respect, confidence, status and recognition)	Status, recognition for achievement, power, trust
Self-actualisation (e.g. self-fulfilment); 'to become everything that one is capable of becoming,' wrote Maslow	Scope to develop new skills and meet new challenges, and to develop one's full potential

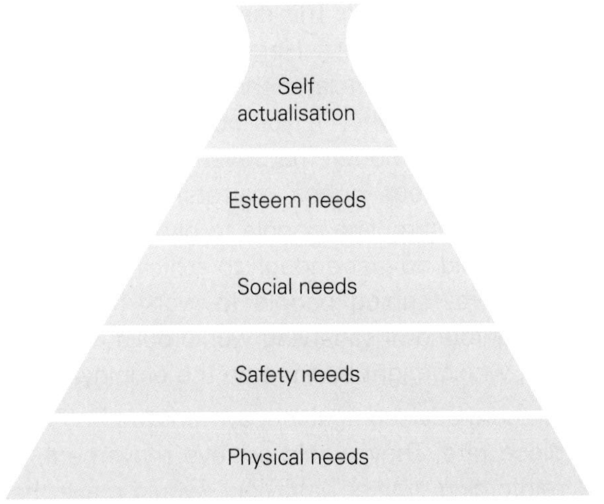

Figure 26.1 Maslow's hierarchy of needs

Ever since Maslow first put his theory forward (in 1940) writers have argued about its implications. Among the key issues raised by Maslow are the following.

- Do all humans have the same set of needs? Or are there some people who need no more from a job than money?
- Do different people have different degrees of need – for example, are some highly motivated by the need for power, while others are satisfied by social factors? If so, the successful manager would be one who can understand and attempt to meet the differing needs of her/his staff.
- Can anyone's needs ever be said to be fully satisfied? The reason the hierarchy diagram (see Figure 26.1) has an open top is to suggest that the human desire for achievement is limitless.

Maslow's work had a huge influence on the writers who followed him, especially McGregor and Herzberg. The hierarchy of needs is also used by academics in many subjects beyond Business Studies, notably Psychology and Sociology.

Herzberg's two factor theory

The key test of a theory is its analytic usefulness. On this criterion, the work of Professor Fred Herzberg (1923–2000) is the strongest by far.

The theory stems from research conducted in the 1950s into factors affecting workers' **job satisfaction** and dissatisfaction. It was carried out on 200 accountants and engineers in Pennsylvania, USA. Despite the limited nature of this sample, Herzberg's conclusions remain influential to this day.

Herzberg asked employees to describe recent events that had given rise to exceptionally good feelings about their jobs, and then probed for the reasons why. 'Five factors stand out as strong

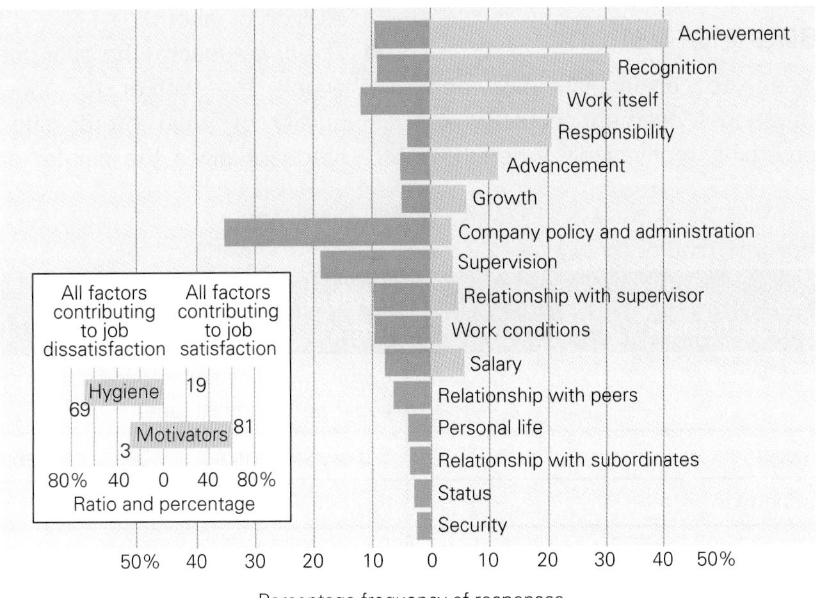

Figure 26.2 Comparison of satisfiers and dissatisfiers

determiners of job satisfaction,' Herzberg wrote in 1966, 'achievement, recognition for achievement, the work itself, responsibility and advancement – the last three being of greater importance for a lasting change of attitudes.' He pointed out that each of these factors concerned the job itself, rather than issues such as pay or status. Herzberg called these five factors 'the motivators'.

The researchers went on to ask about events giving rise to exceptionally bad feelings about their jobs. This revealed a separate set of five causes. Herzberg stated that 'the major dissatisfiers were company policy and administration, supervision, salary, interpersonal relations and working conditions'. He concluded that the common theme was factors that 'surround the job', rather than the job itself. The name he gave these dissatisfiers was '**hygiene factors**'; this was because fulfilling them would prevent dissatisfaction, rather than causing positive motivation. Careful hygiene prevents disease; care to fulfil hygiene factors prevents job dissatisfaction.

To summarise: motivators have the power to create positive job satisfaction, but little downward potential; hygiene factors will cause job dissatisfaction unless they are provided for, but do not motivate. Importantly, Herzberg saw pay as a hygiene factor, not a motivator. So a feeling of being underpaid could lead to a grievance; but high pay would soon be taken for granted. This motivator/hygiene factor theory is known as the 'two factor theory' (see Table 26.2).

Movement and motivation

Herzberg was keen to distinguish between movement and motivation. Movement occurs when somebody does something; motivation is when they *want* to do something. This distinction is essential to a full understanding of Herzberg's theory. He did not doubt that financial incentives could be used to boost productivity: 'If you bully or bribe people, they'll give you better than average performance.' His worries about 'bribes' (carrots) were that they would never stimulate people to give of their best; people would do just enough to achieve the bonus. Furthermore, bribing people to work harder at a task they found unsatisfying would build up resentments, which might backfire on the employer.

Herzberg advised against payment methods such as piece rate. They would achieve movement, but by reinforcing worker behaviour, would make them inflexible and resistant to change. The salaried, motivated employee would work hard, care about quality and think about – even welcome – improved working methods.

Job enrichment

The reason why Herzberg's work has had such an impact on businesses is because he not only analysed motivation, he also had a method for improving it. The method is job enrichment, which he defined as 'giving people the opportunity to use their ability'. He suggested that, for a job to be considered enriched, it would have to contain the following:

- *A complete unit of work:* not just a small repetitive fragment of a job, but a full challenging task. Herzberg heaped scorn upon the 'idiot jobs' that resulted from Taylor's views on the merits of high division of labour.
- *Direct feedback:* wherever possible, a job should enable the worker to judge immediately the quality of what he or she has done; direct feedback gives the painter or the actor (or the

Table 26.2 Herzberg's two factor theory

Motivators (can create positive satisfaction)	**Hygiene factors (can create job dissatisfaction)**
Achievement	Company policy and administration (the rules, paperwork and red tape)
Recognition for achievement	Supervision (especially being over-supervised)
Meaningful, interesting work	Pay
Responsibility	Interpersonal relations (with supervisor, peers or even customers)
Advancement (psychological, not just a promotion)	Working conditions

teacher) the satisfaction of knowing exactly how well they have performed. Herzberg disliked systems that pass quality inspection off onto a supervisor: 'a man must always be held responsible for his own quality'. Worst of all, he felt, was annual appraisal, in which feedback is too long delayed.

- *Direct communication:* for people to feel committed, in control and to gain direct feedback, they should communicate directly – avoiding the delays of communicating via a supervisor or a 'contact person'. In itself, it is hard to see the importance of this. For a student of Business Studies, it leads to an important conclusion: that communications and motivation are inter-related.

Conclusion

Herzberg's original research has been followed up in many different countries, including Japan, Africa and Russia. An article he wrote on the subject in the *Harvard Business Review* in 1968 (called 'Just one more time, how do you motivate employees?') has sold more than one million reprinted copies. His main insight was to show that unless the job itself was interesting, there was no way to make working life satisfying. This led companies such as Volvo in Sweden and Toyota in Japan to rethink their factory layouts. Instead of individual workers doing simple, repetitive tasks, the drive was to provide more complete units of work. Workers were grouped into teams, focusing on significant parts of the manufacturing process, such as assembling and fitting the gearbox, and then checking the quality of their work. Job enrichment indeed.

Table 26.3 Key quotes from Professor Herzberg

On the two factor theory	'Motivators and hygiene factors are equally important, but for different reasons'
On movement	'If you do something because you want a house or a Jaguar, that's movement. It's not motivation'
The risks of giving bonuses	'A reward once given becomes a right'
The importance of training	'The more a person can do, the more you can motivate them'
The importance of always treating staff fairly	'A remembered pain can lead to revenge psychology ... They'll get back at you some day when you need them'
On communication	'In industry, there's too much communication. And of course it's passive ... But if people are doing idiot jobs they really don't give a damn'
On participation	'When participation is suggested in terms of control over overall goals, it is usually a sham'

Issues for analysis

- In an exam context, the starting point is to select the most appropriate theory to answer a question. If a case study context suggested poor relations between management and workforce, Elton Mayo's would be very suitable. If motivation was weak, Herzberg's theory provides a comprehensive analysis.
- When applying a theory, the analysis is strengthened by using a questioning approach. Herzberg's theory is admirable, but it is not perfect. It provides insights, but not necessarily answers – and certainly not blueprints. A job enrichment programme might be highly effective in one situation, but a disappointment in another.
- This leads on to another key factor: the success of any new policies will depend hugely on the history of trust – or lack of it – in the workplace. Successful change in the factors involved in motivation may be very difficult and slow to achieve. There are no magic solutions.
- Accordingly, when a firm faces a crisis, changes in factors relating to motivation will rarely provide an answer. A crisis must be solved in the short term, but human motivation requires long-term strategies.

Motivation in theory – an evaluation

Most managers assume they understand human motivation, but they have never studied it. As a result they may underestimate the potential within their own staff, or unthinkingly cause resentments that fester.

The process of managing people takes place in every part of every organisation. By contrast, few would need to know the financial concept of 'gearing' in their working lives. So lack of knowledge of motivation theory is particularly unfortunate – and has exceptionally widespread effects. In some cases, ignorance leads managers to ignore motivation altogether; they tell themselves that control and organisation are their only concerns. Other managers may see motivation as important, but fail to understand its subtleties.

For these reasons, there is a case for saying that the concepts within this unit are the most important in the whole subject.

Key terms

Division of labour: subdividing a task into a number of activities, enabling workers to specialise and therefore become very efficient at completing what may be a small, repetitive task.

Hygiene factors: 'everything that surrounds what you do in the job', such as pay, working conditions and social status – all potential causes of dissatisfaction, according to Herzberg.

Job satisfaction: the sense of well-being and achievement that stems from a satisfying job.

Piece rate: paying workers per piece they produce (e.g. £2 per pair of jeans made).

Productivity: output per person (i.e. a measure of efficiency).

Trades union: an organisation that represents the interests of staff at the workplace.

Further reading

Herzberg, F. (1959) *The Motivation to Work*. Wiley International.

Maslow, A. H. (1987) *Motivation and Personality*. HarperCollins (1st edn 1954).

Mayo, E. (1975) *The Social Problems of Industrial Civilisation*. Routledge (1st edn 1949).

A Revision questions *(35 marks, 35 minutes)*

1 Which features of the organisation of a McDonald's could be described as Taylorite? (3)

2 Explain the meaning of the term 'economic man'. (3)

3 Explain how workers in a bakery might be affected by a change from salary to piece rate. (3)

4 Give a brief outline of Mayo's research methods at the Hawthorne plant. (4)

5 How may 'group norms' affect productivity at a workplace? (3)

6 Explain the meaning of the term 'the Hawthorne effect'. (2)

7 Which two levels of Maslow's hierarchy could be called 'the lower-order needs'? (2)

8 Describe in your own words why Maslow organised the needs into a hierarchy. (3)

9 State three business implications of Maslow's work on human needs. (3)

10 Herzberg believes pay does not motivate, but it is important. Why? (3)

11 How do motivators differ from hygiene factors? (3)

12 What is job enrichment? How is it achieved? (3)

Revision exercises

Data response

Look back at Figure 26.2. It shows the results of Herzberg's research into the factors that cause positive job satisfaction and those that cause job dissatisfaction.

Questions *(25 marks; 25 minutes)*

1 Which of the factors had the least effect on satisfaction or dissatisfaction? (1)

2 One of Herzberg's objectives was to question whether good human relations were as important in job satisfaction as claimed by Elton Mayo. Do you think he succeeded? (6)

3 Responsibility had the longest-lasting effects on job satisfaction. Why may this be the case? (6)

4 On the basis of Herzberg's findings and your own views, discuss which of the factors is the most important motivator. (12)

Case study

Tania was delighted to get the bakery job and looked forward to her first shift. It would be tiring after a day at college, but £52 for eight hours on a Friday would guarantee good Saturday nights in future.

On arrival, she was surprised to be put straight to work, with no more than a mumbled 'You'll be working packing machine B.' Fortunately, she was able to watch the previous shift worker before clocking-off time, and could get the hang of what was clearly a very simple task. As the 18.00 bell rang, the workers streamed out, but not many had yet turned up from Tania's shift. The conveyor belt started to roll again at 18.16.

As the evening wore on, machinery breakdowns provided the only, welcome, relief from the tedium and discomfort of Tania's job. Each time a breakdown occurred, a ringing alarm bell was drowned out by a huge cheer from the staff. A few joyful moments followed, with dough fights breaking out. Tania started to feel quite old as she looked at some of her workmates.

At the 22.00 meal break, Tania was made to feel welcome. She enjoyed hearing the sharp, funny comments made about the shift managers. One was dubbed 'Noman' because he was fat, wore a white coat and never agreed to anything. Another was called 'Turkey' because he strutted around, but if anything went wrong, got into a flap. It was clear that both saw themselves as bosses. They were not there to help or to encourage, only to blame.

Was the bakery always like this, Tania wondered? Or was it simply that these two managers were poor?

Questions *(25 marks; 30 minutes)*

1 Analyse the working lives of the shift workers at the bakery, using Herzberg's two factor theory. (8)

2 If a managerial follower of Taylor's methods came into the factory, how might he or she try to improve the productivity level? (7)

3 Later on in this (true) story, Tania read in the local paper that the factory was closing. The reason given was 'lower labour productivity than at our other bakeries'. The newspaper grumbled about the poor attitudes of local workers. Consider the extent to which there is some justification in this view. (10)

Motivation in practice

Definition

Assessing how firms try to motivate their staff and how successful these actions appear to be. In this context, companies take 'motivation' to mean enthusiastic pursuit of the objectives or tasks set out by the firm.

Introduction

There are four main variables that influence the **motivation** of staff in practice:

1. the financial reward systems
2. job design
3. empowering the employees
4. working in teams.

All four will be analysed with reference to the theories outlined in Unit 26.

Motivation: famous sayings

'The worst mistake a boss can make is not to say well done.' *John Ashcroft, British executive*

'Motivation is everything. You can do the work of two people, but you can't be two people. Instead, you have to inspire the next guy down the line and get him to inspire his people.' *Lee Iacocca, successful boss of Chrysler Motors*

'I have never found anybody yet who went to work happily on a Monday that had not been paid on a Friday.' *Tom Farmer, Kwik-Fit founder*

'Motivating people over a short period is not very difficult. A crisis will often do just that, or a carefully planned special event. Motivating people over a longer period of time, however, is far more difficult. It is also far more important in today's business environment.' *John Kotter, management thinker*

'My best friend is the one who brings out the best in me.' *Henry Ford, founder of Ford Motors*

(Source: Stuart Crainer: *The Ultimate Book of Business Quotations*, Capstone Publishing)

Financial reward systems

Piecework

Piecework means working in return for a payment per unit produced. The payment itself is known as piece rate. Pieceworkers receive no basic or shift pay, so there is no sick pay, holiday pay or company pension.

Piecework is used extensively in small-scale manufacturing – for example, of jeans or jewellery. Its attraction for managers is that it makes supervision virtually unnecessary. All the manager needs do is operate a quality control system that ensures the finished product is worth paying for. Day by day, the workers can be relied upon to work fast enough to earn a living (or a good) wage.

Piecework has several disadvantages to firms, however:

- scrap levels may be high, if workers are focused entirely on speed of output
- there is an incentive to provide acceptable quality, but not the best possible quality
- workers will work hardest when they want higher earnings (probably before Christmas and before their summer holiday); this may not coincide at all with seasonal patterns of customer demand

- worst of all is the problem of change; Herzberg pointed out that 'the worst way to motivate people is piece rate ... it reinforces behaviour'; focusing people on maximising their earnings by repeating a task makes them very reluctant to produce something different or in a different way (they worry that they will lose out financially).

Performance-related pay

Performance-related pay (PRP) is a financial reward to staff whose work is considered above average. It is used for employees whose work achievements cannot be assessed simply through numerical measures (such as units produced or sold). PRP awards are usually made after an appraisal process has evaluated the performance of staff during the year.

On the face of it, PRP is a highly attractive system for encouraging staff to work towards the organisation's objectives. The usual method is as follows:

1. Establish targets for each member of staff/management at an appraisal interview.
2. At the end of the year, discuss the individual's achievements against those targets.
3. Those with outstanding achievements are given a Merit 1 pay rise or bonus worth perhaps 6 per cent of salary; others receive between 0 per cent and 6 per cent.

Despite the enthusiasm they have shown for it, employers have rarely been able to provide evidence of the benefits of PRP. Indeed, the Institute of Personnel Management concluded in a report that:

> It was not unusual to find that organisations which had introduced merit pay some years ago were less certain now of its continued value ... it was time to move on to something more closely reflecting team achievement and how the organisation as a whole was faring.

This pointed to a fundamental problem with PRP: rewarding individuals does nothing to promote teamwork. Furthermore it might create unhealthy rivalry between managers – each going for the same Merit 1 spot.

Other problems for PRP systems include the following.

- *Perceived fairness/unfairness:* staff often suspect that those awarded the maximum are being rewarded not for performance but out of favouritism; this may damage working relations and team spirit.
- *Whether they have a sound basis in human psychology:* without question, Professor Herzberg would be very critical of any attempt to influence work behaviour by financial incentives; a London School of Economics study of Inland Revenue staff found that only 12 per cent

A-grade application

Performance-related pay doesn't encourage performance

The clue ought to be in the name. Performance-related pay is pay for performance, and the better performance you turn in and the harder you work, the more you will get to take home. Except, academics are now suggesting, more often than not the opposite may be the case.

New research by the London School of Economics has argued that, far from encouraging people to strive to reach the heights, performance-related pay often does the opposite and encourages people to work less hard.

An analysis of 51 separate experimental studies of financial incentives in employment relations found what the school has described as 'overwhelming evidence' that these incentives could reduce an employee's natural inclination to complete a task and derive pleasure from doing so.

The findings are, of course, deeply controversial, given the depths of anger still felt by many over the role of performance-related pay in causing or contributing to the current economic crisis.

'We find that financial incentives may indeed reduce intrinsic motivation and diminish ethical or other reasons for complying with workplace social norms such as fairness,' argued Dr Bernd Irlenbusch, from the LSE's Department of Management.

'As a consequence, the provision of incentives can result in a negative impact on overall performance,' he added.

Companies therefore needed to be aware that the provision of performance-related pay could result in a net reduction of motivation across a team or organisation, he suggested.

(Source: www.management-issues.com)

believed that PRP had raised motivation at work, while 76 per cent said it had not. Herzberg would approve of the researchers' conclusion that 'The current system has not succeeded in motivating staff to any significant degree, and may well have done the reverse.'

As the last point illustrates, a key assumption behind PRP is that the chance to be paid a bit more than other employees will result in a change in individual behaviour, in increased motivation to work. A survey for the government publication *Employment in Britain* found that pay incentives were thought important for hard work by fewer than one in five, and for quality standards by fewer than one in ten.

So why do firms continue to pursue PRP systems? There are two possible reasons:

1 To make it easier for managers to manage/control their staff (using a carrot instead of a stick).
2 To reduce the influence of collective bargaining and therefore trades unions.

Profit sharing

A different approach to financial incentives is to provide staff with a share of the firm's annual profit. This puts staff in the same position as shareholders as, in effect, they are paid an annual dividend. This offers clear psychological benefits, as outlined below.

- Staff can come to see profit positively. Before, they may have regarded it as an unfair way of diverting pay from their own pockets to those of shareholders.
- Herzberg and other theorists warn that financial incentives distort behaviour. For example, if you pay a striker £500 per goal, wave goodbye to passing in the penalty area. Profit sharing, however, is more of a financial reward than an incentive. It may encourage people to work harder or smarter, but should not stop them working as a team.
- If paid to staff in the form of free shares, the employees may develop a strong sense of identity with the company and its fortunes.

Profit sharing can represent a substantial bonus on top of regular earnings. For instance, the John Lewis Partnership pays an annual bonus that can be worth over 20 per cent of an employee's earnings, typically around £2,000. In other cases, such as Tesco, the profit share amounts to no more than £100 or so. At such a low level it is clearly more of a thank you than a serious incentive.

Fringe benefits

These are forms of reward other than income. Some managers have generous expense accounts; many have company cars where usually all maintenance and running costs are paid by the company. In some cases, even petrol for private mileage can be charged to the employer. Other fringe benefits include:

- membership of clubs or leisure centres
- low-interest rate loans or mortgages
- discounts on the company's products, such as the British Airways' staff perk of air fares at 90 per cent off.

In all cases, fringe benefits are offered to encourage staff loyalty and to improve human relations.

Table 27.1 The pros and cons of profit sharing

Pros	Cons
Encourages staff to think about the whole business, not just their own job	If the employee share is only a small proportion of annual profit, the payouts may be meaninglessly small
Encourages thinking about cost saving as well as revenue raising	Large payouts, though, may either hit shareholder dividends or reduce the investment capital for long-term expansion
Focus on profit may make it easier for staff to accept changes in working practices (i.e. it may lessen resistance to change)	Because no single individual can have much impact on overall profits, there may be no incentive effect

Job design

Herzberg's theory (see Unit 26) emphasised the importance of job design. He wanted employers to create jobs with the maximum scope to be motivating. For example, when Jose Mourinho became manager of Chelsea, he was allowed the independence and authority to buy and sell players as he thought best. He had full power over the tactics and the budget for running the team. Two years later, club owner Abramovic had brought in a managing director and a director of football to restrict the manager's powers. Players were bought against Mourinho's wishes. The result was Mourinho's evident job dissatisfaction during the 2006/07 season. His job had been redesigned in the worst way possible. Instead of being empowered to show what he could do, Mourinho was being held back by his bosses.

Job design is the thought process of deciding what tasks each employee must do, what equipment they will have, what decision-making power they will have and whether they are working alone or in a team. F W Taylor believed that management should design jobs to be simple, repetitive and easily monitored. Today, the term job design usually refers to job enrichment or job enlargement.

Job enrichment

Professor Herzberg defines job enrichment as 'giving people the opportunity to use their ability'. A full explanation of his theory is outlined in Unit 26.

How can job enrichment be put into practice? The key thing is to realise the enormity of the task. It is not cheap, quick or easy to enrich the job of the production line worker or the supermarket checkout operator. The first thought might be to add more variety to the work. The supermarket operator might switch between the checkout, shelf-stacking and working in the warehouse. Known as job rotation, this approach reduces repetition but still provides the employee with little challenge. Herzberg's definition of job enrichment implies giving people 'a range of responsibilities and activities'. Job rotation only provides a range of activities. To provide job enrichment, workers must have a complete unit of work (not a repetitive fragment), responsibility for quality and for self-checking, and be given the opportunity to show their abilities.

Full job enrichment requires a radical approach. Take a conventional car assembly line, for example. As shown in Figure 27.1, workers each have a single task they carry out on their own. One fits the left-hand front door to a car shell that is slowly moving past on a conveyor belt – every 22 seconds. Another worker fits right-hand front doors, and so on. Job enrichment can be achieved only by rethinking the production line completely.

Figure 27.1 Traditional production line

Figure 27.2 shows how a car assembly line could be reorganised to provide a more enriched job. Instead of working in isolation, people work in groups on a significant part of the assembly process. An empty car shell comes along the conveyor belt and turns in to the Interior Group Area. Six workers fit carpets, glove boxes, the dashboard and much else. They check the quality of their own work, then put a rather impressive-looking vehicle back on the conveyor belt. Not only does the teamwork element help meet the social needs of the workforce, but there are also knock-on effects. The workers can

Figure 27.2 Enriched 'teamworking' line

be given a time slot to discuss their work and how to improve it. When new equipment is needed, they can be given a budget and told to get out to meet potential suppliers. In other words, they can become managers of their own work area.

Such a major step would be expensive. Rebuilding a production line might cost millions of pounds and be highly disruptive in the short term. There would also be the worry that team working might make the job more satisfying, yet still be less productive than the boring but practical system of high division of labour.

Job enlargement

Job enlargement is a general term for anything that increases the scope of a job. There are three ways in which it comes about.

1. *Job rotation:* increasing a worker's activities by switching between tasks of a similar level of difficulty. This does not increase the challenge, but may reduce the boredom of a job.
2. *Job loading:* increasing workload, often as a result of redundancies. It may mean having to do more of the same, but often entails one or two extra activities that have to be taken on.
3. *Job enrichment:* this enlargement of the scope of the job involves extra responsibilities and challenges, as well as extra activities/workload.

Of these, only job enrichment is likely to provide long-term job satisfaction. Employers may like to use the term job enrichment, but often they are really carrying out job rotation or job loading.

Empowerment

Empowerment is a modern term for delegation. There is only one difference between the two. The empowered worker not only has the authority to manage a task, but also some scope to decide what that task should be. An IKEA store manager has power delegated to him/her, but head office rules may be so rigid that the manager has little scope for individual judgement. An empowered store manager would be one who could choose a range of stock suited to local customers, or a staffing policy that differs from the national store policy.

Empowerment means having more power and control over your working life, having the scope to make significant decisions about how to allocate your time and how to move forward. It is a practical application of the theories of Mayo and Herzberg. It may lead to greater risks being taken, but can also lead to opportunities being identified and exploited. Above all else, it should aid motivation.

The only major worry about empowerment in recent years has come from the financial services industry. In the 1990s a trader called Nick Leeson carried out a series of reckless trades that lost hundreds of millions of pounds and brought about the collapse of Barings Bank. Other similar disasters happened, and in most cases, a fundamental problem was that the company bosses did not understand fully the risks that were being taken. Empowerment is highly dangerous in a situation of ignorance, yet highly-paid directors of banks blundered on until the 2007–9 credit crunch revealed their inadequacies.

Team working

Team working is the attempt to maximise staff satisfaction and involvement by organising employees into relatively small teams. These teams may be functional (the 'drive-thru crew' at a McDonald's) or geographic. The key features of such teams are that they should be:

- multi-skilled, so that everyone can do everyone else's job
- working together to meet shared objectives, such as to serve every customer within a minute or produce a gearbox with **zero defects**
- encouraged to think of the future as well as the present, in a spirit of *kaizen* (continuous improvement).

From a theoretical point of view, team working fits in well with Mayo's findings on the importance of group working and **group norms**. It can also be traced back to Maslow's emphasis on social needs. In practical terms, modern managers like team working because of the flexibility it implies. If worker A is absent, there are plenty of others used to dealing with the job and therefore there is no disruption. Team working also gives scope for motivating influences such as job enrichment and quality circles.

Professor Charles Handy suggests in his book *Inside Organisations* (BBC Books, 1990) that 'a good team is a great place to be, exciting, stimulating, supportive, successful. A bad team is horrible, a sort of human prison.' It is true that the business will not benefit if the group norms within the team discourage effort. Nevertheless, team working has proved successful in many companies in recent years. Companies such as Rolls-Royce, Trebor, Rover and Komatsu have reported major improvements in absenteeism and labour turnover, and significant shifts in workforce attitudes.

A-grade application

Motivation at the RNLI

How do you motivate 4,500 unpaid staff? Especially when you require them to put you before everything else, including family? This is the task of Ali Peck, human resources director for the RNLI, the Royal National Lifeboat Institution. If a boat capsizes in stormy weather, the lifeboatmen must stop whatever they are doing, put out to sea, and risk their own lives to save someone else's.

Peck's task is made more difficult because the 230 lifeboat stations are, of course, dotted around the coast. So the only way to bring people together is through training. Every lifeboatman has to go through a retraining programme every three to five years. This takes place at a purpose-built college. This is also where new volunteers are trained. Peck explains that the RNLI spends 50 per cent more per head on training than any comparable organisation. It is crucial, because if the volunteers drifted away from the job, the organisation would fold. In the case of the RNLI, the staff motivations come from the teamwork and from a real sense of personal achievement and pride. The lifeboatmen certainly aren't in it for the money.

Issues for analysis

The key ways to analyse motivation in practice are as follows.

- To select and apply the relevant motivation theory to the method being considered: good analysis of methods such as Performance Related Pay or job rotation require a critical eye.
- To question the publicly stated motives of the organisation or manager concerned: businesses can be very loose in their use of words such as motivation or empowerment. They can be euphemisms for tougher targets and greater pressure. If the recent history of a firm makes employees sceptical of the goodwill of managers, students should be equally questioning.
- As John Kotter has said, 'Motivating people over a short period is not very difficult.' The key test of a new approach to motivation is over a two- to five-year period, not the early months of a new initiative. So always consider the timescale.

Motivation in practice – an evaluation

There are many aspects of business studies that point solely towards money. How profitable is this price or that? What is the forecast net cash flow for April? And so on. In such circumstances it is understandable that human implications may be forgotten. A high price for an AIDS cure may be profitable, but life-threatening to those who cannot afford the medicine. April's positive cash flow might be achieved only by sacking temporary staff.

When covering motivation in practice, there is little excuse for ignoring the implications for people. Exaggerated commissions or performance-related pay can lead sales staff to oversell goods or services, which may cause customers huge difficulties later on, such as cosmetic surgery or questionable investments. Also, within the workplace, serious problems can arise: bullying to 'motivate' staff into working harder, or creating a culture of overwork which leads to stress.

Fortunately, there are many businesses in which the management of motivation is treated with respect – companies which know that quick fixes are not the answer. Successful motivation in the long term is a result of careful job design, employee training and development, honesty and trust. It may be possible to supplement this with an attractive financial reward scheme, but money will never be a substitute for motivation.

Key terms

Division of labour: subdividing a job into small, repetitive fragments of work.

Group norms: the types of behaviour and attitude seen as normal within a group.

Motivation: according to Professor Herzberg, it means doing something because you want to do it; most business leaders think of it as prompting people to work hard.

Zero defects: production that is right first time, therefore requiring no reworking; this saves time and money.

Revision questions *(40 marks; 40 minutes)*

1 'Job design is the key to motivation.' Outline one reason why this might be true, and one reason why it might not. (4)

2 Look at the famous saying by Lee Iacocca on page 180. Explain in your own words what he meant by this. (3)

3 How *should* a manager deal with a mistake made by a junior employee? (4)

4 State three reasons why job enrichment should improve staff motivation. (3)

5 Distinguish between job rotation and job enrichment. (4)

6 How does 'empowerment' differ from 'delegation'? (4)

7 Identify three advantages to an employee of working in a team. (3)

8 State two advantages and two disadvantages of offering staff performance-related pay. (4)

9 What might be the implications of providing a profit share to senior managers but not to the workforce generally? (5)

10 What problems might result from a manager bullying staff to 'motivate' them? (6)

Revision exercises

Data response

In July 2010 Channel 4 showed a programme called 'Undercover Boss'. The Chief Executive of hotel chain 'Best Western' grew a tatty beard, left his suit at home, and worked on the shopfloor for a week. He saw some awful things, but was delighted by Breakfast Supervisor Leona at the Castle Green hotel in the Lake District. Even though she had to work hard, at quite a low wage, she was welcoming, warm and enthusiastic. Each breakfast service can involve 120 breakfasts in three hours, which means intensive, pressured work. Yet she found time for all 'her' staff – and for the customers. When asked why, she said: 'They're so good to you here. You can have an overnight stay, and leisure club membership.' It was clear that she loved working there. Unsurprisingly, the first entry on the online hotel site 'Tripadvisor' suggested that 'the hotel (Castle Green) must be one of the friendliest in the country'.

Questions *(25 marks; 30 minutes)*

1 Why do some managers assume that working people are motivated by money? (6)

2 Analyse two possible reasons why Leona is so well motivated. (8)

3 Evaluate the likely business benefits to the Castle Green hotel of having a well-motivated staff. (11)

Data response

Write a questionnaire for self-completion by full-time employees. Your research objectives are to discover:

- whether there are any policies in place for encouraging workplace involvement/consultation
- whether job enrichment or job rotation measures exist (and what their effect is)
- how your respondents would describe the workplace culture
- whether there are any financial bonuses available, such as piece rate or performance-related pay, and what their effect is on motivation
- how highly motivated they feel themselves to be
- how highly motivated they believe their colleagues are.

This questionnaire should be conducted with at least ten respondents. It is preferable for the questionnaire to be conducted face-to-face, but if that is not possible, self-completion is acceptable.

When the research is completed, analyse the results carefully and write a summary of them in report form.

28 Integrated people in organisations

Introduction

People management affects every aspect of the operations of a business. Clearly, workers are not machines and, despite what some managers may continue to think, treating them as such has been discredited by many theorists as an ineffective approach to managing them. Each worker is unique, with moods and motivations that may change on a daily basis, often affecting performance. This makes human resources management a complex, and at times frustrating, activity. However, like machinery, effective investment in a firm's human resources – in the form of recruitment, training, organisation and motivation – can have a dramatic impact on productivity. All businesses, regardless of size, need to manage all aspects of their human resources carefully. For instance:

- How should the workforce be structured and what job roles should be adopted?
- How should a business choose between the training and development of existing staff and the recruitment of new employees?
- What techniques can be used to improve motivation, and how might these change over time and between different groups of workers?
- How can workforce performance be measured and improved?

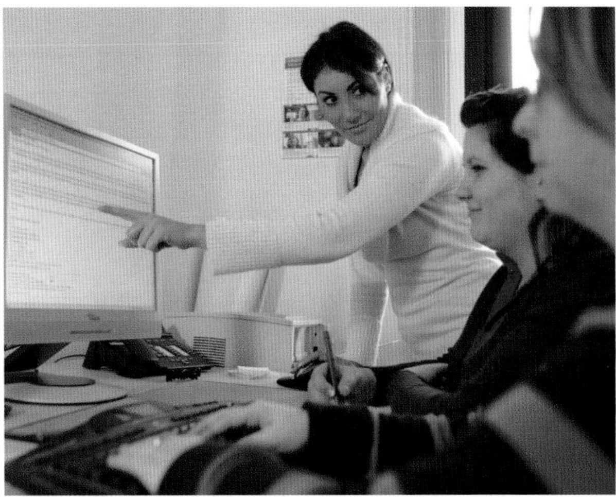

Figure 28.1 Employee training

People in organisations

It is tempting to deal with people in organisations by dividing the area into separate topics – such as recruitment, training and motivation – and tackling them one by one. While this might help the initial learning process, A-grade students need to go further, making connections between individual topics in order to unlock the underlying themes. For example, a sudden decrease in labour productivity may be linked to falling motivation, which, in turn, may result from a change in policy aimed at bringing in new staff to fill a skills gap, rather than promoting existing employees.

There is plenty of scope for misunderstanding within the people section of the specification. Weaker candidates, for example, often fall into the trap of believing that managers should be working towards creating a happier workforce, confusing motivation with contentment. Stronger candidates will recognise the connection between motivation and the benefits of improved productivity, lower costs and greater profits for the firm. A-grade students need more than just an understanding of the people concepts – they need to be able to discuss and assess their relative significance for individual firms and the circumstances they face.

Issue 1: the link between human resources decision making and the business objectives

Regardless of whether a business is struggling to survive or to manage rapid growth, the contribution of the workforce will be crucial. The 'human' element of the business is responsible for generating new ideas, ensuring that production is carried out, and that customers and suppliers receive a service that meets or beats expectations. Employees also represent a major cost to the business and any individual performing below their potential will act as a drain on profits. Ensuring that a business has the right number of people, with the right skills, performing the right roles at the right time, is a major challenge. It is a necessary one, though, if a business is to achieve its long-term objectives.

Issue 2: the link between training and the success of a business

Improving and maintaining the quality of the workforce comes at a cost. Regular training to ensure that employees' skills remain relevant and up to date can be expensive. Any business behaviour that contributes to increased costs should surely be avoided – or should it? Assuming that training is justified and effective in improving the performance of the workforce, it may provide the business with its only way of competing successfully. Investment in training not only creates a skilled workforce but is also likely to produce a more motivated and efficient workforce. Ultimately, a firm's attitude to training will depend on its ability and willingness to accept higher short-term costs in the hope of benefits in the long term.

Revision questions *(60 marks; 60 minutes)*

1 Identify two reasons why a business might use an organisational chart. (2)

2 Explain what is meant by a narrow span of control. (3)

3 Describe one benefit and one drawback for a business of reducing the levels within its hierarchy. (4)

4 Outline two elements required for successful delegation. (4)

5 Give one example of internal communication and one example of external communication. (2)

6 Explain two reasons why good communications can improve the performance of a firm. (4)

7 Outline two potential barriers to communication within a firm. (4)

8 Briefly distinguish between labour productivity and labour turnover. (3)

9 Outline one positive and one negative effect of an increase in labour turnover on a firm's performance. (4)

10 Suggest two ways that a business can reduce its level of labour absenteeism. (2)

11 State two reasons why a business might choose to recruit internally rather than externally. (2)

12 Identify three methods of recruiting staff from outside the business. (3)

13 Explain the difference between on-the-job and off-the-job training. (3)

14 State two benefits to a firm of training its workers. (2)

15 Briefly explain what is meant by motivation. (3)

16 Suggest two reasons why employee motivation is important to a business. (2)

17 Give two examples of hygiene factors and two examples of motivators. (4)

18 Identify three key characteristics of a meaningful and well-designed job. (3)

19 State three ways in which employers can reward staff financially. (3)

20 Briefly explain the difference between job enlargement and job enrichment. (3)

Revision exercises

Data response

Training is the key concern for graduates

Training and development are rated more highly by graduates than the size of their salaries, according to a recent survey. The findings came from a web poll conducted for accountants Ernst & Young. The research found that 44% of the 1,051 graduates who responded rated training opportunities most highly among potential first employers, with only 18% identifying salaries and benefits as their top concern. According to Stephen Isherwood, Ernst & Young's head of graduate recruitment, 'Despite the many concerns students have when thinking about their future employer, it is still critically important for many of them that their new job offers them opportunities to learn, and to develop their own careers.' Other aspects of work rated in the survey included work/life balance (16%), business reputation (12%), and people and culture (8%). Despite the recent interest by businesses in promoting their social credentials, ethical and environmental reputation received only 3% of the vote.

(Source: Adapted from www.bbc.co.uk)

Questions *(25 marks; 25 minutes)*

1 Describe two costs associated with training employees. (3)

2 Using a suitable theory, examine the link between training and worker motivation. (8)

3 To what extent do you believe that the research carried out for Ernst & Young confirms the view that money does not motivate? Explain your answer. (14)

Data response

HRM and social networking

Social networking is a modern phenomenon, with over 500 million users on Facebook alone. While many businesses complain about the amount of time wasted by staff chatting online, others are embracing the trend as an opportunity for more effective recruitment and communication. For instance, accountancy firm Ernst & Young uses Facebook as part of its recruitment strategy, by sponsoring its own page on the site, where graduates can learn more about the firm.

For smaller firms, social networking can provide a cost-effective means of accessing a large pool of potential recruits. Helen Wright, head of people at marketing agency Iris, claims that the sites are the 'perfect medium' for recruitment. Staff can pass on details of job vacancies to suitably qualified friends who can then make their details available to the firm looking to recruit. Developments in the USA suggest that, in the future, recruitment is less likely to happen on the high street and more likely to occur in a virtual world. Computer giant IBM is one of a number of employers who have participated in 'virtual job fairs'. Jobseekers are able to create their own online personas (known as avatars), speak to representatives and even attend interviews.

However, there are also a number of potential problems that could arise from using social networking as a method of recruitment. Judging a candidate on the basis of a social profile may lead to bias, either positive or negative, on behalf of the recruiter. Other firms question the ethics of using the sites to research candidates. According to Donna Miller, European director for Rent-a-Car, the practice is comparable to 'going into somebody's house and searching through their cupboards'.

(Source: PM Online)

Questions *(25 marks; 30 minutes)*

1 Suggest two methods, other than the internet, that a business could use to recruit candidates for a job vacancy. (4)

2 Analyse the main advantages for a small business of using the internet to recruit new staff. (9)

3 To what extent do you agree with the view that, in the future, recruitment is more likely to take place via computer than by using more traditional methods? (12)

Introduction to operations management

Definition

Operations management turns a customer order into a delivery.

Introduction

Operations management is the central business function of creating the product or service and delivering it to the customer (i.e. meeting the customer requirement). Operations management at Ford means designing the cars and the machinery for making them, ordering the supplies, manufacturing the products, delivering them to the car showrooms and handling customer service issues such as warranty claims. Marketing creates the demand; operations management creates the supply to meet the demand. To achieve this, it requires human and financial resources.

The importance of operations management is especially clear in the car industry. Rover Cars once commanded more than a 50 per cent share of the British car market. Its cars were well designed but poorly made and in 2005 the business ceased to exist as a British producer. In the years of Rover's decline, Toyota moved from being outside the top 20 world car producers to its current position as number one. Toyota has never been famous for producing stylish cars, but their quality and reliability have built its reputation worldwide. Toyota's business success has been built not on marketing but on operations management. By 2007, this success brought it annual profits of around £10 billion – more than the rest of the world's car makers put together. Even though Toyota had quality problems in 2010, the fundamental strength of the business (and its customer loyalty) keeps it motoring.

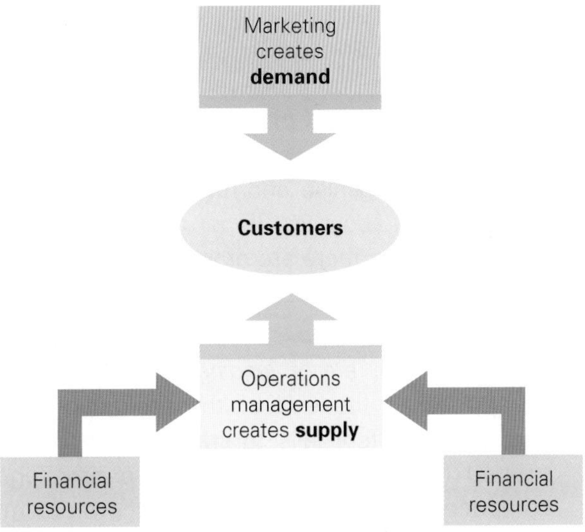

Figure 29.1 The central role of operations management

What is operations management?

Step 1: design

The process starts by designing a product or service to meet the needs or desires of a particular type of customer (see Table 29.1 for examples). The key to this, and every other stage is to be clear about the customer and his/her requirements. If an airline's target customer is a student, the design of the plane interior must be simple, economical and effective – to help keep costs low enough to provide the low prices the student traveller wants.

Step 2: establishing the supply chain

In a manufacturing process, the heart of the operation will be the factory. This is where a collection of materials and parts will be turned into a finished product. In the case of a car, literally thousands of parts are involved in making each vehicle. Components that may cost little to produce, such as metal fixings for seat belts, all combine to turn £4,000 worth of parts into a car worth £10,000.

Table 29.1 Examples of designs that aim to meet customer requirements

Market	Type of customer	Customer needs or wants	Outline operational design
Hotels	Busy traveller and busy worker	Low-cost but comfortable hotel room in city centre	Well-located building with small but very well-equipped rooms; all food and drink from vending machines
Car market	Family with young children	A car to make family journeys more pleasant	Spacious car with good entertainment (seat-back monitors, etc.) and a small refrigerated drinks unit
Mortgages	University students	Students wanting to buy a flat on a joint mortgage – to stop relying on landlords	Flexible, low-cost mortgage, which is easy to get into and out of; available online to students with limited financial histories

This does not mean, though, that the car maker receives £6,000 of profit for every car sold; £6,000 of value has been added to the components, but at what cost? The most obvious cost is labour (i.e. the staff needed to organise and run the factory). This will typically cost about 20–25 per cent of the value of the output. Then there are other things that are a clear waste of money for the business such as those listed below.

- *Production line errors leading to 'wastage':* if a car reaches the end of the production line and, when tested, fails to start, labour time is wasted finding the fault, and more time and components involved in correcting the problem. Modern companies try to eliminate all activities that waste time, but taking care over quality can never make sense for any company that wants to build a long-term future.
- *Breakdowns, perhaps due to faulty maintenance, or just due to wear and tear:* a well-run business uses preventative maintenance – checking machinery and replacing worn parts before a breakdown occurs.

Having established a well-run factory, the business can establish the other key parts of the **supply chain**, as indicated in Figure 29.2.

Step 3: working with suppliers

Very few businesses produce 100 per cent of a product or service – almost all use suppliers. In some cases suppliers may do most of the operational work. Companies that 'bottle' Coca-Cola buy in the aluminium cans (already printed with the can design), the water, the carbon dioxide used to create the fizz and the secret Coke syrup (sent from the Coca-Cola factory in America). They may also

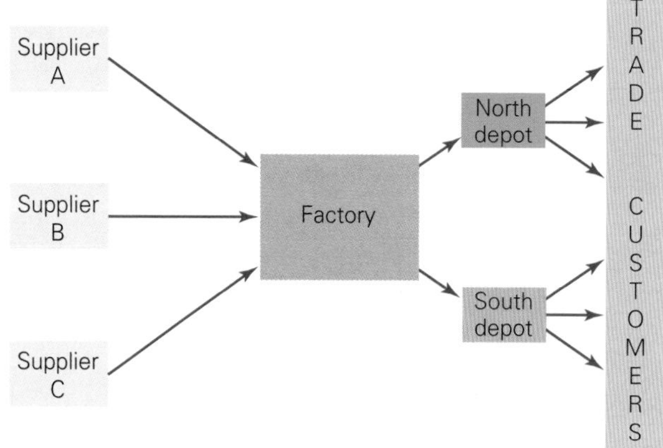

Figure 29.2 The supply chain: from supplier to customer

get a distribution company such as Exel to make all the deliveries to wholesale and retail customers. So what does the Coca-Cola bottler actually do? Well, not a huge amount, clearly. But it must still be responsible for the coordination of all the suppliers and the quality of their work. If Waitrose ordered a container load of Coke Zero to reach its Bracknell depot at 10.00 on a Tuesday morning, did it turn up on time? If not, why not?

For many companies, working with suppliers is a key to success. A homemade ice cream parlour may do all the production operations on-site, but still relies on suppliers of fresh fruit, fresh milk and cream; grocery items such as sugar, wafer biscuits and cones; paper cups and plastic spoons, and so on. To run the parlour successfully, all the operations have to be carried out successfully. If you have run out of cones, the best ice creams can remain unsold.

A company must therefore select suppliers that can deliver the right goods reliably and must negotiate low enough prices for the supplies to make it possible to run the business economically.

Step 4: managing quality

Quality is not easy to define. It is a combination of real factors plus psychological ones. A haircut may be carried out very expertly, yet the customer may go away and cry! A less expert hairdresser may produce a technically worse cut, yet the effect may be just what the customer wants. In this case, providing quality means providing what the customer wants (i.e. delivering customer satisfaction).

Yet what if the customer wants the 'wrong' thing? The traveller may only care about getting to work on time, yet if the train company has safety concerns, the train should be slowed down or stopped. The traveller may get to work, cursing the train company's poor-quality service – but in reality the company has done the right thing.

Ten years ago few shoppers worried about healthy eating, so McDonald's and others made their money 'supersizing' their customers. Were the companies providing a high-quality service? Perhaps not.

Effective operations management requires certain quality objectives:

- the product/service must do what the customer has been promised
- it must arrive on time, in good condition
- it must last at least as long as the customer expects
- customer service should be effective (e.g. phones answered quickly)
- after-sales service should also be effective (e.g. speedy repair if something goes wrong).

These are the basics. On top of these should come the psychological factors that can mean a huge amount (e.g. service with a warm smile, with staff showing warmth towards the customers). Modern business theory suggests that, to stand out, a company needs to achieve 'customer delight' not just customer satisfaction. The easiest way to delight a customer is to be genuinely welcoming; a fake smile is worse than none at all.

Step 5: using technology effectively

Twenty years ago it required a room full of computers to do what a laptop can do today. In ten years there will probably be more computing power in a mobile phone than today's PC. At a time of dramatic change, some firms have come unstuck when upgrading their whole IT system; still more have struggled to make the best use of the internet.

Within the operations department of a business, the key requirement has been to find software that will satisfactorily manage the day-to-day process, from supplies through to delivery. For example, if fashion retailer Zara of Spain suddenly orders 4,000 'Glastonbury' jackets from your clothing factory, you need instantly to know:

- how many metres of cloth to order from your suppliers, and how many metres of lining
- how many buttons and zips to order
- when is the earliest date that all the above can be received, and therefore the job can begin
- how many hours of machine time will be needed
- how much overtime will be needed from staff, if the factory is already busy
- how many extra delivery vehicles will be needed and when
- when Zara can expect delivery of all 4,000 items to its Spanish headquarters.

This should all be available at the touch of a button using **enterprise resource planning** (ERP) software. This software has all the details of the business operation and provides not only the planning but will also monitor on a day-to-day basis whether things are working to schedule.

Issues for analysis

There are several concepts within operations management that are perfect for analysis:

- The idea that the heart of every business is the interface between marketing (demand) and operations (supply) and that operations relies on human and financial resources. Only if all these departments work in harmony can the operation succeed.
- Success in managing operations requires a true understanding of what the customer really wants: a car to get from A to B, or an 'ultimate driving machine' to impress the neighbours?
- A well-run operation should be able to capture all its key information in the form of an ERP software package. In fact, most firms who buy this software find that they lack much of the

information they need; without accurate data, it can be 'garbage in, garbage out'. Exactly this problem happened with Sony in its much-delayed development of the PS3.

Operations management – an evaluation

Every business is different, especially in the status given to operations staff. In Toyota or BMW, top engineers are the stars of the business and the operations department will be at the heart of all major decisions. In a business such as Innocent Drinks, the marketing people lead the business, with the operations changing to suit the market. Usually the importance and power of operations staff will reflect the needs and history of the business. In some cases, though, career politics will have intervened. A company that should be based on strong operations may actually be dominated by marketing and finance people. In which case, key decisions about the future may be taken wrongly. The A-grade student not only analyses the precise circumstances of the business, he or she is also willing to make a judgement on how well the business is being run.

Key terms

Enterprise resource planning (ERP): logs all of a firm's costs, working methods and resources (machinery, labour, stocks of materials) within a piece of software. This provides a model of the business that can be used to answer questions such as 'When do we need to start working to get stocks made in time for delivery before Christmas?'

Supply chain: the whole path, from suppliers of raw materials through production and storage on to customer delivery.

A Revision questions *(25 marks; 25 minutes)*

1 Why may the quality of product design be less important for some businesses than others? (3)

2 Explain two key elements of operations management for:
- a) a children's shoe shop (4)
- b) a new, all-business-class airline. (4)

3 Choose one of the examples in Table 29.1 and outline one strength and one weakness of that business idea. (4)

4 Identify three ways in which staff might be at fault in production line errors that cause wastage. (3)

5 Examine the possible effects on a firm such as Coca-Cola of being unreliable in delivering to a big customer such as Waitrose. (5)

6 Outline one possible benefit to a business from 'delighting' rather than 'satisfying' its customers. (2)

B1 Revision exercises

Data response

Lean, green, efficient operations

Recent years have been great for Toyota, largely due to one car: the Prius. It is the car beloved of Hollywood stars due to its green technology – part electric, part petrol engine. The car has sold 'only' two million units, but its impact has been much greater. It has made the Toyota brand stand out in the crowded mass market in

America, and helped Toyota become the world's number one car maker. Without doubt it is the world's richest, with more than £8,000 million cash in its bank account. Now Citroën wants to muscle in on Toyota's green success.

Of course, it is not enough to simply copy a rival. Citroën decided to tackle the main weakness of the Prius: its price. As the Prius has two engines (one electric, one petrol), its production costs are higher, forcing it to be priced at £2,000–£3,000 more than comparable cars. Citroën's new car is called the C-Cactus and is priced at the level of the comparable petrol-only Citroën C4 model. This is because the C-Cactus has been made with dramatically fewer parts than a normal car. The car's interior, for example, has half the usual number of 400 separate components. That saves time and money in building the car. The C-Cactus therefore is less costly on parts and much less costly on labour than the C4.

Citroën's designers have questioned the need for every component in the car. Where possible they have cut back and simplified – but without risking passenger comfort. The car doors have two parts instead of the twelve on a normal car. The dashboard has gone, with most controls on a touch-screen indicator in front of the driver.

According to Citroën, the C-Cactus will not only drink less fuel, it will also use far fewer labour hours. There is no doubting that it is a designed to be lean and efficient; the only worry is whether customers will accept the very different look and feel of the car. It certainly won't have the luxury touches some car buyers expect.

(Source: www.scoop.co.nz)

Questions *(30 marks; 35 minutes)*

1 a) Outline two features of the C-Cactus that might prove appealing to car buyers. (6)

b) Outline one reason why buyers of large family cars may not buy the C-Cactus. (4)

2 a) On average, Prius cars have sold for £12,000. How much revenue, therefore, has the brand generated for Toyota? (3)

b) Product development on the Prius took eight years and cost an estimated £850 million. Was it worth it? Explain your answer. (5)

3 This unit sets out five important elements of operations management. Discuss which one of the five proved the most important in the development of the C-Cactus. (12)

Data response

Insourcing: Bringing jobs back home

Insourcing means bringing a service back in-house, to be operated by the firm's own personnel. In other words it means reversing the process of outsourcing (to countries such as India). Insourcing seems to have been an increasing trend in America, especially in functions such as customer service and technical support. Why has this pattern occurred? Delta Airlines recently announced that it would no longer handle customer service calls from India and confirmed that these would be handled in-house in the US. 'Customer acceptance of call centre representatives in other countries was low and our customers are not shy about letting us have that feedback.' According to mycustomer.com, the airline has cancelled its contract with offshore services provider Wipro following negative customer feedback received after routing calls to India. The initial outsourcing was expected to save the company £15 million a year. The customer reaction was a less positive side effect.

Other companies to go down the road of insourcing include United Airlines. Originally it was not clear to Indian outsourcing organisations whether these moves were due to customer backlash or an effort on the part of these companies to bring jobs back home to help stimulate the economy. A source at United Airlines EMEA revealed that 165 jobs were made available in the US in April, to be split between Chicago and Hawaii as part of a 'change to the way customer relations are handled.'

Despite the cost-cutting times, the need for quality service to sell a quality product will endure and put firms in a strong position for coming out of the recession. And this quality, many companies find, often begins at home.

Source: Ben Lobel, Supply Chain Digital, 15 March 2010, by permission of White Digital Media

Questions *(25 marks; 30 minutes)*

1 Explain why a business might benefit from bringing its customer service function 'in-house'. (6)

2 From the article, analyse whether Delta Airlines has helped the efficiency of its operations by bringing the customer service and technical support functions back in-house. (8)

3 It is possible that the trend to insource is due to the availability of (cheap) unemployed staff in the USA. Discuss whether it would ever be wise for a customer-focused business to outsource its customer service personnel. (11)

Customer service

Definition

Customer service describes the range of actions taken by a business when interacting with its customers. Effective customer service will meet or surpass the expectations that customers have of the business.

Introduction

The biggest question in relation to this topic is whether firms try to provide good service to their customers or 'customer service'. In other words, is customer service a label used to describe actions that prevent the customer from inconveniencing the organisation? Or is providing a service a genuine part of the company's attitudes and culture?

How is customer service delivered?

Face to face

The most immediate, most powerful situation in which customer service is seen is in direct, face-to-face dealings with customers. Retailers must focus clearly on how shop staff interact with their customers. This is a situation with which you are likely to be highly familiar, perhaps from both sides. Here, the face of the employee is the face of the company to the customer.

Telephone

Much of customer service activity now happens in call centres. From finding out the price of a train from Leeds to Plymouth, to making an insurance claim following a car crash, the telephone is a key factor in customer service. Call centres are thought to be cost efficient, partly because they can be located in Birmingham, Belfast or Bangalore. It is highly questionable, though, as to whether they deliver 'customer service'. Most customers want to talk to an individual, not someone who is reading a script.

Internet

Many online booking systems have eliminated direct human contact from customer service. Behind the scenes, though, the attitudes within the business remain all-important. You may book a bargain flight online, ticking the box for same-day delivery of the tickets. If the business fails to deliver the tickets on time, you are not going on holiday. Will the tickets arrive? Only if the faceless staff do their jobs on time. As customers, we have to trust that an online service will soon fail if it cannot meet its promises.

A-grade application

Customer service at home

Companies looking for a less controversial alternative to basing call centres in Asia may have found an answer in a concept known as home-shoring. An alternative to 'off-shoring' where customer service is provided from a call centre in another country, 'home-shoring' bases customer service assistants in their own homes.

Research evidence seems to suggest that this boosts productivity and increases the level of service provided. The most famous home-shoring success story is US airline JetBlue where over 1,200 staff work at home. The customer complaint level is, amazingly, just one per 300,000 passengers, while staff turnover is just 3.5 per cent, way below that experienced in a traditional call centre. In June 2010 JetBlue was ranked highest among US airlines for customer satisfaction for the sixth year in a row.

Methods of meeting customer expectations

To meet customer expectations, a business needs to follow a four-stage process as illustrated in Figure 30.1.

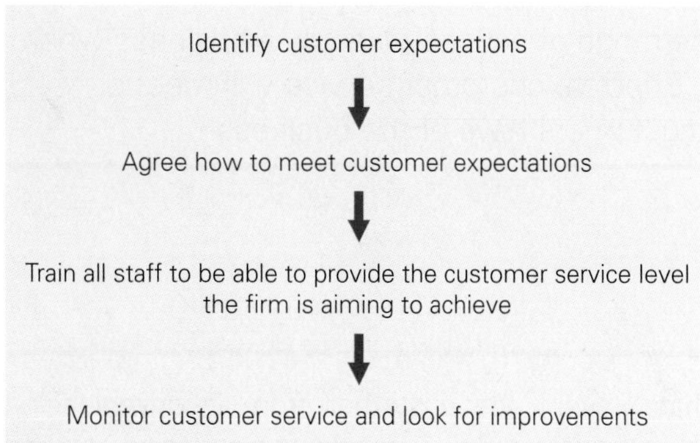

Figure 30.1 Meeting customer expectations

Market research

In order to find out what customers expect, market research will be used. This is likely to be a mixture of quantitative and qualitative research. The qualitative research is designed to probe selected key customers to find what level of support and service they expect from the firm. Such detailed qualitative research will probably enable the firm to gain a clear understanding of the range of expectations that different customers may have. With these identified, quantitative research can be used to assess how many customers expect certain features of customer service. An example may be using research to identify 'acceptable' queuing times when ringing a call centre.

Decision-time

Decisions will need to be made, based on the results of research into customers' expectations, of just what level of service the firm will aim to provide. If money were no object, any firm could provide exquisite customer service. We can only imagine the level of service available from James Bond's Savile Row tailor or Victoria Beckham's Beverly Hills hairstylist. Alternatively, a firm may decide to take a low-cost approach to customer service, perhaps outsourcing enquiries and technical problems to reduce costs. The costs and benefits of spending on customer service will be weighed. For those companies that value their reputation highly, the benefits may outweigh the costs, while for those that rely on low prices to shift their products, they may cut corners on customer service to protect their profit margin.

Training

Staff training can begin once the firm has decided on its customer service policies and practices. Note, however, that firms will have varying levels of commitment to training for staff. Some firms may offer staff just 30 minutes' informal training in customer service. They cannot expect their policies to be implemented as effectively as the firm that sends all new staff to a training centre for a full day's training. In America, McDonald's began a programme of getting staff to work with **zero training**. This was just at the start of the period when the firm's sales and profits collapsed in the period 2002–2005. The zero training approach disappeared when new managers decided that McDonald's needed *more* customer training, not less. At McDonald's, and everywhere else, the cost involved in improving the level of customer service must be set against the cost of not doing so.

Quality

As discussed in Unit 31, firms looking to ensure the quality of anything that they do, face a choice between quality control and quality assurance.

Quality control methods for customer service involve spotting defective service. The problem here is that poor customer service can be spotted only once it has been delivered, and this means at least one unhappy customer. Anyone who has rung a call centre is likely to have heard an announcement that 'Your call may be recorded for quality control purposes.' Those working in the retail sector are at the mercy of '**mystery shoppers**', who are paid to visit stores and report back on the customer service provided. Other methods of quality control involve planned or unannounced management checks.

Quality assurance is the attempt to introduce systems to ensure that quality errors cannot occur. Therefore, quality assuring customer service systems must involve staff training. Given the key role of staff in meeting customer expectations, they will need to be 100 per cent clear on how to deal with any situation they may face. The problem is that staff can start to see themselves, not the customers, as the focal point of the business. Management may keep saying 'the customer is king' or 'the customer is always right', but the staff don't really believe it.

Quality standards

As noted in Unit 31, companies can apply for quality standards certification to show the rest of the world that they are serious about the quality of what they do. The basic **ISO 9000** certification series covers customer service in organisations for which the skill is relevant. However, for customer service specialists, there are customer service-specific standards as follows:

- ISO 10002 – a customer complaint handling standard.
- The BSI runs the CCA Standard – a special quality standard for call centres.
- Charter Mark – administered by the government, this is a customer service standard for public- and voluntary-sector organisations, along with firms that provide a public service in the passenger train and bus, water, gas and electricity supply industries.

Figure 30.2 A mystery shopper may be assessing quality

Table 30.1 Quality control vs quality assurance

Quality control	Quality assurance
'Your call may be recorded for quality purposes'	Thorough, ongoing training in customer service
Mystery shoppers	Customer service is a key feature of company culture
Management checks	Clear systems, set out in writing, about how to deal with each type of customer complaint

Monitoring and improving customer service

With a customer service system in place, the final step is to fight complacency. Systems designed to monitor the effectiveness of customer service must be used in order to ensure that standards do not slip and that the quality systems being used for customer service continue to produce the required results. However, in a spirit of continually trying to improve, most firms will monitor their own customer service standards relative to those of their rivals. Innovations in customer service are likely to be copied fairly quickly in most markets. This is why major changes to customer service, such as the use of the internet in the banking industry, tend to become common features of the industry in such a short time.

Benefits of good customer service

There is no doubt that good customer service has positive effects on a business, not just in terms of keeping from jumping to rival firms.

- *Brand loyalty*: good customer service tends to bring repeat custom. As customers feel positive about the experience they have had with a business, they are most likely to return to that firm for future purchases. Hanging on to existing customers is crucial for any sensible business, since attracting new customers from rivals tends to rely on expensive promotional tools, such as advertising and special offers.
- *Word-of-mouth promotion*: good customer service can actually generate free promotion as happy customers tell their friends. Anecdote suggests that word-of-mouth promotion is the most effective promotional tool available to a business. This is because you are more likely to believe your friends than a company's marketing department.
- *Increased efficiency*: since good customer service is likely to include better advice to customers, firms are less likely to sell inappropriate products

or services that fail to meet customer needs. This should mean fewer complaints and therefore a reduced need for 'second phase' customer service back-up, such as customer complaint lines or product returns.

A-grade application

The best and worst …

The UK Customer Service Institute regularly publishes the results of its survey of customer service in the UK. This provides data on the best and worst-performing sectors when it comes to customer service. It also highlights prime examples of excellent customer service. In the 2010 survey, the top three performers were all retailers – John Lewis, Waitrose and Marks and Spencer (Food). Meanwhile, the UK's worst-performing sector for customer service was the utility companies (gas, water, electricity). It is interesting to note that all three of the UK's customer service leaders undoubtedly experience commercial benefits from the reputation their customer service brings.

(Source: www.ukcsi.com)

Issues for analysis

- With so much customer service being provided by phone, call centres feature high in the customer service agenda. Churchill Insurance is just one of many companies now stating clearly in its promotional literature that it uses only UK call centres. Why should it use UK call centres when the cost is far higher than for those located in India, and the staff in a UK call centre will be less qualified than their Indian counterparts? Customer service could be argued to be more qualitative than quantitative. Perceptions of customers are probably more important than the service they actually receive; the link between this area of operations management and the marketing department is strong.
- Some companies, notably DIY chain B&Q, believe that some types of people are better at customer service than others. Many major retailers use students and school-leavers as a huge portion of their shop-floor staff. However, B&Q feels that students and school-leavers are naturally less polite than older members of staff. The result is that B&Q actively encourages retired and semi-retired people to apply for positions in its stores, since it believes that these staff can provide the most effective customer service.

Customer service – an evaluation

Good customer service is unlikely to be provided by unmotivated staff. Although systems for ensuring customer service – such as market research, training and quality control systems – do help to improve customer service, it is the staff that will be the vital determinant. The message for businesses is therefore one that stresses the need to look after all staff. Often, a business may pay particular attention to motivating its managers, at the cost of ignoring the needs of staff lower down the organisation's hierarchy. However, in the majority of businesses, the front-line providers of customer service are the staff at the lowest level of the hierarchy. No matter how motivated the store management team, an unmotivated supermarket checkout assistant may well be the main determinant of a customer's shopping experience.

Key terms

Culture: within a business, this means 'the way we do things round here' (i.e. the attitudes and behaviours of staff within an organisation).

ISO 9000: the International Standards Organisation (ISO) has a quality assurance certification system called ISO 9000.

Mystery shoppers: employed to test customer service by visiting a shop or sales outlet unannounced, and therefore have the same experience as customers.

Zero training: the opposite of customer service, in that it implies that staff need neither skills nor positive attitudes to work for the business.

Revision questions *(35 marks; 35 minutes)*

1 List three methods of meeting customer expectations. (3)

2 Explain how the use of a mystery shopper can help to maintain standards of customer service. (4)

3 Briefly explain how the following businesses might benefit from providing excellent customer service:
   a) a café
   b) a manufacturer of washing machines
   c) a bank. (9)

4 For a business that you use regularly where you feel customer service could be better, briefly explain:
   a) your own customer expectations
   b) how the business could identify what your expectations are
   c) how the business could try to meet your expectations. (9)

5 Explain why a small local plumber might benefit from offering better customer service than all her local rivals. (4)

6 Explain two benefits that an electricity supplier such as npower might find as a result of gaining a customer service quality standard such as the Charter Mark. (6)

Data Response

Harry Ramsden's Fish 'n' Chips

In July 2010, Channel 4's 'Undercover Boss' series featured Marija Simovic, Chief Executive of Harry Ramsden's. She spent a day working as a waitress at the chain's most profitable branch, right by Blackpool tower. Within an hour she had a customer complaint. The fish and chips she served were cold. The reason was simple. There was no system for telling waiting staff that their order was ready to serve.

Furthermore, poor store layout created a bottleneck just where the food was cooked, so it was impossible to hang around waiting for the hot food to be ready.

Despite these problems, Marija was enormously impressed by the friendliness of the customer service. Two waiting staff especially caught her eye. They were warm, friendly and always willing to provide customers with a great experience ('Would you like some extra hot chips, love?'). Marija decided to ask these two staff to get involved in a national training programme on customer service. She also addressed the problem of cold food by investing in a personal buzzer system which would vibrate in the pockets of individual waiting staff when their food was ready to be served.

Overall, the Chief Executive could see that good service was a combination of staff attitudes and motivation, together with organisational and physical factors such as equipment, store layout and store investment.

Questions *(25 marks; 30 minutes)*

1 Explain why customer service is so important to a business such as Harry Ramsden's. (6)

2 The problems at the Blackpool store were easily solvable by the Chief Executive. Why may local managers be unable to solve the day-to-day customer service problems they face? (6)

3 TV programmes such as this persuade Chief Executives to solve the immediate issues they see. Discuss the broader lessons a Chief Executive such as Marija should learn about how to improve customer service throughout her business. (13)

Data response

Twinkle.com

Twinkle.com is an internet service provider, aiming for the top end of the market in a marketplace that has experienced enormous growth over the past ten years. Twinkle knows the importance of customer service, but has experienced a number of problems over the past year. Its management is disappointed in this because this year it has spent more than ever before on a promotional campaign to recruit new customers. Disappointed with the results produced by its online and telephone customer service teams, Twinkle.com has called in a consultant to improve customer service levels. She has gathered the data shown in the table below.

Table 30.2

	Quarter 1 (Jan–Mar)	Quarter 2 (Apr–Jun)	Quarter 3 (Jul–Sep)	Quarter 4 (Oct–Dec)
Complaints per month	864	967	932	902
% of complaints dealt with within 24 hours	28	24	29	34
Customer service training expenditure (£000s)	12	12	12	10
Overall customer service rating from monthly customer survey	6	5	5	4
Increase/decrease in total customer numbers	+3%	+2%	−3%	−12%

Questions *(30 marks; 35 minutes)*

1 Briefly explain how the table shows evidence of poor customer service. (3)

2 Identify and explain a possible cause of poor customer service performance suggested by the table above. (4)

3 Analyse two other possible causes of poor customer service within the business. (6)

4 Analyse the reasons why customer service may be especially important for an ISP (internet service provider). (8)

5 To what extent can an external consultant help to improve the customer service levels offered by a firm such as Twinkle.com? (9)

31 Effective quality management

Definition

Quality management means providing what the customer wants at the right time, with the right level of quality and consistency, and therefore yielding high customer satisfaction.

What is quality?

W Edwards Deming, the American quality guru, said that 'quality is defined by the customer'. The customer may insist on certain specifications, or demand exceptional levels of customer comfort. Another definition of quality is 'fit for use'. Although hard to define, there is no doubt that customers are very aware of quality. Their perception of quality is a key part of the buying decision.

Customers will accept some **trade-off** between price and quality. There is, however, a minimum level of quality that is acceptable. The customer wants the product to work (be fit for use), regardless of the price. If the customers think that the quality is below a minimum level, they will not buy the product. Above the minimum level of acceptable quality, customers will expect to get more as they pay more.

The importance of quality is related to the level of **competitiveness** in the market. When competition is fierce, the quality of the product can tip the balance in the customer's decision making. Dell is a hugely successful computer manufacturer, which sells directly to customers through the internet or newspaper advertising. Its mission statement is: 'Customers must have a quality experience and be pleased, not just satisfied.'

For all customers, quality is about satisfying their expectations. The customer will take into account the total buying experience. Customer service and after-sales service may be as important as the product itself. The way the product is sold, even *where* it is sold, all contribute to the customer's feelings about the quality of the product.

Quality is a moving target: a quality standard that is acceptable today may not be in the future. Customer expectations of quality are constantly changing. As quality improves, customer demands also increase.

A-grade application

Toyota

Toyota has long had a reputation for superior quality. All this was threatened when some of its cars appeared to suffer from accelerator pedal problems in the USA. Initially Toyota was slow to react but eventually had to recall 2.3 million vehicles across the world. The damaged reputation inevitably led to lower sales.

The president of Toyota, Akio Toyoda, said the company had identified 2003 as the turning point for its decline in quality. This was when it passed 6 million vehicles and the subsequent growth across the world made it difficult to apply its quality principles for which it was renowned. In June 2010 Toyota announced that all its new cars sold in the UK would come with a five-year warranty.

'Our new five-year warranty is tangible evidence of our commitment to quality and to our customers – both those who are loyal to the brand, and those who are considering switching to Toyota for their next car,' said Miguel Fonseca, Toyota GB managing director.

'By taking this major initiative we are giving our customers complete peace of mind. We want to reassure them that, in choosing a Toyota, they are getting the best in quality, reliability and durability.'

Quality:

- is satisfying (preferably beating) customer expectations
- applies to services as well as products
- involves the whole business process, not just the manufacturing of the product
- is an ever-rising target.

Quality defined by customer specifications

Where the customer is in a powerful position, quality is directly defined by the customer. Many firms lay down minimum standards for their suppliers. Large businesses, such as supermarkets and chain stores, are able to insist on quality standards. They have the buying power to force their suppliers to conform. For many years, Marks & Spencer has worked with suppliers to ensure that standards are met. Other large purchasers, such as government departments and local authorities, are also able to insist on high standards for supplies. As new roads and motorways are built, their surface is checked to ensure its quality. If the surface does not conform to the required standards, the contractor will have to re-lay the area.

Other firms, and in particular local and central government agencies, will insist that their suppliers have obtained ISO 9000 (see box). This ensures that suppliers are operating within a quality framework.

ISO 9000

ISO 9000 is an international standard for quality systems. It is a British standard that is recognised worldwide and companies that are registered can display the BSI symbol. In order to register, companies have to document their business procedures, prepare a quality manual and assess their quality management systems. They are assessed by an independent assessor. After obtaining the award, businesses are visited at regular intervals to ensure compliance. It is necessary that everyone in the organisation follows the processes outlined in the quality manual. Firms who have registered say that this has provided a range of benefits to the business. These include:

- less waste
- cost savings
- fewer mistakes
- increased efficiency
- improved competitiveness
- increased customer satisfaction
- increased profits.

Why is quality management important?

Quality is an important competitive issue. Where the consumer has choice, quality is vital. For a new business, effective quality management may mean the difference between success and disaster. If the product or service cannot get a good reputation, the business will not last long.

A reputation for good quality brings marketing advantages and a good-quality product will:

- generate a high level of repeat purchase, and therefore a longer product life cycle
- allow brand building and cross-marketing

Table 31.1 Implications of poor product or service quality

Marketing costs	Business costs
Loss of sales	Scrapping of unsuitable goods
Loss of reputation	Reworking of unsatisfactory goods – cost of labour and materials
May have to price-discount	Lower prices for 'seconds'
May impact on other products in range	Handling complaints/warranty claims
Retailers may be unwilling to stock goods	Loss of consumer goodwill and repeat purchase

- allow a price premium (this is often greater than any added costs of quality improvements; in other words, quality adds value – it generates additional profit)
- make products easier to place (retailers are more likely to stock products with a good reputation).

A-grade application

Product recalls

Looking at the Food Standard Agency's website www.food.gov.uk could lead you to think that there are many quality problems with food in the UK. On this site you will find details of products that have been recalled (the customer is asked to return the product) or withdrawn (the product is removed from shelves in stores). In May 2010 Nestlé issued a recall notice for their Nescafé Collections range of coffee. This applied to 100 g jars of their Collections range. The reason given for the recall was that the jars may contain small pieces of glass. Another product, Hovis Hearty Oats Loaf, was recalled in June 2010 because the bread might contain small pieces of glass.

Product recalls are not only expensive in terms of the cost of destroying and replacing the goods, but inevitably they damage the brand.

How can firms detect quality problems?

Ideally quality problems should be detected before they reach the customer. This can be done by:

- inspection of finished goods before sale – this has been the traditional method; it may be all goods or only a sample
- self-inspection of work by operatives – this is being used more as businesses recognise that quality needs to be 'everyone's business'
- statistical analysis within the production process – this can be used to ensure that specifications stay within certain limits. For example, Mars might set a target weight for 100 g bags of Maltesers of between 96 and 104 g (see Figure 31.1). Only if the weight slips outside this range will an alarm indicator be triggered to warn that the specifications are not being met; staff could then stop the production line and readjust the machine to ensure that the correct weight is being given.

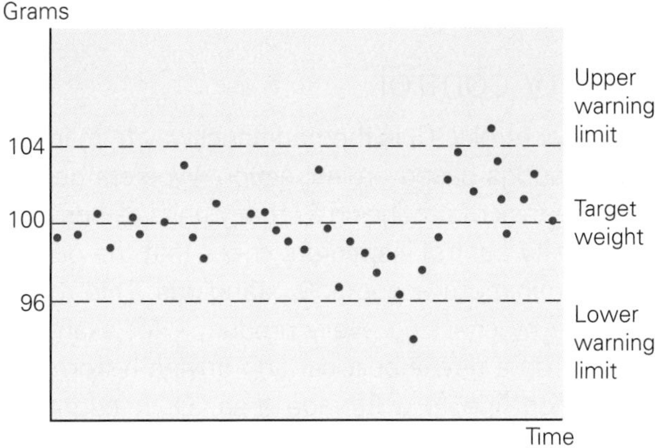

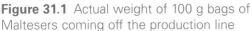

Figure 31.1 Actual weight of 100 g bags of Maltesers coming off the production line

Quality quotes

'Reducing the cost of quality is in fact an opportunity to increase profits without raising sales, buying new equipment, or hiring new people.' *Philip Crosby, American quality guru*

'Quality is remembered long after the price is forgotten.' *Gucci slogan*

'The only job security anybody has in this company comes from quality, productivity and satisfied customers.' *Lee Iacocca, successful boss of Chrysler Motors*

'Good management techniques are enduring. Quality control, for instance, was treated as a fad here, but it's been part of the Japanese business philosophy for decades. That's why they laugh at us.' *Peter Senge, US business author*

'Quality has to be caused, not controlled.' *Philip Crosby*

'Quality is our best assurance of customer allegiance, our strongest defence against foreign competition, and the only path to sustained growth and earnings.' *Jack Welch, General Electric chief*

(Source: Stuart Crainer; *The Ultimate Book of Business Quotations*, Capstone Publishing)

How do businesses manage quality?

This depends on the size of the business. A small new business will be able to inspect every item and ensure that each customer is satisfied. As the business grows, keeping checks on quality needs to be more systematic. In large manufacturing businesses, quality control has traditionally been the responsibility of the production department. Most quality control processes were concentrated in the factory. These were intended to prevent faults leaving the factory. Today, firms are more likely to see quality as having product and service aspects.

There are four stages to quality management that apply to all businesses. These are prevention, detection, correction and improvement.

Prevention

This tries to avoid problems occurring. It requires thought and care at every stage:

- in the initial product design, to 'build in' quality
- in purchasing raw materials and components (i.e. not just trying to buy the cheapest supplies, but caring about quality)
- designing the factory layout to minimise production errors
- ensuring that all staff feel empowered to care about quality; at Toyota car plants, any factory worker with a quality concern can pull an alarm (*jidoka*) cord that stops the whole assembly line; this shows how seriously management takes quality.

Detection

This ensures that quality problems are spotted before they reach the customer. This has been the traditional emphasis of quality control. The use of electronic scanning has given firms better tools to detect faults.

Correction

This is not just about correcting faults. It is also about discovering why there is a problem. Once the problem is identified, steps can be taken to ensure it does not recur.

Improvement

Customer expectations of quality are always changing so it is important that businesses seek to improve quality. Therefore, staff need to be encouraged to put forward ways in which their jobs can be done better; the Japanese term *kaizen* (meaning continuous improvement) has become common in British manufacturing.

Programmes for managing quality

As the importance of quality for both marketing and cost control has been recognised, there has been a growth in initiatives to control and improve quality. Techniques for quality control, such as inspection and statistical control, continue. They have been supplemented by other policies aimed at controlling and improving quality. These include total quality management, quality control and quality assurance.

Total quality management

Total quality management (TQM) was introduced by American business guru W Edwards Deming in the early 1980s. He worked with Japanese firms, and his techniques are said to be one of the reasons for the success of Japanese businesses. TQM is not a management tool: it is a philosophy. It is a way of looking at quality issues. It requires commitment from the whole organisation, not just the quality control department. The business considers quality in every part of the business process – from design right through to sales. TQM is about building-in rather than inspecting-out. It should draw closely on the Japanese experience with *kaizen*, set out below.

Quality control

Quality control (QC) is the traditional way to manage quality and is based on inspection. Workers get on with the task of producing as many units as possible and quality control inspectors check that the output meets minimum acceptable standards. This might be done by checking every product – for example, starting up a newly built car and driving it from the production line to a storage area. Or it might be done by checking every 200th KitKat coming off the end of the factory's production line. If one KitKat is faulty, inspectors will check others from the same batch and, if concerned, may scrap the whole batch. The problem with this system is that faulty products can slip through, and it stops staff from producing the best quality: all they need focus on is 'good enough' to pass the checks. TQM is therefore a superior approach.

Quality assurance

Quality assurance (QA) is a system that assures customers that detailed systems are in place to govern quality at every stage in production. It would start with the quality-checking process for newly arrived raw materials and components. This includes schemes such as ISO 9000. Companies have to have in place a documented quality assurance system. This should be an effective quality system that operates throughout the company and involves suppliers and subcontractors. The main criticism of QA is that it is a paper-based system and therefore encourages staff to tick boxes rather than care about quality.

Table 31.2 Pros and cons of TQM, QC and QA

	TQM	QC	QA
Pros	Should become deeply rooted into the company culture (e.g. product safety at a producer of baby car seats) Once all staff think about quality, it should show through from design to manufacture and after-sales service (e.g. at Lexus or BMW)	Can be used to guarantee that no defective item will leave the factory Requires little staff training, therefore suits a business with unskilled or temporary staff (as ordinary workers needn't worry about quality)	Makes sure the company has a quality system for every stage in the production process Customers like the reassurance provided by a badge such as 'ISO 9000'; they believe they will get a higher-quality service and may therefore be willing to pay more
Cons	Especially at first, staff sceptical of management initiatives may treat TQM as 'hot air'; it lacks the clear, concrete programme of QC or QA To get TQM into the culture of a business may be expensive, as it would require extensive training among all staff (e.g. all British Airways staff flying economy from Heathrow to New York)	Leaving quality for the inspectors to sort out may mean poor quality is built in to the product (e.g. clothes with seams that soon unpick) QC can be trusted when 100% of output is tested, but not when it is based on sampling; Ford used to test just 1 in 7 of its new cars, which led to quality problems	QA does not promise a high-quality product, only a high-quality, reliable process; this process may churn out OK products reliably QA may encourage complacency; it suggests quality has been sorted, whereas rising customer requirements mean quality should keep moving ahead

Other quality initiatives

Continuous improvement (*kaizen*)

This is a system where the whole organisation is committed to making changes on a continual basis. The Japanese call it *kaizen*. It is an approach to doing business that looks for continual improvement in the quality of products, services, people and processes. In 1991 a book was published in Japan about Toyota, called *40 Years; 20 Million Ideas*. This alerted western business to the amazing ability of the Japanese car companies to get suggestions for improvement from their factory employees.

Six Sigma

A programme developed by America's General Electric Company, which aims to have fewer defective products than 1 per 300,000. To achieve this, staff are trained to become 'Green Belt' or 'Black Belt' quality experts. Although gimmicky, this has been followed widely by other companies.

Quality circles

A quality circle is a group of employees who meet together regularly for the purpose of identifying problems and recommending adjustments to the working processes. This is done to improve the product or process. It is used to address known quality issues such as defective products. It can also be useful for identifying better practices that may improve quality. In addition, it has the advantage of improving staff morale through employee involvement. It takes advantage of the knowledge of operators.

Zero defects

The aim of **zero defects** is to produce goods and services with no faults or problems. This is vital in industries such as passenger aircraft production or the manufacture of surgical equipment.

Benchmarking

Benchmarking is a process of comparing a business with other businesses. Having identified the best, businesses attempt to bring their performance up to the level of the best, by adopting its practices.

Most of these initiatives rely on employee involvement. In addition to quality improvements and cost reductions, most businesses find that the initiatives in themselves deliver benefits. These include better working practices, improved employee motivation, increased focus on tasks and the development of team working.

Is quality expensive or free?

The traditional belief was that high quality was costly: in terms of materials, labour, training and checking systems. Therefore, managements should beware of building too much quality into a product (the term given to this was 'over-engineered'). The alternative approach, put forward by the American writer Philip Crosby, is that 'quality is free'. The latter view suggests that getting things **right first time** can save a huge amount of time and money.

- The time required to make it work – quality initiatives take time. Workers may be away from their jobs while attending training or quality groups.
- Short-term versus long-term viewpoints – there may be a conflict between short-term costs and longer-term results. Shareholders may want returns today, but often quality initiatives require a long-term view. The investment will be a current cost. The benefits, however, may take some time to show. They may also be difficult to measure.

If quality control is to be effective, it must balance the costs against the advantages; 100 per cent quality is possible but it may make the product so expensive that it cannot be sold.

Issues for analysis

When looking at quality issues in an exam question, you should consider the following:

- The importance of quality to the business: this will depend on the type of business, the type of product or the service. It will also depend on the market in which the business is operating.
- Whether the firm has adopted the right approach to quality management: perhaps a firm using quality assurance should switch to TQM.
- Quality issues are often closely interwoven with other parts of the business. The role of the employee in quality control is an important issue. Interlinked with this are the changes in management styles and philosophies that come with many of the quality initiatives.

Remember that quality is not just about manufacturing; it is about the whole experience of contact with the business. A poor call centre could just as easily lose a sale as a faulty product.

Effective quality management – an evaluation

In recent years there has been a change in the emphasis on quality. The quality business has itself grown – the management section of any book shop will reveal several titles dedicated to quality management. The growth of initiatives such as TQM and continuous improvement goes on. The number of worldwide registrations for ISO 9000 increases by more than 25 per cent each year. Not all of these are from British businesses – there has been a rapid rise in overseas registrations. With an increase in the international awareness of quality, British businesses will have to ensure that they continue to be competitive.

This growth in emphasis on quality has undoubtedly brought benefits to business. Increased quality brings rewards in the marketplace. Companies have also found that the initiatives, especially where they are people-based, have brought other advantages: changes in working practices have improved motivation and efficiency and have reduced waste and costs.

This change in emphasis has not been without problems, however. The shift to a focus on the customer and the role of the employee could result in additional costs. Unless this results in increased profits, shareholders may feel that they are losing out. Some businesses have found that changing cultures is not easy and resistance from workers and management has often caused problems.

Key terms 

Benchmarking: comparing a firm's performance with best practice in the industry.

Competitiveness: the ability of a firm to beat its competitors (e.g. Galaxy is a highly competitive brand in the chocolate market).

Right first time: avoiding mistakes and therefore achieving high quality with no wastage of time or materials.

Trade-off: accepting less of one thing to achieve more of another (e.g. slightly lower quality in exchange for cheapness).

Zero defects: eliminating quality defects by getting things right first time.

A Revision questions *(35 marks; 35 minutes)*

1 State two reasons why quality management is important. (2)

2 How important is quality to the consumer? (3)

3 Suggest two criteria customers might use to judge quality at:
   a) a budget-priced hotel chain (2)
   b) a Tesco supermarket (2)
   c) a McDonald's. (2)

4 Why has there been an increase in awareness of the importance of improving the quality of products? (3)

5 Give two marketing advantages that come from a quality reputation. (2)

6 What costs are involved if the firm has quality problems? (3)

7 What are the four stages of quality management? (4)

8 What is total quality management? (4)

9 Outline two benefits of adopting quality circles to a clothing chain such as Topshop. (4)

10 Outline two additional costs that might be incurred in order to improve quality. (4)

B1 Revision exercises

Data response

Trac Parts

Trac Parts is a major manufacturer of parts for farm and construction machinery. It has been operating from a new centralised warehouse for four years. This year the company applied for ISO 9000 and gained accreditation. The main reason for applying was that several large customers had indicated that they would only deal with ISO 9000 companies when negotiating new contracts. The warehouse manager has been pleasantly surprised by the operational performance figures since accreditation:

- orders completed on time up from 75 to 84 per cent
- errors in completing orders reduced by 40 per cent
- average time from order receipt to dispatch reduced by two days.

Questions *(25 marks; 30 minutes)*

1 What is ISO 9000? (3)

2 Why might a business want to become ISO 9000 approved? (4)

3 Examine the benefits to Trac Parts of the performance improvements identified in the text. (6)

4 In order to be accepted by ISO 9000, the firm had to introduce procedures to ensure that levels of quality are maintained. Using the four stages of quality control (prevention, detection, correction and improvement), examine the actions it might have taken. (12)

B2 Case study

Manufacturing defects – producer comparisons: PcNow

PcNow is a small computer manufacturer based in the East Midlands. It tailor-makes computers and accessories based on customers' own specifications. Although business grew steadily initially, it is now worried about falling sales. It believes it is losing sales to Japanese and American companies that have set up manufacturing facilities in Europe, as well as to other European and UK-based firms. An industry survey has produced data on industry levels of production defects. It has added its own figures and produced the chart shown in Figure 31.2.

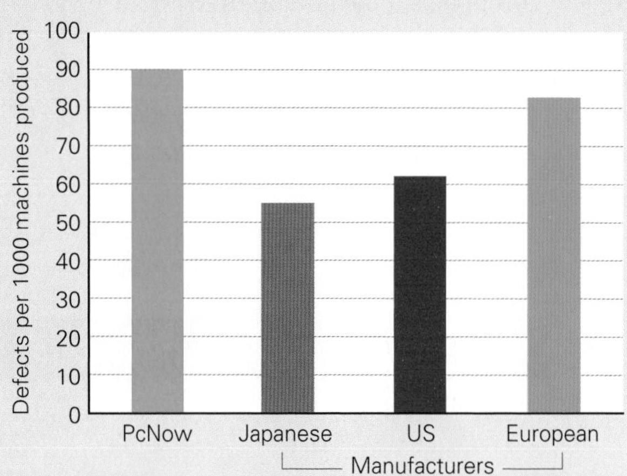

Figure 31.2 Manufacturing defects – producer comparisons

The firm realises that survival depends upon addressing the quality problems. It has decided to employ a quality manager, Cara Davenport, to address the issues. Her first suggestion is to get together workers from each department to discuss the problems and issues. Following a survey of the factory, she has also suggested that the layout of the production facilities should be changed. This will be an expensive exercise, and management is reluctant to make the changes as they will require production to stop for a week and there will need to be investment in new equipment. The firm's weak cash flow position makes it hard for the owners to accept new capital spending. The other area that Cara has identified is a problem with one particular component. She has suggested that a new supplier should be found, or that she should work with the existing supplier to improve the quality of the component.

Questions *(40 marks; 45 minutes)*

1 a) What does the chart show? (2)

b) What further data would help to make the bar chart more useful? (4)

2 From the case study, identify two reasons for the quality problems experienced by PcNow. (2)

3 What are the marketing implications for PcNow of the data in the bar chart? (8)

4 Outline the advantages PcNow might get from the discussion group formed to discuss the quality problems. (8)

5 How might Cara convince the firm's management to change the layout of the production facilities? (6)

6 Once these changes have been made, the firm needs to ensure that quality is maintained and improved. Discuss the implications for the firm of implementing a total quality management initiative. (10)

C Essay questions (40 marks each)

1 'Quality control is about building quality in, not inspecting it out.' Discuss.

2 Consider whether quality management is solely a matter for the production department.

3 To what extent is quality a major competitive issue in service businesses?

32 Working with suppliers

Definition

Suppliers are other businesses that provide products or services to a firm. The relationship with suppliers is likely to have a critical impact on a firm. Operational success demands high-quality supplies delivered on time in the right quantities.

Key factors to consider when choosing suppliers

Cost

Cheaper supplies mean higher profit margins. The incentive to find a cheap supplier is huge for any firm; therefore, the price charged by a supplier will be a key factor in the relationship between a firm and its suppliers. Large businesses may be able to almost dictate prices to their suppliers. This is because the quantities they purchase may account for the whole output of the supplier, giving a huge amount of power to the buyer. However, for small businesses with limited purchasing power, the supplier may have the upper hand.

As a result of this, small businesses may be advised to shop around, looking for the cheapest supplier they can find. However, this may not always be the most sensible course of action – there are other important factors to consider when choosing suppliers.

Quality

There is frequently a trade-off between the price charged by suppliers and the quality of their offering. The cheapest supplier may be one with a poor reputation for the quality of its products or service. Choosing to use a supplier with quality problems is likely to lead to operational problems. Poor-quality supplies can lead to machinery breakdowns, along with poor-quality output. This can lead to problems with customer complaints, guarantee claims or reputation. Choosing the cheapest supplier may sow the seeds of long-term problems for a business.

Reliability

Supplies at the right price and of a high quality may be of little use if they arrive late. It is important that a supplier can offer reliability to a business. Failure to deliver on time can stop a manufacturing process or leave shop shelves empty. Suppliers' reliability will be easy to assess once a business has started working with them. However, a new business or a business sourcing new supplies may need to rely on word-of-mouth reputation to inform its choice. Larger firms may be able to impose certain penalties on suppliers who prove unreliable but, again, small businesses will be in a weaker position if trying to threaten a supplier.

Frequency

Depending on the type of business and the production system it uses, frequent deliveries may be needed from suppliers. Firms selling fresh produce will need to ensure that they are using suppliers that can supply and deliver frequently – probably a new batch each day. Similarly, a firm that uses a **just-in-time (JIT)** production system will need very frequent deliveries to feed its production system without it having to hold stock (Honda, for example, requires hourly deliveries of parts to its Japanese car factories). For firms such as these, it makes sense to look for a local supplier – they are far more likely to be willing to deliver with a greater level of frequency.

Flexibility

In a similar way to ensuring the right frequency of supplies, many firms will need to find a supplier with the capacity to cope with widely varying orders. Businesses selling products with erratic demand patterns, caused by changes in the weather or fashion, will need to find themselves suppliers that can meet their ever-changing needs. Probably the most common scenario is to ensure that suppliers have the spare capacity available to cope with sudden rush orders. In addition, some firms will need to find suppliers that can supply at the right time – perhaps night-time deliveries are needed for firms in congested town centres, or in areas where lorries are banned during the day. A key to supplier flexibility is a short **lead time** (i.e. there should not be too long a period between placing an order and receiving a delivery).

Figure 32.1 Flexible suppliers may be able to deliver at night

Payment terms

Most business transactions are on credit, not for cash. If Tesco wants to order 2,000 cases of Heinz Beans, the bill is unlikely to be paid until 30 or more days after the goods have been delivered. This gives time for the goods to be sold, providing the cash to make it easy to pay the bill. Small business start-ups will struggle to get the same terms. A newly opened corner shop will not be given credit by Heinz. The supplier will want to be paid in cash until the new business has shown that it can survive and pay its bills. So a new small firm has to pay up front, placing extra strain on its cash flow. This should not be a problem as long as it has been anticipated (i.e. built in to its start-up cash flow forecast).

A-grade application

In the driver's seat

Each spring for the past eight years, key ('Tier 1') suppliers to the six major North American car producers have shared with us their experiences of working with Chrysler, Ford, General Motors (GM), Honda, Nissan and Toyota.

This year, the previous pattern of working relationships has changed significantly. For the first time in the study's eight-year history, a US carmaker – Ford – was ranked in the top three, along with, but well behind, Honda and Toyota, who held their respective first and second places. While GM continues in the 'very poor/poor' range, its supplier relations are improving rapidly. Notwithstanding Nissan's slight improvement last year, Honda, Toyota, and Nissan continue their slow four-year downward trend of steadily worsening supplier relations.

The real question behind the annual study and, for that matter, for any company interested in achieving strong supplier relations is – why should they care? The answer is simple. For many years, the study has shown that automakers with the best rankings, specifically Toyota and Honda, receive the greatest benefit from their suppliers in a variety of areas including lower costs, higher quality, increased price reduction concessions, and supplier innovation.

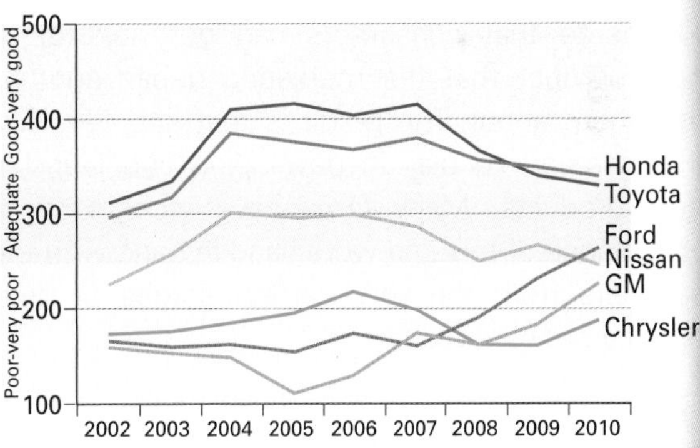

Figure 32.2 OEM Supplier working relations

(Source: www.supplymanagement.com 24 June 2010. John W Henke Jr is president of Planning Perspectives, a consultancy specialising in SRM. He is also professor of marketing at Oakland University)

The role of suppliers in improving performance

Some businesses enjoy telling their shareholders how tough they are with their suppliers – after all, the lower the supply cost, the higher the profit. Many firms encourage competition between rival suppliers by threatening to go elsewhere if the terms are not what they want. This approach has been important in building the hugely profitable business of many high-street stores, which find cheap goods by negotiating toughly in Cambodia, China or the Philippines.

An alternative approach was followed in the past by Marks & Spencer, and today by car firms such as Toyota and Honda. These companies build long-term relationships with their suppliers, with the aim of working with, rather than against, them. There are many potential benefits from this approach, as discussed below.

Working together on new product development

Developing new products involves many considerations. One of these will be how the product is to be manufactured, what materials will be used and what properties will be needed. Meanwhile, launching a new product will require careful production planning to ensure that consumers can get hold of the new product that the marketing department has told them about. The result is that suppliers have a major part to play in developing and launching new products. Many firms have recognised the importance of this and work hand in hand with their suppliers from the very earliest stages of developing a new product.

Flexibility

A strong relationship with a supplier should mean it is willing to make special deliveries if a business is running low on stock. A strong relationship may also allow some flexibility on payment. A toy shop may be struggling for cash in the months leading up to Christmas, so a trusting supplier may accept a delay in payment. This could be the lifeline required for the small firm. However, no supplier is likely to be able to sustain this generosity for a long period.

Sharing information to improve the efficiency of the supply chain

Large businesses with sophisticated IT systems have direct links between their cash tills and their suppliers. Cadbury knows at any hour of the day how many Creme Eggs are selling at Tesco. This enables Cadbury to plan its production levels (e.g. pushing up output if sales are proving better than expected). The supermarket can even allow Cadbury to make the decisions on how much stock to produce and deliver on the basis of the information it is receiving.

Small grocers use the same laser scanning software at their tills, but it would be rare for a small business to have a direct electronic link with a supplier. This means the shopkeeper has to make the purchasing decisions, or go to a wholesaler to buy the goods, which is much less efficient than the electronic systems of the big companies.

A-grade application

Why do it yourself if suppliers can help?

Wickes is a DIY retailer that has worked hard to develop closer relations with its suppliers. The company invested in improved IT systems to enable better transfer of information between retail outlets and suppliers. Store-level sales and stock data are sent daily to suppliers to allow them to improve their production planning, ensuring the right amount is available to be delivered to each Wickes store. The system has also enhanced the role played by suppliers in the planning and development of new own-brand products for the stores. In the future, the group is hoping to move towards a system where store stock levels are actually monitored and managed by the suppliers themselves.

Issues for analysis

- Although firms are likely to try to build a long-term relationship with their suppliers, there will be times when a business will consider changing supplier. This is an issue that has a number of aspects that need consideration, in addition to the standard factors covered earlier. There will be an existing relationship with the current supplier and this may bring advantages that would not be available with a brand new supplier. Meanwhile, the cliché that 'the grass is always greener on the other side' may be a factor in the motive for changing.
- When analysing any choice between suppliers, be sure to consider the consequences of the differences between them. Failure to consider consequences will lose analysis marks. Think through the consequences in your answers with lines of argument such as 'poor-quality materials may lead to poor-quality output, which could lead to customer disappointment, which will hit reputation, probably damaging future sales'.

Working with suppliers – an evaluation

Evaluative themes relating to suppliers will centre on judgements that firms make as to which supplier to choose. This unit has covered a range of factors that need to be considered, but effective evaluation will, as always, come from a willingness to appreciate which factors are most important for the particular business being considered. A retailer that sells high volumes of cheap products at low prices may be right to compromise on quality to use the cheapest suppliers. The reverse would be the case for a firm with a luxury image or targeting socially conscious consumers. Take some time before putting pen to paper to work out which factors will be most important for the firm mentioned in the question.

Another judgement that should improve your answers is who has the most power in the relationship between company and supplier. Larger firms tend to have more power – indeed there are concerns over the way Britain's huge supermarket chains treat small farmers. However, size may not be the only factor to consider. A supplier with a patent on a particular component will need to be dealt with even if it fails to prove 100 per cent reliable. Evaluation will shine through if a candidate judges effectively where power lies in the specific business relationship featured in an exam question.

Key terms

Just-in-time (JIT): ordering supplies so that they arrive 'just in time' (i.e. just when they are needed); this means operating without reserves of materials or components held 'just in case' they are needed.

Lead time: the time the supplier takes between receiving an order and delivering the goods.

A Revision questions (30 marks; 30 minutes)

1 Explain why the cheapest supplier may not be the best choice. (4)

2 Identify two businesses for which daily deliveries may be absolutely crucial. (2)

3 Briefly explain two problems that may arise when a firm uses a supplier with poor levels of quality. (4)

4 Describe why attractive credit terms from a supplier will be particularly useful for a new business. (4)

5 Outline two reasons why a firm might choose to change its supplier of an existing component. (4)

6 Examine one benefit a mobile phone shop might receive from encouraging several suppliers to continually compete with each other for every month's order of components. (4)

7 What benefits might the mobile phone shop miss out on by not building a long-term relationship with its suppliers? (4)

8 Describe how a car manufacturer such as Volkswagen might benefit from including its component suppliers in the development process when designing a new car. (4)

Revision exercises

Data response

Supplier choice

KMH Ltd is a small manufacturer of children's toys. Having developed a brand new child's doll, it is considering which supplier to use for the plastic used in moulding the doll (see table). Having started up only 12 months ago, the firm has done well and is eagerly anticipating the Christmas rush that will begin soon. The management hopes that the new doll will be a best-seller this Christmas.

Supplier	A	B	C
Price per unit (£s)	3.20	3.50	3.65
Reject rate (per 000 products delivered)	28	18	5
Credit terms (days)	0	60	30
Lead time (days)	7	1	4

Questions *(20 marks; 20 minutes)*

1 Which supplier offers the best:
   a) quality
   b) lead time
   c) credit terms? (3)

2 Explain why lead time is important. (5)

3 Which supplier should the firm choose, and why? (12)

Data response

Crepe Heaven

Carla Turner set up Crepe Heaven in early 2010. As the only creperie in her local area, she attracted some attention with the launch of her small café specialising in French pancakes. Business was more brisk than she had expected and she often found herself popping out to the local supermarket to buy extra ingredients halfway through the day. The supermarket was more expensive than her catering suppliers, but Carla found it hard to predict sales in the early months of the business. Her stock of eggs, milk and fruit for fillings had a very limited life and the last thing

Having been trading successfully for six months, Carla had an encouraging letter from the catering supplier she had been using, telling her that it was now willing to make an afternoon delivery if she needed extra supplies. This lowered her running costs – just what was needed as the interest payments on her bank loan were now biting hard into her cash flow. She also realised that she would need a second crepe-making machine if she was to make sure that waiting times during busy periods were kept to a minimum. She contacted the French supplier the model she wanted. Furthermore she would have to pay cash on delivery – something she could ill afford.

Shopping around on the internet, she found a supplier in America who could deliver in a week. This was great news as she knew that some customers took one look at her peak-period queues and headed off to other cafés in the area. She was also grateful that the supplier was willing to accept a small deposit on order followed by 60 days' interest-free credit. This seemed perfect and she placed her order immediately.

The delivery went smoothly, though she had some trouble installing the new machine as it was rather different to her existing one. Worse was to come some months later, as the new machine started smoking when in use for more than a couple of hours. The American supplier was unhelpful, insisting that the fault must have been due to Carla failing to install the machine properly. The next few months were tough for Carla, as she struggled to get her money back from the US supplier. Fortunately, the shop remained popular and within six months she replaced the second machine with one from her original supplier.

Questions *(30 marks; 30 minutes)*

1 Explain why Carla tended to under-order ingredient supplies in the early days of the business. (5)

2 Explain which two factors may have been most important to Carla when originally choosing her ingredient supplier. (6)

3 Analyse the benefits to Carla of choosing the American supplier for her second crepe machine. (8)

4 To what extent does the case study support the view that building a long-term relationship with a supplier is a better approach than shopping around for 'the best deal'? (11)

33 Capacity utilisation

Definition

Capacity utilisation is the proportion of maximum possible output that is currently being used. A football stadium is at full capacity when all the seats are filled. A company producing 1,500 units a week when the factory is capable of 2,000 units has a capacity utilisation of 75 per cent.

Operational targets

To run a successful operation such as Primark requires brilliant organisation and clear targets. The role of the targets is to help all staff to aim to achieve the same goal. The target at a hotdog stand outside a concert venue is to serve as many people as possible as quickly as possible, before and after the show. To achieve this, the stallholder will plan ahead, cooking the sausages in advance and getting the onions ready. The most efficient stallholder will almost always make more money than the best cook. It is all down to clear targets and clear objectives.

There are three main targets focused on by operations managers:

1. Quality targets (e.g. to have no more than 1 in 100 customers demand a refund).
2. Capacity utilisation targets (e.g. that the factory should be working at 85–95 per cent of its maximum possible capacity).
3. Unit costs (e.g. keeping the average cost per unit below £1.99, in order to keep the selling price below £2.99).

How is capacity utilisation measured?

Capacity utilisation is measured using the formula:

$$\frac{\text{current output}}{\text{maximum possible output}} \times 100$$

What does capacity depend upon? The amount a firm can make is determined by the quantity of buildings, machinery and labour it has available. Maximum capacity is achieved when the firm is making full use of all the buildings, machinery and labour available. The firm is said to be working at full capacity, or 100 per cent capacity utilisation.

For a service business, the same logic applies, though it is much harder to identify a precise figure. This is because it may take a different time to serve each customer. In a shop or a bank branch, demand may exceed capacity at certain times of the day, in which case queues will form. At other times the staff may have little to do. A service business wishing to stay cost-competitive will measure demand at different times of the day and then schedule the staffing level to match the capacity utilisation.

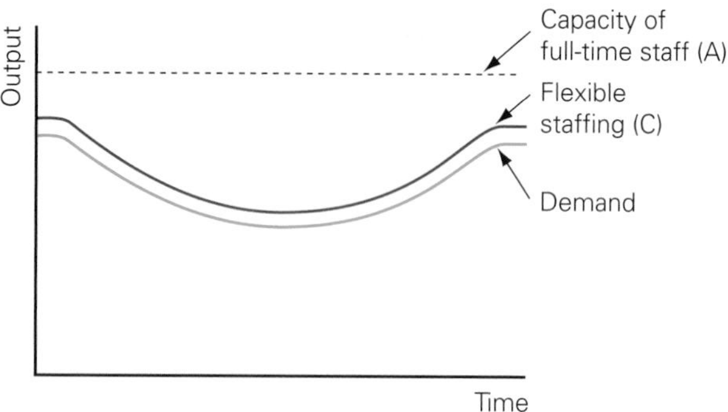

Figure 33.1 How flexible staffing (C) can reduce wastage implied by having under-used full-time staff (A)

Many service businesses cope with fluctuating demand by employing temporary or part-time staff.

These employees provide a far greater degree of flexibility to employers. Part-time hours can be increased, or extra temporary staff can be employed to increase capacity easily. If demand falls, temporary staff can be laid off without redundancy payments, or part-time staff can have their hours reduced, thus reducing capacity easily and cheaply. Many businesses like this flexibility as it limits wastage on staff costs. However, the situation may not be as appealing for employees, who have fewer rights than their full-time salaried predecessors. Figure 33.1 shows how flexible staffing (C) can reduce the wastage implied by having under-used full-time staff (A).

Fixed costs and capacity

It is vital to understand clearly the relationship between fixed costs and capacity utilisation. Fixed costs are fixed in relation to output. This means that whether capacity utilisation is 50 per cent or 100 per cent, fixed costs will not change. The implication of this is clear: if a football club invests in a huge, expensive playing staff (whose salaries are a fixed cost), but matches are played to a half-empty stadium, the fixed costs will become a huge burden. This is because the very fact that fixed costs do not change *in total* as output changes means that they do change *per unit* of output/demand. A half-empty stadium means that the fixed costs per unit are double the level at maximum capacity (see Table 33.1).

When the stadium capacity utilisation is at 50 per cent, £10 of the ticket price is needed for the players' wages alone. The many other fixed and variable costs of running a football club would be on top of this, of course.

The reason why capacity utilisation is so important is that it has an inverse (opposite) effect upon fixed costs per unit. In other words, when utilisation is high, fixed costs are spread over many units. This cuts the cost per unit, which enables the producer either to cut prices to boost demand further, or to enjoy large profit margins. If utilisation is low, fixed costs per unit become punishingly high. In March 2010 an African newspaper reported that manufacturers in Nigeria were operating at only 27 per cent of capacity, largely due to electricity shortages. This would make fixed costs per unit almost four times higher than necessary – an almost impossible situation.

The ideal level of capacity utilisation, therefore, is at or near 100 per cent. This spreads fixed costs as thinly as possible, boosting profit margins. There are two key concerns about operating at maximum capacity for long, however. These are:

1 The risk that if demand rises further, you will have to turn it away, enabling your competitors to benefit.
2 The risk that you will struggle to service the machinery and train/retrain staff; this may prove costly in the long term, and will increase the chances of production breakdowns in the short term.

The production ideal, therefore, is a capacity utilisation of around 90 per cent.

A-grade application

Gordon Ramsay: footballer, chef, TV personality ... and business guru?

In his TV series *Ramsay's Kitchen Nightmares*, the renowned chef spent a lot of time swearing and criticising chefs for the way they cooked. The series placed Gordon at a failing restaurant for a week. His task was to wave a magic wand and turn it into a profitable business. In almost every episode of the series, Ramsay identified each restaurant's failure to use anything near its full capacity. Commonly, he suggested the introduction of a simple lunchtime menu to boost trade during the day, in addition to speeding up service in the evenings to ensure that every table would see at least two sittings in the main evening session. Ramsay's advice, delivered in his own inimitable way, was simply a call to push capacity utilisation higher in order to spread each restaurant's fixed costs over more units of output (customers). The advice usually worked.

Table 33.1 Fixed costs and capacity

	Full stadium	Half-empty stadium
	50,000 fans	25,000 fans
Weekly salary bill (fixed costs)	£250,000	£250,000
Salary fixed cost per fan	£5	£10
	(£250,000 ÷ 50,000)	(£250,000 ÷ 25,000)

How to work towards full capacity

If a firm's capacity utilisation is an unsatisfactory 45 per cent, how could it be increased to a more acceptable level of around 90 per cent? There are two possible approaches, as discussed below.

Increase demand

Demand for existing products could be boosted by extra promotional spending, price cutting or, more fundamentally, devising a new strategy to reposition the products into growth sectors. If supermarket own-label products are flourishing, perhaps offer to produce under the Tesco or Sainsbury's banner. If doubling of sales is needed, it is unlikely that existing products will provide the whole answer. The other approach is to launch new products. This could be highly effective, but implies long-term planning and investment.

Cut capacity

If your current factory and labour force is capable of producing 10,000 units a week, but there is demand for only 4,500, there will be a great temptation to cut capacity to 5,000. This might be done by cutting out the night shift (i.e. making those workers redundant). This would avoid the disruption and inflexibility caused by the alternative, which is to move to smaller premises. Moving will enable all fixed costs to be cut (rent, rates, salaries, and so on), but may look silly if, six months later, demand has recovered to 6,000 units when your new factory capacity is only 5,000.

A-grade application

Odeon: filling seats with anyone it can

Odeon is acutely aware of the dangers of having capacity empty during quiet times. In an attempt to increase capacity utilisation during the day and on quieter evenings, Odeon has introduced a number of specialised film showings, catering for groups who are more likely to visit the cinema during 'quiet periods':

- Odeon kids – Saturday and Sunday mornings and every day during school holidays.
- Senior screen – mid-morning showings of traditional and modern classics for 'mature guests', with free tea and coffee.
- Odeon Newbies – for parents with babies, mid-morning showings with volume quieter than usual and lights higher than usual, to try to create a calming environment for babies and parents.
- Director's Chair – showing foreign-language, independent and art-house films for serious film buffs, one quiet evening per week.

Figure 33.2 Odeon Newbies

Selecting the best option

A key factor in deciding whether to cut capacity or boost demand is the underlying cause of the low utilisation. It may be the result of a known temporary demand shortfall, such as a seasonal low point in the toy business. Or it may be due to an economic recession, which (on past experience) may hit demand for around 18–24 months. Either way, it might prove a mistake in the long run to cut capacity. Nevertheless, if a firm faces huge short-term losses from its excess fixed costs, it may have to forget the future and concentrate on short-term survival.

Why and how to change capacity

Firms may find themselves with **excess capacity** if demand for their products slows down. Unless the reduction in demand is just a short-term glitch, a firm will seek to find ways to reduce its maximum capacity. This process is commonly called **rationalisation** – it means reorganising in order to boost efficiency. The three main elements of rationalising are as follows.

1 Closing down and selling off a factory or part of a factory if the space will not be needed in the foreseeable future. Alternatively, the firm may decide to lease out factory space to other companies on a short-term basis. This will enable it to get the extra space back if demand improves.

2 Machinery can be sold off second-hand or for scrap. A more flexible solution is to rent machinery rather than buy it outright in the first place. This would enable the firm to return machinery in times when capacity needs to be reduced.

3 Redundancy is the obvious answer for a firm with too large a workforce. As this can prove expensive, firms may **redeploy** their employees to other jobs. This may be difficult for the employee, who feels pushed towards a job he or she had never wanted. Many firms with excess labour will cut down the length of time worked by employees, perhaps by shortening shifts.

Dealing with non-standard orders

Firms organise their operations around the amount they expect to sell in coming months. For a brand such as Marmite, which has sold quite steadily for more than 100 years, the factory can be set up to mass produce Marmite around the clock. Sales of the brand are not especially seasonal, and change little year on year. So an automated production line can be set up, requiring a minimum of labour and therefore minimal costs.

A problem arises, though, when a non-standard order arrives. Perhaps China, not known for its Marmite eating, is influenced by a TV programme into deciding that it loves, rather than hates, the taste. Chinese shops suddenly put through a series of huge orders to the UK Marmite factory. How can it cope if it is already being run at a high capacity utilisation?

The answer may lie in subcontracting. In other words, the main Marmite factory may have a permanent arrangement with a food-processing factory that it will supply Marmite, when ordered, within an agreed lead time. So, the extra order can be accepted, the product delivered within, perhaps, two weeks and the customer will be happy. The subcontracted production will have to be checked extra carefully for quality, but that is not difficult. Marmite itself will probably make less profit from subcontracted production than when using its own factory, yet it will still work out far better than permanently running an under-utilised factory just in case an extra order comes along.

Issues for analysis

When developing an argument in answer to a case study or essay question, the following lines of analysis should be considered.

- The time frame of the question: is spare capacity caused by a short-term fall in demand or is there a longer-term downward trend? Only if the demand decline is a long-term trend should capacity be cut. It must be remembered, though, that it is always hard to be sure of these things. In the early 1990s, falling attendance at football matches meant that when clubs such as Manchester United and Newcastle rebuilt their stadiums, they cut the crowd capacity. Looking back, with Arsenal playing in the new Emirates stadium and Liverpool's new, bigger Anfield about to be built, it is easy to say they were wrong. At the time, they made what seemed the right decision. So consider the timescale, but be careful of sounding too definite about the 'right' solution.
- The link between capacity utilisation, fixed costs per unit and profitability: if dealing with a question about how to improve profitability, increasing capacity utilisation could well be a valid solution. If profits are poor, be sure to ask what capacity utilisation is at present.
- Modern production theory praises systems such as just-in-time, **flexible specialisation** and lean production: successful management of all three of these approaches is likely to mean capacity utilisation that is well below 100 per cent. This is because all these approaches require flexible responses to customer requirements/orders. In turn, this requires spare capacity. Can lean production yield enough other benefits to compensate for the poor capacity utilisation?

Capacity utilisation – an evaluation

Most firms will aim to operate close to full capacity, but probably not at 100 per cent. A small amount of spare capacity is accepted as necessary, bringing a certain degree of flexibility in case of need. In this way, sudden surges of demand can be coped with in the short run by increasing output, or **downtime** can be used for maintenance. Spare capacity can be a good thing, particularly in small doses.

Firms operating close to full capacity are those that may be considering investing in new premises or machinery. Building new factories takes time, as well as huge quantities of money. Can the firm afford to wait 18 months for its capacity to be expanded? Perhaps the firm would be better served subcontracting certain areas of its work to other companies, thus freeing capacity.

Capacity utilisation also raises the difficult issue of cutting capacity by rationalisation and, often, redundancy. This incorporates many issues of human resource management, motivation and social responsibility. There are fewer more important tests of the skills and far-sightedness of senior managers.

When tackling case studies, it is important that you take a step back from any that deal with such a situation, to consider the cause and the effect. Is excess capacity the problem or an indicator of another problem, such as declining market share? By showing the broader picture in this way you can also show the skill of evaluation.

Key terms

Downtime: any period when machinery is not being used in production; some downtime is necessary for maintenance, but too much may suggest incompetence.

Excess capacity: when there is more capacity than justified by current demand (i.e. utilisation is low).

Flexible specialisation: a production system based upon batches of goods aimed at many market niches, instead of mass production/mass market.

Rationalisation: reorganising in order to increase efficiency. This often implies cutting capacity to increase the percentage utilisation.

Redeploy: to allocate a member of staff to a new job role, probably because their old job is now redundant.

Revision questions (30 marks; 30 minutes)

1 What is meant by the phrase '100 per cent capacity utilisation'? (3)

2 At what level of capacity utilisation will fixed costs per unit be lowest for any firm? Briefly explain your answer. (4)

3 What formula is used to calculate the capacity utilisation of a firm? (2)

4 How can a firm increase its capacity utilisation without increasing output? (3)

5 If a firm is currently selling 11,000 units per month and this represents a capacity utilisation of 55 per cent, what is its maximum capacity? (4)

6 Use the information in the table below to calculate profit per week at 50, 75 and 100 per cent capacity utilisation. (9)

7 Briefly explain the dangers of operating at 100 per cent capacity utilisation for any extended period of time. (5)

Maximum capacity	800 units per week
Variable cost per unit	£1,800
Total fixed costs per week	£1.5 million
Selling price	£4,300

Revision exercises

Data response

R Sivyer & Co was founded 50 years ago. It has a successful history of manufacturing high-quality bicycle chains, which are supplied direct to retailers. In recent years, orders from retail customers have fallen, meaning that the firm is now manufacturing and selling only 12,000 chains per month.

The following cost information has been made available:

Materials cost per unit	80p
Shop floor worker's salary	£10,000 pa
Salary paid to other staff	£12,000 pa
Manager's salary	£32,000 pa
Maximum capacity	20,000 units per month
General overheads	£40,000 per month
Current selling price	£5.80
Number of managers currently employed	3
Number of shop floor staff currently employed	10
Number of other staff currently employed	4

The finance manager has called the other two managers to a meeting to discuss the firm's future. She puts forward two alternative courses of action:

1 Make four shop floor and two other staff redundant, thus cutting the firm's fixed costs, and reducing maximum capacity to 12,000 units per month.

2 Sign a contract to supply a large bicycle manufacturer with a fixed quantity of 8,000 chains per

month at £5.80 each for the next four years; breaking the contract will lead to heavy financial penalties.

Questions (30 marks; 35 minutes)

1 What is the firm's current monthly profit? (5)

2 Calculate the monthly profit that would result from each of the two options. (10)

3 Explain the advantages and disadvantages of each option. (10)

4 State which of the two options you would choose, and list any other information you would need before making the final decision. (5)

Data response

Out of the red and into success

Steven Carragher had decided to set up a specialist sports goods store after injury cut short his football career. With limited business experience, but plenty of local contacts, he bought a ten-year lease on a large high-street shop with plenty of floor space, along with storage on the two floors above the shop. He felt confident that business would be brisk as there were few specialised sports stores in Cheshire at the time. He blew most of his budget in preparing for the start-up, paying for the lease, a refit, staff training and plenty of stock to fill his stock rooms. With a little left over for a launch marketing campaign, he was optimistic on opening day. The first week was busy, with plenty of people coming in but few actually buying. By the end of the first month's trading, the picture had turned decidedly negative, with revenues failing to cover running costs and the store far from break-even.

Steven's old colleague Robbie knew a little about business and he pointed out that Steven was trying to run a small business in the sort of premises that a major chain store would expect to use. Robbie's solution had two main features:

1 Turn the top floor of the building into a three-bedroom flat that could be rented out to cover 50 per cent of the rent that Steven was paying.

2 Divide the shop in two, renting half the shop space to another retailer to help Steven cover the rent and bills.

When the two met again in 12 months, Steven paid for lunch. With both the flat and smaller shop unit rented out, he was now covering the costs of his shop comfortably. Meanwhile, Steven had set up an online ordering service that was proving to be highly successful.

Questions (25 marks; 30 minutes)

1 Using the concept of capacity utilisation, analyse why Steven's business had initially failed to cover its costs. (6)

2 a) Explain why Robbie's ideas were always likely to improve Steven's profit. (4)

b) What crucial assumptions did Robbie make when offering his advice? (3)

3 Steven had few other options as a result of the length of his lease on the property. Use this case as a starting point to discuss why flexibility is vital in a small business start-up. (12)

Making operational decisions

Definition

Operations management is the engine room of the business that turns plans into delivered products or services. Operational decisions are therefore the key to the success of the business day by day.

Operational targets

The starting point for every operations manager is to obtain a plausible forecast of demand (i.e. how many products will be needed and when). This enables **operational targets** to be set. When the iPhone was launched in America in 2007, Apple ensured that it had stockpiled enough units to meet sales of 300,000 phones in the first day and a half. Often the launch of a new product such as this get bogged down with inadequate supplies and frustrated customers. A well-run organisation will do all it can to avoid this.

Setting targets can be helpful in any business context, as they give staff something to work towards and give the firm something against which to check its actual performance. Achieving these targets is the fundamental indicator of successful operations management. Targets are the key to most operational decisions.

Different firms will have different operational targets, including:

- unit costs
- quality
- capacity utilisation.

A-grade application

Getting the sums right

Before the iPhone was launched in 2007, many financial analysts made forecasts of the likely level of sales. As can be seen from Table 34.1, the variations were extraordinarily wide. This shows that getting operational targets correct is especially difficult when a new product is being launched.

Table 34.1 Apple iPhone: sales forecasts

	Sales to Sept 2007	Sales in year to Sept 2008
American Technology Research	250,000	–
Bear Stearns Ltd	650,000	–
Credit Suisse	1,700,000	12,300,000
Pacific Crest Securities	800,000	4,800,000
Piper Jaffray & Co	1,200,000	8,000,000
UBS AG	950,000	8,100,000
Apple Innovation Blog	1,500,000	10,500,000

Source: analysts' research reports, reported at Bloomberg.com

In fact, Apple later reported that the actual sales volume was 1,120,000 in the period up to the end of September 2007, so Piper Jaffray & Co produced a brilliant short-term forecast. Sales in the year to September 2008 turned out to be 11.6 million phones, so Piper Jaffray proved less impressive for the second part of their forecast.

Unit costs

The cost of one unit of output is a raw measure of the efficiency of a firm's operations. Unit cost is calculated by dividing the total cost of production for a period by the number of units produced, as shown below:

$$\frac{\text{Total cost}}{\text{Total output}} = \text{unit cost}$$

For example:

$$\frac{\text{Total cost for March} = \text{£64,000}}{\text{Total output for March} = \text{32,000 units}} = \text{£2 per unit}$$

Unit costs can be reduced in one of three ways:

1 By cutting variable costs, perhaps by running the business with lower wastage levels.
2 By cutting fixed costs.
3 By increasing sales volumes so that the firm's existing fixed costs are spread over more units of sale.

If a firm can lower its unit costs, it can make a decision between two attractive alternatives:

1 Cut the selling price to boost customer demand; if the product is **highly price elastic**, this would probably be the most attractive choice.
2 Keep the selling price constant, but make a **higher profit margin** on each unit sold; that would be the sensible approach if the product's price elasticity was low.

Such a desirable choice explains why so much management energy is focused on trying to reduce unit costs through increases in efficiency. However, unit costs themselves are not the only operational target that a business will set itself.

Capacity utilisation

Since a high level of capacity utilisation means that fixed costs are spread across more units of output, ensuring that a firm's capacity is nearly fully used all the time is an excellent way of keeping unit costs low. Therefore, many firms will set themselves targets for capacity utilisation. Though operating at 100 per cent capacity utilisation will bring the lowest unit costs, most capacity utilisation targets will be set just below that level. This is to allow for time to carry out routine maintenance, space to accept special orders, or just a slight margin for error in case of breakdowns.

Quality

The race to produce output as quickly as possible and reduce labour costs per unit can lead to mistakes. Setting targets for unit costs and capacity utilisation is risky unless targets for quality levels are also taken seriously. As discussed in Unit 31, poor-quality output has a number of negative consequences. Errors in products will lead to higher unit costs as a result of wasted materials or correcting the faults. This will slow production rates as a result of needing to correct the mistakes.

Matching production to demand

Many factors can cause sales levels to fluctuate, including:

- fashion
- temperature and weather
- marketing activity
- competitors' actions.

Some of these are predictable and others are unpredictable. Sales forecasting can help in production planning, especially for predictable changes in demand. However, the fundamental issue is the same for most businesses: how to organise their operations to cope with varying levels of demand for their products or services.

The issue of matching production to demand considers a firm's ability to make sure that whenever customers want to buy, there is something to supply them with. A factory manufacturing lawnmowers may be an ideal illustration. Sales are likely to follow a monthly pattern, as shown in Figure 34.1. Every spring time there will be a sales peak as people decide to replace their old lawnmowers – unused all winter.

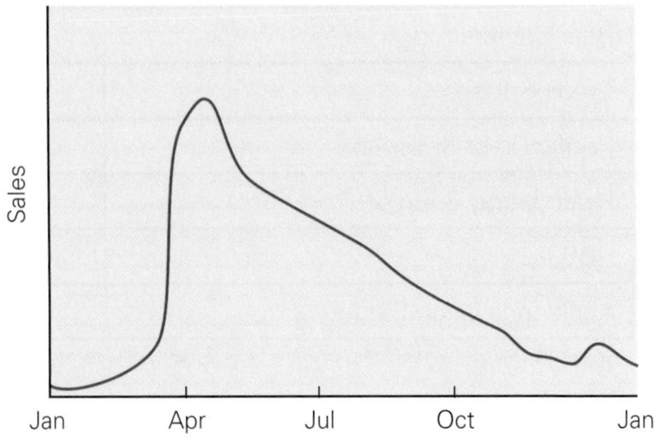

Figure 34.1 Lawnmower sales

The question facing the firm is, how should production be spread through the year? Figure 34.2 offers two alternative extremes: option A is where the firm maintains a constant production level throughout the year; option B shows a scenario where the firm exactly matches monthly production with monthly demand.

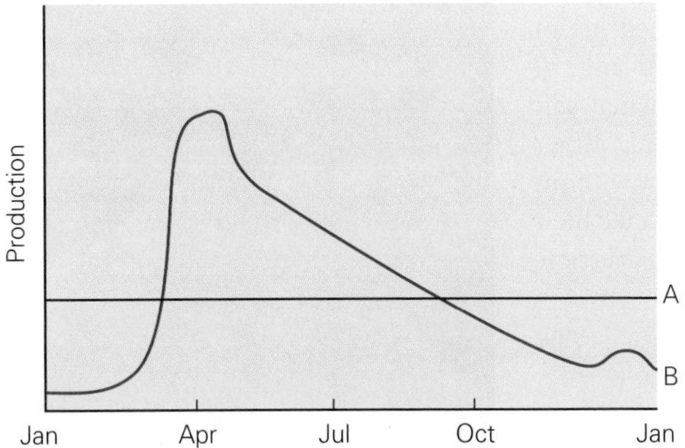

Figure 34.2 Possible production options

There are a number of issues raised by each option (and some possible solutions).

Key issues

Option A is to hold production constant. Surprisingly, this is how Cadbury's produces its Creme Eggs, even though sales only really take place in the lead-up to Easter. This approach offers the easiest solution in terms of planning, since it largely ignores demand fluctuations, and keeps production at a stable level. This has clear benefits: high capacity utilisation and maintaining a skilled and loyal workforce.

However, the cost involved in keeping stock may be huge. It is not just the physical costs of keeping stock, such as space for storage and the people whose job it is to organise the storage facilities – many businesses will find that stock becomes worthless over time. Food manufacturers may be forced to throw out stock that has passed its sell-by date, while fashion-related manufacturers and retailers do not want to find themselves heavily discounting last season's stock in a desperate attempt to empty their stock rooms. Service providers such as hairdressers face an even greater problem in that they cannot keep stock. If the salon is capable of dealing with 50 customers every day, but this demand level occurs only on Friday and Saturday, costs per customer will be unnecessarily high. Stylists are at work, being paid, but cannot generate revenue when there are no customers.

The result is that many firms look towards option B: tailoring staffing and capacity levels to cope with expected demand. To achieve this, firms need to find ways to operate more flexibly; in particular, they need staff to be more flexible. The main ways to achieve this are through:

- overtime
- hiring temporary and part-time staff
- subcontracting.

Overtime

Paying staff extra to work longer hours than their contracts state may be a way of coping with busy periods. Of course, this requires staff that are willing to work overtime. Furthermore, staff generally expect a higher rate of pay if they are working overtime – pushing up labour costs.

Hiring temporary and part-time staff

Temporary and part-time staff give extra flexibility to an employer. Temporary staff can be hired on fixed-term contracts designed to last only as long as the expected busy period. Most tourist attractions keep very few full-time staff, relying instead on an army of summer temps to run their attractions. Part-time staff can be hired with contracts that include flexible working hours, offering employers the chance to call them in during busy periods to work longer shifts. This is a phenomenon common among A-level students working in retail over the Christmas period. Through the use of temporary or part-time staff, a company can reduce its fixed salary costs, thus reducing the break-even point to a level that is sustainable during quiet periods.

However, there are drawbacks. Motivating and communicating with temporary staff and part-timers can be much harder than with a stable workforce of full-timers. Quality and customer service issues may arise that have a damaging effect on a firm's reputation.

Subcontracting

Subcontracting is the term used to describe a situation where one firm is doing the work of another. A company struggling to cope with a rush of demand may subcontract its excess work to another. This depends on a good relationship with another company, and is also reliant on the other company having the capacity to cope with the order. On the other hand, a firm that finds its capacity is under-used may try to win work from other businesses looking to subcontract some of

A-grade application

Britvic staff hit the slopes, not the beach

Britvic is Britain's second largest soft drinks manufacturer, producing brands such as Pepsi, Robinsons and Tango. Their main canning factory, in Rugby, has to cope with large fluctuations in demand caused by the weather. Typically, sales in a warm June will be three times a typical December. Meanwhile, Britvic are constrained by the short shelf-life of many of their products, preventing them from stockpiling in advance of busy periods. In order to boost capacity during hot periods when soft drink sales boom, employees come in to work seven days per week, rather than the usual five. This leads to a 40 per cent increase in capacity without the need to take on and train extra staff. Staff are encouraged to take their holidays during the winter to ensure they are available to work overtime in hot summer periods.

Source: www.britvic.com and adapted from *Operations Management* by Slack, Chambers and Johnston.

Figure 34.3 Demand for Britvic's products rises in hot weather

their work. This practice can be found not just in the manufacturing sector but in the service sector too. An insurance company whose call centres are overwhelmed with work may look to subcontract some of its claims to other call centres. Similarly, busy builders often subcontract some of their work to other building companies.

Other types of operational decision

Rationalisation

Longer-term reductions in demand may require long-term solutions to matching production with demand. Firms which find that sales have fallen due to changes in technology may choose **rationalisation** (i.e. to increase efficiency by permanently reducing overall capacity). This may be done by closing entire branches or factories, or simply shedding staff across the whole firm. In 2009 British Airways underwent a rationalisation programme to cut 3,700 jobs by March 2010. Rationalisation programmes must be handled carefully to minimise damage to the morale of the remaining staff and to minimise bad external publicity. Redundancies are never popular, but voluntary redundancy is a more attractive proposition than compulsory redundancy; however, neither is as pain-free as using **natural wastage** to rationalise.

Stock management

The issues already covered show the importance of managing stocks effectively. Stocks of finished goods waiting to be sold may be seen as a buffer against sudden surges in demand. However, keeping too much stock is a dangerously expensive habit. The balancing of stock levels is one of the major issues facing operations managers. Meanwhile, stock of raw materials and components presents similar problems. A lack of production inputs may force production to grind to a halt, while too much stock may lead to wasted materials or space.

Non-standard orders

Sometimes firms will be approached by customers with special orders at a different price to their regular selling price. A customer with special requirements, such as a different design or a very short delivery date, may offer a price above the norm. In other cases customers may try to buy special orders at especially low prices. Retailers such as Lidl and Tchibo sell cheaply to the public because of their skill at buying cheaply.

High-price special orders

In these cases, the order is likely to look profitable at first glance. However, the special nature of the order is such that it will be more expensive to produce and this will mean that unit costs are going to be higher. Perhaps overtime or subcontracting will be necessary to meet a tight order deadline or to adjust the standard design to meet the customer's needs. In these cases, extra costs must be factored into any calculation of the possible profit from the order.

Low-price special orders

There are several reasons why a firm may consider accepting an order at lower than the usual selling price. The key is whether a firm has enough under-used capacity to meet the order and if the order will generate a positive contribution per unit. If the firm is already breaking even, a low-price order that generates a positive contribution per unit will generate extra profit. A further reason to accept the order is the possibility that it could lead to a new customer becoming a regular if they are happy with the quality and delivery of the order.

A-grade application

The world's biggest private jet

In 2012 a mystery middle-eastern buyer will take delivery of a customised A380 'double-decker' plane. The giant Airbus plane can take 700 passengers, but this version will have:

- a garage for a Rolls Royce
- a huge spiral staircase
- a concert hall
- a sauna
- bedrooms for 20 guests.

The plane is believed to have a price tag of £300 million, more than twice the normal price of an A380. It is the ultimate non-standard order.

Issues for analysis

- Whenever operational targets are missed, managers will want to know why. In these cases it is vital that you show a clear understanding of cause and effect. There will clearly be links between the three major target variables of unit cost, quality and capacity utilisation. Good analytic arguments will show a clear understanding of which events have caused which consequences. For example, an answer could suggest that unit costs have risen as a result of operating at a lower than anticipated level of capacity. This may have been the result of a fall in demand caused by a poor reputation, which itself was caused by poor quality levels the previous month.
- It is useful to experiment by taking each of the three target variables as a starting point, then thinking through the impact on the other two. For example, if capacity utilisation falls, what is the impact on unit costs and what might be the effect on quality? Or, what if quality performance falls?
- Another major analytical theme is likely to be an awareness of the arguments for and against keeping a stable production level month by month, as opposed to attempting to exactly match production with demand. Logically constructed arguments on both sides of this question are likely to lead to effective judgements when asked to evaluate.

Making operational decisions – an evaluation

Operational decisions are at the very heart of any business. Efficiency is king – without it, no firm will last long. Few customers are willing to wait for an unavailable product, while few firms have the financial resources to indefinitely fund inefficient stock-holding. The magical formula for matching production to demand does not exist. Instead, it is important to show an awareness that the forecasting skills and experience of operations managers will need to go hand in hand to ensure that a business is operationally efficient.

Key terms

Highly price elastic: when customers are so focused on price that a small price change can cause a big switch in customer demand (e.g. price up 5 per cent, sales down 20 per cent).

Higher profit margin: a wider gap between price and unit cost; if sales volumes stay the same, this must increase total profit.

Natural wastage: the 'natural' annual fall in staff levels caused by employees retiring, moving away or finding better jobs elsewhere.

Operational targets: the numerical goals set by management at the start of the year (e.g. output of 220,000 units with a quality wastage rate of no more than 1 per cent).

Rationalisation: reorganising in order to increase efficiency; this usually leads to redundancies.

A Revision questions *(35 marks; 35 minutes)*

1 Briefly explain what is meant by capacity utilisation. (2)

2 Explain why a high level of capacity usage makes cost per unit fall. (2)

3 Calculate the unit cost for a firm that manufactured 23,000 units with total costs of £11,500. (3)

4 Explain why quality targets may suffer if management is concerned only with meeting unit cost targets. (4)

5 Explain what is meant by the term rationalisation. (2)

6 Explain two methods that could be used to improve the level of capacity utilisation in a clothing factory. (4)

7 Explain two possible drawbacks to a farmer of relying on temporary staff when picking strawberries. (4)

8 Explain two benefits to a farmer of using temporary staff to pick strawberries. (4)

9 Explain two reasons why a company might agree to provide a customer with a special order at a selling price lower than its average unit cost. (4)

10 Outline three possible reasons why a cake manufacturer may try to closely match production with demand in order to reduce stock levels to a minimum. (6)

Revision exercises

Data response

Hotel Torres

Hotel Torres is a part of the Hoteles Benitez group of hotels in Spain. For hotels, the main operational target is occupancy rates: the percentage of rooms that are occupied at any time. The chain's head office is assessing last year's performance at each branch and is particularly interested in the data shown below relating to the Hotel Torres in Barcelona.

Table 34.2

	Quarter 1	Quarter 2	Quarter 3	Quarter 4
Average occupancy rate (%)	53	66	84	62
Target occupancy rate (%)	55	70	90	75
Group average occupancy rate (%)	58	72	90	75
Cost per guest (euros)	64	58	50	60
Target cost per guest (euros)	62	55	40	55

Questions *(20 marks; 20 minutes)*

1 Explain what the table reveals about Hotel Torres's operational efficiency during the year. (4)

2 Use the data in the table to explain the possible link between room occupancy performance and cost per guest. (6)

3 Analyse the benefits that the hotel might gain by setting targets for occupancy rates and cost per guest. (6)

4 Briefly explain two possible reasons why Hotel Torres failed to meet its targets. (4)

Data response

DWS Ltd is a toy manufacturer, operating in the UK from a factory in the north-east. Having been running for 20 years, DWS is used to the particular problems posed by operating in such a seasonal industry. With 70 per cent of sales being made in November and December, the managers have experience of battling to match production to demand. Their problem is intensified by the short product life cycles involved in manufacturing toys designed to tie in with the latest television and films. Table 34.3 shows units sold, output and maximum capacity month by month for last year.

The firm uses a range of methods to boost its maximum capacity during busy periods. These include overtime, temporary staff and subcontracting work to another trusted local manufacturer.

DWS has been approached by a major UK greetings card retailer, which is looking for a manufacturer of stuffed toys themed around various holidays, including Valentine's Day, Easter and Halloween. The initial contract would cover a 12-month period and would mean that sales levels would treble in January, March and October. The firm would pay a price equivalent to 5 per cent above the variable cost of each unit of output.

Table 34.3

	Sales (units)	Output (units)	Maximum capacity (units)
January	10,000	5,000	20,000
February	10,000	10,000	20,000
March	15,000	15,000	20,000
April	15,000	15,000	20,000
May	20,000	20,000	20,000
June	20,000	20,000	20,000
July	20,000	20,000	40,000
August	30,000	30,000	40,000
September	60,000	100,000	120,000
October	100,000	280,000	300,000
November	380,000	300,000	300,000
December	320,000	300,000	300,000

Questions *(35 marks; 45 minutes)*

1 a) Draw a graph to show units sold, output and maximum capacity. (6)

b) Shade the areas on the graph that represent under-use of capacity. (2)

2 Analyse the problems that DWS might experience by maintaining a consistent level of production all year round in order to avoid using overtime, temporary staff and subcontracting. (9)

3 Describe the pros and cons of two possible methods of increasing maximum capacity in the three affected months. (6)

4 Discuss whether DWS should accept this special order. (12)

35 Using technology in operations

Definition

Technology means the computer hardware and software used to automate systems, and to handle, analyse and communicate business data.

Introduction

Information technology (IT) applications in business are various and rapidly changing. Often, though, the changes are to processing speed and business jargon – the essential tasks remain the same. In recent years, the most important business IT innovation has been the emergence of the internet. This will be covered relatively briefly, because the pace of change means that magazine articles will provide a more up-to-date understanding of the internet's business potential than is possible here.

Key applications of technology are:

- automated stock control systems
- computer-aided design (CAD)
- robotics
- information technology, including electronic data interchange (EDI) and the internet
- database management (the organisation behind efficient delivery systems such as Tesco Home Delivery).

Automated stock control systems

Modern stock control systems are based on laser scanning of bar-coded information. This ensures the computer knows the exact quantity of each product/size/colour that has come into the stockroom. In retail outlets, a laser scanning till is then used to record exactly what has been sold. This allows the store's computer to keep up-to-date records of current stocks of every item. This data can enable a buyer to decide how much extra to order or an electronic link with the supplier can re-order automatically (see the section on EDI, below).

All this information will be held in the form of a database. This makes it easy for the firm to carry out an aged stock analysis: the computer provides a printout showing the stock in order of age. Table 35.1 shows a list of stock in a clothes shop, with the oldest first. It enables the manager to make

Table 35.1 An example of aged stock analysis

Garment	Received (days ago)	Number received	In stock today
Green *Fabrice* dress, size 8	285	2	1
Blue *Channelle* dress, size 14	241	1	1
Red *Channelle* dress, size 8	241	2	2
Red *Grigio* jacket, size 10	235	4	3
Black *Grigio* dress, size 8	205	3	2
Black *Fabrice* dress, size 12	192	2	1
Blue *Florentine* suit, size 8	179	1	1

informed decisions about what to do now and in the future. In this case:

- big price reductions seem to be called for on the first five items – they have been around too long
- there should be fewer orders in future for size 8 dresses.

Design technology

Computer-aided design (CAD) has been around for more than 20 years, but is now affordable and hugely powerful. Before CAD, product designers, engineers and architects drew their designs by hand. A CAD system works digitally, allowing designs to be saved, changed and reworked without starting from scratch. Even better, CAD can show a 3D version of a drawing and rotate to show the back and sides.

For multinationals such as Sony, a product designed in Tokyo can be sent electronically to Sony offices in America and Europe, for local designers to tweak the work to make it better suited to local tastes. And when work is behind schedule, designers in Tokyo can pass a design on to London at the end of the Japanese working day, then the design is sent on to America. The time differences mean that 24-hour working can be kept up.

The benefits of CAD systems to successful design are as follows.

- The data generated by a CAD system can be linked to computer-aided manufacturing (CAM) to provide integrated, highly accurate production.

Figure 35.1 Guggenheim Museum, Bilbao, designed by Frank Gehry

- CAD systems are hugely beneficial for businesses that are constantly required to provide designs that are unique, yet based on common principles (e.g. designing a new bridge, car or office block).
- CAD improves the productivity of designers and also helps them to be more ambitious; the extraordinary buildings of Frank Gehry could not have been produced without CAD (because only computers could calculate whether an unusual structure would fall down in a high wind).

A-grade application

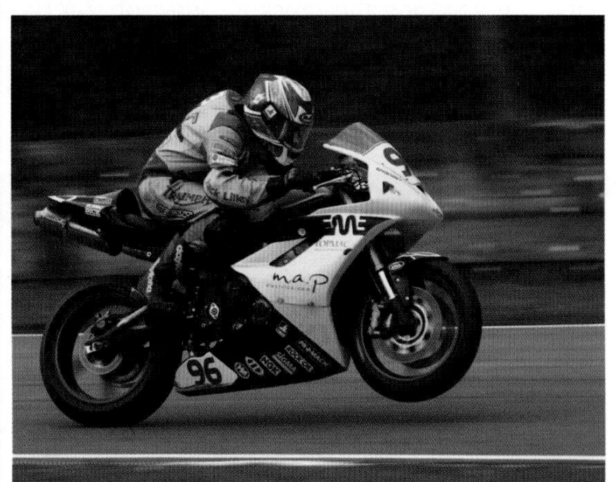

Figure 35.2 A Triumph bike

A Triumph

The Triumph motorbike business collapsed in 1983, and people said Britain could no longer make things such as bikes. But entrepreneur John Bloor bought the name and rebuilt the company. The first new Triumph hit the streets in 1991 and, incredibly, the business now has 1,400 employees, a turnover of £300 million and a 5% share of the world market for motorbikes.

The success has been built on design. Triumph has the biggest motorcycle design department outside Japan. The designers work on up-to-date CAD systems, to ensure that the bikes have the key combination of looks and performance. Although some of the production takes place in the Far East, all the research, design and engineering jobs are in Britain.

(Source: *The Independent*, 13 May 2010)

Robotics

Industrial robots are fundamental to the car industry worldwide, and are becoming increasingly important in the production of electrical goods such as TVs and computers. Nevertheless, it remains a bit of a surprise that robots have not become a more powerful force in industry. Thirty years ago, people assumed that few workers would be left in factories – the robots were coming. In Britain today there are fewer than 50 robots per 10,000 workers. Even in Japan (with more than 40 per cent of the world's robots) the figure is only 350 robots per 10,000 manufacturing workers.

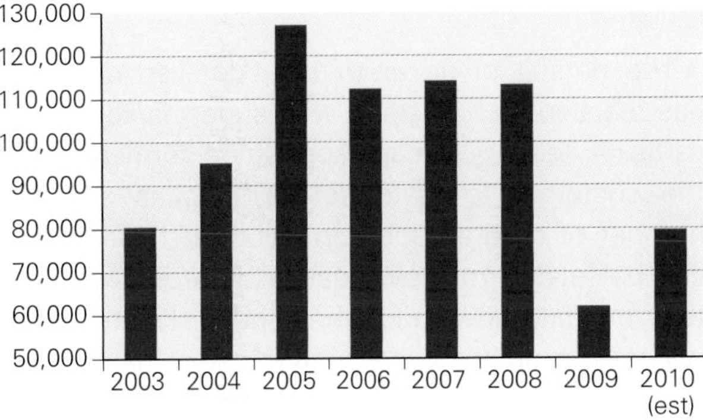

Figure 35.3 Industrial robot sales worldwide 2003–2010

(Source: World Robotics Report, IFR Statistical Department)

Figure 35.3 shows that worldwide sales of industrial robots were rising until the 2008/2009 recession. The industry expects that there will be a full recovery in sales by 2012/2013.

Industrial robots have important advantages over human labour. They are programmed to do the same thing over and over again, so repetitive tasks can be completed with 100 per cent consistency. This can be vital – for example, in the production of components for aircraft engines, or in the production of heart pacemakers. Robots are also likely to prove cheaper than people, as long as the business is able to use them effectively (e.g. for 20 hours a day).

Yet robots are clearly not a magic solution, or else they would have taken over. They are inflexible, so they cannot easily switch jobs in the way that people can, and they have rarely proved as reliable as they perhaps should be.

A-grade application

Toshiba robots

Three Toshiba robots are used at a pet food factory in Bremen, northern Germany. The company has made substantial investment in factory automation in order to improve productivity. Toshiba Machine robots now package birdseed sticks at a rate of 90 per minute. Where once there were seven people working on the application across three shifts, now three Toshiba Machine TH350 robots achieve the same results. The people have been redeployed across the plant.

The robots are part of a production line that manufactures birdseed sticks that are like a fat-based lollypop, embedded with nuts and seeds. The sticks are fed down three conveyors, each with a ceiling-mounted robot at its end. As this happens, the boxes are fed down another conveyor. A robot gripper then picks up the seed sticks and transfers them into boxes on a moving conveyor. Ceiling-mounted SCARA robots make the best use of the available work area.

Communication with customers

There are two main ways firms communicate electronically with their customers. The first is a website – for example, easyJet receives over 95 per cent of its bookings in this way. The second is through careful database management. A database is a store of information that can be rearranged and sorted in numerous ways. For example, if you had a database of all your friends, classmates and work colleagues, you might like to:

- sort them by birthday, so that you never missed the chance of a party invitation
- sort them by activity, so that you could rustle up a football or hockey team when needed
- sort them by location, to give you a mailing list for organising a school reunion.

For businesses, the ability to store information on thousands, perhaps millions, of customers is invaluable. In order to maximise the speed and flexibility of a database, every type of information needs to be held in a different 'field'. Field 1 may be the surname, field 3 the address, field 7 the age, and so on. This enables the data to be sorted, or picked out, in different ways. If you have a new product aimed at the over-40s, those aged 40 and over can be picked out and a mailing list produced in seconds.

To obtain this data, businesses use various approaches:

- asking customers to fill in their name and address when purchasing goods
- recording the information on product warranty cards
- supplying 'loyalty' cards, such as Tesco's Clubcard
- buying databases from companies that specialise in gathering data.

If building a database, firms are legally required to register it with the Data Protection Registrar. The Data Protection Act 1984 gives people the right to see their personal file – for example, one held by a bank on a customer's creditworthiness.

Marketing and database management

Mailing lists have existed for decades. American Express, *Reader's Digest* and many others have built their business through well-targeted direct mail (sometimes referred to as 'junk mail'). They achieved this through the use of large, expensive mainframe computers. Nowadays even the smallest firm can afford a computer and some database software. Customers can be sorted into regular, light and occasional users, and be sent an appropriate mailshot. Each letter can be personalised (e.g. 'Dear Miss Hendrick ...') and is therefore better suited to building a relationship with the customer. Alternatively, telephone sales staff can make direct contact to check on customer satisfaction and inquire whether any extra services are required.

The pursuit of an up-to-date, detailed database has reached its high point with supermarket loyalty cards. A Tesco Clubcard application form requires the customer to state details such as address, number of children, job and income. These details can be related to their lifestyle by recording what they buy and how much they spend. If Tesco then wants to promote wine costing more than £8 per bottle, it can invite to an in-store tasting all those who have spent over £6 on a bottle of wine over the past six months. Having an accurate database minimises the waste, and therefore the cost, of such mailings. This makes them a more attractive proposition when compared to other advertising media.

These are all ways in which technology can cut costs, reduce waste, improve customer service quality and increase productivity.

Communication with suppliers

Electronic data interchange (EDI)

EDI is a permanent link between computers on different sites, enabling specified types of data to be exchanged. By establishing an EDI link, firms can ensure that the latest information is available instantly to other branches of their business, or even to other businesses. For example, Heinz's link with Tesco enables it to see how sales of soups are going this week. If chicken soup sales have pushed ahead 20 per cent (perhaps because they were featured on a TV programme), production increases can be planned even before the Tesco head office phones through with a large order. This makes a just-in-time operation far more feasible.

Of course, Tesco does not want Heinz to have access to all its computer files, so the EDI link covers only specified data. Heinz might allow Tesco access to its stock levels and production plans in exchange for Tesco's daily sales data. This cooperation can help ensure that shelves are rarely empty.

EDI used to be for large companies only. Today, however, the availability of low-cost internet-based EDI means that any small supplier can keep this direct link with a retail customer. Sainsbury's, for example, set up JSnet for its smaller suppliers.

Electronic point of sale (EPOS)

EPOS equipment is at the heart of data collection by retailers. Laser scanning systems gather data from bar codes, which allow the computer to record exactly what has been bought and at what price. This forms the basis of the stock control system and also the recording of sales revenues. As with other aspects of IT, rapid falls in the cost of EPOS systems make them increasingly affordable for small shops.

Issues for analysis

Information technology provides a series of tools that can be used to help businesses operate more effectively. This raises many issues for analysis, a couple of which are discussed below.

- Will electronic shopping mean shops are on the way out? The answer is probably no. But internet shopping will put new competitive pressures on high streets and shopping centres. If this book could be ordered in minutes on the internet and arrive in three days' time, would it make sense to go and look for it in a bookshop where it might not be in stock? Retailers are going to have to think very hard about whether they are offering the level of personal service that makes a visit worthwhile.
- Most managers and staff accept that new technology is necessary for businesses to keep up with their competitors. Yes, there are often problems when the time comes to update technology. Staff may worry that suggested 'improvements' are excuses for making people redundant. Managers need to be sensitive to people's fears, and win them over by honesty and openness.

Using technology in operations – an evaluation

Years ago the managers at Guinness thought change management was a technical question. When a change was needed, such as a new distribution system, they hired consultants, whose main focus was to establish effective information and communications technology (ICT) links. Time after time they were disappointed by the results. Improvements began only when they realised that the key variable was not the technology but the people. Not only were results better if staff were consulted fully, but also the new systems were successful only if staff applied them with enthusiasm and confidence.

Technology is only a set of tools. It can form the basis of a major competitive advantage, as with easyJet's initiative with internet bookings. More often, though, the successful application of IT relies on good understanding of customer and staff needs and wants. This suggests that good management of information technology is no different from good management generally.

Revision questions *(35 marks; 35 minutes)*

1 A database could be used by an aircraft manufacturer such as Boeing to record the supplier and batch number of every part used on every aircraft. How might this information be used? (3)

2 State two benefits of good database management in achieving efficient stock control. (2)

3 Read the A-grade application on Triumph. Identify one benefit and one drawback of keeping all design work in the UK. (2)

4 Look at Figure 35.3. Explain one possible implication for:
   - a) a UK factory owner feeling under pressure from competition from China (3)
   - b) a UK worker, with few qualifications or skills, thinking of taking a job in a factory. (3)

5 Explain one benefit and one drawback of computer-aided manufacture (CAM). (4)

6 From your reading of the whole unit, outline three ways in which technology can lead to improved quality. (6)

7 How significant might internet retailing become for each of the following types of business:
   - a) a music shop specialising in 1960s classic pop and rock (2)
   - b) a builders' merchant (selling bricks, cement, etc.) (2)
   - c) a mail-order clothing firm? (2)

8 From your reading of the whole unit, explain two ways in which technology can reduce waste within a business. (6)

Revision exercises

Data response

Robots

Recently TM Robotics (Europe) Ltd worked with a major UK manufacturer to fit three Toshiba robots as part of an automated system to increase its output of valves.

The managers had to consider: the cost of the robots; the cost of installation and maintenance; the training required for key staff to manage the operation. All of this has to be weighed up against the cost of a manual alternative. One must also bear in mind potential downtime if the automated system is replacing an existing manual one.

The key factors in the success of the automation process were accuracy and flexibility. Accuracy was provided by the +/−0.02 mm repeatability of the Toshiba robot, and flexibility allowed the system to cope with 240 different product variants, all consisting of at least five component pieces.

One of the key factors in the installation process was ensuring a quick changeover period between different product variants, in order to minimise downtime. This is where a manual process can be advantageous – the worker simply finishing a batch of one product type and collecting the components for another, with no long changeover period required. Careful design ensured that the average changeover time was just 15 minutes, giving an impressive operating efficiency of 90 per cent.

The total cycle time for the three robots to assemble the fitting is just 7.8 seconds, 4.2 seconds faster then the manual method. Furthermore, the automation has the obvious advantage of constant running. It doesn't slow down when it's tired, it doesn't take coffee breaks and never takes long lunches. Faster production time and constant output mean that the robot quickly pays for itself.

(Source: adapted from www.tmrobotics.co.uk)

Questions *(30 marks; 35 minutes)*

1 **a)** Explain in your own words the meaning of 'downtime'. (3)

b) Why may firms be keen to minimise downtime? (4)

2 Examine the importance to this 'major UK manufacturer' of the accuracy and flexibility of these three robots. (6)

3 **a)** Calculate the percentage increase in production speed now that robots rather than people are producing. (3)

b) Analyse two ways in which the manufacturer can benefit from the extra speed. (6)

4 Using the information in the case study and your own knowledge, discuss two ways in which human workers may be more valuable than robots. (8)

Data response

An architect and her iPhone

Patti the Architect, a small architectural firm based in Florida, is turning Apple's iPhone into a productivity-boosting mobile resource for construction-site communications.

With the Apple iPhone, architect Patricia 'Patti' Stough and her staff can now easily access their full library of design and construction documents on the move. The firm designs all its projects in CAD on high-performance Mac hardware, making the files effortlessly portable and displayable on iPhone's high-res widescreen display.

This mobility enables the firm to more easily communicate design intentions to customers on the site, as well as consult more effectively with builders, subcontractors and regulatory inspectors. And even if they had forgotten a document, they can easily retrieve it wirelessly via iPhone's Wi-Fi.

With a slight tap or pinch of their fingers, users can easily zoom in and out of drawings and 3D high-resolution photos on iPhone, drilling down to the finest of details or panning out for a big picture view via iPhone's revolutionary touchscreen interface. 'The days of hauling scrolls of paper drawings to job sites only to discover I forgot a critical document are over,' says Stough. 'I can now carry even the largest, most complex and detailed CAD models in the palm of my hand. The ability to bring 3D digital drawings on site is a huge advantage, enabling me to better communicate and coordinate with everyone involved in the project.'

Patti the Architect is an award-winning architectural firm that specialises in beachfront townhouses, hotels, churches, schools, offices, retail additions and commercial interior renovations. Stough says that the huge productivity gains of designing in and working with 3D virtual building models are further enhanced through the mobility of iPhone.

Source: adapted from www.architosh.com

Questions *(25 marks; 30 minutes)*

1 Outline three benefits of the CAD system to this architectural business. (6)

2 Explain how the iPhone-linked CAD has reduced time wastage for the business. (4)

3 Examine Patti Stough's suggestion that having CAD on the iPhone leads to 'huge productivity gains'. (6)

4 To what extent is the portable CAD system likely to improve Patti's customer service? (9)

Essay Questions *(40 marks each)*

1 Information technology is reducing the need to meet people face to face. Discuss the implications of this for running a successful business.

2 If industrial robots become cheap enough, they may replace almost all unskilled factory workers in the future. Discuss the benefits and costs of this to society.

3 'Internet retailing will mean the death of the high street.' Discuss.

36 Integrated operations management

Introduction

According to the AS specification, 'Candidates should understand how operations management can help a business to be more effective and the role that can be played in this by technology.'

Operations management is at the heart of what every business does. The most cleverly conceived promotional campaign for a sub-standard product will not assure success – only those products that result from careful and inspired development and delivery succeed in the long term.

Operations management is often misinterpreted as a more modern way of referring to production. In fact, the term covers a much wider range of activities and can be applied equally to organisations that provide services and those involved in the production of goods. These activities are key to maximising the productive efficiency of a business and ensuring its ability to compete effectively. For instance, all businesses need to consider the following questions:

- How can efficiency be improved?
- What does quality mean to different businesses and how can quality standards be maintained?
- How can a business continue to develop new products (goods or services)?
- What role do suppliers play in improving operational performance?
- How can the use of technology improve the performance of a business?
- What methods can a business use to deliver effective customer services?

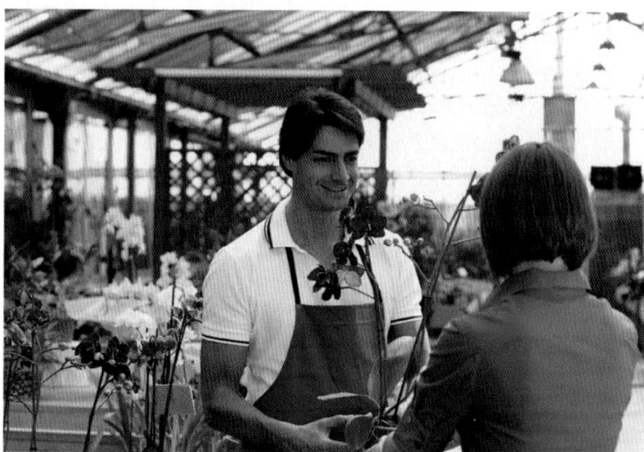

Figure 36.1 Customer service is an important part of operations management

Operations management

A-grade operations management requires not only a thorough understanding of the subject matter, but also a sound grasp of the major underlying themes and issues, including those discussed below. This requires an ability to evaluate the wider significance of the concepts covered in the context of individual firms.

Issue 1: the link between efficiency and profitability

It is worth remembering the formula for calculating profit at this point:

Profit = revenue − costs

Effective operations management can contribute to improved profitability in a number of ways. For example, the introduction of efficient quality systems can lead to cost savings by reducing wastage and the time and resources spent on reworking faulty products. Reliable suppliers can reduce the need to hold high stock levels, eliminating the costs associated with their storage. Adopting new technology can lead to long-term cost savings by improving productivity.

Clearly, then, keeping costs down plays a major

role in achieving greater profitability. Maintaining profits helps ensure an internally generated source of finance that can be used to improve performance, by investing in new machinery, by training workers or by directing funds towards more effective advertising. However, are UK firms fighting a losing battle, given the ever-increasing competition from firms based in low-cost countries? To what extent can UK firms offer superior quality, continuous innovation and flawless customer service over competitors, and will this be enough to guarantee sales?

Issue 2: the link between operations management and the rest of the business

The management of operations ties in very closely with the other main business functional areas. Operational managers are required, by definition, to manage their workers. The way in which the workplace is organised, the allocation of tasks and the leadership style of those in charge will have a major impact on the motivation and, therefore, performance of the workforce.

Good quality, innovation and customer service not only help to reduce costs but also contribute to a firm's marketing function. These areas may be just as, if not more, important as the ability to offer competitive prices in winning a slice of the market. However, achieving the right balance internally may still not be enough – external factors such as high exchange rates may ruin the competitiveness of even the most efficient firms.

Revision questions *(60 marks; 60 minutes)*

1 What is meant by the term capacity utilisation? (2)

2 A firm's fixed costs are £100,000, its variable costs per unit are £2.50 and its maximum output is 20,000 units a week. Calculate the cost per unit of production for the firm if it operates at:

a) 50% capacity (3)

b) 90% capacity. (3)

3 Suggest two benefits for a firm from increased capacity utilisation. (2)

4 Outline two ways in which a firm could increase its capacity utilisation. (4)

5 Explain why a firm may choose not to operate close to 100 per cent capacity utilisation over long periods of time. (3)

6 Explain why average costs are likely to fall as production increases. (4)

7 Briefly explain what is meant by total quality management (TQM). (3)

8 Identify three features of TQM. (3)

9 Explain, using examples, what is meant by quality. (3)

10 Identify two costs for a business that fails to meet acceptable quality standards for its products. (2)

11 Briefly explain the distinction between quality control and quality assurance. (3)

12 Identify two areas of business where technology could be introduced to improve performance. (2)

13 Identify two ways in which a restaurant could introduce technology to improve the service offered to its customers. (2)

14 Give two reasons why it is important for a business to establish and maintain good relationships with its suppliers. (2)

15 State three factors that might affect the choice of supplier for a business. (3)

16 Outline one benefit and one problem of operating a just-in-time (JIT) system of stock control. (4)

17 Explain why customer service is so important to a modern business. (4)

18 What is the difference between a customer and a consumer? (3)

19 Identify three criteria that could be used to assess the quality of customer service at a hotel. (3)

20 Suggest two ways in which a high-street retailer such as Debenhams could improve the service offered to its customers. (2)

Revision exercises

Data response

Lily's Kitchen

Lily's Kitchen is the UK's first organic and holistic pet food company. It was launched by Henrietta Morrison in November 2008 after concerns about her own dog's health led her to take a closer look at the ingredients contained in pet foods. She became convinced that there would be many other people who, like herself, wanted to feed their pets healthily but did not have the time or the knowledge to prepare complicated recipes themselves. She decided to set about creating a range of dog and cat foods that animals would enjoy and that would also help to keep them healthy.

Henrietta spent two years getting advice from vets, food technologists, nutritionists and herbalists, as well as the British Association of Holistic Nutrition and Medicine (BAHNM) in order to develop the Lily's Kitchen range. She also had to search across the UK and Europe to find kitchens that would be prepared to produce pet food in small batches in order to create a 'home made' style. Only ingredients that have been certified as organic are used in the pet food range and are sourced from around 30 small suppliers, growers and cooperatives, all committed to providing ingredients of the highest standards. Lily's Kitchen products do not contain artificial additives, sugars or fillers such as wheat, soya or corn. The kitchens used by the company must also be certified as organic, requiring very high standards of cleanliness to prevent any traces of non-organic food. Information regarding the product range and the ingredients and the processes used to produce it is contained on the company's website, as well as the products' recyclable packaging.

The Lily's Kitchen range is sold in Harrods, Whole Foods Market and over 200 independent vets and organic outlets. Customers are encouraged to bring their pets along to shops for in-store taste testings, as well as providing regular feedback to the company via its website.

Source: www.lilyskitchen.co.uk

Questions *(20 marks; 25 minutes)*

1 Explain how Lily's Kitchen attempts to meet customer expectations. (4)

2 State two factors that Henrietta might consider when choosing suppliers for the Lily's Kitchen range (6)

3 Analyse two possible consequences for Lily's Kitchen of continuing to maintain high standards of quality (10)

Data response

The perfect curry – in a box!

When Ketan Varu left for Sheffield University in 1996, his parents were determined to ensure that their son ate healthily while he was away from home. So they made special, easy-to-use packs of curry spices and ingredients, to help him cook for himself. Ketan began making up packs for friends who were put off making curry by the fact that most of the necessary ingredients were sold in bulk and stocked only by specialist stores. The popularity of the packs led Ketan to turn the idea into a business. In April 2005, he set up a company, Spice-N-tice, to manufacture and sell curry kits. These were made up of fresh pre-blended herbs and spices, easy-to-follow recipe cards and shopping lists – in fact, everything necessary to create authentic Indian food at home.

The product range is produced at the company's factory in Leicester. The herbs and spices are hand-blended according to secret recipes. Machines are used to fill the sachets, which are then packed with the recipe cards into small boxes. The business initially relied on family support but now employs six staff. According to Ketan, one of the main challenges faced by Spice-N-tice was the transformation of a cottage-sized industry into a business with sufficient operational capability to supply on a national and even international basis. In the first two years, the company's trade customers grew from 5 to 150, including retailers in France, Spain and Dubai. It also had over 3,000 online customers buying the packs via the Spice-N-tice website

(Source: www.spicentice.com)

Questions (30 marks; 35 minutes)

1 Describe one advantage and one disadvantage to Spice-N-tice of blending its herbs and spices by hand. (6)

2 Examine two ways in which the introduction of technology could increase productive efficiency at the company. (10)

3 Discuss the main operational implications for Spice-N-tice from further expansion of the business. (14)

Data response

A unique service from the Pink Ladies

Concerns over female safety led Tina Dutton and Andrea Winters to create a car hire service aimed exclusively at women. Pink Ladies Cars was launched by the two business partners in Warrington in June 2005. The decision to provide the service was based on research claiming that a high proportion of women had concerns about using taxis driven by unknown men. A number of relevant organisations, including the Suzy Lamplugh Trust, were also contacted to find out more about risks to women in general. In order to overcome charges of discrimination, the company operates as a private members' club, rather than a taxi service, meaning that passengers have to pre-book cars, instead of hailing them on the street.

Pink Ladies' focus on customer safety ensures high levels of customer care. The distinctive bright-pink Renault Kangoo cars used by the business are staffed only by women drivers, who are all trained in customer service, self-defence and first aid. The cars are fitted with up-to-date GPRS tracking and satellite navigation so that they can be constantly tracked. Customers are rung twice when their car is two minutes away to avoid the need to wait outside. The company's 'through the door' policy means that drivers are trained to wait until passengers are safely inside their destination before departing. In order to reduce the risk of attack, no money is carried by drivers. Instead, customers are given top-up cards allowing payment via the telephone or internet. Even the cars' tyres are filled with a revolutionary gel, almost eliminating the chances of a puncture and, therefore, reducing the risk of a breakdown.

After various arguments with the local Warrington council, Pink Ladies reorganised the business as a not-for-profit organisation in 2009. Its website says it has 1,500 members, which is a huge number of Pink Ladies.

(Source: www.pinkladiesmembers.co.uk)

Questions (30 marks; 35 minutes)

1 Explain, using examples, the difference between internal customers and external customers. (6)

2 Describe two ways of monitoring the levels of customer service provided by Pink Ladies Cars. (6)

3 Analyse the main methods used by Pink Ladies to meet customer expectations. (8)

4 To what extent do you believe that Pink Ladies' approach to customer service will guarantee its long-term success? (10)

37 An introduction to effective marketing

Definition
Effective marketing achieves the firm's sales and profit targets by convincing customers to buy the firm's products again and again.

What is effective marketing?

The term 'marketing' is widely misunderstood by people who have not studied business and management. Many people still think that 'marketing' is just another interchangeable term for selling, advertising and other forms of promotion (e.g. sponsorship). Some people even think that marketing is about persuading consumers to buy or use a product they do not want. So, if marketing isn't just about designing glitzy advertising, or aggressive high-pressure 'selling', what is it?

Marketing is the business function that aims to identify, influence and then satisfy consumer wants profitably. Effective marketing starts with identifying an opportunity, just as Nintendo did with its Wii console. Instead of assuming that all consoles had to target players of shoot-em-up games, Nintendo identified other opportunities among girls (e.g *Nintendogs*) and older people (e.g. *Brain Training*).

In many small businesses the owner will come into regular contact with customers. This allows the owner to hear first-hand the needs and wants of the target market. In large businesses, formal market research is undertaken because head office managers cannot feel sure that they know what customers think and want. Once consumer wants have been identified, products and services will need to be designed to match consumer preferences. Finally, a launch marketing mix must be decided. This involves decisions such as setting price, choosing an appropriate distribution channel and setting a promotional strategy.

Why is effective marketing important?

Consumers tend to be quite rational. They will seek out fairly priced products that satisfy their needs. In a competitive market, firms stand or fall according to their ability to satisfy the needs of the consumer. Generally, firms that fail will lack customer loyalty and be punished automatically by the market. These firms will lose market share and profit. Firms with products and services that offer genuine consumer benefits will attract revenue and profit.

Consumer tastes do not tend to stay the same for very long. Therefore, a key aspect of effective marketing is the ability to respond quickly to any change in consumer tastes. Firms that fail to adapt their business model, at a time when consumer tastes are changing, are normally forced out of business. In recent years retail chains such as KwikSave, Unwins and the Gadget Shop have collapsed.

A-grade application

Fopp

In June 2007 the music retailer Fopp announced that it was closing down all 105 of its UK stores. The management of Fopp had failed to react fast enough to a change in consumer preferences for buying music. In the last five years there has been a growing trend towards purchasing music via internet downloads. Fopp tried to respond by lowering its prices. Unfortunately for Fopp, this tactic failed to generate the revenues required by the company to break even, proving that low prices alone cannot save a business from closure, especially if consumers no longer wish to purchase the product that the business concerned sells.

The characteristics of effective marketing

Identifying the target market

When a business creates a new market (as Richard Branson is attempting currently with space tourism) it can aim its product at everyone who can afford the product. Some time later competitors will arrive, and usually focus on one segment of the market. In space tourism, perhaps some firms will focus on thrill-seekers, while others target wealthy, older travellers seeking a super-safe, luxury version of the same thrill.

To succeed at marketing you need to know and understand the customers within your target market: what do they *really* want from your product? The satisfaction of using/having the product, or the satisfaction of showing it off to friends? What are their interests and lifestyle?

Having a clear idea of the age, sex, personality and lifestyle of the target market enables the business to do the following things.

- *Focus market research by interviewing only those who make up the target market:* this should make the findings far more reliable. If the target market is clearly defined, the firm's market research budget can be spent with greater effect. Quota sampling could be used instead of a wide random sample; only those that meet the specific criteria for the target market will be interviewed, saving the firm time and money.
- *Focus advertising spending on the people most likely to buy the product:* one national TV commercial can cost £500,000; it will reach millions of people, but how many are really in the target market? Men do not need to know that 'Maybe it's Maybelline'. A product targeting young women would be advertised far more cost-effectively in magazines such as *More* or *Look*.

Segment markets

Most markets are not made up of identikit consumers who all want exactly the same product. In practice, consumer preferences can vary greatly. Firms that market their products effectively in this situation produce a range of products, each targeted at specific market segments.

A good example of a company that has used market segmentation to great effect is British Sky Broadcasting (BSkyB); in 2010 the company made an operating profit of £1,096 million.

Before Sky joined the market, the choice of what to watch on TV was limited. The BBC, ITV and Channel 4 tried in vain to produce a range of programmes in an attempt 'to be all things to all people'. Today Sky offers subscribers a choice of over 800 different channels. Among the target segments are kids, sports fans (mainly men), ethnic minorities and fans of different music types, e.g. MTV Base and Performance (classical music). The output of each channel is carefully matched to a particular consumer interest or hobby. Many of these channels attract additional charges, which has helped BSkyB to increase its monthly income (see Figure 37.1).

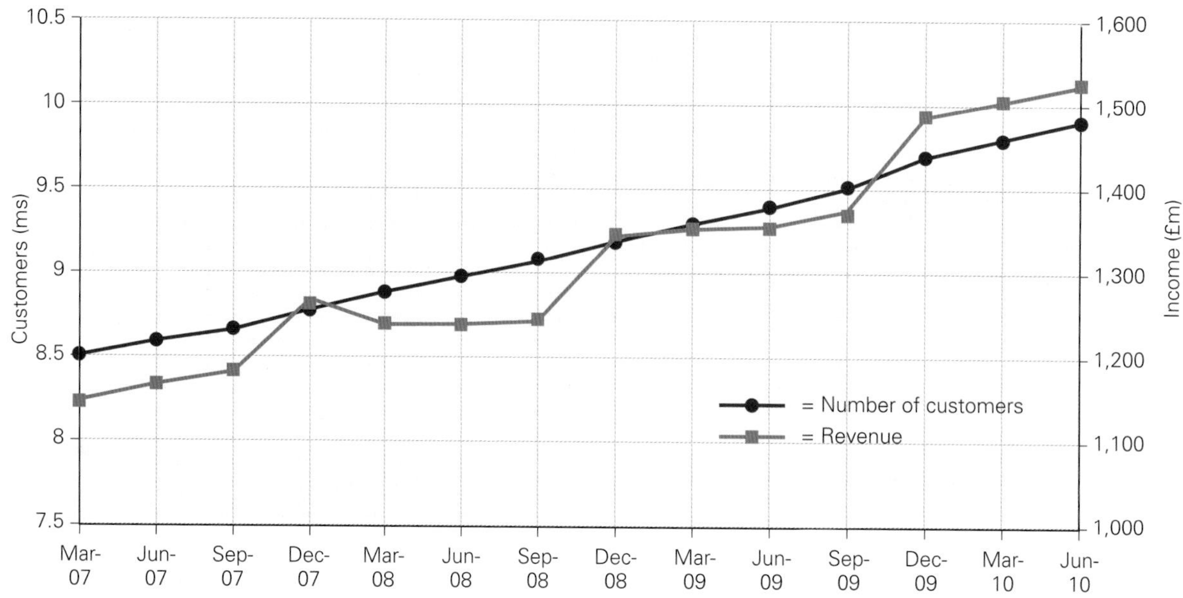

Figure 37.1 BSkyB growth 2007–2010

Market-orientated marketing

Effective marketing is usually based around an approach that is market-orientated rather than production-orientated. In a market-orientated business, managers take into account the needs of the consumer before making any decision: they put the customer at the heart of the decision-making process.

Some firms still use a production-orientated approach to marketing. Production orientation leads managers to focus on what the firm does best; internal efficiency comes before consumer preferences. The production-orientated approach to marketing may lead the business towards the following approaches:

- *The hard sell:* employing a large sales force to go out and convince consumers that they should buy your product. Individualised sales targets, low basic salaries and high rates of commission ensure that sales staff will be 'motivated' to hit their targets, ensuring that the firm sells the products that it has already produced.
- *Cutting costs and prices:* if a production-orientated firm's products are not selling very well, managers tend to respond to this crisis by cutting costs. If costs can be cut, retail prices can also be cut without any loss of profit margin.

On the other hand, there are some weaknesses in market orientation. The death of Rover Cars (once one of the world's biggest car producers) was partly due to this. Rover management seemed convinced that customers could be attracted by marketing gimmicks such 'special edition' cars or cars with angular steering wheels. A greater focus on the quality and reliability of the product would have been far more effective. The ideal approach is that of a firm such as BMW, which is hugely proud of its products, but always makes sure that it understands what its customers really want from them.

A coherent brand image

Firms that market their products successfully use the marketing mix in an integrated manner to create a coherent and attractive brand image that appeals to the target market. Marketing success depends upon getting all four marketing mix decisions right. A good product that is properly priced and promoted will still fail if distribution is poor. Firms use the marketing mix to create an attractive and coherent brand image for each of the products that they sell. Creating the right brand image is important. If the brand image created by the marketing mix appeals to the target market, there should be an increased chance that the product will succeed.

The most important thing to remember is that all four elements of the mix must be coordinated. If the marketing mix is not coordinated, mixed product messages will be sent out to the target

A-grade application

Gap

By 2010, Gap's Chief Executive, Patrick Robinson, had seen sales fall by 14 per cent since his appointment in 2007. And the American clothes retailer has been overtaken by Zara as the world's number one clothing retailer.

Gap has suffered from falling sales and market share because it has failed to keep up to date with changes in fashion. Gap built its reputation around selling 'preppy' clothes. Consumer tastes have moved on, but Gap has not. To survive, Gap will probably have to abandon its 'preppy' clothes and instead switch to a more market-orientated approach. Market research needs to be given a bigger role. Focus groups could be carried out to identify popular contemporary style and fashion. New lines of clothing can then be designed that will have a better chance of appealing to Gap's target market.

Figure 37.2 The clothing retailer Gap

market. This could create confusion, leading to disappointing sales. The key, then, is to think through the brand image that you want to create *before* making any other decisions about your product, such as how you might want to price it, promote it and distribute it.

Marketing is everyone's job

Many Japanese firms do not have a marketing department. Firms that adopt this approach believe that every employee has a part to play in marketing their business. Marketing should not be the preserve of a specialised marketing department – it is everyone's responsibility. However, to be successful the management has to create the right culture. Every member of staff must see their role as to better serve the needs and wants of the consumer.

Short-termist marketing = ineffective marketing

Short-termism describes a business philosophy whereby a firm pursues strategies that might boost profit in the short run, even if these strategies damage the firm's long-run profitability. Some examples of short-termist marketing strategies are given below.

High prices designed to exploit consumer loyalty or a dominant market position

In the short run, firms that operate in a market where there is little competition might be tempted to raise their prices to boost revenues and profits. In recent years both Manchester United and Chelsea have tried to exploit the loyalty of football fans by raising ticket prices. In the short run this can work; however, in the longer term fans may rebel against the price increases and drift away from the game completely. There are signs that this has already started to happen. For example, in September 2009 Chelsea sold fewer than 25,000 tickets for a Champions League game.

A decision to exploit consumers by charging high prices is definitely not a good example of effective marketing. High prices can also encourage new competitors to join the industry.

Short-run sales-driven marketing

Some managers believe that their employees can only be motivated to work hard if they are set targets that are linked to bonuses and other performance-related payments. An over-reliance on targets and performance-related pay can create a ruthless and dishonest culture that can affect a firm's marketing. For example, a 2007 BBC investigation suggested that staff at a high-street bank were encouraged by their supervisors to lie to the bank's customers in order to hit their personal sales targets. Mis-selling inappropriate financial products to customers can improve a bank's profitability in the short run; however, if the unethical marketing practices are exposed, the resulting wave of bad publicity may hit demand for the firm's products.

Issues for analysis

- Weak exam answers present marketing as a set of simple tools: the 4Ps. In fact, effective marketing is remarkably difficult, even for the biggest and best companies. A survey by *The Grocer* magazine placed Coca-Cola as Britain's most valuable brand. Yet Coca-Cola has been responsible for some dreadful new product flops in this country recently, including Dasani water, Coke Blak (coffee-flavoured Coke!) and Vanilla Coke. Good exam answers acknowledge that marketing is difficult because it is based on judgements about the future: future competition, future consumer tastes and future consumer attitudes.
- Achieving success depends on devising a genuinely new type of product that meets an actual consumer need or desire. Apple's iPhone did exactly that, as did Innocent Drinks when they made smoothies an everyday drink for wealthy young adults.

An introduction to effective marketing – an evaluation

To judge the likely effectiveness of a firm's marketing plans requires a full understanding of the market. Therefore, just as the marketing manager must research the market, so you must take care to study the evidence available within the case material. An exam question based on Cadbury might lead to very different answers to the same question based on Mars or Nestlé – even though they all make chocolate. Good judgement comes from good application to the market and to the company.

Revision questions (30 marks; 30 minutes)

1 In your own words, explain the meaning of the term 'marketing'. (3)

2 Explain why some firms choose not to carry out market research. (3)

3 Why do you think most firms decide to review their marketing strategy at fairly regular intervals? (3)

4 What is meant by the phrase 'target market'? (2)

5 Outline two reasons why it is important for firms to be able to identify their target market. (4)

a) Distinguish between a production-orientated and a market-orientated approach to marketing. (3)

b) Outline whether a production-orientated or market-orientated approach would be better for *one* of the following companies:

i) Manchester United FC

ii) easyJet

iii) Topshop (4)

6 Explain how market segmentation has helped companies such as BSkyB to improve their profitability. (4)

7 What are the marketing advantages of not having a specialised marketing department? (4)

Revision exercises

Data response

The role of luck

Figure 37.3 Car production at Morgan

Effective marketing usually comes about as a result of careful planning and market-orientated decision making. However, in some cases, firms stumble across a successful marketing strategy by chance. Morgan cars is a conservatively run private business. The production methods used by the company have hardly changed at all in 40 years. Cars are still made largely by hand. Morgan's best-selling cars are based on designs that have not been changed for decades. In most industries this approach would be a recipe for disaster. Fortunately for Morgan, the cars continue to sell well within a tiny niche comprised of customers that want to purchase a hand-built British sports car, built in the Brooklands tradition. Morgan has not deliberately engineered its niche market position, it has just happened accidentally – it has just been fortunate.

Questions *(30 marks; 35 minutes)*

1 From your reading of the text, is it really true that all Morgan's success is down to luck? (12)

2 Discuss marketing problems the business might face if it attempts to expand. (18)

Case study

Wimbledon Quality Cars

Wimbledon Quality Cars (WQC) sells second-hand cars. The business was set up five years ago when the economy was still booming. The owner of the business, Roger Raymond, believes that most businesses over-complicate their marketing. According to Roger, 'marketing is just a set of tools to sell more products, in my case, cars'. The marketing mix of WQC could be summarised as follows.

- *Price:* according to Roger, the bulk of second-hand car buyers are interested in only one thing – low prices. Most of the cars sold by WQC are sold for less than £2,000 – an important psychological pricing point.
- *Promotion:* Roger spends £300 per week advertising his cars in the south London press. He also employs two salesmen, Andy and John, who are paid a basic wage of £200 per week and a flat rate commission of £250 per car sold.
- *Product:* Roger believes that the bulk of his customers are not fussy about the make or model of car that they buy. 'Most of my punters want a cheap run-around. The majority of them don't know a good car from a death trap. In our market, quality always comes second to a low price.' Roger buys most of his cars from car auctions.
- *Place:* WQC has an old, run-down car showroom, just opposite Wimbledon dog track.

Last year WQC enjoyed its most profitable year yet: sales were up 40 per cent on the previous year. Unfortunately, events took a dramatic turn for the worse last month. To Roger's horror, WQC was the subject of a TV documentary investigating sharp practice in the second-hand car market. The programme alleged that WQC sold cars that were not roadworthy. The implication was that Roger was happy to put the profits of WQC before his customers' safety. Ex-customers of WQC claimed that they had been tricked into buying poor-quality cars by WQC salesmen who failed to disclose faults with the cars.

Questions *(30 marks; 30 minutes)*

1 According to Roger, 'Marketing is just a set of tools to sell more products.' Explain the possible drawbacks of this approach. (7)

2 How would you describe WQC's marketing philosophy? Is it production orientated or is it market orientated? (7)

3 Using the example of WQC, explain why an unethical approach towards marketing can often yield profitable results in the short-term. (8)

4 Outline two internal and two external factors that might affect the effectiveness of WQC's marketing. (8)

Niche vs mass marketing

Definition

Mass marketing means devising products with mass appeal and promoting them to all types of customer. Niche marketing is tailoring a product to a particular type of customer.

Mass marketing

Mass marketing is the attempt to create products or services that have universal appeal. Rather than targeting a specific type of customer, mass marketing aims the product at the whole market. The intention is that everyone should be a consumer of the product. Coca-Cola is a good example of a firm that uses mass marketing techniques. The company aims its product at young and old alike. Its goal has always been to be the market leader and it still is today. The ultimate prize of mass marketing is the creation of **generic brands**. These are brands that are so totally associated with the product that customers treat the brand name as if it was a product category. Examples include 'Hoover' (vacuum cleaner) and 'Bacardi' (white rum).

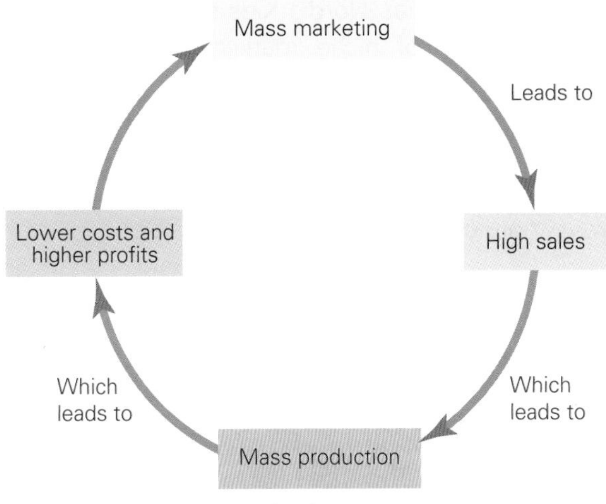

Figure 38.1 Mass marketing

As shown above, when mass marketing is carried out successfully it can be highly profitable. Firms such as Ryanair set out to be high volume, mass market operators and achieve handsome profits. However, it is important to note that mass marketing does not have to go hand in hand with low prices. For example Apple, when it launched the iPod, decided to become *the* MP3 player. Brilliant launch advertising and – most importantly – the development of *iTunes* meant that it achieved mass market sales while keeping its prices high. Even now, with its sales entering the decline phase of its product life cycle (see Figure 38.2), it remains the dominant brand in its market. The clever marketing of the iPod provided the necessary **product differentiation** to sell high sales volumes without the need to cut prices.

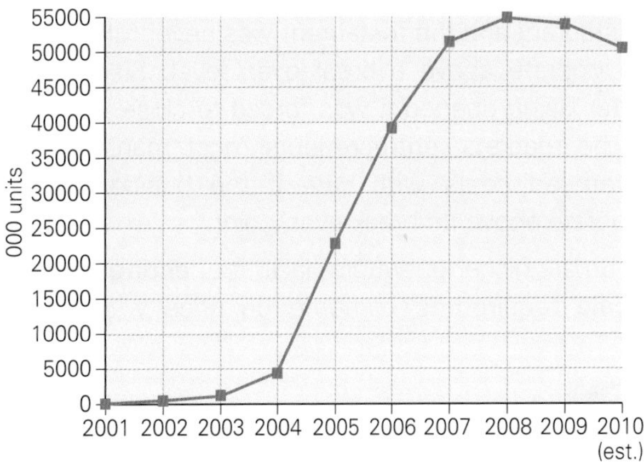

Figure 38.2 Worldwide annual sales of Apple iPod (2001–2010)

(Source: Apple annual accounts)

Niche marketing

A niche market is a very small segment of a much larger market. Niche marketing involves identifying the needs of the consumers that make up the niche. A specialised product or service is then designed to meet the distinctive needs of these consumers. Niche market products tend to sell in relatively low volumes. As a result, the price of a niche market product is usually higher than the mass market alternative. Niche market operators often distribute their products through specialist retailers, or directly to the consumer via the internet.

An entrepreneur wanting to set up a niche market business must first identify a group of people who share a taste for a product or service that is currently unsatisfied. A product or a service must then be designed that is capable of meeting this unsatisfied need. To stand a good chance of success, the new niche product will need to be superior to the mass market equivalent that is currently available. Finally, the niche must be large enough to support a profitable business. Many new niche market businesses fail because the revenue generated from their niche market business is not high enough to cover their operating costs.

A good example was a small neighbourhood restaurant called Bajou that tried, unsuccessfully, to make a business out of selling Cajun food in south Croydon. At the weekend the restaurant was never completely empty, proving that a gap in the market did exist. Unfortunately, this gap in the market was not large enough to cover the overheads of running a restaurant and the restaurant was never full enough to operate above a break-even level. Six months after Bajou opened it was forced to close down. In niche markets, entrepreneurs must manage their overhead costs with care if the business is to operate above its break-even point.

Small niche operators lack the **economies of scale** required to compete on price with larger, established operators. Instead, the small firm could try to find a small, profitable niche. The amount of profit generated by this niche needs to be high enough for the small firm, but too trivial for big business. In Birmingham's city centre, Rubicon Exotic is a profitable line of soft drinks; but with a market share of less than 1 per cent, Coca-Cola will not be worried. The profit generated is enough to satisfy the requirements of Rubicon Drinks, with its low overheads. Small, niche market businesses survive on the basis that they occupy a relatively unimportant, low profit market niche. Larger firms operating in the mass market are happy to ignore the niche businesses because they pose no threat.

Niche market businesses sell specialised, differentiated products that are designed to appeal to their very specific target market. Firms selling niche market products can exploit the low price sensitivity created by product differentiation by raising price. Total revenue will rise after the price increase because, in percentage terms, the fall in sales volume will be less than the price increase.

Successful niche marketing in practice

Until recently, catalogue retailing has suffered from a down-market image. Operators such as Argos based their success on selling mass market products at budget prices. However, in the last few years internet retailing has seen a host of new niche market players entering the market. Companies such as Nordic Kids sell a highly differentiated range of niche market premium quality designer clothes that are not available on the high street. In this case the niche market is affluent middle class parents seeking, according to the company's website, 'effortless Scandinavian cool' (www.nordickids.co.uk).

Are niche markets safe havens for small businesses?

In the past many large companies stuck to mass markets and ignored small market gaps and the small companies that filled them. To fill lots of small niches would require lots of short production runs (e.g. 90 minutes on the printing press producing the Hartlepool FC fanzine, and 60 minutes producing the Darlington one). This has always been expensive, because it takes a long time to re-set machinery.

Now, however, improvements in technology mean that production lines are increasingly set up by computer, enabling them to be re-set almost instantly. So large firms can build the sales volumes they need by producing a large variety of low-volume niche market products. Small scale producers are coming under threat from larger companies that have begun to target their niches.

Fortunately, small firms are often quicker on their feet, so when a large firm lumbers towards the market, the smaller one may still be able to win the competitive war. When the multi-billion dollar PepsiCo bought the smoothie business PJ's, Innocent Drinks thought that the market might become very difficult for them. In fact, Innocent kept its market share rising within the small smoothie niche within the soft drinks market.

A-grade application

Flares

A good example of a successful business that uses the niche marketing approach is the Flares nightclub chain. 'Flares' targets a niche market comprised, mostly, of ageing clubbers in their forties that want a 1970s retro night out. Each Flares nightclub tends to be relatively small, so even a small number of customers will make the club look reassuringly busy. The small capacity also helps to reduce overheads, decreasing the number of customers required each week to break-even. The interior design of a typical Flares nightclub is deliberately garish; an exaggerated version of what a typical nightclub looked like in the 1970s, complete with features such as mirror-balls and an under-lit glass dance floor. The music policy of a typical Flares nightclub holds no surprises either: 1970s funk and other kitsch retro classics such as ABBA that are likely to appeal to the ageing clubber.

(Source: www.flaresbars.co.uk)

Figure 38.3 Hitting the retro dance floor

Issues for analysis

- It is useful to analyse niche marketing in relation to **price elasticity**. Niche market products are invariably designed to meet the needs of customers looking for something different. This means that buyers of niche market goods are likely to be less price sensitive than consumers of mass market brands. This is especially true for the first brand to open up a niche market. Consumers may regard the originator of the market segment as 'the real thing'. An example would be Marmite, in the relatively tiny market for savoury spreads (most people prefer sweet things on their toast, such as honey or jam). This allows Marmite to charge extraordinarily high prices such as £4 for a jar the same size and weight as a £1 jar of honey.
- Fundamentally there are two approaches to making profit. The first is to be a high-volume, low-profit margin operator, such as Ryanair. The second is to charge higher prices and be a low-volume, high-profit margin business, such as Marmite. This is the route taken by those who adopt niche marketing tactics.

Niche vs mass marketing – an evaluation

Which is better? Mass or niche marketing? The answer is that it depends. In the bulk ice cream market, large packs of vanilla ice cream have become so cheap that little profit can be made. Better by far, then, to be in a separate niche, whether regional (Mackie's Scottish ice cream) or upmarket such as Rocombe Farm or Häagen-Dazs. The latter can charge ten times as much per litre as the mass-market own-label bulk packs.

Yet would a film company prefer to be selling a critic's favourite or a blockbuster smash hit? The latter, of course. In other words, the mass market is great, if you can succeed there. Businesses such as Heinz, Kelloggs and even Chanel show that mass marketing can be successful and profitable in the long term.

Key terms

Economies of scale: factors that cause costs per unit to fall when a firm operates at a higher level of production.

Generic brands: brands that are so well known that customers say the brand when they mean the product (e.g. 'I'll hoover the floor').

Price elasticity: the responsiveness of demand to a change in price.

Product differentiation: the extent to which consumers perceive your brand as being different from others.

A Revision questions (20 marks; 20 minutes)

1 Identify two advantages of niche marketing over mass marketing. (3)

2 Give three reasons why a large firm may wish to enter a niche market. (3)

3 Why may small firms be better at spotting and then reacting to new niche market opportunities? (3)

4 Give two reasons why average prices in niche markets tend to be higher than those charged in most mass markets. (2)

5 Outline two reasons why information technology has made niche marketing a more viable option for large firms. (4)

6 Explain why it is important for a large firm to be flexible if it is to successfully operate in niche markets. (2)

7 In your own words, explain why the price elasticity of niche market products may be lower than for products in the mass market. (3)

B1 Revision exercises

Data response

The return of mass marketing

For many years car manufacturers such as Toyota and Nissan have sought out market niches in an attempt to improve profitability. Cars such as the Toyota Prius, a hybrid electric powered vehicle, are not intended to sell in high volumes. Instead, niche market cars sell for high prices, delivering a higher profit margin per car than more conventional mass market models.

However, in the last couple of years, there are signs that car manufacturers have sought a return to conventional mass marketing, particularly in Asia where rapid rates of economic growth have created a growing middle class. At present both the Indian and the Chinese car markets are unsaturated. For example, in India car ownership is only 8 per 1000, whereas in the USA and the UK the corresponding figures are 477 and 373 respectively. Income per head, while increasing rapidly, is still low by American and European standards, and so far this has limited the demand for new cars in India.

Now car manufacturers have spotted a gap in the market for a basic, low cost car. The first company to fill this gap in the market was the Indian car manufacturer, Tata Motors. It sells its basic 'People's car' for less than 100,000 rupees (£1,500). Multinationals such as Renault and General Motors are now opening their own Indian factories to produce similar mass market cars sold at ultra-low prices. The challenge for these producers will be to manufacture the cars cheaply enough to make the low prices profitable.

Environmentalists have expressed their concerns that these new cheap cars will add to the problem of global warming and climate change. This year Tata Motors expects to sell a quarter of a million new cars in India.

Questions *(30 marks; 35 minutes)*

1 a) What is a niche market product? (2)

b) Explain why the Toyota Prius is a good example of a niche market product. (2)

2 Explain two reasons why the Indian car market has grown (4)

3 a) What is a mass market product? (2)

b) Explain why the Tata Motor's 'People's car' is a good example of a mass market product. (4)

4 Analyse two advantages and two disadvantages for European car manufacturers, such as Renault, of mass marketing £2,000 cars in India. (8)

5 Cars costing £2,000 can be profitably made in India. Explain why UK consumers are unlikely to benefit from similar low prices. (4)

6 Discuss whether companies such as Tata Motors should take into account the concerns of environmentalists when making their business decisions. (4)

B2 Data response

Winter melon tea

Mass market soft drinks such as Coca-Cola and Pepsi are very popular in countries such as Hong Kong and Singapore. In an attempt to survive against the imported competition, local producers of soft drinks have managed to establish a flourishing niche market for traditional Asian drinks sold in 33cl cans. Sales of these niche market products have been rising but from a very low level.

Consumers that make up this niche market are encouraged to believe, through advertising, that traditional drinks such as winter melon tea and grass jelly drink are healthier than their mass market alternatives. Other firms use economic nationalism to sell their drinks, using slogans such as 'Asian heritage' in their advertising.

However, producers of traditional drinks could now become a victim of their own success. Foreign multinationals have noticed the rapid growth of this market niche, and in response, they have launched their own range of traditional drinks.

Questions *(20 marks; 25 minutes)*

1 a) What is a niche market product? (2)

b) Explain why Asian traditional drinks are examples of niche market products. (2)

2 Explain two ways in which the producers of traditional drinks, such as winter melon tea and grass jelly drink, created product differentiation. (4)

3 Niche market products are normally more expensive than most mass-market products. Using the example of traditional Asian drinks, explain why this is usually so. (4)

4 Discuss whether the local producers of Asian traditional drinks will be able to survive in the long term given that their products now have to compete against similar brands produced by foreign multinationals such as Coca-Cola and Pepsi. (8)

Designing an effective marketing mix

Definition

The marketing mix is the balance between the four main elements of marketing needed to carry out the marketing strategy. It consists of the '4Ps': product, price, promotion and place.

Components of the marketing mix

When working out how to market a product successfully, there are four main variables to consider (the **marketing mix**).

1 *Product:* the business must identify the right product (or service) to make the product both appealing and distinctive. To do this, it needs to understand fully both its customers and its competitors. No product will have long-term success unless this stage is completed successfully.

2 *Price:* having identified the right product to appeal to its target market, the business must set the right price. The 'right' price for a Versace handbag might be £1,200 – it is a great mistake to think that low prices or special discounts are the path to business success.

3 *Promotion:* marketing managers must identify the right way to create an appropriate image for the product and present it to the right target audience. This might be achieved best by national TV advertising, but specific markets can be reached at far lower cost by more careful targeting (e.g. advertising lawnmowers in magazines such as *Amateur Gardening*). 'Promotion' includes both media advertising (TV, press, cinema, radio) and other forms of promotion (e.g. special offers, public relations, direct mail and online).

4 *Place:* for products, 'place' is how to get your product to the place where customers can be persuaded to buy. This might be through a vending machine or on a Tesco shelf, or positioned just by the till at a newsagent (the prime position for purchases bought on impulse). For service businesses, place may be online or in the location of a retail outlet (e.g. Tesco Direct and Tesco stores).

The units that follow this one deal with each of these factors in turn.

A-grade application

Both McVitie's Jaffa Cakes and Burton's Jammie Dodgers are well-known biscuit brands, but the former is distributed in 90 per cent of retail outlets, whereas the latter is in only 64 per cent. Clearly this restricts sales of Jammie Dodgers, because few customers would make a special journey to find them. Both companies have a similar view of the right outlets for their products (e.g. supermarkets, corner shops, garages, canteens and cafés), so why may Burton's be losing out to McVitie's in this particular race? Possible reasons include:

- Jaffa Cakes have higher consumer demand, therefore retail outlets are more willing to stock the product.
- Jammie Dodgers may have more direct competitors; high product differentiation may make Jaffa Cakes more of a 'must stock' line.
- If Jaffa Cakes have more advertising support, retailers know customers will ask for the product by name while the advertising campaign is running.
- McVitie's has a much larger market share; therefore, the company is in a stronger position to cross-sell (i.e. persuade a shopkeeper to buy a range of McVitie's brands).

How is the marketing mix used?

The marketing mix can be used by a new business to develop ideas about how and where to market a product or service. A very small business start-up may look no further than leaflets to be handed out or posted in neighbouring front doors. In a larger business, a senior manager is likely to set a maximum budget and then the individual marketing managers will look at each of the ingredients in the mix. They then decide what marketing actions need to be taken under each of the headings. If marketing activity is to be effective, each ingredient needs to be considered.

For each market situation, managers are trying to set the ideal combination of the ingredients based on a balance between cost and effectiveness. The ingredients need to work with each other as a good product poorly priced may fail. If the product is not available following an advertising campaign, the expenditure is wasted. A successful mix is the one that succeeds in putting the strategy into practice (see Figure 39.1).

A different mix for each market

The focus of the marketing mix will vary according to the market in which the firm is operating. Careful market research should reveal the attitudes and tastes of the target market. An important issue will be whether the goods are:

- regular purchases
- impulse purchases
- emergency purchases.

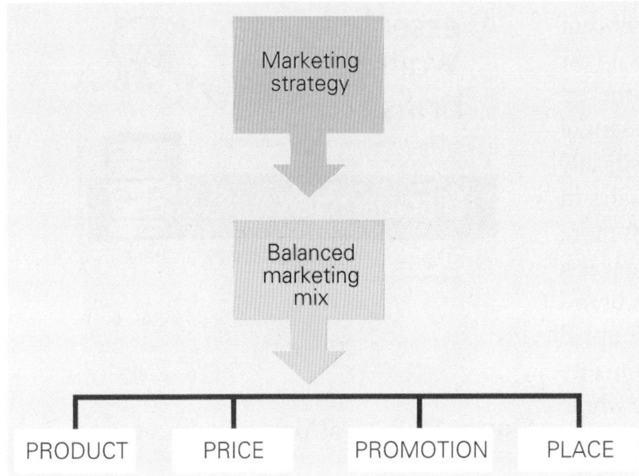

Figure 39.1 A balanced marketing mix

Impulse purchases (such as chocolate brands) are interesting because they require strong branding, great distribution and display and eye-catching packaging. In other words, the mix focuses on place and promotion. Price is much less important and the quality of the product may not be hugely important.

Table 39.1 Different types of purchasing and the marketing mix

Type of purchasing	Most important elements of the mix
Regular purchases	Product, promotion and price
Impulse purchases	Place and promotion (including packaging)
Emergency purchases	Place and product

Different segments within the market

The differences in customers and buying habits result in many 'markets within markets'; these are known as market segments and each segment will require its own marketing mix. The fashion industry is one example: at one end of the market, cheap and cheerful clothing with mass availability is the key; at the other end exclusivity, quality workmanship and a famous brand name are important.

Ingredients are not equally important

In most cases the product is the vital ingredient and no amount of marketing effort will make a poor product succeed. When selling to other businesses, reliability and quality will probably be far more important than brand image. However, a good product without good support may also fail. The balance will vary. In a price-sensitive market, pricing will be important – this is seen in the petrol market. If one company reduces its price, the others follow rapidly.

Influences on the marketing mix

Finance

Every marketing director is attempting to achieve the best mix of marketing factors to enable the marketing strategy to be a success. He must decide how big a budget is needed to market the product successfully, and then how to divide the budget between the 4Ps. If £1 million is available, should it all be put into a TV advertising campaign, or should half the budget be kept for offering special discounts to retailers who stock the product for the first time?

If the budget is big enough, the company will be able to do all the things it wants. Yet even Cadbury, with a £12 million **marketing budget** for its Dairy Milk brand, cannot do everything. This is not surprising, given that a single week of strong TV advertising nationally would cost more than £1 million.

If the budget is very tight, the business may have to be clever about setting the right marketing mix. Small, upmarket food producer Klein Caporn started with a strategy based on advertising in classy magazines and distribution through small, independent food shops. After 12 months it became clear that this would never be profitable because of the costs of delivery to lots of small shops. So bosses Paddy Klein and Ed Caporn changed their approach, cutting their price level and targeting the main supermarkets. Waitrose provided distribution in its London stores and then the company made a breakthrough into Sainsbury's outlets nationally. They also changed their promotional strategy, hiring a public relations company to get them features in the press instead of spending on advertising. The new approach is working well.

Technology

In the past, a peak-time advertisement on ITV could reach 33 per cent of the population. Now it would reach only 15 per cent, and less than 10 per cent of the key market of 15–24 year olds. Fewer and fewer families sit together through a night's television: grannies are on Google, while the 15–24 year olds may be in their bedroom on Facebook, playing *Halo 3* or swapping digital files with WiFi-connected friends.* Long-term success in marketing requires that firms keep up with changes and invest in technology. Tesco showed the sharpness of its management by going into online sales and delivery

A-grade application

Waitrose bucks the trend

High-end stores like Waitrose are not expected to do well in a recession. Business theory would expect it to lose customers to other supermarkets offering lower prices. However, profit is up 25 per cent and it is planning to expand by building 10 new supermarkets a year and to continue to roll out convenience stores. So how has it bucked the trend? One major factor has been the introduction of its 'essential range'. This range of 1,400 new 'everyday' products is specifically designed for shoppers on a budget. It has created £500m of sales in the first year and Waitrose estimates that it is getting 400,000 more customers each week. The introduction of the essential range was a change in marketing strategy. Previously marketing had been brand based. The new 'essential' campaign emphasised price and coupled it with the company's reputation for quality. The strapline 'Quality you'd expect at prices you wouldn't' sums up the message. The whole campaign was backed by considerable advertising on TV, posters, direct mail and online.

Figure 39.2 Waitrose's 'essential range'

* By definition this sentence will probably be out of date by the time you read it.

in the 1990s. Now almost every retail outlet makes its goods available online. Online sales are estimated to be 8 per cent of total sales and they are growing at a faster rate than store-based sales. Amazon makes considerable investment in technology to ensure that its sites are customer friendly.

Market research

If finance and technology are important to a successful marketing mix, market research is vital. Note that this does not have to be formal research (questionnaires, group discussions, and so on). All firms are in daily contact with their customers, but it is usually only small firms that can capture this information. If a Pizza Hut customer complains that a pizza is too greasy, the head office manager for pizza supplies is very unlikely to ever hear the bad news. At a small Italian restaurant, the chef should hear straight away and think hard about whether the dough has too much oil in it.

Medium-sized and large firms need primary research to keep the senior managers in touch with the customers they rarely see. Small firms should constantly be listening to what customers say – in praise or in criticism. There is no better form of market research, because getting the product right is the key to all marketing success.

A-grade application

Amazon success due to customer focus

Amazon.com has been ranked the 'financially healthiest' retailer in the US for the second year in a row by an investment advice firm. A 2009 survey found that Amazon was the UK's favorite music and video retailer, and third overall retailer. Sales in 2009 were 15 times higher than 10 years ago. So what is the secret of the undoubted success of this business? Its 2009 letter to shareholders makes interesting reading.

It says 'The financial results for 2009 reflect the cumulative effect of 15 years of customer experience improvements: increasing selection, speeding delivery, reducing cost structure so we can afford to offer customers ever-lower prices. This work has been done by a large number of smart, relentless, customer-devoted people across all areas of the company. We are proud of our low prices, our reliable delivery, and our in-stock position on even obscure and hard-to-find items. We also know that we can still be much better, and we're dedicated to improving further'.

(Source: Extract from Amazon.com Inc 2009 letter to shareholders, dated 14 April 2010)

Where does the mix fit into marketing planning?

In **marketing planning**, the marketing mix should follow on from the **marketing strategy**. Managers need an excellent understanding of the market if they are to mix the ingredients effectively.

- Statistical analysis should highlight trends and further investigation will reveal the reasons for them.
- Market research should provide:
  - an understanding of the product's place in the market, the market segments and target customers
  - customers' views on the product
  - reasons for the success or failure of the product
  - an understanding of competitive activity.
- The marketing strategy should follow from this analysis. The marketing mix will put the strategy into practice (see Figure 39.3).

Figure 39.3 The 4Ps and marketing planning

Issues for analysis

When answering questions on the marketing mix, consideration should be given to the following points:

- How well the mix is matched to the strategy; only if every aspect of the mix is coordinated and focused will it be effective.
- The relative importance of the ingredients in the marketing mix. Although the product is likely to be the most important element of the mix, every case is different. Taste tests show Coca-Cola to be no better than Pepsi, yet Coke outsells its rival by up to 20 times – in nearly every country in the world.
- How each of the mix ingredients can be used to achieve effective marketing. The mix elements must be tailored to each case. One product may require (and afford) national television advertising, but in another case, small-scale local advertising might be supported by below-the-line activity to increase distribution. There is never a single answer to a question about the marketing mix. The best approach depends on the product, its competitive situation, the objectives and the marketing budget

Designing an effective marketing mix – an evaluation

The concept of the marketing mix has remained unchanged since it was first introduced in the 1950s and it has proved to be a useful marketing tool. However, many believe that there are strong arguments for adding a fifth ingredient – people. Many also feel that it should not be presented as a list of equally important parts but that the mix should be seen with the product at the core, supported by the other ingredients.

With the growing importance of customer service and good sales staff, it is legitimate to extend the marketing mix to include people. A customer who feels the salesperson is rude or lacks knowledge will go elsewhere. The type of people employed, and their attitude, can be used to build the company's image. Disney employees have to be smart, without facial hair, and be 'upbeat'. Particularly in service businesses, people matter. Good exam answers do not simply repeat a theory, they show a willingness to criticise it. It is worth remembering that not everyone agrees that the mix should have only 4Ps.

Although the 4Ps are presented as a list, there is no doubt that in almost every case the product is the most important ingredient. A successful marketing mix should be matched to the marketing strategy. And that strategy is rooted in how well the product is matched to the segment of the market being targeted.

Key terms

Marketing budget: the sum of money provided for marketing a product/service during a period of time (usually a year).

Marketing mix: the elements involved in putting a marketing strategy into practice; these are product, price, promotion and place.

Marketing planning: producing a schedule of marketing activities based on decisions about the marketing mix. This will show when, what and how much will be spent on a product's advertising, promotions and distribution over the coming year.

Marketing strategy: the medium- to long-term plan for meeting the firm's marketing objectives.

Revision questions (30 marks; 30 minutes)

1 Briefly outline each of the four ingredients of the marketing mix. (8)

2 Pick the marketing mix factor (the 'P') you think is of most importance in marketing any two of the following brands. Give a brief explanation of why you chose that factor.
   a) The *Sun* newspaper
   b) The iPod
   c) Cadbury's Creme Eggs
   d) A top-of-the-range BMW (6)

3 Outline how the marketing mix for Mars bars may affect their level of impulse sales in a small corner shop. (4)

4 What is meant by a market segment? (3)

5 Explain why new products are so important to businesses. (3)

6 List three different ways of promoting a product. (3)

7 Explain why it might be difficult for a new, small firm to get distribution in a supermarket chain such as Sainsbury's. (3)

Revision exercises

Discussion point: Cadbury Cocoa House

In October 2010, after five years' planning, the Cadbury Cocoa House opened in Bluewater Shopping Centre in Kent. It is the first of 50 planned cafes. Oddly, Cadbury is stepping back to the eighteenth-century origins of chocolate in Britain: drinking cocoa in a cafe. Cadbury has witnessed a decade of profitable growth for cafes such as Costa. Why not have a chocolate-themed, upmarket cafe? Not a place for a fry-up, but a place to take your aunt.

Cadbury Cocoa House has a menu of hot chocolate varieties, from white chocolate to 70% cocoa. It also offers lunches plus ice cream sundaes: a place for a treat.

Remarkably, this new business is not really a Cadbury operation. The initiative came from David Morris, former director of Harrods Foods, who approached Cadbury five years ago and agreed a 20-year licensing deal. Morris and his two co-founders are funding and managing the chain; Cadbury will simply enjoy the licensing income. This seems clever for Cadbury, as the company trialled the same concept in Bath in 2000, and ended up closing it down.

The Harrods background seems to have influenced a bold pricing strategy. The menu pricing points are higher than at Starbucks or Costa. For example, in December 2010, classic hot chocolate was £3.50, chestnut hot chocolate £6.95, a bacon butty £5.50 and a chicken sandwich £8.50. A Curly Wurly or Fruit and Nut sundae was £11.50. The founders must be hugely confident that the Cadbury name justifies these prices.

On launching, the business relied on two main forms of promotion:

- Public relations, including a TV news clip about the 2,000 job applicants for the cafe
- Passing traffic as the cafe has a big site at a busy junction in Bluewater.

In the long term, success will depend on whether £11.50 sundaes are special enough to bring customers back. The Cadbury name can generate product trial, but repeat custom is the only way to make enough profit to finance those big expansion plans.

Questions (25 marks; 30 minutes)

1 Using the marketing mix, analyse the proposal to open the Cadbury Cocoa Houses. (10)

2 Do you think it is a good idea? Explain your reasons. (15)

Case study

The battle for customers

A leading UK supermarket chain is considering expanding into India. It sees this as a relatively untapped market. The home market is saturated, and price wars and loyalty cards have reduced profit margins. In the UK, the supermarkets have been blamed for the disappearance of the corner shop. In India, the situation is very different. A recent survey by an Indian market research firm concluded that small grocery shops will continue to dominate the food retailing market for the foreseeable future. Several firms, which have been lured to India by its rapid economic growth and over 1 billion mouths to feed, have not been successful in their attempts to establish supermarkets in India's largest cities. Neither of the two main contenders have managed to break-even since opening in the early 1990s. They are continuing to expand and hoping that, eventually, economies of scale will permit lower prices and hopefully improve their standing and their profitability.

These new supermarkets have faced several problems.

- The local stores do not stock as many brands as the supermarkets, but they will stock an item if a customer wants it. If they do not have what the customer wants, they will get it.
- The local stores offer a free delivery service and allow customers credit.
- The supermarkets cannot match the cost base of the local store. The poor infrastructure makes operational costs very expensive.
- Government laws limiting urban development mean that property prices are high. The smaller stores have often been in the family for generations, and so the initial cost of the site has long since been forgotten.

To try to gain customers, one of the supermarket chains has introduced promotions such as coupons and has advertised in local newspapers. Another has teamed up with local manufacturers and obtains staples such as lentils and rice locally. These are then packaged and branded by local manufacturers. This has helped to lower prices for customers and improve margins. A recent entrant into the market is trying to stay ahead of the competition. It has invested in air-conditioning and additional telephone lines to ensure that customers do not have to wait when they call.

The UK chain has looked at the existing market in India and feels it can succeed. However, the managers know they will do this only after a struggle to change customer attitudes.

Questions *(30 marks; 40 minutes)*

1 What is meant by 'the home market is saturated'? (2)

2 What are the marketing implications for a business in a saturated market? (6)

3 Why might expansion allow economies of scale? (4)

4 What problems might a British retailer have in marketing its product in India? (6)

5 Using the marketing mix, analyse the existing market and evaluate the UK firm's chances of success. (12)

40 Product and product differentiation

Definition

A product is a good or service that is bought and sold within a market. Products are developed so that they satisfy a specific consumer need or want that has been targeted by the business.

Physical and psychological benefits of a product

Successful products are normally bought by consumers for more than one reason. Products such as Coca-Cola and Stella Artois deliver both physical and psychological consumer benefits. Both products taste good, delivering a fairly obvious physical benefit for the consumer. In addition, both brands offer consumers psychological benefits: both products have brand images that consumers want to buy into.

The key to having a good product is achieving consumer satisfaction. A restaurant can improve the quality of its product in many ways, the most obvious method being to improve the quality of food sold. Purchasing new superior tables and chairs could also improve the 'product'. However, the restaurant's product could also be improved by providing waiting staff with better training so that customer service improves. For service-sector businesses, such as hotels, a major element of the 'product' is the staff. Motivating employees so that they provide high standards of customer care is vital in terms of producing a high-quality product.

A-grade application

The iPad

Netbooks, portables and tablet computers had been around for years before Apple introduced its iPad. Observing the many previous flops in this sector, many analysts suggested that iPad would struggle to make an impact. Yet people queued to get their hands on the new computer and within six months, it had achieved an amazing 84 per cent market share within its sector of the US market.

The explanation for its success has been as much to do with marketing as to do with technical excellence. Apple created a remarkable buzz about the product before it was unveiled in early 2010, and then ran expensive advertising campaigns in Europe and America. This was surprising because the product was often sold out as production struggled to keep up with demand. Of course, beautiful product design was a huge help, especially iPad's good looks and pin-sharp screen. The highly differentiated package allowed Apple to price it markedly higher than its rivals.

Figure 40.1 The iPad

By late July 2010 analysts were suggesting that the iPad's sales would achieve double the launch expectations, at 13 million units, with sales of 50 million expected for 2012.

Influences on the development of new products

Technology

Technological advances can provide firms with opportunities to produce new products that offer consumers new benefits. According to 'Moore's law', computer speed and capacity doubles every two years. Advances in computer technology have enabled firms to develop new and improved mobile phones and laptop computers that offer consumers new features. These new features enable the firm that was first to the market with these new products to steal market share away from its rivals.

Rapid technological advances in computing have major implications for computer and mobile phone producers. Product life cycles are very short in both markets. As a consequence, component suppliers face tremendous timescale pressures to launch new components before they become technologically obsolete. Even a delay of just a month could be the difference between a successful new product and a failed launch.

Competitors' actions

Firms operating in competitive markets may try to emulate a successful new product produced by one of their rivals by launching their own 'me-too' version of the product. A me-too is a new brand that is largely an imitation of an existing product. Me-toos normally sell at a price discount compared to the original product.

Entrepreneurial skills of managers and owners

Most firms use market research findings to help them identify profitable new gaps in the market. Once these gaps in the market have been found, firms will then try to design new products that possess the characteristics required by the target market. Entrepreneurs need to be good at spotting gaps in the market; they also need to develop systems within their business that enable it to react first to changes in market trends.

Entrepreneurial managers can launch their new products quickly enough to benefit from '**first-mover advantage**'. Firms that can launch their new products before their rivals have the opportunity to charge premium prices until competition arrives. In most markets **brand loyalty** tends to be established at a very early stage. Businesses run by managers with weaker entrepreneurial skills, which launched their new products late, will probably find it very difficult to gain a foothold in the market.

A-grade application

Mercedes-Benz: innovative technology at your service

Sleeping at the wheel is one of the major causes of road fatalities. To combat this problem, Mercedes-Benz is trying to develop the technology necessary to detect driver fatigue. Teams of engineers, computer scientists and psychologists at Mercedes are working on the idea of installing an infra-red camera directed at the driver's eye. If eye-blink frequency drops below a critical level, indicating the onset of sleep, an audible alarm will sound inside the car to re-awaken the driver.

A-grade application

Zara's fast fashion revolution

Zara is one of Europe's fastest-growing fashion retailers. The company has based its success on fast fashion. The aim of this strategy is to launch new lines of cheap clothing that replicate exclusive designs, shown just a week earlier at major fashion shows. To make this strategy possible, the founder of Zara, Amancio Ortega, used lean production techniques first developed by the car maker Toyota to reduce new product development times.

Product differentiation and USP

Product differentiation is the degree to which consumers perceive that your brand is different from its competitors. A highly differentiated product is one that is viewed as having unique features, such as Marmite or the iPhone. A highly differentiated product may have substitutes. However, if differentiation is strong enough, consumers won't even bother looking at these other brands when making their purchasing decisions. The substitutes available are *not acceptable* to the consumer. A product's point of differentiation is often described as a **unique selling point** or proposition (USP).

Creating product differentiation

Product differentiation can be created in two ways.

1 *Actual differentiation*: this type of differentiation creates genuine product advantages that benefit the consumer in some way. Actual product differentiation can be created by:
   - a unique design that is aesthetically pleasing to the eye (e.g. Scandinavian furniture from IKEA)
   - a unique product function (e.g. a mobile phone with a new feature)
   - a unique taste (e.g. Dr Pepper)
   - ergonomic factors (e.g. a product that is easier to use than its rivals)
   - superior performance (e.g. a Dyson vacuum cleaner).

2 *Imagined differentiation*: this type of differentiation involves creating differences that exist only in the mind of the consumer. A product can be differentiated by psychological factors despite the fact that the product is not physically different from a similar product produced by the competition. Imaginary product differentiation can be created via persuasive advertising, celebrity endorsements and sponsorship. When a product is consumed it is not just the product itself that is consumed – buyers also enjoy 'consuming' the brand's image too. Many people are prepared to pay a price premium for a product that has a brand image that appeals to them.

Issues for analysis

When developing an argument in answer to an exam question, product differentiation offers the following main lines of analysis:

- Firms operating in competitive markets need to sell products that have a strong USP if they are to hold on to market share.
- Product differentiation reduces consumer price sensitivity. The brand loyalty created by the differentiation means that prices can be increased without having to worry about a substantial fall in sales volume. Total revenue should rise when prices are increased because highly differentiated products tend to be price inelastic.
- Product differentiation boosts value-added because it makes premium prices possible.

Product and product differentiation – an evaluation

Product differentiation is rarely permanent. Changes in consumer tastes and technological advances can make a product's point of differentiation ineffective. Can the idea be easily copied? Is there patent protection?

Which is more effective: imagined differentiation or actual differentiation? It could be argued that imagined differentiation, created by persuasive advertising, might be more long-lasting than actual differentiation because it might be harder for a me-too to replicate a brand's distinctive personality. Magners' original differentiation was relatively weak. Competitors quickly realised that they could also package their premium ciders in pint bottles, promoting the brand to be drunk over ice. If Magners is to hold on to its market share, it must identify a new USP.

Globalisation has increased the availability of products to consumers. As a result firms now face increased competitive pressure. In order to survive, firms must continually develop new, ever more powerful USPs for their products. Will small firms with modest research and development resources be able to compete against their larger rivals?

Key terms

Brand loyalty: the desire by customers to stick with one brand; perhaps to always buy that brand (e.g. always buying Galaxy instead of Cadbury's).

First-mover advantage: the benefits of being the first business into a new market sector (as Coca-Cola once was – in 1886!).

Unique selling point: one feature that makes a product different from all its rivals (e.g. Bounty – the only mass-market chocolate bar featuring coconut).

Revision questions *(40 marks; 40 minutes)*

1 Outline two reasons that might explain the success of products such as Coca-Cola and Stella Artois. (4)

2 Analyse how training might be used to improve the quality of the product produced by a service-sector business such as a supermarket. (3)

3 Explain how technological advances can influence the direction of new product development. (3)

4 What is first-mover advantage? State two benefits firms receive if they can achieve first-mover advantage. (4)

5 What is a me-too product and why do some firms choose to launch them? (4)

6 Explain the meaning of the term product differentiation, using your own example. (4)

7 Outline two ways in which a clothes shop might differentiate itself from its competitors. (6)

8 Explain two benefits a firm can gain from selling a differentiated product. (4)

9 Why is it particularly helpful to have a product that is differentiated by a USP? (4)

10 Outline two examples of USPs in current products or services you buy. (4)

Revision exercises

Data response

San Paulo is a highly successful Brazilian company that runs over 2,000 coffee bars across South America. The idea for the business came ten years ago when the founder of the business, Roberto Carlos, visited Italy for a family holiday. During his holiday Carlos was impressed by the décor and ambience of the traditionally-styled Italian coffee shops that he visited.

On his return to Brazil, Carlos decided to set up his own Italian-styled coffee bar. To ensure authenticity and a strong unique selling point, Carlos imported all the fixtures and fittings for his café from Italy. The business was an overnight success. At the time, nothing like it existed in his home town of Campo Grande, and the business quickly expanded by opening up new franchised outlets in other cities across Brazil and Argentina. Over time, trading conditions have become tougher as new competitors have entered the market. Most of these competitors have sought to replicate San Paulo's original unique selling point: classic Italian interior design. Today, San Paulo is still the market leader; a significant percentage of customers see San Paulo as being the original coffee bar of its type. However, in an attempt to grow market share, Carlos recently took the decision to reduce San Paulo's price premium.

The company now has plans to enter the UK market and the first bar will be set up in Croydon. The management of San Paulo believe that they will have to charge their UK consumers substantially more than their South American customers to overcome higher European wages and rents. The UK coffee bar market is extremely competitive. Will San Paulo be able to survive against companies such as Costa, Caffè Nero and Starbucks?

Questions *(25 marks; 30 minutes)*

1 a) Define the term 'unique selling point'. (2)

b) Identify the original unique selling point that made San Paulo a successful business in South America. (2)

2 Using the data in the case as a starting point, discuss whether constant innovation is required to maintain product differentiation. (12)

3 You have been hired to manage the new bar in Croydon. Despite your concerns about the strength of the competition locally, your English boss wants you to charge high prices. Outline three ways that could be used to create the high product differentiation required for your coffee bar. (9)

Data response

Absolut vodka

Absolut vodka was developed by the Swedish state-owned monopoly provider of strong alcohol, Systembolaget, in the late 1970s. The government's goal was to create a premium-priced product that would sell well in America. Blind product tests showed that consumers were not able to tell the difference between one brand of vodka and another. The challenge, then, was to create a consumer preference for Absolut vodka where there was no real difference.

To create the product differentiation required, the advertising agency appointed to market Absolut had to create a unique image for the brand that would appeal to consumers. The first step was to create a distinctive award-winning bottle that reflected the brand's Scandinavian origins. The second step was more controversial. A brand heritage for Absolut was required to convince American consumers that the brand was authentic. Advertisements claimed that the brand was over 400 years old. Unfortunately, this was not true: Absolut was first sold in Sweden in 1879 and, for many years, the brand had been withdrawn and was unavailable for sale – production of Absolut only restarted in 1979, just before the brand's relaunch. Less controversially, differentiation was also built up by the decision to use world-famous artists such as Andy Warhol to promote the brand. In America the company also sponsored arts and cultural events to enhance the image of the brand. The strategy worked and today, Absolut holds over 30 per cent of the American vodka market.

Questions *(25 marks; 30 minutes)*

1 What is a premium-priced product? (2)

2 Explain why product differentiation can create premium prices. (4)

3 Outline two factors that might influence the direction of new product development in the alcoholic drinks industry. (4)

4 Analyse two ways in which product differentiation was created for the Absolut brand. (6)

5 Discuss the ethics of the marketing of Absolut vodka. (9)

Product life cycle and portfolio analysis

Definition
The product life cycle is the theory that over time all products follow a similar pattern of development, birth, growth, maturity and decline.

Product life cycle

The product life cycle shows the sales of a product over time. When a new product is first launched, sales will usually be slow. This is because the product is not yet known or proven in the market. Retailers may be reluctant to stock the product because it means giving up valuable shelf space to products that may or may not sell. This involves a high risk. Customers may also be hesitant – many may want to wait until someone else has tried the product before they purchase it themselves.

If the product does succeed, then its sales will grow and it enters the growth phase of the product life cycle. However, at some point sales are likely to stabilise; this is known as the maturity phase. This slowing down of the growth of sales might be because competitors have introduced similar products or because the market has now become saturated. Once most households have bought a dishwasher, for example, sales are likely to be relatively slow. This is because new purchases will mainly involve people who are updating their machine, rather than new buyers.

At some point sales are likely to decline, perhaps because new technology means the product has become outdated. An example is the way CD sales have fallen due to the rise of downloading music from the internet. A decline in sales may also be because competitors have launched a more successful model or you have improved your own product (e.g. the iPad has taken sales from the iPhone).

The five key stages of a product's life cycle are known as development, introduction, growth, maturity and decline. These can be illustrated on a product life cycle diagram. The typical stages in a product's life are shown in Figure 41.1. (Refer back to Figure 38.2, the iPod life cycle, as well.)

Do remember that many products never make it as far as being launched. Many would-be entrepreneurs have what they think are great ideas. Unfortunately, it turns out they are not financially viable or they cannot find a way of successfully getting them to market. Just think how many ideas are rejected each series on the BBC TV show *Dragons' Den*, because the investors do not think demand is going to be high enough.

Even well-established firms will find that many of their new ideas do not prove commercially viable. Cadbury's rejects twenty new product ideas for every one that reaches the market. Apple's iPod may have been a great success, but its internet software, Cyberdog, lasted about a year, and its first phone – launched with Motorola in 2005 and called the ROKR – was a flop. (Its second effort, the iPhone, did rather better!) Thousands of products are taken out of production each year because they fail to hit their initial sales targets and have not reached the growth stage of the life cycle.

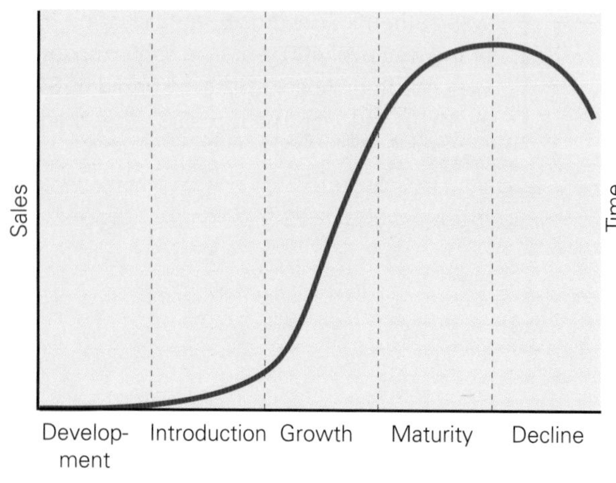

Figure 41.1 The product life cycle

Purpose of the product life cycle

The product life cycle model helps managers plan their marketing activities. Marketing managers will need to adjust their marketing mix at different stages of the product life cycle, as outlined below.

- In the introduction phase the promotion may focus on making customers aware that a new product exists. In the maturity phase it may focus more on highlighting the difference between your product and competitors that have arrived since.
- At the beginning of the life cycle, a technologically advanced product may be launched with a high price (e.g. the iPhone), but over time the price may fall as newer models are launched. By considering the requirements of each stage of the life cycle, marketing managers may adjust their marketing activities accordingly.

Managers know that the length of the phases of the life cycle cannot easily be predicted. They will vary from one product to another and this means the marketing mix will need to be altered at different times. For example, a product may be a fad and therefore the overall life of the product will be quite short. Many fashions are popular only for one season and some films are popular only for a matter of weeks. Other products have very long life cycles. The first manufactured cigarettes went on sale in Britain in 1873. By chance, sales hit their peak (120,000 million!) exactly 100 years later. Since 1973 sales have gradually declined.

It is also important to distinguish between the life cycle of a product category and the life cycle of a particular brand. Sales of wine are growing, but a brand that was once the biggest seller (Hirondelle) has virtually disappeared as wine buyers have become more sophisticated. Similarly, confectionery is a mature market but particular brands are at different stages in their life cycles: Mars bars are in maturity while Trident chewing gum is in its growth stage.

Table 41.1 Examples of how the marketing mix may vary at different stages of the product life cycle

	Development	Introduction	Growth	Maturity	Decline
Sales	Zero	Low	Increasing	Growth is slowing	Falling
Costs per unit	High; there is investment in product development but only a few prototypes and test products are being produced	High, because sales are relatively low but launch costs are high and overheads are being spread over a few units	Falling as overheads are spread over more units	Falling as sales are still growing	Still likely to be low as development costs have been covered and reduced promotional costs are needed to raise awareness
Product	Prototypes	Likely to be basic	May be modified following initial customer feedback; range may be increased	Depends – may focus on core products and remove ones in the range not selling well; may diversify and extend brand to new items	Focus on most profitable items
Promotion	As development is nearly finished, it may be used to alert customers of the launch	Mainly to raise awareness	Building loyalty	May focus on highlighting differences with competitors' products	

Table 41.1 contd.

	Development	Introduction	Growth	Maturity	Decline
Distribution	Early discussions with retailers will help in finalising the product packaging	May be limited as distributors wait to see customers' reactions	May be increasing as more distributors willing to stock product and it is rolled out to more markets	May focus on key outlets and more profitable channels	Lower budgets to keep costs down
Price	Not needed	Depends on pricing approach – a high price if skimming is adopted (if demand is high and not sensitive to price); a low price if penetration is adopted to gain market share	Depends on demand conditions and strategy adopted; with a skimming strategy the price may now be lowered to target more segments	May have to drop price to maintain competitiveness	Likely to discount to maintain sales

A-grade application

Falling sales of CDs

Towards the end of 2009 Linn Products announced that it would stop producing CDs. The niche producer based in East Renfrewshire will now focus on producing digital streaming equipment. The newer digital machines will allow streaming through other operating systems such as home computers. However, the company will continue to make turntables for vinyl records as demand continues for the sound quality of this older technology.

Compact discs (CDs) began to be used for commercial music in 1982, replacing cassette tapes and vinyl records. The CD is now being replaced by digital recordings. In 2009 there were 117 million sales of single and individual tracks; nearly 99 per cent of these were digital downloads. However, in terms of albums, CD sales continue to dominate even though their market share is falling. In 2006 there were 154 million album sales, of which CDs accounted for 151m and digital for 2.7m. In 2007, with 138m sales, 131m were CDs and 6.2m were digital. In 2008, there were 137m album sales, with 123m CDs and 10.3m digital downloads. Vinyl records, cassettes and other formats accounted for around 300,000 sales.

Product life cycle and capacity

When considering the future sales of the business, managers will need to link their forecasts to their plans for the firm's capacity. The capacity of an organisation is the maximum it can produce given its existing resources. If managers choose a capacity level that is relatively low, this means that a sudden increase in sales (e.g. if the product enters the growth phase quickly) may mean customers have to be turned away. On the other hand, if the chosen capacity level is high, if the product is not successful the business will have invested in facilities that are not required; this is inefficient and expensive. Trying to match the capacity of the business to the likely sales is a difficult challenge for managers.

Cash flow and the product life cycle

In the development phase before a product is launched, cash flow will be negative. The firm will be spending money on research and development, market research and production planning, but no revenue is yet being generated. Prototypes and models are being made (Dyson produced 5,000 prototypes of the Dyson vacuum cleaner before launching it) but income is zero. The business may also decide to test-market the product, which again costs money.

Once the product is on sale, cash should begin to come in. However, at this stage, sales are likely to be low and the firm will still be promoting the product heavily to generate awareness. Overall cash flow may continue to be negative for some time. In many cases, the cash flow will not become a positive figure until some way into the growth stage of the life cycle. It may only be at that stage that the firm reaches operational break-even. Cash flow should then continue to improve until the decline stage, when the volume of sales and the amount of cash coming in begin to fall.

It is important, therefore, for firms to manage their cash flow effectively during the life cycle and to plan ahead. Although a product may prove successful in the long term, it may also cause the firm severe cash flow problems in the short term unless its finances are properly managed. Careful budgeting is important at this stage, to avoid overspending.

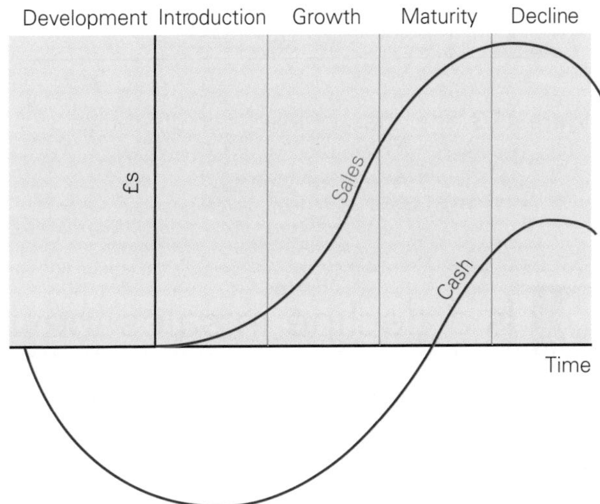

Figure 41.2 The product life cycle and cash flow

A-grade application

Ocado is an online grocer that is in partnership with the supermarket Waitrose. Ocado was established in 2001 and, within its first six years, had gained sales of £300 million a year. Even so, it was still not making a profit because of the huge costs of establishing the business. For example, Ocado has invested in an enormous central warehouse where the products are stocked and packed. This is the size of seven football pitches and six storeys high. By 2007 the warehouse was still operating at 35 per cent capacity.

In 2010 Ocado floated on the stock market to become a public limited company. The firm raised about £200m from the share sale to build a second depot for fulfilling customer orders. Its sales at this stage were £427.3m but it had still not made a profit! Investors were willing to bet that the huge cash investment would eventually pay off.

Extension strategies

The aim of an extension strategy is to prevent a decline in the product's sales. There are various means by which this can be achieved, as described below.

- *By targeting a new segment of the market:* when sales of Johnson & Johnson's baby products started to fall, the company repositioned the product and aimed it at adults. Alternatively, a new geographic market may be targeted.
- *By developing new uses for the product:* the basic technology in hot-air paint strippers, for example, is no different from that in a hairdryer.
- *By increasing the usage of a product:* Actimel's 'challenge' was for consumers to eat one pot a day for a fortnight – a wonderful way to encourage increased consumption.

The continued success of products such as Coca-Cola and Kellogg's cornflakes is not just due to luck; it is

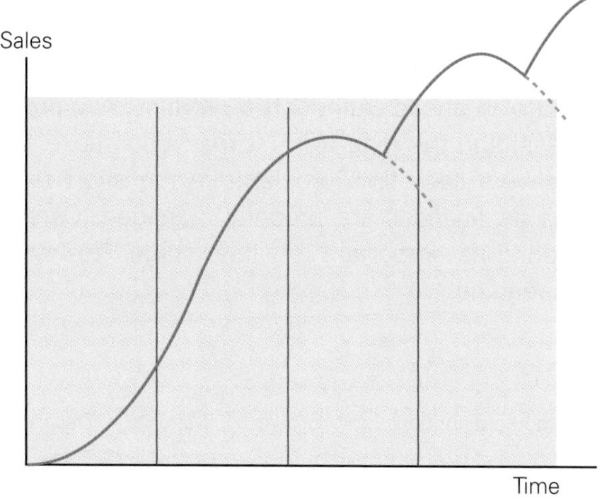

Figure 41.3 The effect of extension strategies

down to sophisticated marketing techniques, which have managed to maintain sales over many years despite fierce competition. The Kellogg's logo is regularly updated, new pack sizes are often introduced, and various competitions and offers are used on a regular basis to keep sales high. The company has also tried to increase the number of students and adults eating its products. It has run advertising campaigns to encourage people to eat the product throughout the day as well as in the morning.

Given the fact that developing a product can involve high costs and that there is a high failure rate of new products, it is not surprising that if a product is successful managers will try to prolong its sales for as long as it is profitable. Who would have thought, in the 1880s, that a frothy drink would still be a huge seller more than 125 years later? Clever Coke.

Is a decline in sales inevitable?

In the standard product life cycle model it seems as if a decline in sales is inevitable. This may be true in some situations. For example, developments in technology may make some products obsolete. On the other hand, the decline in sales may be the result of poor marketing. Effective extension strategies may ensure that a product's sales are maintained. The long-term success of products such as Monopoly and Kit-Kat shows that sales can be maintained over a very long period of time. Creative marketing can avoid the decline phase for a substantial period of time – but only if the product is good enough to keep buyers coming back for more.

One of the reasons for sales decline may be that some managers assume the product will fail at some point and so do not make enough effort to save it. This is known as 'determinism': managers think sales will decline and so sales do fall because of inadequate marketing support. Instead of adapting their marketing strategy to find new ways of selling the product, they let it decline because they assume it cannot be saved.

It is important to remember that a life cycle graph only shows what has happened – it is not a prediction of the future. Top marketing managers try to influence the future, not just let it happen. They try to shape the product life cycle rather than let it shape their success.

A-grade application

UK soft drinks market

The soft drinks market in the UK is worth about £13 billion. In this market, new product development is critical. Soft drinks have increasingly come under attack for their impact on children, because the sugar content can lead to obesity and artificial additives can lead to hyperactivity. These criticisms could have led to a decline in sales in the market. However, producers have responded by developing products with a healthier image, to keep sales growing. Claims about the lack of additives, preservatives and low/no/reduced sugar drinks are now almost essential. Retail value sales of soft drinks are expected to grow by 17 per cent between 2009 and 2014.

The product portfolio

Product **portfolio analysis** examines the existing position of a firm's products. This allows the firm to consider its existing position and plan what to do next. There are several different methods of portfolio analysis. One of the best known was developed by the Boston Consulting Group, a management consultancy, and is known as the Boston Matrix.

The Boston Matrix shows the market share of each of a firm's products and the rate of growth of the markets in which they operate. By highlighting the position of each product in terms of market share and market growth, a business can analyse its existing situation and decide what to do next and where to direct its marketing efforts. This model has four categories, as described below.

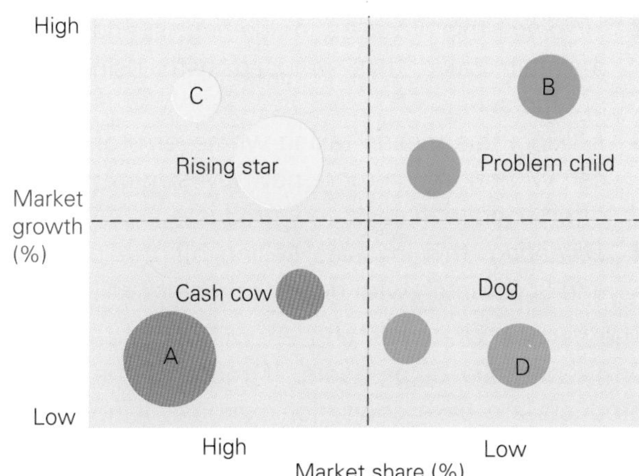

Figure 41.4 Product portfolio: the Boston Matrix

Cash cow: a high share of a slow-growing market

In Figure 41.4, product A has a high market share of a low-growth market. The size of the circle depends on the turnover of the product. This type of product is known as a **cash cow**. An example of a cash cow might be Heinz Baked Beans. The overall market for baked beans is mature and therefore slow growing. Within this market, the Heinz brand has a market share of more than 50 per cent. This type of product generates high profits and cash for the company because sales are relatively high, while the promotional cost per unit is quite low. Consumers are already aware of the brand, which reduces some of the need for promotion. High and stable sales keep the cost per unit relatively low. Heinz can therefore 'milk' cash from baked beans to invest in newer products such as Heinz Organic Ketchup.

Problem child: a low share of a fast-growing market

Product B, by comparison, is in a high-growth market but has a low market share. This type of product is known as a **problem child** (also called a 'question mark'). A problem child may well provide high profits in the future; the market itself is attractive because it is growing fast and the product could provide high returns if it manages to gain a greater market share. However, the success of such products is by no means certain and that is why they are like problem children – they may grow and prosper or things may go wrong. These products usually need a relatively high level of investment to promote them, get them distributed and keep them going. A new Heinz recipe might be in this position.

Rising star: a high share of a growing market

Rising stars such as product C have a high market share and are selling in a fast-growing market. These products are obviously attractive – they are doing well in a successful market. However, they may need protection from competitors' products. Once again, the profits of the cash cows can be used to keep the sales of rising stars growing. Heinz Organic Soups are in this category. They are very successful, with fast-growing sales, but still need heavy promotion to ensure their success.

Dogs: a low share of a stable or declining market

The fourth category of products are known as **dogs**. These products (like product D in Figure 41.4) have a low share of a low-growth market. They hold little appeal for a firm unless they can be revived. The product or brand will be killed off once its sales slip below the break-even point.

Purpose of product portfolio analysis

Product portfolio analysis aims to examine the existing position of the firm's products. Once this has been done, the managers can plan what to do next. Typically this will involve four strategies:

1 *Building*: this involves investment in promotion and distribution to boost sales; it is often used with problem children (question marks).
2 *Holding*: this involves marketing spending to maintain sales; this is used with rising star products.
3 *Milking*: this means taking whatever profits you can without much more new investment; this is often used with cash cow products
4 *Divesting*: this involves selling off the product and is common with dogs or problem children.

The various strategies chosen will depend on the firm's portfolio of products. If most of the firm's products are cash cows, for example, it needs to develop new products for future growth. If, however, the majority are problem children, then it is in quite a high-risk situation; it needs to try to ensure some products do become stars. If it has too many dogs then it needs to invest in product development or acquire new brands.

Both the product life cycle and product portfolio analysis are marketing tools to help firms with their marketing planning. By analysing their existing situation, they can identify what needs to be done with the marketing mix to fulfil their objectives. However, like all planning tools, simply being able to examine the present position does not in itself guarantee success. Firms still have to be able to select the right strategy and implement it successfully.

Issues for analysis

When analysing the importance of the product life cycle and portfolio model, it might be useful to consider the following points:

- Portfolio analysis examines the position of all the firm's products, and helps managers decide what to do with each of them (e.g. invest more or milk them).
- The models do not in themselves tell the firm what to do; managers must interpret their findings and decide on the most effective course of action.
- Managers must avoid letting these models become self-fulfilling (e.g. deciding the product is in decline and so letting its sales fall).
- Product life cycles are generally becoming shorter due to rapid developments in technology and increasing levels of competition in most markets.
- As well as the life cycle for a particular product, it can be useful to study the life cycle of a category of products (e.g. examining the life of Flora margarine and the life cycle for the whole margarine market).

Product life cycle and portfolio analysis – an evaluation

The product life cycle model and portfolio analysis are important in assessing the firm's current position within the market and make up an important step in the planning process. However, simply gathering data does not in itself guarantee success. A manager has to interpret the information effectively and then make the right decision. The models show where a business is at the moment; the difficult decisions relate to where the business will be in the future.

Product portfolio analysis is especially useful for larger businesses with many products. It helps a manager look critically at the firm's product range, enabling decisions to be made on how the firm's marketing spending should be divided up between different products. By contrast, the product life cycle is of more help to a small firm with one or two products. A company called Filofax made a fortune in the 1990s marketing a paper-based 'personal organiser'. When people switched to electronic products such as the BlackBerry, Filofax wasted years (and many millions) persisting with its paper product. The business needed to acknowledge when a life cycle decline was unstoppable.

Key terms

Cash cow: a product that has a high share of a low-growth market.

Dog: a product that has a low share of a low-growth market.

Extension strategy: marketing activities used to prevent sales from declining.

Portfolio analysis: an analysis of the market position of the firm's existing products; it is used as part of the marketing planning process.

Problem child: a product that has a small share of a fast-growing market.

Rising star: a product that has a high share of a fast-growing market.

Revision questions (35 marks; 35 minutes)

1. Identify the different stages of the product life cycle. Give an example of one product or service you consider to be at each stage of the life cycle. (4)
2. Explain what is meant by an 'extension strategy'. (4)
3. Outline the likely relationship between cash flow and the different stages of the life cycle. (4)
4. How is it possible for products such as Barbie dolls to apparently defy the decline phase of the product cycle? (6)
5. What is meant by 'product portfolio analysis'? (3)
6. Distinguish between a cash cow and a rising star in the Boston Matrix. (4)
7. Explain how the Boston Matrix could be used by a business such as Cadbury. (4)
8. Firms should never take decline (or growth) for granted. Therefore, they should never take success (or failure) for granted. Explain why this advice is important if firms are to make the best use of product life cycle theory. (6)

Data Response

Fire Angel

Sam Tate and his partner have developed an innovative smoke detector called Fire Angel. This product is placed in a light fitting and its energy supply is automatically recharged when the light is turned on. This way the danger of your smoke detector failing to work because of flat batteries should be reduced and, because it recharges itself, customers don't need to buy new batteries. Fire Angel is now stocked in around 6,000 stores.

Before launching Fire Angel, Sam did lots of market research. He spoke to the Fire Brigade and the government office responsible for fire safety, to ensure that there was a need for this sort of product, and to estimate the market size and market growth. He then interviewed people in the street to see what they thought, as well as analysing competitors' products. He also examined different ways of getting the product to market and eventually decided that selling through the supermarkets was the key to achieving a high volume of sales.

The average price of smoke detectors is between £15 and £20 but Sam felt he could charge a premium price because his product does not need a battery and lasts for up to ten years, so he set the price of the Fire Angel at £30. He felt it was better to go in with a higher price than a lower one because it is more difficult to lower the price than increase it later on. It took three years to get the Fire Angel from the idea stage to the launch stage; most of this time was spent on design and testing, but it did take many months to convince some of the retailers to stock it.

(Source: adapted from Business Link)

Questions *(30 marks; 35 minutes)*

1 What is meant by 'market growth'? (2)

2 Outline the unique selling point of the Fire Angel and explain how this can benefit the business. (6)

3 Analyse the possible benefits to Sam of undertaking market research before launching the Fire Angel. (7)

4 Explain why Sam might have had cash flow problems in the first few years of his business. (6)

5 At the moment the Fire Angel is still in its growth phase. Discuss the ways in which the marketing mix of the Fire Angel might change as it enters the maturity phase. (9)

B2 Data response

Mackie's ice cream

Mackie's is a luxury ice cream maker, based in Scotland.

All Mackie's ice cream is made at its farm in Aberdeenshire. Its production chain includes the wind that provides the business with renewable energy, its own crops that feed its cattle and its own cows that produce the milk and cream for the ice cream. 'It's a real plough to plate – or cow to cone story,' says the company.

Mackie's employs 70 people and produces over 7 million litres of luxury ice cream a year.

Mackie's ice cream is well established as the brand leader in the luxury ice cream market in Scotland, has an increasing market share in England and is being exported to Seoul, South Korea and Norway.

The Mackie family have been farming at Westertown Farm since the turn of the century, but it was only in 1986 that it started pilot trials for an ice cream. In 1993 some of the farm's facilities were converted to a modern ice cream dairy capable of producing more than 10 million litres a year. In 1996 the New Product Development Kitchen was added. In 2006 production machinery was added to raise capacity in the ice cream dairy to 6,000 litres per hour. It sells through shops, restaurants and ice cream parlours.

Its luxury ice cream products include traditional vanilla (this is its cash cow), raspberry, honeycomb, strawberry and cream, chocolate mint and absolutely chocolate. These are available in a variety of sizes. It also produces 100% fruit frozen smoothies, sorbets and organic ice cream.

Figure 41.5 The Mackie family

(Source www.mackies.co.uk)

Questions *(30 marks; 35 minutes)*

1 What is meant by the term 'market share'? (2)

2 Explain the factors that Mackie might have considered before expanding its capacity. (5)

3 Explain how the promotion of a new Mackie's ice cream might vary at different stages in its life cycle. (5)

4 Examine the possible benefits to Mackie of having a portfolio of products. (8)

5 Consider whether new product development is likely to be essential for success in the ice cream market. (10)

Promotion

Definition

Promotion is the part of the marketing mix that focuses on persuading people to buy the product or service.

I know that half the money I spend on advertising is wasted, but I can never find out which half. *(Lord Leverhulme, British industrialist)*

Promotion

Promotion is a general term that covers all the marketing activity that focuses on letting the customer know about a product and persuading them to buy that product. It is not just about advertising. The different elements of promotion can be grouped into two broad categories: those that stimulate short-term sales and those that build sales for the long term.

Types of promotion for building long-term sales

These include branding, persuasive advertising and public relations, as discussed below.

Branding

One of the best forms of promotion is branding. Branding is the process of creating a distinctive and lasting identity in the minds of consumers. Establishing a brand can take considerable time and marketing effort, but once a product brand is established, it becomes its own means of promotion. The brand name is recognised and this makes it more likely that the customer will buy the product for the first time. If the experience is satisfactory the customer is very likely to continue to choose the brand. Once established, branding has many advantages, such as:

- it enables the business to reduce the amount spent on promotion
- customers are more likely to purchase the product again (repeat purchases)
- it is easier to persuade retailers to put the products in their stores
- other products can be promoted using the same brand name.

Persuasive advertising

Persuasive advertising is designed to create a distinctive image. A good example is BMW, which has spent decades persuading us that it produces not a car but a 'Driving Machine'. Advertising of this kind has also helped create clear consumer images for firms such as Tesco and L'Oréal (see Table 42.1).

Public relations

This is the attempt to affect consumers' image of a product without spending on media advertising. It includes making contacts with journalists to try to get favourable mentions or articles about your product. It would also include activities such as sponsorship of sport or the arts. The London Olympic Games in 2012 has Lloyds TSB as one of its main sponsors. This allows the business to advertise and use its logo alongside the Olympic logo.

Table 42.1 Examples of persuasive advertising

Company	Slogan	Meaning
Tesco	'Every little helps'	We understand your needs and we try to help (we're not just a great big, greedy business)
L'Oréal	Because you're worth it'	Go on, spoil yourself. You can afford that bit extra, so buy our products, not our competitors'
Innocent Drinks	'Nothing, but nothing, but fruit'	Our products are pure (whereas others are not)

A-grade application

Social advertising – Nike

Social networks are the latest trend in getting your products in front of potential consumers. Social network sites such as Facebook, Twitter and YouTube are increasingly being used to promote products. Coca Cola and Ikea are two of the big brands that are using Facebook. During the 2010 World Cup, Nike scored a major goal. An advertising video originally shown on TV was then shown on YouTube. The number of hits (over 16 million after a few months) showed that this reached a much greater audience than the original TV ad.

Figure 42.1

Types of promotion for boosting short-term sales

These include sales promotions, direct selling and merchandising, as discussed below.

Sales promotions

These range from on-pack competitions to in-store offers such as buy-one-get-one-free (BOGOF). These can be very effective at boosting sales, but there are risks involved, such as: customers may stock up at (in effect) half price, then not need to buy more items in the weeks following the offer; special offers may undermine the brand image (what would it say to consumers if Apple started offering 'buy one iPhone get one free'?). These risks are worthwhile only if the promotion succeeds in attracting brand new customers, who come for the offer and then stay loyal after the offer has ended (which is asking a lot).

Direct selling

Potential customers are approached directly. At one time this would be done by door-to-door salesmen. Nowadays, the main mechanism for direct selling is telesales. Both approaches are expensive, because one-to-one selling implies high labour costs. A TV advertisement sounds expensive at, perhaps, £100,000, but that money would buy you an audience of 5 million people. Therefore, the cost per person is £100,000 ÷ 5m = £0.02 (i.e. 2p). Just think how much more expensive it would be to pay someone to travel to you and spend time selling a product to you personally (2 hours @ £8 an hour + £4 travel costs = £20, and that's the absolute minimum). Direct selling is affordable only if there are huge financial rewards to the seller (e.g. selling financial products or double glazing).

Merchandising

This requires staff to visit shops to ensure that a brand's display looks eye-catching and tidy. Merchandisers may set up 'dump bin' displays at the end of shopping aisles, perhaps featuring a newly launched product. The shop will charge rent for the space, but the extra sales can more than make up for this. Merchandisers may also offer shoppers free product samples, to encourage them to make their first trial purchase.

Promotional mix

Few businesses would use just one method of promotion. A snack bar might do no more than hand out leaflets, but most firms will have a mixture of activities. This is known as the **promotional mix**. An example would be Innocent Drinks, whose promotional mix has been successful enough to build the company's sales from £0.5 million to £100 million in less than ten years. Its mix includes:

- TV advertising (to build brand awareness)
- newspaper advertising to target high-income young adults (who do not watch much TV)
- an annual 'Fruitstock' free concert, to build loyalty among existing customers
- continually working on its website, so that regular customers return to find out the latest new product ideas or recipes.

The mix of promotional activities chosen by a company will depend on the following factors:

- *The size of the market:* if the market is large the business will primarily use advertising through the mass media. If the market is very small this method will be too expensive and inefficient. Direct marketing or selling will probably be the best focus.
- *The type of product:* a consumer product will require different promotion to an industrial product.
- *The cost:* a small or new business is unlikely to be able to spend large amounts of money on promotion. This means that some forms of promotion, such as TV advertising, are out of the cost range of the business. The business will need to find cheaper alternatives, such as local advertising and direct marketing or selling.

Getting the promotional mix right will require the business to understand the nature of its product, its customers and its competitors. Good **market research** will provide the essential information to make the right decisions about the promotional mix.

A-grade application

Lloyds TSB – London 2012 Olympic sponsor

In March 2007 Lloyds TSB became the first official British sponsor of the London Olympic Games in 2012.

The sponsorship is thought to have cost Lloyds TSB £80m. It will be the only high street bank to have marketing rights for the London 2012 Olympics and will be able to use the Games' logo in its promotions. The bank will help sell and distribute tickets to the Games when they go on sale in 2011.

Lloyds TSB said: 'Our partnership with the London 2012 Olympic and Paralympic Games places Lloyds TSB at the heart of the most exciting world event to take place in the UK for many decades. As a truly British company serving customers across the UK, we wanted to demonstrate our commitment to Britain and our confidence that 2012 will be the best Games ever.'

Eric Daniels, the chief executive of Lloyds TSB Group, said: 'The 2012 Games represent a unique opportunity to create a lasting legacy for sport and youth in this country and we are proud to be associated with it. Every day, our staff work with customers to help them realise their goals and aspirations, and in many ways, that is what 2012 is all about.'

London 2012 chief executive, Paul Deighton, said: 'London 2012 is a once in a lifetime opportunity for businesses in the UK to access the powerful benefits associated with staging the Olympic and Paralympic Games.

'The commercial value of a London 2012 partnership will be realised long before the opening ceremony in 2012, and can be sustained as a legacy for decades after the final race is won.'

Choosing the right promotional activity for the marketing strategy

The type of promotion used and the level of promotional activity will vary not only from company to company and product to product but also in terms of the marketing strategy being followed. Different forms of promotion will achieve different purposes and much will depend on what the business is trying to achieve (see Table 42.2).

Table 42.2 Marketing strategies and types of promotion

Marketing strategy	Promotion needs to:
Launching a new product	● be informative ● reach target customers
Differentiating the product	● identify special features of the product ● persuade customers it is different/better than rival products
Extending the life of an existing product	● reinforce the reasons for customers choosing it ● highlight any new features ● attract new customers
Increasing market share	● attract new customers ● reinforce buying in existing customers
Building brand identity	● increase awareness of the company/product name ● create customer recognition and loyalty

The correct promotional mix will be achieved only if the business has clear marketing objectives. Once the objectives and strategy are determined it is much easier for the business to develop an effective promotional campaign.

Promotion and market research

In order to develop the best promotional campaign it is important that market research is carried out so that the business has the necessary knowledge about the product and the market. The more information the business has about its customers and its competitors, the easier it will be to develop an effective promotional campaign.

- If the business knows who is likely to buy the product it can determine its target audience and specifically target that group with its promotional activity.
- If the business understands why customers are choosing a rival product, it can specifically design promotional material that addresses these issues.
- If the business understands what makes its product attractive to customers, it can use this knowledge to reinforce the promotional message.

Market knowledge is always important if promotional activity is to be effective and it is vital for a new business. If the business is unable to target the right **market segment** or to persuade customers to buy the product, then the promotional expenditure will be wasted. Ultimately no sales means no business.

Promotion needs to be effective

Being effective means striking a balance between coverage, cost and results. TV advertising is expensive but has huge coverage. However, if the target customers are a small segment of the population, the coverage may be wasted. There is no point in advertising table tennis equipment on TV at peak viewing times – it is more effective to use a specialist magazine for table tennis players; if players belong to clubs, they could also be targeted by direct mail.

The business needs to constantly monitor promotional activity to see if it is having the desired effect. A prime-time TV advert may reach a huge audience but is ineffective if it does not increase sales.

There are many ways that businesses can monitor the effect of any promotional campaign. The most obvious is to see if there is any increase in sales. Other ways include using market research to see if the campaign has affected public perception of the product.

How important is promotion?

Promotion is vital for a new business – how else will customers know that it exists and what its products are? Although existing businesses may need to do less promotion, the importance of promotion will depend on the following factors:

- *The competitiveness of the market:* where no alternatives are available, the consumer will have less choice; there will be less need to persuade the customer to buy.
- *Availability:* if the product is in short supply, there will be little need to promote it. Where several products are competing for customer approval in crowded markets, promotion becomes very important.
- *How easily the product can be differentiated in the market:* if the differences are obvious to the customer, there may be less need for promotion.
- *The stage of the product life cycle:* a new product will usually need promotional support. Promotion will tell customers that the product is available and will persuade them to try the new product. If the product has been altered, promotion will tell customers of the changes.

In **industrial markets**, where one business is selling to another, there may be less need for promotion. This is particularly true where a business is supplying products to the customer's specification and has established a long-term relationship with the buyer.

Issues for analysis

- Promotion is about telling the customer about the product and persuading them to make a purchase. It is therefore vital when answering a question on promotion to consider the business, its product and the market. Analysis should consider the different promotional methods that are available but should concentrate on those that are suitable for the particular business. There is no point suggesting that a new small business should look at advertising on TV or consider promoting a major sporting event.
- The single best form of analysis, though, is to consider promotion in relation to the timescale of the firm's objectives. If it wants to build a brand for the long term, it can do damage by using short-term tactics such as price promotions. Carefully targeted advertising designed to build the 'right' image is the key – 'right' being the image that best suits the customers being targeted. Over-60s may respond very well to secure, warm images, whereas the 16–25 age group may want images based on fun and celebrity.

Table 42.3 Advantages and disadvantages of various promotion methods

	Advantages	Disadvantages
Advertising (e.g. on TV)	• Reaches a large audience • Increases prestige of the product/ company • Can be targeted to viewing groups	• Very expensive • Can be too broad-based to reach target customers
Direct selling	• With good research, enables the customer to be targeted directly	• Can get a reputation as a nuisance caller • Unless properly researched, can be difficult to target
Direct marketing	• With good research, can be cost effective	• Wide coverage often produces only a small response
Merchandising	• Good product displays can increase the rate of impulse purchase and can build brand awareness	• Expensive as it relies on personal calling by sales staff
Sales promotions (such as buy one get one free)	• Increases sales immediately and, possibly, dramatically	• Customers may have bought anyway
Public relations (PR)	• Publicises the company name	• Hard to measure effectiveness

Promotion – an evaluation

Promotion is generally considered to be a good thing for businesses to do. But is it? How does the business know if it is money well spent? It is very hard to measure the effect of promotion and if the business is using a mix of promotional methods, it is very difficult to separate the effect of one from the other.

Key terms

Industrial markets: where businesses sell to other businesses (not directly to the public).

Market research: gathering information about customers and competitors.

Market segment: a smaller part of a larger market.

Promotional mix: the combination of promotional methods used by a business in marketing its products.

Revision questions *(35 marks; 35 minutes)*

1 Why is promotion an important element of the marketing mix? (4)

2 Outline one advantage and one disadvantage of TV advertising. (4)

3 What is meant by the promotional mix? (2)

4 Explain what form of promotion you think would work best for marketing:

a) a new football game for the PS3 (3)

b) a small, family-focused seaside hotel (3)

c) organic cosmetics for women. (3)

5 Why is it important for businesses to monitor the effect of their promotional activity? (4)

6 What is meant by the phrase 'promotion needs to be effective'? (3)

7 Explain why promotion is essential for new businesses. (4)

8 Discuss whether Pepsi-Cola would be wise to sponsor the *X-Factor* TV programme. (5)

Revision exercises

Data response

Getting your furniture noticed

Simon Heaton and Lyndon Jeremiah were bored with teaching and decided to set up their own business. Heaton & Jeremiah now employs ten staff but the business struggled before the pair hit upon a unique marketing ploy. Heaton and Jeremiah wanted to combine their backgrounds: furniture design and software development. They investigated the household market but found it saturated. Then they hit upon the idea of corporate logos inlaid in office furniture.

The pair tried a variety of marketing approaches, including product cards, adverts in retail magazines, the *Yellow Pages* and designer handbooks, but they were not reaching their target market. While the marketing generated interest, it tended to be members of the public 'phoning up for a bedside table worth £20,' said Jeremiah.

They decided to take a more proactive approach. They made up a hit list of the big companies in their area – such as Jaguar and British Airways – and started to work out how they could reach them. The approach had to be daring. The annual round of multinational companies exhibiting at Birmingham's National Exhibition Centre gave them an idea. They managed to get hold of a copy of the exhibition schedule and produced tables for ten exhibitors. The tables were smuggled in at the start of the day. 'The show started at 9 am and we were receiving calls from companies at 8.45 am to say thanks', says Jeremiah. Heaton and Jeremiah extended their 'knocking on doors technique' to companies not at the exhibition, making tables to leave in reception areas. 'We were showing them a product they didn't know they wanted until they got it,' said Lyndon.

It was a big, but calculated, risk. They drew up a prototype budget and with their hit list focused only on companies that could provide them with big contracts. The product was sold through persistence. 'We had such a unique product that unless we got in people's faces it didn't really work,' said Lyndon. They now have a full order book and work is booked for two months in advance. The business now survives on word of mouth – the best form of marketing!

(Source: © Startups MMVII (www.startups.co.uk))

Questions *(30 marks; 35 minutes)*

1 a) What is a corporate logo? (2)

b) Why do companies have logos? (2)

2 What is meant by 'target market'? (4)

3 The initial promotional efforts did not reach the target market. Explain why this might have happened. (4)

4 a) Explain how promoting a unique product might differ from promoting a mass-market product. (4)

b) Discuss the advantages and disadvantages of two forms of promotion for a unique product such as Heaton & Jeremiah's. (8)

5 Discuss why word of mouth might be the best form of advertising for a new business. (6)

Data response

Tabasco® launches UK TV ad campaign

In 2009, Tabasco® Brand Pepper Sauce launched its first ever UK TV advertising campaign.

It's hard to believe that this iconic pepper sauce brand has never advertised on UK TV before. The campaign, in association with Pizza Hut Delivery, strengthens the link between Tabasco® and pizza and demonstrates it in a humorous way. The Tabasco® advert featured a young man shaking Tabasco® generously over his pizza; while he eats the pizza, a mosquito lands and bites him, as the mosquito flies off it explodes from the heat. The advert was broadcast over an eight-week period on both Channel 4 and E4, during programmes such as *Hollyoaks*.

An on-pack promotion featured a Pizza Hut Delivery 2-for-1 pizza offer with every bottle of Tabasco® Red Pepper Sauce purchased. And to coincide with the campaign, Tabasco® launched the brand-new official UK Fan Club website, www.tabascofanclub.co.uk. The site was not only linked to the campaign through the redemption of the on-pack offer, but also provides Tabasco® fans with opportunities to learn more about Tabasco®, download Tabasco® screensavers and access some recipes.

Chris Tebben, Retail Marketing Director, Pizza Hut Delivery, said: 'We're excited to be linking up with Tabasco® Pepper Sauce for its first ever TV campaign. Tabasco® and pizza are a classic combination, and this commercial, coupled with the on-pack 2-for-1 Pizza Hut Delivery offer, will help reinforce that.'

Did it work? According to the PR agency Food Matters, 'Tabasco® now enjoys cult status and a growing, loyal consumer base. The brand receives an unprecedented and regular level of press and broadcast coverage. Used by all leading chefs, it has also achieved table top presence in many leading restaurants. The brand's sales have increased dramatically in the UK'.

(Source: adapted from an article in *The Grocery Trade*, 11 June 2009 and www.foodmatters.co.uk/tabasco.htm)

Questions *(30 marks; 35 minutes)*

1 What is meant by 'iconic brand'? (4)

2 What is meant by the expression 'achieved table top presence' and why is this important? (4)

3 Why would a company want to appeal to a lower age group? (6)

4 Why do you think that Tabasco® linked its marketing to Pizza Hut? (6)

5 Tabasco® has not used TV advertising before. Consider the advantages and disadvantages of using this form of advertising. (10)

43 Pricing

Definition

Price is the amount paid by the customer for a good or service.

How important is price?

Price is one of the main links between the customer (demand) and the producer (supply). It gives messages to consumers about product quality and is fundamental to a firm's revenues and profit margins. As part of the marketing mix, it is fundamental to most consumer buying decisions. The importance of price to the customer will depend on several factors, as discussed below.

Customer sensitivity to price

Consumers have an idea of the correct price for a product (see Figure 43.1). They balance price with other considerations. These include:

- *the quality of the product*: products seen as having higher quality can carry a price premium; this may be real or perceived quality
- *how much they want it*: all purchases are personal; customers will pay more for goods they need or want
- *their income*: customers buy products within their income range; consumers with more disposable income are less concerned about price; uncertainty about future income will have the same effect as lower income; if interest rates are high, hard-pressed home-buyers will be much more sensitive to price; they need to save money and so they check prices more carefully and avoid high-priced items.

Level of competitive activity

The fiercer the competition in a market, the more important price becomes. Customers have more choice, so they take more care to buy the best-value item, whereas a business with a strong **monopoly** position is able to charge higher prices.

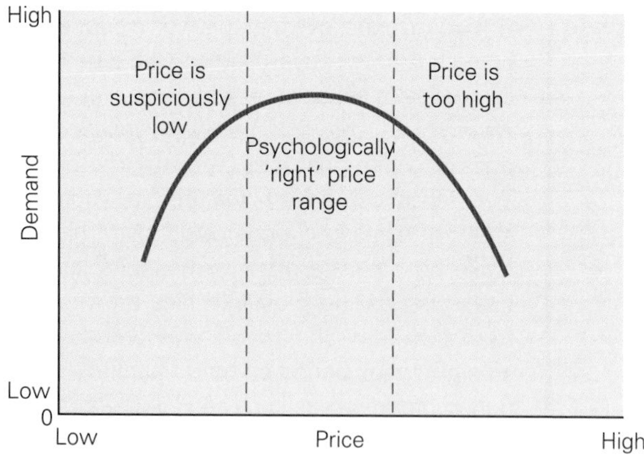

Figure 43.1 The 'right price'

Table 43.1 Price sensitivity in practice

Products, services and brands that are highly price sensitive	Products, services and brands that are not very price sensitive
No-frills air travel	Business-class air travel
Fiat and Ford cars	BMW and Mercedes cars
Children's white school shirts	Babies' disposable nappies
Monday-night cinema tickets	Saturday-night cinema tickets

Availability of the product

If the product is readily available, consumers are more price conscious. They know they can go elsewhere and find the same product – perhaps cheaper. Scarcity removes some of the barriers to price. This is why perfume companies such as Chanel try to keep their products out of supermarkets and stores like Superdrug – they want to avoid shops price-cutting brands such as Chanel No 5.

Price determines business revenue

Pricing is important to the business. Unlike the other ingredients in the marketing mix, it is related directly to revenue through the formula:

revenue = price × units sold.

If the price is not right the business could:

- lose customers – if the price is too high, sales may slump and therefore revenue will be lost; it will depend on the **price elasticity** of the product (see Unit 44); if goods remain unsold, costs of production will not be recovered
- lose revenue – if the price is too low, sales may be high, but not high enough to compensate from the low revenue per unit.

Pricing therefore involves a balance between being competitive and being profitable.

How do businesses decide what price to charge?

At certain times during a product's life cycle pricing is especially important. Incorrect pricing when the product is launched could cause the product to fail. At other stages in the product's life, pricing may be used to revive interest in the brand.

There are two basic pricing decisions: pricing a new product and managing prices throughout the product life. Both decisions require a good understanding of the market – consumers and competitors.

Pricing decisions require an understanding of costs. These costs must include purchasing, manufacturing, distribution, administration and marketing. Cost information should be available from the company's management accounting systems.

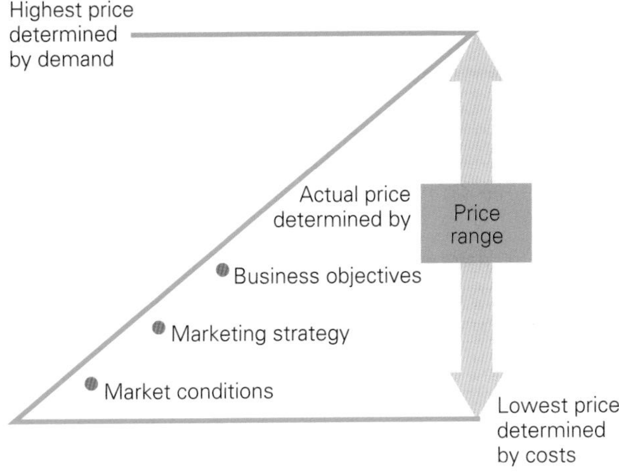

Figure 43.2 Determining price

The lowest price a firm can consider charging is set by costs. Except as a temporary promotional tactic (a loss leader), businesses must charge more for the product than the variable cost. This ensures that every product sold contributes towards the fixed costs of the business.

The market determines the highest price that can be charged. The price that is charged will need to take account of the company objectives – the right price will be the one that achieves those objectives.

There are several ways that businesses obtain market information:

- market research can provide consumer reactions to possible price changes
- competitive research tells the company about other products and prices
- analysis of sales patterns shows how the market reacts to price and economic changes
- sales staff can report on customer reactions to prices.

When making changes to product prices, the business needs to understand the relationship between price changes and demand. Demand for some products is more sensitive to price changes than for others. Price elasticity of demand measures how sensitive demand is to price changes. If demand for a product is sensitive to price changes, an increase in price could cut total revenue.

A-grade application

Hoxton Hotel

If you put '£1 hotel rooms' into Google, London's Hoxton Hotel pops up in front of you. This 200-room hotel sells five rooms per night at £1 – and another five at £29. The other 190 are at the 'normal' rate of £189! The Hoxton uses this device to get customers to register as members of the Hoxton Fan Club. Only they are told when the sale is taking place of £1 rooms (to cover the next three months). The website boasts that in each sale, 1,000 rooms are sold in 20 minutes. So this pricing trick makes sure that Hoxton has a terrific e-mailing list of people interested in hotel rooms.

Pricing strategies

A pricing strategy is a company's plan for setting its prices over the medium to long term. In other words it is *not* about deals such as 'This week's special: 40% off!' Short-term offers are known as tactics. Medium- to long-term plans are called strategies.

For new products, firms must choose between two main pricing strategies: skimming and penetration.

Skimming is used when the product is innovative. As the product is new there will be no competition and the price can therefore be set at a high level. Customers interested in the new product will pay this high price. The business recovers some of the development costs, making sure that enthusiasts who *really* want the product pay the high price they expect to pay. For example, the first DVD players came onto the UK market at a price of around £1,000. Firms use the initial sales period to assess the market reaction. If sales become stagnant, the price can be lowered to attract customers who were unwilling to pay the initial price. The price can also be lowered if competitors enter the market.

Penetration pricing is used when launching a product into a market where there are similar products. The price is set lower to gain market share, then once the product is established the price can be increased. It is hoped that high levels

Table 43.2 Advantages and disadvantages of price skimming and price penetration

	Price skimming	Price penetration
Advantages	High prices for a new item such as the iPhone help establish the product as a must-have item **Early adopters** of a product usually want exclusivity and are willing to pay high prices, so skimming makes sense for them and for the supplier Innovation can be expensive, so it makes sense to charge high prices to recover the investment cost	Low-priced new products may attract high sales volumes, which make it very hard for a competitor to break into the market High sales volumes help to cut production costs per unit, as the producer can buy in bulk and therefore get purchasing costs down Achieving high sales volumes ensures that shops will provide high distribution levels and good in-store displays
Disadvantages	Some customers may be put off totally by 'rip-off pricing' at the start of a product's life When the firm decides to cut its prices its image may suffer Buyers who bought early (at high prices) may be annoyed that prices fell soon afterwards	Pricing low may affect the brand image, making the product appear 'cheap' It may be hard to gain distribution in more upmarket retail outlets, due to mass-market pricing Pricing on the basis of value for money can cause customers (and therefore competitors) to be very **price sensitive**

of initial sales will recover development costs and lead to lower average costs as the business benefits from bulk-buying benefits.

Pricing strategies for existing products

For existing products the key is to be clear about where your brand stands in the market. Pricing strategy on the latest Mercedes sports car will be based on the confidence of the company in the strength of its brand name. Mercedes will not worry what Ford or Mazda charge for a sports car, nor even the prices of its BMW or Lexus rivals. The Mercedes will be a 'price leader': where it sets prices, others will follow. Weaker brands, such as Chrysler or Fiat, are the followers. They are 'price takers' (i.e. they have to take the lead set by the strong brands, usually pricing their own products at a lower level).

Price leader

This is where the price is set above the market level. This is possible when the company has strong brands or there is little effective competition. In Britain the accepted price of chewing gum is set by Wrigley's, which has a 90 per cent market share. Other brands have little choice but to charge at or below the level set by Wrigley's.

Price taker

This is when the price is set at the market level or at a discount to the market. This happens in highly competitive markets or in markets where one brand dominates. When Branston Baked Beans were launched in 2006, they were priced at 41p, compared to the 44p charged by the price leader, Heinz. By 2010 Branston was 62p to the 64p of Heinz, implying that Branston is still a price taker, but in a slightly stronger position now than then.

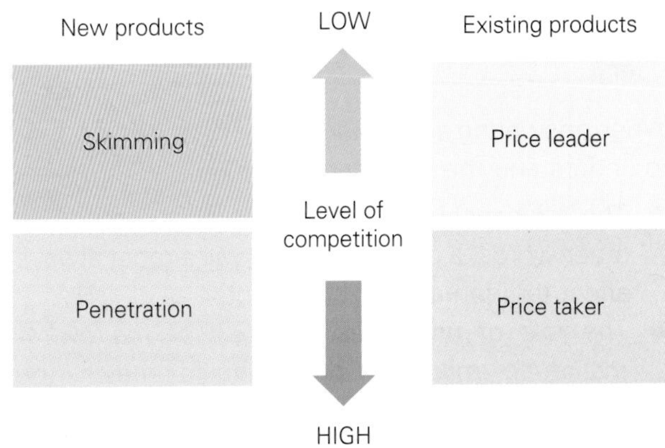

Figure 43.3 Factors affecting choice of pricing strategy

Choosing a pricing strategy

The choice of pricing strategy will depend on the competitive environment. Figure 43.3 shows how the choice of pricing strategy will vary according to the level of competition.

Pricing tactics

Whichever pricing strategy has been selected, there are a number of pricing tactics that should also be considered. They can be part of normal pricing or used as one element in the firm's promotional tactics. They include the following:

- *Loss leaders:* prices are set deliberately low – so low that the firm may make a loss on every unit sold. The idea is to encourage customers to buy other products or **complementary goods** that generate profit. Supermarkets commonly use this approach, for example, at Christmas they may attract custom by selling tree lights for 49p – confident that shoppers will end up with a full trolley of other goods. Children's sticker albums may also be offered very cheaply – but the packs of stickers to go inside are often expensive.
- *Psychological pricing:* prices are set at a level that seems lower to the customer. Without thinking about it, customers see a price of £9.99 as quite significantly lower than £10.50. The loss of 51p per item is more than made up for by higher sales.
- *Special offer pricing:* for example, buy-one-get-one-free, or offers made for a period of time or to clear stocks.

Issues for analysis

When answering a question on pricing it is important to understand the following points:

- *The relationship between price and demand:* in other words, a change in price will almost always affect the demand for a product.
- *The role of pricing as one part of the overall marketing mix:* the price should match the image suggested by the product design, advertising, branding and distribution outlets; an expensive-looking perfume displayed in Harrods would have its image undermined if it were priced at £4.99.
- *The influence of price upon profitability:* many products have profit margins of only 20 per cent; therefore a 10 per cent price cut will halve profit per unit. It would take a huge increase in demand to compensate.
- *The factors influencing pricing:* for example, cost, customer psychology and competitors.

Pricing – an evaluation

Economists think of price as a neutral factor within a marketplace. Its impact upon demand can be measured, predicted and captured in the concept of price elasticity (see Unit 44). However, many businesses would disagree – especially those selling consumer goods and services. The reason is that consumer psychology can be heavily influenced by price. A '3p off' flash makes people reach for the Mars bars, but if they are half price people wonder whether they are old stock or have suffered in the sun – they are *too* cheap.

When deciding on the price of a brand new product, marketing managers have many options. Pricing high might generate too few sales to keep retailers happy to stock the product, yet pricing too low carries even more dangers. Large companies know there are no safe livings to be made selling cheap jeans, cheap cosmetics or cheap perfumes.

If there is a key to successful pricing, it is to keep it in line with the overall marketing strategy. When Häagen-Dazs launched in the UK at prices more than double those of its competitors, many predicted failure. In fact the pricing was in line with the image of adult, luxury indulgence and Häagen-Dazs soon outsold all other premium ice creams. The worst pricing approach would be to develop an attractively packaged, well-made product and then sell it at a discount to the leading brands. In research, people would welcome it, but deep down they would not trust the product quality. Because psychology is so important to successful pricing, many firms use qualitative research, rather than quantitative, to obtain the necessary psychological insights.

Key terms

Complementary goods: products bought in conjunction with each other, such as bacon and eggs, or Gillette shavers and Gillette razors.

Early adopters: consumers with the wealth and the personality to want to be the first to get a new gadget or piece of equipment; they may be the first to wear new fashion clothes and the first to get a new (and expensive) computer game.

Monopoly: a market dominated by one supplier.

Price elasticity: a measurement of the extent to which a product's demand changes when its price is changed.

Price sensitive: when customer demand for a product reacts sharply to a price change (i.e. the product is highly price elastic).

Revision questions (35 marks; 35 minutes)

1 Explain why price 'is fundamental to a firm's revenues'. (3)

2 Look again at Figure 43.1. Outline two factors that would affect the 'psychologically right price range' for a new Nokia phone. (4)

3 Explain how the actions of Nike might affect the footwear prices set by Adidas. (4)

4 Look at Table 43.1 on the price sensitivity of products, brands and services. Think of two more examples of highly price sensitive and two examples of not-very-price-sensitive products, services or brands. (4)

5 Explain the difference between pricing strategy and pricing tactics. (2)

6 For each of the following, decide whether the pricing strategy should be skimming or penetration. Briefly explain your reasoning.

a) Richard Branson's Virgin group launches the world's first space tourism service (customers are launched in a rocket, spend time weightless in space, watch the world go round, then come back to earth). (4)

b) Kellogg's launches a new range of sliced breads for families in a hurry. (4)

c) The first Google phone is launched (called G-Fone) with free, instant WiFi access to Google. (4)

7 Is a cash cow likely to be a price maker or a price taker? Explain your reasoning. (3)

8 Identify three circumstances in which a business might decide to use special offer pricing. (3)

Revision exercises

Data response

On 1 August 2010, Tesco Pricecheck provided the following information on the prices of shampoo brands. Study the table then answer the questions that follow.

Product description	Tesco price	Asda price
Tresemme Fresh Start 200 ml	£2.99	£4.28
Pantene Volume & Body 250 ml	£2.27	£1.00
Head & Shoulders 250 ml	£2.39	£2.38
Elvive Anti-Breakage 250 ml	£2.40	£2.40
John Frieda Sheer Blond 250 ml	£5.00	£5.00
Own-brand kids/baby 250 ml	£1.00	£0.98
Own-brand budget shampoo 400 ml	£0.80	£0.80
Bob Martin dog shampoo 300 ml	£2.62	£2.62

Questions (25 marks; 25 minutes)

1 Briefly explain why it might be fair to describe Pantene Volume & Body shampoo as a price-taker. (4)

2 John Frieda shampoo is priced at more than ten times the level of supermarket budget shampoos (per ml). Explain why customers might be willing to pay such a high price. (6)

3 Examine the position of the long-established brand Head & Shoulders within the UK shampoo market. What pricing strategy does it seem to be using and why might it be able to use this approach? (7)

4 Discuss whether dogs should have 'better' shampoo than kids. (8)

Data response

The $100 laptop

Computer enthusiasts in the developed world will soon be able to get their hands on the so-called '$100 laptop'

The organisation behind the project has launched the 'give one, get one' scheme, which will allow US residents to purchase two laptops for $399 (£198). One laptop will be sent to the buyer while a child in the developing world will receive the second machine. The G1G1 scheme, as it is known, will offer the laptops for just two weeks.

Figure 43.4 The $100 laptop

Price hike

The XO laptop has been developed to be used by children and is as low cost, durable and simple to use as possible. It packs several innovations, including a sunlight readable display so that it can be used outside. It has no moving parts, can be powered by solar, foot-pump or pull-string powered chargers, and is housed in a waterproof case.

The machine's price has recently increased from $176 (£88) to $188 (£93), although the eventual aim is to sell the machines for $100 (£50).

Governments can buy the green and white machines in lots of 250,000. Hardware suppliers have been given the green light to ramp-up production of all the components needed to build the low-cost machines. The decision suggested that the organisation had met or surpassed the three million orders it needed to make production viable. The names of the governments that have purchased the first lots of machines have not been released.

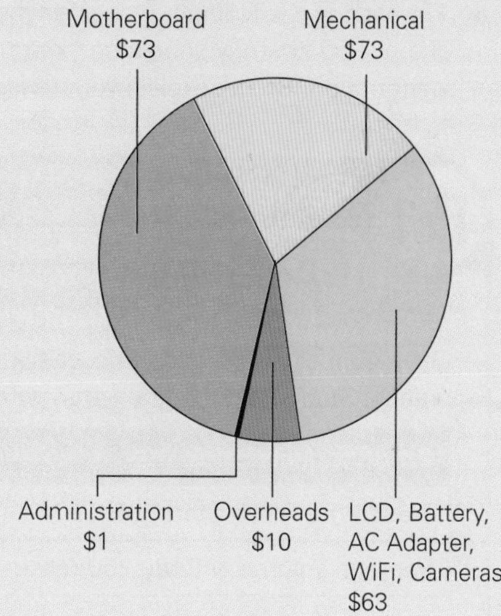

Figure 43.5 Breakdown of costs

Early adopter

The first countries to receive the donated laptops will be Cambodia, Afghanistan, Rwanda and Haiti. Other least developed countries (LDCs), as defined by the UN, will be able to bid to join the scheme. The laptops will go on sale for just two weeks through the xogiving.org website. They will only be available for two weeks to ensure OLPC can meet demand and so that machines are not diverted away from countries that have already placed orders.

(Source: Adapted from www.bbc.co.uk)

Questions *(30 marks; 35 minutes)*

1 Describe the objectives behind the pricing of the XO laptop. (4)

2 a) Compare the 'breakdown of costs' pie chart in Figure 43.5 to the text to work out the recent profit per unit made on selling the XO laptop. (3)

b) Given that level of profit, how could the company hope 'to sell the machines for $100'? (4)

3 a) Explain what is meant by an 'early adopter'? (3)

b) Why may early adopters be important to a business? (4)

4 Some people see the XO laptop as a brave, charitable idea; others see it purely as a clever form of penetration pricing strategy. To what extent can you agree with either view? (12)

Price elasticity of demand

Definition

Price elasticity measures the extent to which demand for a product changes when its price is changed.

Introduction

When a company increases the price of a product, it expects to lose some sales. Some customers will switch to a rival supplier; others may decide they do not want (or cannot afford) the product at all. Economists use the term 'the law of demand' to suggest that, almost invariably:

Price up ⟶ Demand down

Price down ⟶ Demand up

Price elasticity looks beyond the law of demand to ask the more subtle questions such as 'When the price goes up, by how much do sales fall?' and 'Do they collapse or do they fall only slightly?' Elasticity measures the extent to which price changes affect demand.

Price elasticity of demand

In the short term, the most important factor affecting demand is price. When the price of the *Guardian* newspaper increased from 70p to 80p in 2007, sales fell by 8 per cent, whereas a 50p increase in the price of the *Financial Times* newspaper in the same year cut sales by just 1.5 per cent. Readers of the *Guardian* proved much more price sensitive than readers of the *Financial Times*, therefore the owners of the *Financial Times* could feel delighted with their pricing decision. Selling 1.5 per cent fewer papers but receiving 30 per cent more for each one sold meant that revenue rose by more than a quarter.

The crucial question is *how much* will demand change when the price is changed? This question can be answered by calculating the price elasticity of demand. Price elasticity is not about whether demand changes when price changes, it is about the degree of change. Consequently, price elasticity is a unit of measurement rather than being a thing in itself. A price cut will not cause price elasticity to fall; instead the price elasticity figure explains the effect the price cut is likely to have on demand. Will demand rise by 1 per cent, 5 per cent or 25 per cent following the price cut? The answer can be known only by referring to the product's price elasticity of demand. Price elasticity measures the *responsiveness* of demand to a change in price.

Some products are far more price sensitive than others. Following a 5 per cent increase in price, the demand for some products may fall greatly, say by more than 20 per cent, whereas the demand for another type of product may fall by less than 1 per cent.

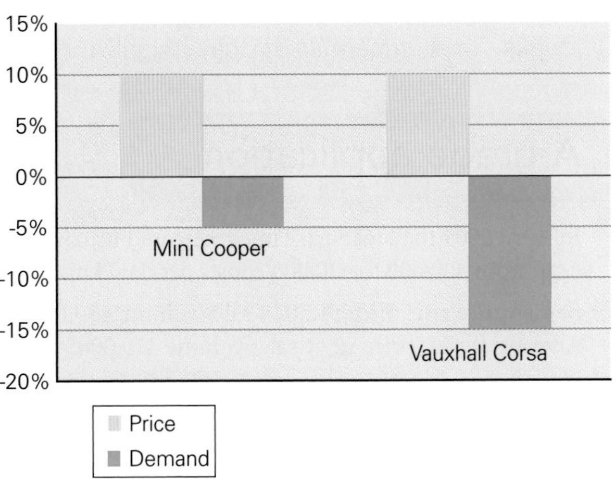

Figure 44.1 Measuring price elasticity of demand for cars

Price elasticity can be calculated using the formula shown below:

$$\text{Price elasticity} = \frac{\%\ \text{change in quantity demanded}}{\%\ \text{change in price}}$$

Price elasticity measures the percentage effect on demand of each 1 percent change in price. So if a 10 per cent increase in price led demand to fall by 20 per cent, the price elasticity would be 2. Strictly speaking, price elasticities are always negative, because price up pushes demand down and price down pushes demand up.

For example:

$$\frac{-20\%}{+10\%} = -2$$

The figure of −2 indicates that, for every 1 per cent change in price, demand is likely to change by 2 per cent. All price elasticities are negative. This is because there is a negative **correlation** between price and quantity demanded. In the short term, a price cut will always boost sales and a price rise will always cut sales.

Determinants of price elasticity

Why do some products, services or brands have low price elasticity and some high elasticity? Why is the price elasticity of Branston Baked Beans higher than that of Heinz Baked Beans? Or the price elasticity of the *Financial Times* as low as 0.05 while the elasticity of *Look* magazine is as high as 2.0 (i.e. 40 times higher)?

The main determinants of price elasticity are as follows:

- *The degree of product differentiation:* that is, the extent to which customers view the product as being distinctive compared with rivals. *Look* may be an excellent magazine, but it is offering the same mix of fashion, shopping and celebs as many other magazines aimed at young women. So if the cover price is increased, it is easy for readers to switch to an alternative, whereas readers of the *Financial Times* have nowhere else to go. Therefore the higher the product differentiation, the lower the price elasticity.
- *The availability of substitutes:* customers may see Tango and Fanta as very similar orange drinks. In a supermarket they might buy the cheaper of the two. At a cinema, though, only Fanta may be available. At a train station vending machine, almost certainly Fanta will be the only orange drink. This is because it is a Coca-Cola brand and the distribution strength of Coke places Fanta where Tango never goes. When Fanta is on its own, its price elasticity is much lower; therefore the brand owner (Coca-Cola) can push the price up without losing too many customers.
- *Branding and brand loyalty*: products with low price elasticity are those that consumers buy without thinking about the price tag. Some reach for Coca-Cola without checking its price compared to that of Pepsi, or buy a Harley-Davidson motorcycle even though a Honda superbike may be £4,000 cheaper. Strong brand names with strong brand images create customers who buy out of loyalty. Note that some strong brands create very little loyalty, such as BP; when buying petrol, drivers buy the cheapest they can, and therefore the price elasticity of retail petrol brands such as BP is very high.

A-grade application

In April 2009 the Financial Times increased its cover price by 50p to £2. This caused its circulation to fall by 2.5 per cent, from 430,000 to 420,000 copies per day. This caused the following effect on daily revenue:

Before price rise: price £1.50 × sales volume 430,000 = £645,000
After price rise: price £2 × sales volume 420,000 = £840,000

In other words, sales revenue rose by £195,000 per day – a 30 per cent increase – and as the change could only reduce total costs (because of the fall in variable costs), the boost to the paper's profit would be huge.

The significance of price elasticity

Being able to estimate a product's price elasticity is a hugely valuable aid to marketing decision making. When Wigan FC was promoted to the Premiership, its managers assumed that the attractions of Arsenal, Manchester United and the rest would make it easy to push up the price of match tickets. In fact ticket sales proved much worse than expected, forcing the club to cut its prices halfway through the season. A firm that knows its price elasticity can make better decisions than one that is in ignorance.

Data on a product's price elasticity can be can used for two purposes, as outlined below.

Sales forecasting

A firm considering a price rise will want to know the effect the price change is likely to have on demand. Producing a sales forecast will make possible accurate production, personnel and purchasing decisions. For example, in 2009 Sony cut the price of its Playstation 3 (PS3) by 25 per cent, from $399 to $299. In January–March 2010, sales rose by 120 per cent. At that time, the price elasticity of the PS3 proved to be:

$$\frac{+120\%}{-25\%} = -4.8.$$

Sony could then use that knowledge to predict the likely impact of future price changes. Another price cut of 10 per cent could lead to a sales increase of 48 per cent ($-10\% \times -4.8 = +48\%$). This is valuable information to know. Before implementing the price cut, the company could make sure to produce an extra 48 per cent more stock to cope with the extra orders.

Pricing strategy

There are many external factors that determine a product's demand and therefore its profitability. For example, a soft drinks manufacturer can do nothing about a wet, cold summer that drastically reduces sales and profits. However, the price the firm decides to charge *is* within its control and it can be a crucial factor in determining demand and profitability. Price elasticity information can be used in conjunction with internal cost data to forecast the implications of a price change on revenue.

Example

A second-hand car dealer currently sells 60 cars each year. Currently he charges his customers £2,500 per car. This means the business has a revenue of:

Total revenue = £2,500 × 60 = £150,000

From past experience the salesman believes the price elasticity of his cars is approximately −0.75. The dealer is thinking about increasing his prices to £3,000 per car, an increase of 20 per cent. Using the price elasticity information, a quick calculation would reveal the impact on revenue:

Percentage change in demand = +20% × −0.75
= −15%

A 15 per cent fall in demand on the existing sales volume of 60 cars per year will produce a fall in demand of nine cars per year. So demand will fall to 51 cars per year after the price increase. On the basis of these figures, the new revenue would be:

Total revenue = new price × new sales volume
= £3,000 × 51 cars
= £153,000

So, even though the price rise cuts sales to 51 cars, the revenue actually increases. Obviously, in this case, the car dealer should change his pricing strategy. However, this is all based on two assumptions:

1. that the price elasticity of the cars actually proves to be -0.75
2. other factors that could also affect demand remain unchanged following the price increase.

Classifying price elasticity

Price-elastic products

A **price-elastic product** is one with a price elasticity of above 1. This means that the percentage change in demand is greater than the percentage change in price that created it. For example, if a firm increased prices by 5 per cent and as a result demand fell by 15 per cent, price elasticity would be:

$$\frac{-15\%}{+5\% \times 100} = -3$$

For instance, for every 1 per cent change in price, there will be a 3 per cent change in demand. The higher the price elasticity figure, the more price elastic the product. Cutting price on a price-elastic product will boost total revenue. This is because the extra revenue gained from the increased sales volume more than offsets the revenue lost from the price cut. On the other hand, a price increase on a price-elastic product will lead to a fall in total revenue.

It is important to note that price cutting can damage brand image, because customers often associate high prices with high quality. In addition, a price-cutting decision is usually difficult to reverse due to consumer resistance to price increases. Finally, the actions of the competition must also be taken into account. If your price cut prompts a **price war**, the much needed gains in sales volume might not arise.

Price-inelastic products

Price-inelastic products have price elasticities below 1. This means the percentage change in demand is less than the percentage change in price. In other words, price changes have hardly any effect on demand – perhaps because consumers feel they *must* have the product or brand in question: the stunning dress, the trendiest designer label or – less interestingly – gas for central heating. Customers feel they must have it, either because it really is a necessity, or because it is fashionable. Firms with price-inelastic products will be tempted to push the prices up. A price increase will boost revenue because the price rise creates a relatively small fall in sales volume. This means the majority of customers will continue to purchase the brand but at a higher, revenue-boosting price.

Problems measuring price elasticity

What is the price elasticity of Kit Kat? Naturally, owners Nestlé would like to know, so that the right pricing decisions can be made. Therefore, the company will do all it can to work out the price elasticity figure for this £100 million-plus brand. But how? All a firm can do is to work out what the price elasticity has been in the past, because it can only be calculated using past data. For example, if demand fell by 8 per cent on the last occasion the price of Kit Kat was pushed up by 10 per cent, the calculation is that the price elasticity was −0.8 (−8%/+10%).

Yet if that was a year ago, will the same be true today? Competition today may be a bit fiercer, making the price elasticity a bit higher. And today's consumer may be that much more sensitive about eating fatty foods, making a price rise a reason to stop buying Kit Kats altogether.

The price elasticity of a brand is a complex combination of how fashionable it is, the number of direct competitors it faces and the loyalty of its existing customers. All these things can change over time, causing the elasticity to go up or down. It is also possible that elasticity changes over a product's life cycle. It may be highly price elastic at the start, when people are suspicious of a new product. In its growth phase it may become trendy, making it less sensitive to price. In its decline phase people may hang on to the product only if the price is attractive, making it price elastic again.

In conclusion, it is unwise to talk about a product's price elasticity as if it is a fact. Firms make decisions using their assumptions or estimates about the price elasticity of their products. These assumptions are usually based on data that may now be out of date.

Strategies to reduce price elasticity

All businesses prefer to sell price-inelastic products. Charging more for a price-inelastic product guarantees an increase in short-term profit. If a firm has price-elastic products it will always feel vulnerable, as a rise in costs may be impossible to pass on to customers. And if a firm is tempted to cut the price of a price-elastic product, sales will probably rise so sharply that competitors will be forced to respond and a price war may result.

Figure 44.2 The brand of designer jeans makes a statement about the wearer

It is important to realise that the price elasticity of a brand is not set in stone. Price elasticity is not an **external constraint**. The most important influence on a brand's price elasticity is substitutability – if consumers have other brands available that they think deliver the same benefits, price elasticity will be high. So, to make a brand price inelastic, the firm has to find ways of reducing the number of substitutes available (or acceptable). How can this be done?

Increasing product differentiation

Product differentiation is the degree to which consumers perceive that a product is different (and preferably better) than its rivals. Some products are truly different from others, such as a Britain's only business newspaper, the *Financial Times*. Others are successfully differentiated by image, such as Versace Jeans or Coca-Cola. The purchasers of highly differentiated products like Versace Jeans often remain brand loyal despite price rises. The reason for this low price elasticity is that wearing Versace Jeans makes a statement about the wearer, even if the cloth itself is no different from that used by Levi's or Wrangler.

Predatory pricing

Predatory pricing is a deliberate attempt to force a competitor out of a market by charging a low, loss-making price. Once the competitor has been forced out of the market, the consumer has one less source of supply. The reduction in the number of substitutes available to the customer allows the predator to raise prices successfully. If there are no cheaper substitutes available, the customer is forced to pay the higher prices or go without. The same effect can be achieved by takeover bids (e.g. the purchase by Adidas of Reebok sportswear).

Issues for analysis

In examinations, elasticity of demand is a key discriminator between good and weak candidates. Really weak candidates never bring the concept into their answers at all. Better candidates apply it, but imprecisely. Top-grade students see where it is relevant and show a clear understanding of the concept and its implications. Here are two ways to use price elasticity for business analysis:

- Whenever answering any question about pricing, elasticity is a vital factor. Even if a firm faces severe cost increases, a price rise will be very risky if its products have a high price elasticity. Pricing decisions must always start with careful consideration of price elasticity.
- People naturally assume that marketing (especially advertising) is always about trying to increase sales. In fact, most firms are far more interested in their image (a glance at any commercial break will confirm this). Companies focus upon their image because that is the way to differentiate themselves from others. That, in turn, is the way to reduce price elasticity and therefore give the company stronger control over its pricing.

Price elasticity of demand – an evaluation

For examiners, elasticity is a convenient concept. It is hard to understand, but very easy to write exam questions on! But how useful is it in the real world? Would the average marketing director know the price elasticities of his or her products? In many cases the answer is no. Examiners and textbooks exaggerate the precision that is possible with such a concept. The fact that the price elasticity of the *Financial Times* appeared to be -0.05 in 2007 does not mean it will always be that low. Price elasticities change over time, as competition changes and consumer tastes change.

Even though elasticities can vary over time, certain features tend to remain constant. Strong brands such as Apple and Coca-Cola have relatively low price elasticity. This gives them the power over market pricing that ensures strong profitability year after year. For less established firms, these brands are the role models: everyone wants to be the Coca-Cola of their own market or market niche.

Key terms

Correlation: the relationship between one variable and another.

External constraint: something outside the firm's control that can prevent it achieving its objectives.

Predatory pricing: pricing low with the deliberate intention of driving a competitor out of business.

Price-elastic product: a product that is highly price sensitive, so price elasticity is above one.

Price-inelastic product: a product that is not very price sensitive, so price elasticity is below one.

Price war: when two or more companies battle for market share by slashing prices, perhaps selling at or below cost.

A Revision questions *(35 marks; 35 minutes)*

1 a) If a product's sales have fallen by 21 per cent since a price rise from £2 to 2.07, what is its price elasticity? (4)

b) Is the product price elastic or price inelastic? (1)

2 Outline two ways in which Nestlé might try to reduce the price elasticity of its Aero chocolate bars. (4)

3 A firm selling 20,000 units at £8 is considering a 4 per cent price increase. It believes its price elasticity is −0.5.

a) What will be the effect upon revenue? (5)

b) Give two reasons why the revenue may prove to be different from the firm's expectations. (2)

4 Explain three ways a firm could make use of information about the price elasticity of its brands. (6)

5 Identify three external factors that could increase the price elasticity of a brand of chocolate. (3)

6 A firm has a sales target of 60,000 units per month. Current sales are 50,000 per month at a price of £1.50. If its products have a price elasticity of -2, what price should the firm charge to meet the target sales volume? (4)

7 Why is price elasticity always negative? (2)

8 Explain why the manager of a product with a price elasticity of -2 may be reluctant to cut the price. (4)

Revision exercises

Data response

A firm selling Manchester United pillow cases for £10 currently generates an annual turnover of £500,000. Variable costs average at £4 per unit and total annual fixed costs are £100,000. The marketing director is considering a price increase of 10 per cent.

Questions *(20 marks; 25 minutes)*

1 Given that the price elasticity of the product is believed to be 20.4, calculate:

- **a)** the old and the new sales volume (3)
- **b)** the new revenue (3)
- **c)** the expected change in profit following the price increase. (6)

2 If the firm started producing mass-market white pillow cases, would their price elasticity be higher or lower than the Manchester United ones? Why is that? (8)

Data response

Love it or hate it

In 2009 UK sales of Marmite were £38.1m, 5.3% up on 2008. This was despite an 8% fall in sales volume, to 3.81 million kilos.

	2008	2009
Marmite price per kilo		£10
Marmite sales volume (kilos)	4.14m	3.81m
Marmite sales value	£36.2m	£38.1m

In 2009 Marmite's share of the market for Yeast Extracts was 82%. It was the only brand that spent any money on advertising, spending £1.5 million in the year.

Marmite is an interesting product because it started life as a waste product from the brewing industry. Instead of throwing it away, it was turned into a food and, later, a brand. Despite this, it is noticeably more expensive for consumers to buy than anything else you might choose to spread on bread. Strawberry jam contains far more expensive ingredients, yet jams were priced, in 2009, at an average of £2.60 per kilo compared with the £10 charged for Marmite.

Within the market for jam, there were huge changes in customer behaviour. Sales of own-label economy lines grew by 51%, while own-label premium and organic jam sales fell by 7.1% and 9.7% respectively. Although Hartleys and Bonne Maman are the market leaders, neither has more than a 15% market share.

(Source: *The Grocer*, 9 January 2010, reporting data from TNS Worldpanel, which uses a sample of 25,000 UK households)

Questions *(30 marks; 35 minutes)*

1
- **a)** Calculate the price per kilo charged for Marmite in 2008 (round the answer to the nearest penny) (2)
- **b)** Calculate the percentage price increase for Marmite in 2009 compared with 2008. (3)
- **c)** Calculate the apparent price elasticity of Marmite in 2009. (5)
- **d)** Outline two reasons why Marmite's price elasticity might prove different in 2010 than in 2009. (6)

2 Examine the possible reasons why the price of Marmite is nearly four times the price of jam. (9)

Data response

The iPhone

The date 9 November 2007 was going to be an important one for Apple geeks. It saw the UK launch of the iPhone. Already a sensation in the USA, with sales of more than one million units, it was the most eagerly awaited product launch in years. The appeal was simple: the best-looking phone ever, with the easiest user interface.

But what price should Apple charge for the phone, and how should it distribute it? To help keep competition down, it struck a deal to make O_2 – Britain's largest mobile operator – its exclusive British network for the handset. Apple knew from the outset that it could not take UK sales for granted. Nokia and Sony Ericsson are both bigger brands here than in the USA, so competition would be fiercer. Even more important, perhaps, would be the missing power: by late 2007 more than 20% of UK phones were on the powerful 3G connection, making internet access fast and easy. The iPod was a more backward 2.5G.

A marketing analyst was quoted in the *Financial Times* as saying: 'On November 8th there will be iGeeks waiting outside the Apple store on Regent Street [London] with their sleeping bags and cups of coffee ... There will be a big surge of interest in the beginning but, after that, there will be some difficulty in sustaining demand in the face of some very credible competition.'

Apple decided to price the iPhone at £269. On top of this, users would have to sign up to an 18-month contract with a minimum payment of £35 a month, making the whole commitment a whopping £899. This compared with a 3G Sony Walkman phone priced at £120 or a Samsung Slimline 3G, available for nothing as a contract upgrade.

(Source: adapted from various articles, including the *Financial Times*, 19 September 2007)

Questions *(20 marks; 25 minutes)*

1. Explain the likely logic behind Apple's decision to sign an exclusive deal with the O_2 network. (6)
2. Use your understanding of price elasticity to discuss whether or not Apple was right to price the iPhone in this way. (14)

45 Place

Definition

Place is about availability – how to get the product to the right place for customers to make their purchases. Place includes both the physical place and the availability and visibility of the product. The key questions facing firms are: 'What are the best outlets for reaching potential customers?' 'How can I convince those outlets to stock my products?' 'What is the most effective way to get my products to those outlets?'

Introduction

The word 'place' can be unhelpful, because it suggests that manufacturers can place their products where they like (e.g. at the entrance of a Tesco store), but the real world is not like that. Obtaining distribution at Tesco stores is a dream for most small producers – and a very hard dream to turn into reality. For new firms in particular, place is the toughest of the 4Ps.

Persuading retailers to stock a product is never easy. For the retailer, the key issues are opportunity cost and risk. As shelf space is limited, stocking a particular chocolate bar probably means scrapping another. Which one? What revenue will be lost? Will one or two customers be upset? ('What! No Coffee Walnut Whips any more?') The other consideration is risk. A new, low-cal chocolate bar endorsed by a supermodel may be a slimmer's delight, but high initial sales may then flop, leaving the shopkeeper with boxes of slow-moving stock.

Choosing appropriate distributors

When a new business wants to launch its first product, a key question to consider is the distribution channel – in other words, how the product passes from producer to consumer. Sold directly, as with pick-your-own strawberries? Or via a wholesaler, then a retailer, as with newspapers bought from your local shop? This decision will affect every aspect of the business in the future, but especially its profit.

In 2011 entrepreneur James Seddon will launch his Eggxactly egg cooker in the UK. Since his appearance on the BBC TV series *Dragons' Den*, retailers such as John Lewis have made clear their interest in stocking the product at launch. But James has decided to start by selling purely from his own website. His reasoning is that this will transform his cash flow position. Instead of getting 50,000 machines produced in China (with the cash to be paid in advance), he could get them made in England in response to orders. This way, the customer cash is received before he has to pay out to get the machines made. This would solve another problem: instead of having to guess how many red and how many blue ones to make, he would respond to customer orders.

Manufacturers must decide on the right outlets for their own product. If Chanel chooses to launch a new perfume, 'Alexa', backed by Alexa Chung, priced at £49.99 a bottle, controlling distribution would be vital. The company will want it sold in a smart location where elegant sales staff can persuade customers of its wonderful scent and gorgeous packaging. If Superdrug or Tesco want to stock the brand, Chanel will try hard to find reasons to say no.

Yet the control is often not in the hands of the producer, but of the retailer. If you came up with

Figure 45.1 The right outlet for a high-profile new perfume

a wonderful idea for a brand new ice cream, how would you get distribution for it? The freezers in corner shops are usually owned by Walls and Mars, so they frown upon independent products being stocked in 'their' space. Offering a third freezer free would be hugely expensive, leading to impossibly high costs per unit, especially if you had only one product line to sell. Furthermore, shopkeepers would lack the floor space to be willing to accept your 'free' gift. To the retailer, every foot of shop floor space has an actual cost (the rental value) and an opportunity cost (the cost of missing out on the profits that could be generated by selling other goods). In effect, then, your brand new ice cream is likely to stay on the drawing board, because obtaining distribution will be too large a barrier to entry to this market.

Distribution channels

There are three main channels of distribution.

1 *Traditional:* small producers find it hard to achieve distribution in big chains such as B&Q or Sainsbury's, so they usually sell to wholesalers who, in turn, sell to small independent shops. The profit mark-up applied by the 'middleman' adds to the final retail price, but there is no way that a small producer can afford to deliver individually to lots of small shops.

2 *Modern:* Tesco, B&Q and WHSmith do not buy from a wholesaler. They buy direct from producers and then organise their own distribution to their outlets. Their huge selling power gives them huge buying power. Therefore, they are able to negotiate the highest discounts from the producers.

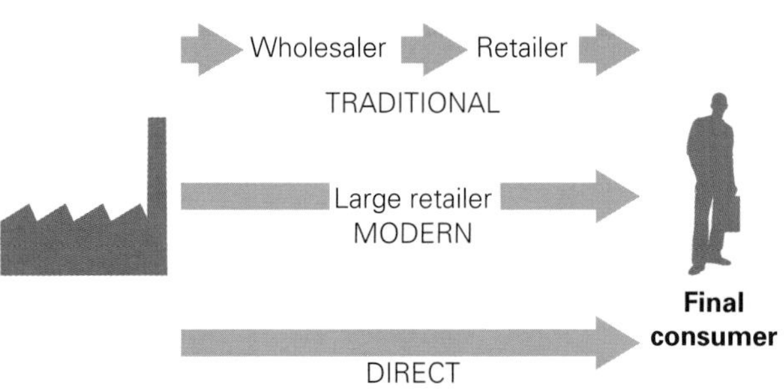

Figure 45.2 Channels of distribution

A-grade application

Tesco Online

In 2009/2010, Tesco Online enjoyed a 12 per cent rise in its sales revenue. This compared with a 4 per cent sales increase in Tesco's UK stores. This repeats a growth pattern typical within the company in the last few years. Interestingly, Online is more profitable for Tesco than its normal shop business. The figures in Table 45.1 show that Tesco Online gives higher net profit margins than the traditional business. No wonder Tesco has extended its internet business by launching Tesco Direct, which will deliver Tesco clothes and other non-food items direct to the consumer's door.

Table 45.1 Tesco stores vs Tesco Online, Year to February 2010

	Tesco plc	Tesco.com
Sales	£56,910m	£2,100m
Operating (net) profit	£3,412m	£136m
Net profit margin	6.0%	6.5%

(Source: Tesco plc, 2010 Annual Report and Accounts)

3 *Direct (i.e. the producer selling directly to the consumer):* manufacturers can do this through mail order or – far more likely today – through a website. This ensures that the producer keeps 100 per cent of the product's selling price. Often a manufacturer receives only half the shop selling price of an item, after the retailer and the wholesaler have taken their cut. So the benefit of the direct distribution channel is that the producer's higher profits can finance more spending on advertising or on new product development.

How does a small firm obtain good distribution?

To obtain distribution for the first time, a small firm producing, for example, organic biscuits would have to take the following steps:

- Announce, display and hand out free samples of the product at a trade exhibition and/or use direct mail to send advertising messages and product samples to trade buyers. (However, the firm will need a good mailing list, since a company like McVitie's will know every key decision maker in the grocery retail trade.)
- Advertise in the trade press (e.g. *The Grocer* magazine). The advertisement will show the attractiveness of the packaging and will emphasise the market gap that has been identified, the generous trade profit margins available, the heavy consumer advertising support and the package of point-of-sale (POS) display materials that are being provided to increase the level of **impulse purchasing** within the store.
- Identify and agree distribution and sales targets for each area of the country and type of outlet. A major company such as McVitie's is likely to be confident of achieving distribution targets as high as 80 per cent, whereas a new small firm may find it very difficult to gain distribution at even 15 per cent of stores. Having set distribution targets, the firm should send sales representatives to visit each of the main wholesale and retail buyers. A possible way to break into major multiples is to agree on an exclusive arrangement (e.g. that the new product will be stocked only at Tesco for its first six months). This gives the retailer the possibility of a worthwhile benefit: Tesco scores a minor triumph in its competitive battle against Sainsbury's and the others.

A-grade application

Even the biggest firms can struggle to keep their products on the shelves. In July 2010 Pepsi had to admit that low sales of its Pepsi Raw brand had led to several major retailers withdrawing it from distribution. In the year to 26 June 2010, its total UK retail sales were £704,000, a pinprick in the huge market for soft drinks. When it was launched into the retail sector in October 2008, Pepsi had said it would 'rejuvenate' the £400 million cola market. Instead it has become too small a niche to be worth allocating precious shelf space.

Issues for analysis

For exam purposes there are two key factors to consider about 'place'.

- A successful business must find where customers want to buy the product, then get it stocked at that place. If the product is ready-to-eat popcorn, the place must be the cinema; if it's unpopped corn, the place must be in the grocery store. Naive businesspeople try to get their product stocked everywhere, without thinking about the high costs of delivery, advertising materials and ongoing customer service. Today's customers value convenience highly, so the right product must be available in the right place at the right time. Clever firms look for appropriate outlets, not simply as many as possible.
- Anyone can have a brilliant new idea; anyone can decide on the price and the name of this new product – but getting shops to take a chance

on a newcomer is more of a problem. Many new small manufacturers have been defeated by the costs, the slowness and the difficulty of obtaining product distribution. Therefore 'place' (sometimes called 'the silent P') is a critical part of the marketing mix.

Place – an evaluation

Place is of particular importance in Business Studies because it can represent a major barrier to entry, especially for new small firms. The practical constraint on the amount of shop floor space available makes it hard for new products to gain acceptance, unless they are genuinely innovative. Therefore, existing producers of branded goods can get quite complacent, with little serious threat from new competition. Famously, in the nineteenth century, Ralph Waldo Emerson said that 'If a man can make a better mousetrap, though he builds his house in the woods, the world will make a beaten path to his door.' In other words, if the product is good enough, customers will come and find you. In a modern competitive world, though, the vast majority of products are not *that* exciting or different from others. So it is crucial to provide customers with convenient access to your products and/or shelf space in an eye-catching location. Getting products into the right place should not be taken for granted.

Key terms

Barrier to entry: factors that make it hard for new firms to break into an existing market (e.g. strong brand loyalty to the current market leaders).

Impulse purchasing: buying in unplanned way (e.g. going to a shop to buy a paper, but coming out with a Mars bar and a Diet Coke).

A Revision questions *(30 marks; 30 minutes)*

1 Outline the meaning of the term 'place'. (2)

2 Explain in your own words why it may be that 'place is the toughest of the 4Ps'. (3)

3 Outline what you think are appropriate distribution channels for:
   a) a new magazine aimed at 12–15-year-old boys (2)
   b) a new adventure holiday company focusing on wealthy 19–32 year olds. (3)

4 Retailers such as WHSmith charge manufacturers a rent on prime store space such as the shelving near to the cash tills.
   a) How might a firm work out whether it is worthwhile to pay the extra? (3)
   b) Why might new small firms find it hard to pay rents such as these? (4)

5 Explain in your own words what is meant by the phrase 'a better mousetrap'. (4)

6 Outline three reasons for the success of direct distribution over the internet in recent years. (9)

B1 Revision exercises

Data response

Getting distribution right

Secondary data can be hugely helpful to new companies looking for distribution of their first products. A company launching the first 'Kitten Milk' product has to decide where to focus its efforts. Where does cat food sell? Is it in pet shops, in corner shops or in supermarkets? Desk research company BMRB reports that, whereas 65 per cent of dog owners shops for pet food at supermarkets, 81 per cent of cat owners do the same. A different source (TNS) puts the cat food market size at £829 million. TNS also shows that the market is rising in value by around 2.5 per cent each year.

Further secondary data shows that pet food shoppers spend only 80 per cent of the amount they intend to when they go to a shop. This is because poor distribution stops them finding what they want. And 50 per cent of shoppers will not return to the same store after being let down twice by poor availability.

Questions *(20 marks; 25 minutes)*

1 State the meaning of the term 'market size'. (2)

2 a) The Year 1 sales target for Kitten Milk is £5 million. What share of the total market for cat food would that represent? (3)

b) Explain why it might be hard to persuade retailers to stock a product with that level of market share. (6)

3 The marketing manager for Kitten Milk is planning to focus distribution efforts on getting the brand placed in pet shops. Discuss whether this seems wise. (9)

B2 Data response

An arm's length from desire

From its origins in America in 1886, Coca-Cola has been a marketing phenomenon. It was the world's first truly global brand; it virtually invented the red, jolly Christmas Santa, and its bottle design (1919) was the first great piece of packaging design.

Yet a 1950 *Time* magazine article quoted another piece of marketing genius: 'Always within an arm's length of desire.' The marketing experts at Atlanta (home of Coca-Cola) realised nearly 60 years ago that sales of Coca-Cola were limited mainly by availability. Especially on a hot day, a cold Coke would be desired by almost anyone who had it an arm's length away. This led the company to develop a distribution strategy based on maximum availability, maximum in-store visibility and therefore maximum impulse purchase.

From then on, Coca-Cola targeted four main types of distribution:

1 in supermarkets and grocers

2 in any kiosk in a location based on entertainment (e.g. a bowling alley or a cinema)

3 in any canteen, bar or restaurant

4 in a vending machine near you; automatic vending proved one of the most valuable ways of building the market until worries about healthy eating saw them banned in schools; a vending machine is the ultimate barrier to entry.

Overall, though, the Coca-Cola approach to distribution set out in 1950 what most companies still try to do today.

Questions *(25 marks; 30 minutes)*

1 Explain how a vending machine can be a 'barrier to entry' to new competitors. (5)

2 Explain what the text means by the difference between 'maximum availability' and 'maximum visibility'. (5)

3 Explain why 'an arm's length from desire' might be less important for a business that does not rely upon impulse purchase. (7)

4 From all that you know about today's Coke, Diet Coke and Coke Zero, discuss whether Coca-Cola's distribution strategy was at the core of the firm's marketing success. (8)

Marketing and competitiveness

Definition

Competitiveness measures a firm's ability to compete (i.e. it compares its consumer offer with the offers made by its rivals).

Competitive markets

In the past, markets were physical places where buyers and sellers met in person to exchange goods; street markets are still like that. Today, some buyers and sellers never meet each other, a good example being eBay.

Some markets are more competitive than others. In general, a competitive market could be described as one where there is intense rivalry between producers of a similar good or service. The number of firms operating within a market influences the intensity of competition; the more firms there are, the greater the level of competition. However, the respective size of the firms operating in the market should also be taken into account. A market consisting of 50 firms may not be particularly competitive, if, for instance, one of the firms holds a 60 per cent market share and the 40 per cent is shared between the other 49. Similarly, a market composed of just four firms could be quite competitive because the firms operating within this market are of a fairly similar size.

Consumers enjoy competitive markets, but the reverse is true for the firms that operate in these markets. In competitive markets, prices and profit margins tend to be squeezed. As a result, firms operating in competitive markets try hard to minimise competition, perhaps by creating a unique selling point (**USP**) or using **predatory pricing**.

It could be argued that marketing is vital no matter what the level of competition is within the market. Firms that fail to produce goods and services that satisfy the needs of the consumers that make up their target market will find it hard to succeed in the long term. Ultimately, consumers will not choose to waste their hard-earned cash on products that fail to meet their needs.

The degree of competition within a market

One dominant business

Some markets are dominated by one large business. Economists use the word 'monopoly' to describe a market where there is a single supplier, and therefore no competition. In practice, pure textbook monopolies rarely exist; even Microsoft does not have a 100 per cent share of the office software market (though it does have a 90 per cent share).

Monopolies are bad for consumers because they restrict choice and tend to drive prices upwards. For that reason, most governments regulate against monopolies and near monopolies that exploit consumers by abusing their dominant market position. The UK government's definition of a monopoly is somewhat looser. According to the Competition Commission, a monopoly is a firm that has a market share of 25 per cent and above.

Deciding whether or not a firm has a monopoly is a far from straightforward task. First of all, the market itself has to be accurately defined – for example, Camelot has been granted a monopoly to run the National Lottery; however, it could be argued that Camelot does not have a dominant market position because there are other forms of gambling, such as horse racing and the football pools, available to consumers in the UK. Second, national market share figures should not be used in isolation because

Figure 46.1 Apple's iPhone 4

some firms enjoy local monopolies. In 2007 the Competition Commission accused Tesco of abusing its market position in towns such as Inverness and Slough by occupying sites previously occupied by its rivals. In both towns, consumers had to travel more than 15 minutes by car to reach another supermarket chain.

Firms implement their marketing strategy through the marketing mix. In markets dominated by a single large business, firms do not need to spend heavily on promotion because consumers are, to a degree, captive. Prices can be pushed upwards and the product element of the marketing mix should be focused on creating innovations that make it harder for new entrants to break in to the market. Apple spends millions of dollars on research and development in order to produce cutting-edge products such as the iPhone 4 (see Figure 46.1). To ensure that Apple maintains its dominant market position, new product launches are patented to prevent me-too imitations from being launched by the competition.

Competition between a few giants

The UK supermarket industry is a good example of a market that is dominated by a handful of very large companies. Economists call markets like this **oligopolistic**. The rivalry that exists within such markets can be intense, because firms know that any gains in market share will be at the expense of their rivals. The actions taken by one firm affect the profits made by the other firms that compete within the same market.

In markets made up of a few giants, firms tend to focus on **non-price competition** when designing the marketing mix. Firms in these markets tend to be reluctant to compete by cutting price. They fear that the other firms in the industry will respond by cutting their prices too, creating a costly price war where no firm wins.

Fiercely competitive markets

Fiercely competitive markets tend to be fragmented, made up of hundreds of relatively small firms, each of which competes actively against the others. In some of these markets, competition is amplified by the fact that firms sell near identical products, called commodities. Commodities are products such as flour, sugar or blank DVDs that are hard to differentiate. Rivalry in commodity markets tends to be intense. In markets such as this, firms have to manage their production costs very carefully because the retail price is the most important factor in determining whether the firm's product sells or not. If a firm cannot cut its costs, it will not be able to cut its prices without cutting into profit margins. Without price cuts, market share is likely to be lost.

In fiercely competitive markets, firms will try, where possible, to create product differentiation. For example, the restaurant market in Croydon, Surrey, is extremely competitive. There are over 70 outlets within a two-mile radius of the town centre. To survive without having to compete solely on price, firms in markets like this must find new innovations regularly because points of differentiation are quickly copied.

A-grade application

Fancy a holiday in Barcelona? There are many different airlines that will fly you there. The three main UK ones are Ryanair, British Airways and easyJet. In August 2010 it was possible to book return flights for March 2011 from Gatwick Airport to Barcelona for the following prices:

British Airways:	£103.90
easyJet:	£60.98
Ryanair:	£49.58

This is a ferociously competitive market, because many airlines are offering a very similar service on exactly the same route. Here, the traveller has a choice based on price and on the customer service image of each airline. It will be hard for any of these three airlines to make a profit on such low prices. By contrast, Virgin Rail can use its monopoly position to charge £200 for a return fare from London to Birmingham.

Determinants of competitiveness

The key to competitiveness is customer satisfaction. If consumers are satisfied with quality and value for money, the firm concerned should be competitive. Competitive firms find it easier to hold on to, or even gain, market share. Competitiveness is a function of internal factors that are within the firm's control, and external factors, which are not.

Efficiency

Ryanair is a highly efficient company that manages its costs very effectively. The company's business model focuses on cost minimisation, by:

- avoiding airports that have high take-off and landing charges; instead, Ryanair prefers flying from secondary airports, some of which actually pay it for using them
- operating only one type of aircraft – the Boeing 737; staff employed to pilot or service Ryanair's aircraft need only be trained on one plane, minimising staff training and stock holding costs (for plane components)
- cutting out free food, drinks and newspapers: passengers that wish to consume these items have to pay for them; charging for food and drink has converted a cost into an important source of revenue.

Cost-efficient businesses such as Ryanair can charge lower prices than their less efficient rivals, yet make the same or more profit per unit supplied. In highly competitive commodity markets, such as low-cost air travel, price cutting is a highly effective way of gaining market share.

Design

Some firms are highly competitive because they sell products that have been differentiated by their design. In countries such as the UK, where wage rates are relatively high, manufacturers cannot compete on price alone. Production costs are too high compared with rivals in countries where wage rates are lower. By using design as a USP, British manufacturers can compete on quality rather than price, making them less vulnerable to competition from China and India. Good-looking design can add value to a product. For example, the BMW Mini relies upon its retro 1960s styling to command its price premium within the small car market.

Brand image

In many markets brand image is crucial. The results of blind tests indicate that, in many cases, consumers are unable to tell the difference between supermarket own-label products and premium-priced brands. Clever branding and advertising may be the only thing ensuring that Stella Artois carries on outselling Tesco's Premium Lager.

External factors

Competitiveness is also partially determined by external factors that are beyond the firm's control. The going wage rate in a country is an excellent example of an external factor that is beyond any single firm's control. High wages tend to drive up costs, making a firm less competitive. On average, factory workers in the USA get paid somewhere in the region of $15–$30 per hour. In China the corresponding figure is less than $1 per hour. Firms try to improve their competitiveness by making internal changes to help compensate for factors, such as labour costs, that are beyond their control. European car manufacturers such as VW and Mercedes have decided to close down some of their European factories and re-open them in low-cost countries such as China in an attempt to improve their competitiveness.

Methods of improving competitiveness

Training

Some firms aim to improve their efficiency by increasing the amount they spend on staff training. Well-trained staff create the following competitive advantages:

- *Lower costs:* training tends to increase the productivity of labour because trained staff can work faster and make fewer mistakes; if output per worker increases, unit labour costs will tend to fall.
- *Improved product quality:* trained staff know what they are doing; improving the build quality of the finished product could give the firm concerned a competitive advantage in the market.
- *Better customer service:* effective training can

dramatically improve customer service, for example, in some supermarkets untrained staff are still sent straight to the checkouts to learn how to use the till on the job, leading to queues and irritated customers.

Management

The quality of management has an important impact on the competitiveness of a business. For many years newspapers blamed British workers for the decline of UK car producers such as Rover. Yet, today, the Nissan plant in Sunderland is the most productive car factory in Europe. This implies that British management methods were at fault, as the Nissan plant's workforce is British. Improving the quality of management within an organisation is notoriously difficult, requiring a change in an organisation's culture.

Modernisation and investment

Some firms try to improve their competitiveness by purchasing new machinery and technology designed to improve efficiency. For example, a car manufacturer could drive down unit costs by replacing labour with the latest CAM (computer-aided manufacturing) technology. It is hoped that the new machinery will boost efficiency by driving up productivity, while at the same time reducing the firm's wage bill.

Issues for analysis

- Every firm is different, and so is every market. It is always essential to think hard about the structure of the market, as this can affect every aspect of management within individual firms. Facing the same opportunity (e.g. for robot window-cleaners), a small firm may react very differently from a large one.
- It is then necessary to remember the huge difference between what firms do and what is right. Many firms try to improve their competitiveness by cost-cutting, such as the attempt by McDonald's to operate a 'zero training' policy. From a marketing point of view, that was a poor idea as it would inevitably affect customer service.

Marketing and competitiveness – an evaluation

Competitiveness is a much wider issue than marketing. It is affected by the quality of the design and build of the products, and by the enthusiasm of the staff. These are clearly operations and personnel issues. Nevertheless, marketing is at the heart of competitiveness for many firms. Mars knows how to produce Galaxy chocolate, so the key to the firm's success next year is how well the brand can be marketed. The managers must understand the customers and then have the wisdom and the creativity to find a way to make the product stand out.

Key terms

Non-price competition: rivalry based on factors other than price (e.g. advertising, sales promotions or 'new improved' products).

Oligopolistic: a market in which a few large companies have a dominant share (e.g. the UK chocolate market with a 70 per cent share divided between Cadbury, Nestlé and Mars).

Predatory pricing: when a large company sets prices low with the deliberate intention of driving a weaker rival out of business.

USP (unique selling point): a point of genuine difference that makes one product stand out from the crowd (e.g. the Toyota Prius 'hybrid synergy drive').

Revision questions (35 marks; 35 minutes)

1 What is a competitive market? (3)

2 Explain how the marketing mix of Virgin Trains might be affected by a decision by government to allow other train operating companies to compete on Virgin's routes. (3)

3 Describe the main features of an oligopolistic market. (3)

4 a) What is a price war? (3)
b) Why are price wars rare? (3)

5 Explain why product differentiation becomes more important as competition within a market increases. (3)

6 Identify four factors that could be used to identify whether or not a business is competitive. (4)

7 How might the size of an organisation affect its efficiency? (3)

8 Why might a firm that is struggling to be competitive increase its training budget? (3)

9 Explain how the quality of management can impact upon an organisation's efficiency. (4)

10 Apart from market research, how might a firm achieve its goal of attempting to get closer to the consumer? (3)

Revision exercises

Data response

At the beginning of the 1960s Indian food was a niche market business: there were just 500 Indian restaurants in the whole of the UK. As the table below illustrates, in the two decades that followed, the UK Indian restaurant market grew at a spectacular rate. In more recent times the market has continued to grow, however the rate of growth has declined. Today, the Indian restaurant market is firmly established and the industry is one of Britain's largest, employing over 60,000 people.

Table 46.1 Number of Indian restaurants in UK

Year	No. of restaurants	Market growth rate (%)
1960	500	–
1970	1200	140
1980	3000	150
1990	5100	70
2000	7940	56
2004	8750	10
2010	8900	2

The Indian restaurant market is extremely decentralised and is made up of thousands of small, independent operators. In most British high streets there are several Indian restaurants that compete aggressively against one another. Indian food is very popular: over 23 million portions of Indian food are sold in restaurants each year. In the 1960s and 1970s, the growing affluence and cosmopolitan nature of the British public boosted takings at most Indian restaurants. Indian restaurateurs began to make serious money from the industry. Most owners chose to use some of their profit to upgrade their facilities. Gradually the Indian restaurant scene became more sophisticated (e.g. luxurious-looking tables, chairs and tablecloths, piped Indian music, air conditioning, dinner-jacketed waiters and flock wallpaper). Some 30 years ago all Indian restaurants tended to look the same and most had fairly similar menus too. As a result, Indian restaurants were forced into competing against each other on price. Unfortunately, intense price competition led to falling profit margins. Indian restaurateurs began to realise the importance of product differentiation as a competitive weapon. The first real attempt to create differentiation occurred in the early 1960s when a handful of forward-looking Indian restaurants, such as the Gaylord in Mortimer Street, London, imported tandoors. A tandoor is a special type of oven made from clay that gives the food cooked inside it a distinctive taste. Restaurants using tandoor ovens found that they could charge slightly higher prices without emptying their restaurants. Today, Indian restaurants use a variety of tactics to compete including those listed below.

- *Décor and design*: in recent times several now famous London-based Indian restaurants, such as the Cinnamon Club (opened in 2001 at a cost of £2.6 million in the Old Westminster Library), ditched the old-style traditional Indian restaurant décor in favour of a more upmarket-looking, modern, minimalistic interior design style. This change inspired many other Indian restaurants up and down the land to upgrade their fixtures and fittings in the hope that they too could charge Cinnamon Club-style premium prices (e.g. smoked rack of lamb with Rajasthani corn sauce and pilau rice for £22.00).
- *Exotic-sounding premium-priced menu items:* for example, Seabass Kaylilan prepared with fenugreek and tamarind.

Other restaurants have adopted a different approach. For example, the Khyber in Croydon has tried to win customers by emphasising its authenticity. The restaurant's website informs the reader that 'Our success is based on more traditional recipes.' The slogan 'It's just how mum would cook it back home' also features prominently on its internet menu. It also offers:

- balti cooking, including the super-sized big-as-your-table Naan breads!
- a prestigious imported German lager on draught, or a selection of fine wines
- flying in celebrated curry chefs from the Indian subcontinent for a limited period to cook up special food for a Curry Festival – the equivalent of a nightclub flying in a celebrity DJ.

Figure 46.2 Modern Indian restaurant décor

Questions *(35 marks; 40 minutes)*

1 Using the table, explain what has happened to the degree of competition within the UK Indian restaurant market over the last 50 years. (6)

2 Giving your reasons, discuss whether the Indian restaurant market in the UK is an example of a fiercely competitive market. (6)

3 a) Explain how efficiency might affect the competitiveness of an Indian restaurant. (4)

b) How might an Indian restaurant go about improving its efficiency? (4)

4 Identify and explain three internal factors that might affect the competitiveness of an Indian restaurant. (6)

5 Product differentiation is essential if an Indian restaurant is to survive in the long run. Discuss. (9)

Case study

The £9 toaster

The prices of consumer electronics, such as toasters, satellite TV set-top boxes and MP3 players, have tumbled in recent years. Supermarket chains now sell DVD players that previously cost hundreds of pounds for under £10. So, why have the prices of these goods fallen? In part, the price falls reflect the falling price of the components that go into consumer electronics. Low prices also reflect the fact that there is now more competition in the market. In the past, consumers typically bought items such as TVs and computers from specialist retailers such as Currys and Dixons. Today, the situation is somewhat different: in addition to these specialist retailers, consumers can now buy electrical goods over the internet and from supermarkets. Some industry analysts also believe that some of the supermarket chains are using set-top boxes and DVD players as loss leaders.

In today's ultra-competitive environment, manufacturers of consumer electronics face intense pressure from retailers to cut costs so that retail prices can be cut without any loss of profit margin. To cut prices without compromising product quality, manufacturers such as the Dutch giant Philips have transferred production from the Netherlands to low-cost locations such as China.

Questions *(35 marks; 40 minutes)*

1 Describe three characteristics of a highly competitive market. (6)

2 Why has the market for consumer electronics become more competitive? (4)

3 Explain three factors that would affect the competitiveness of a manufacturer of consumer electronics. (6)

4 What is a loss leader and why do supermarkets sell them? (3)

5 How might the degree of competition impact upon the marketing mix used by a Chinese manufacturer of own-label toasters? (6)

6 In today's increasingly competitive market for consumer electronics, firms must constantly cut costs and prices if they are to survive. Discuss. (10)

47 A-grade concepts for AS level

To achieve an A grade requires far more than simply knowing all the subject matter – you need to be able to weave ideas together to generate mature analysis from which judgements (evaluation) can be made. You need concepts that enable your answers to rise above those of the majority. There are two categories of 'A grade' concept: those that are transferable and those that are naturally analytic.

Transferable concepts

A transferable concept is one that can be used to answer a wide variety of questions. You may have been taught the concept in relation to one issue, but the A-grade student sees the scope for using it more often. At AS level, the main transferable concepts are:

- opportunity cost
- objectives
- strategy
- risk.

Opportunity cost

This is the cost of missing out on the next best alternative when making a decision. Opportunity cost in the context of new business start-ups was introduced in Unit 5. However, you also need to see the many other ways in which the concept can be used, for example, any answer to a question about decisions or strategies would benefit from consideration of opportunity cost. Table 47.1 shows the scope that exists.

The rule: every decision and every action has an opportunity cost, because there is a limited amount of time and money. Always think about what a business misses out on when making a decision.

Objectives

These are the goals set (or agreed) by the business, by the department or by the individual. Exam answers on decision making are usually rooted in profit (i.e. they assume that the business will do whatever generates the highest revenue or lowest cost). In fact, business decisions are based on the overall or personal objectives. A manager with a £400,000 budget for advertising will spend it all, even if the last £100,000 is not really useful, because spending the budget is the manager's objective. This might sound daft but it is absolutely true (and one of the weaknesses of a strict system of budgets). A business with the objective of growing to become the market leader will charge lower prices than one attempting to maximise its profits.

The rule: business decisions (good and bad) are based on corporate and personal goals. These may be focused on profit, but may also be focused on growth or on survival or on a social goal such as

Table 47.1 Using opportunity cost in exam answers

AS question	The opportunity cost answer
Recommend what the XYZ Co should do to improve its profits	Actions taken will have an opportunity cost (e.g. cutting staff levels will cut costs but may reduce customer service and hit the ability to develop new products)
Examine how the XYZ Co could reduce its labour turnover	Could redesign jobs to enrich them, but this may mean missing out on the opportunity to improve productivity (e.g. by automation)
Should the XYZ Co choose Chinese suppliers, as they are the cheapest?	This will mean missing out on the opportunity to develop good design links with suppliers, and will make it harder to respond quickly to fashion change (which is why Zara gets supplies only from Europe)

improving the environment. A good exam answer is based on the circumstances of the specific business; in this case, what exactly are its objectives?

Strategy

A strategy involves the creation of a medium- to long-term plan for meeting the objectives. Clearly this will be successful only if (a) the plan is a good one and (b) managers put it into practice effectively.

The key to an A-grade answer is to see the differences between strategy and tactics. Tactics are short-term responses to opportunities or threats. For example, Burger King might choose to cut its prices sharply in August in Scunthorpe because a new McDonald's Drive-thru is opening; meanwhile in August in Bournemouth it pushes prices up because so many holidaymakers arrive. Overall, though, Burger King's long-term pricing strategy has been to charge higher prices than McDonald's.

Any question on objectives must lead through to strategy; after all, objectives mean nothing without a plan to make them happen. Beware, though, of straying away from strategy into tactics. Questions about how to achieve marketing objectives are often answered with reference to BOGOF (buy-one-get-one-free) or other short-term tactical sales promotions.

The rule: strategy is medium to long term; tactics are short term.

Risk

Risks are the chance elements within a decision that need to be assessed before carrying on. Second-rate managers in second-rate organisations may have a long career without ever doing anything risky. If bosses hate 'mistakes', they will hate decisions involving risk. Yet no decision worthy of the name is risk-free. Just because launching new products is risky, this should not mean that no new products are launched; clearly that would sign the death warrant of the business.

Entrepreneurs are, by definition, willing to accept risk as part of the decision-making process – so are good managers in good companies. One of the world's biggest companies is Unilever. A recent chairman was Niall Fitzgerald. Before being promoted to chairman, Fitzgerald had been responsible for an awful new product flop called Persil Power. Appointing Fitzgerald sent a very positive message to all staff: 'We know that if you take risks, some won't come off; but the odd failure won't stop you getting to the top.'

The rule: risk is part of business because the future cannot be known. Good entrepreneurs and good businesses take risk in their stride; it is just part of a calculation about the positives versus the negatives when making a decision.

Naturally analytic concepts

These are ideas that are quite complex, but if you can master them, you can show a quality level that sets you apart from other exam candidates. At A2 level there are many analytic concepts, but at AS level there are really only three:

1 Distinguishing between cash flow and profit (re-read Unit 20, then tackle Data response B1, below).
2 Competitiveness.
3 The business context.

Competitiveness

Competitiveness is the ability of a business to compete effectively against its rivals. This term is invaluable. It has two aspects: the ability to compete on price and the ability to compete in other ways.

Price competitiveness is based on costs. In the long term you can compete with Ryanair on price only if you can keep your costs as low as Ryanair's. Look at the extraordinary staff cost comparisons for 2010 shown in Table 47.2.

Table 47.2 Airline staff cost comparisons, 2010

	Passengers flown	Wage bill	Wage cost per passenger
Ryanair	66.5 million	£335m	£5.04
British Airways	32.0 million	£1,998m	£62.44

(Source: Data extracted from British Airways and Ryanair annual accounts, year ending 31 March 2010)

These figures show that British Airways' wage bill per passenger is 12 times higher than Ryanair's.

Non-price factors

Fortunately for British Airways, there are other ways to stay competitive. Its most profitable route is Heathrow to New York. Here it has managed to stay among the leaders for offering a great business-class service (at prices of up to £4,000 return). Its quality of service helps it to remain competitive in a sector that is less concerned by price.

Figure 47.1 New York, a British Airways destination

Key non-price factors that can make customers willing to pay high prices include:

- great design
- prestige brand names
- high-quality production
- terrific personal service and after-sales service
- a satisfied glow (e.g. organic, environmentally sound).

The rule: if a business has no strategy for competitiveness, it may not be around for long. Directors must decide whether to aim for price competitiveness or to stand out from rivals using one or more of the non-price factors.

The business context

A-grade answers show real understanding of the specific business situation set by the examiner. This is not announced in advance, so the 300 words of text have to provide all the clues needed for success. For an A-grade student, it should not matter what the context is: all the key information is in the text. Among the things to look for are those listed below:

- *Is it a manufacturing or a service business?* Usually service businesses have direct customer contact, so staff motivation is critical to the brand image. Also, manufacturing firms are more likely to face direct competition from low-cost producers such as China, so they have more serious competitiveness issues than service firms
- *Is it a recent start-up or an established business?* Even if the firm is small, a few years of success can make it quite easy to cope with a difficult period; the finances might be quite strong and a loyal customer base may exist. For brand new companies, even a temporary problem, such as flooding, may wreck the business plan. Every new firm needs a bit of luck.
- *What is the external context for the business?* The economy may be strong, with confident consumers – or weak, with worried customers keeping their hands in their pockets. The market for your product might be trendy and booming or tired and slipping. Competition may be fierce, perhaps from big well-financed firms, or it may be quite mild, with many small firms keeping to their local area.

The rule: never start answering a business question until you have given yourself the time to ask 'What's special about this particular business?' Its unique features will give you the scope for developing an A-grade answer.

Key terms

Competitiveness: the ability to compete (i.e. highly competitive means in a great position to beat the competition).

Corporate: the company as a whole, so corporate objectives affect the whole business.

Revision questions (35 marks; 40 minutes)

1 Why is it better to spend more revision time on transferable concepts than any other? (2)

2 Outline the opportunity cost to Innocent Drinks of spending £2 million to buy up a German producer of smoothies. (4)

3 Identify whether each of the following is an objective, a strategy or a tactic:
   a) to run a 'Blue Cross day', with 25 per cent off all stock this Sunday
   b) to become the first carbon-neutral car manufacturer
   c) to boost sales by 20 per cent within the next two years
   d) to concentrate advertising spending on TV
   e) to give a huge office party to celebrate winning a big order. (5)

4 Outline three risks faced by a school-leaver who borrows £5,000 to start an online auction site specialising in Manchester United football programmes. (6)

5 Explain one key factor in making each of these companies competitive:
   a) Mercedes cars
   b) Primark
   c) L'Oréal cosmetics. (6)

6 a) Outline two important features of the UK economy over the past six months. (4)
   b) Explain the effect that each of these trends might have on a business start-up focusing on loft extensions and other costly building work. (8)

Revision exercises

Data response: the furniture shop

Section 1

A furniture shop has been operating for six months with regular income of £100,000 in monthly sales. Its monthly fixed costs are £50,000 and it sets its prices by doubling the variable costs of buying supplies in from the manufacturers (i.e. variable costs are half the sales revenue).

1 a) Calculate the monthly profit/loss being made. (3)

A bright young manager carries out some research and finds that sales can be doubled by making an offer of 'buy now, get interest-free credit for three months'.

   b) Calculate the new monthly profit/loss when sales double. (3)

Section 2

The business decides to go ahead with this offer and plans to introduce it on 1 February. This will boost profit, but what will it do to the firm's cash flow? Copy the grid below and fill it in carefully (in pencil, preferably). Note that the business has £50,000 in the bank at the start of January.

2 Fill in the cash flow table. (12)

(All figures in £000s)

	Jan	Feb	Mar	Apr	May	June
Cash at start	50					
Cash in						
Cash out						
Net cash						
Cash at end						−300

(Keep trying this until you get *minus* £300,000 in the bottom right-hand corner.)

Section 3

After running the interest-free offer for five months, it is decided that the offer will be closed at the end of June. Draw up the cash flow position for the business from July–October.

3 Fill in the cash flow table below. (8)

(All figures in £000s)

	July	August	September	October
Cash at start	−300			
Cash in				
Cash out				
Net cash				
Cash at end				+300

Section 4

Now that the offer is over, it is possible to see the difference between profit and cash flow.

4 Draw a line graph to show cumulative cash and cumulative profit over the period January to October. Label the graph carefully and then shade in the area that indicates the difference between profit and cash flow. (14)

48 Tackling AQA Unit 1

What subject matter does Unit 1 cover?

Unit 1 will ask questions solely on Unit 1 of the AQA specification. That is, it asks you questions about the activities of a business before it starts trading. This is the start of a story that continues through the entire AQA specification. Unit 1 mainly covers issues relating to business planning. This means that it encompasses a wide range of Business Studies topics to give you a good appreciation of the breadth of the subject. However, all of these are dealt with at an introductory level and developed later in the course.

Because Unit 1 covers starting a business, the focus of the specification is obviously on small businesses, and the examination will reflect this. When tackling the Unit 1 examination, you will encounter 'start-up' topics such as developing and protecting business ideas, business plans, market research and locating a business. The unit also covers a range of financial planning issues such as costs, revenues and profits, break-even analysis and budgets. Although this element is a smaller part of the Unit 1 specification than 'Starting a Business', it is no less important.

The Unit 1 specification includes a fair amount of numerical material including market growth, share and size, as well as break-even, cash flow, budgets and profits. Understanding and using numerical information is an important and integral part of your success in this unit.

What are the key features of a Unit 1 paper?

All Unit 1 papers will *not* be exactly the same. There will be variation in the way the text is written and presented, in the number of questions and the marks allocated to each question. However, there will be a number of common features and knowing about these will help you to prepare for the examination.

- The examination paper will be based on an unseen case study. This case will present the story of a business start-up and will provide a range of information about it. It will give some indication of the planning process that the entrepreneur has followed.
- The story will be supplemented by some numerical information. This could relate to the entrepreneur's planning of cash flows or profits/losses, or it could provide some detail on aspects of the market, such as market size or growth. This information might be a part of the text or presented in tables, graphs or charts.
- The types of business that appear on the Unit 1 paper will vary – some will provide services, others might be manufacturers or in the primary sector of the economy.
- The Unit 1 examination will have a number of questions, which may be split into two sections.
  - The first few questions on the examination paper will require relatively brief answers and will usually have low mark allocations (7 marks or under will be common). Such questions might ask you to define a term such as 'primary market research', or to carry out a calculation. These questions will normally test knowledge and application.

- Later questions will be more challenging, require more time to answer and carry larger mark allocations. These questions will ask you to develop arguments and make judgements. A typical question might ask you to evaluate the quality of the entrepreneur's business plan.
- The Unit 1 paper will carry a total of 60 marks and you have an hour and a quarter to complete it.

Key features of AQA Unit 1

- Based on a case study of the start-up of a business
- Covers all of the Unit 1 specification
- A mix of short-answer and extended-response questions
- 60 marks in total for this paper
- The time available is 1 hour and 15 minutes
- Unit 1 represents 40% of your AS marks and 20% of the entire A level.

How should I prepare for and tackle Unit 1?

Revision

Unit 1 offers 21 marks (35% of the total marks) for knowledge. This is a high proportion and means that you have to revise thoroughly for this examination. It is important that you learn the definitions of the terms that are listed in the specification. So, you should be able to define entrepreneur, market niche, market segmentation and budgets, as well as the other terms listed in the Unit 1 specification. It is ideal if you can define these terms in a single sentence. You also need to learn key formulae such as that for calculating profits, break-even and market share.

Your revision should also mean that you have mastered the relevant theory. For example, you need to be able to explain why demand for the product is important to entrepreneurs, the benefits of trading as a private limited company or the problems in setting budgets.

As part of your revision for this examination, it is vital that you go through the Unit 1 specification and tick off all the subjects that you have studied. Make sure that you identify and take action over any gaps that remain. You can be sure that if you miss something out it is certain to be on the paper!

Practising sample papers

You must practise using past papers. There is a mock exam paper in the book (Unit 49) which you can use to test yourself. Your teacher or lecturer will have copies of the sample papers that have been written, as well as any papers that have been issued. Past papers are available on the AQA website (www.aqa.org.uk). Practising past papers will help you to develop the skills listed below.

Making effective use of the information in the case study

Most of the questions in Unit 1 relate to, or apply to, the case study. This means that you need to have relevant knowledge and apply it to the circumstances in the case study. Thus, for example, questions about the quality of market research or the best location should be answered thinking about *the business in the case study*, and not just any business. A total of 17 (of the 60) marks on the paper are for applying your knowledge to the case study. Any calculation on this paper will require you to apply your knowledge as you will have to combine your knowledge (possibly in the form of a formula) with numerical information from the case study.

This means that you must read the case study carefully – do not rush it as you should not be short of time. Identify the distinctive features of the case. These may include issues such as the experience and skills of the entrepreneur, the type and/or uniqueness of the product idea, the extent and appropriateness of the market research and the quality of the financial planning. Other important information could relate to competitors or market size. Remember, some of the most important information might be expressed in numerical terms.

Recognising the differing demands of questions

- *Knowledge questions:* some questions require brief answers and just knowledge to answer. Examples are 'What is meant by the term market segmentation?' or 'State two items of financial information that might be included in a business plan.' These questions do not require you to apply your answers to the case study and will have low mark allocations. Most questions (apart from those above) will ask you to apply your knowledge to the circumstances of the case study, and not to answer in general terms. This is why you must read the case study carefully.
- *Calculations:* it is highly likely that a Unit 1 examination paper will ask you to complete calculations. Do expect this and also to be asked what the results of your calculations mean. For example, you might be asked to complete a cash flow forecast. This information might be used as part of a later question about the quality of the entrepreneur's cash flow planning.
- *Analysis questions:* some questions will require you to write analytically – that is, to develop arguments. Such questions will ask you to examine or analyse as part of the question. An example would be: 'Examine two possible benefits to the Natural Foods restaurant from drawing up budgets before it starts trading.' This means you have to *explain why* Natural Foods would benefit from drawing up budgets. This will require you to write a number of linked sentences to develop your point. You'll need to practise writing in this way.

Table 48.1 Unit 1 examination skills

Skill	Marks/60	Percentage
Marks for knowledge	21	35
Marks for applying answers to case study	17	28
Marks for analysis	12	20
Marks for making judgements or decisions	10	17

- *Evaluation questions:* these are tough, high-mark questions that ask you to make a judgement or a decision. You will be able to recognise them by the use of words such as evaluate, discuss or justify, or the phrase 'to what extent'. You will be expected to consider different arguments and to reach and support a decision. An example of such a question could be 'Do you think that the success of Martin's business was due to luck or high-quality planning? Justify your view.'

Using time effectively

Answering past papers is essential to develop a number of important skills, and this includes managing time effectively. The Unit 1 paper lasts 75 minutes and is worth 60 marks. If you spend 15 minutes during the examination reading the case study and any data, that allows you to spend one minute on a question for each mark allocated to it. It is important that you follow this rule to make sure you have enough time to tackle the high-mark questions at the end of the paper. So, only spend a maximum of two minutes on a two-mark definition, no matter how much you know about it! The spaces in the answer booklet will also guide you as to how long to spend on a question.

Key points to remember for Unit 1

- The paper has a relatively large number of questions (a typical paper may have nine) and can therefore ask questions on most areas of the specification. Therefore, *thorough revision* is essential.
- *Reading the case study* thoroughly and carefully is vital. This may include numerical information, which you must not ignore. Make sure you know the story.
- *Apply your answers to the scenario.* Most questions require you to relate your knowledge and *not* to write general answers.
- Be prepared to *carry out calculations* and also to understand what the answers to your calculations mean.
- The high-mark questions are at the end of the paper. You must *manage your time carefully* so that you can write full answers to these questions and demonstrate your knowledge, as well as examination skills such as analysis and evaluation.

In this exam you must answer *all* the questions. You will need up to ten minutes to skim read and then re-read the text, making brief notes in the margin. That leaves one mark per minute for answering the questions and five minutes to check your work.

The quality of your English will be assessed in your answers to questions 2b and 2c. Be careful to write fully developed prose (i.e. avoid bullet points and abbreviations) and make sure to check your written work carefully.

It would be best to tackle this mock exam in timed conditions, even if you are doing it at home.

49 Mock exam for unit 1

Mock exam for AQA Unit 1 (60 marks; 75 minutes)

XDream Holidays Ltd

Two years ago Karl and Natalia took up parachuting. They both worked at a solicitor's, Natalia as the office manager and Karl as the accountant. Soon their week's work was purely a filler between the important thing in life – parachuting. Then Natalia had an idea.

Why not start a holiday business focusing on parachuting? The modern, adventure-seeking traveller would love a parachute drop in a beautiful part of mid-Wales, with a group leader who would then have to guide the group – on foot – to the nearest town. The next day, they would move on to another part of Wales. Today Wales, tomorrow Austria or Brazil.

They talked to other parachuters and to friends who went on diving and other active holidays. All loved the idea. One said: 'I've never bothered with parachuting because I thought it would always be into the same dull field. This would definitely get me interested.' And what would people expect to pay for a parachuting holiday in Wales? Or in Brazil? Broadly, the answer was £1,500 and £2,500 respectively.

Natalia did some research into hiring planes in Wales – not as expensive as she thought – and the cost of 3-star hotels. Assuming a group size of twelve, it was quite easy to see that a profit could be made. Weekly fixed costs came out at £8,000, variable costs at £500 per person and the price would be £1,500. Natalia said with confidence: 'If we just run one parachute holiday per week in Wales in the six months May–October, there's still enough profit to make a good living. And if one of us is the group leader and the other one the emergency back-up, we'll have free parachuting all summer long.' They also discussed taking on extra staff to run more courses.

Karl's worry was about how to build up to the necessary numbers of customers. Twelve customers a week would be great, but what if there were only six? He carried out some research by dropping in to eight adventure-travel agencies in Manchester and Birmingham. After that he felt

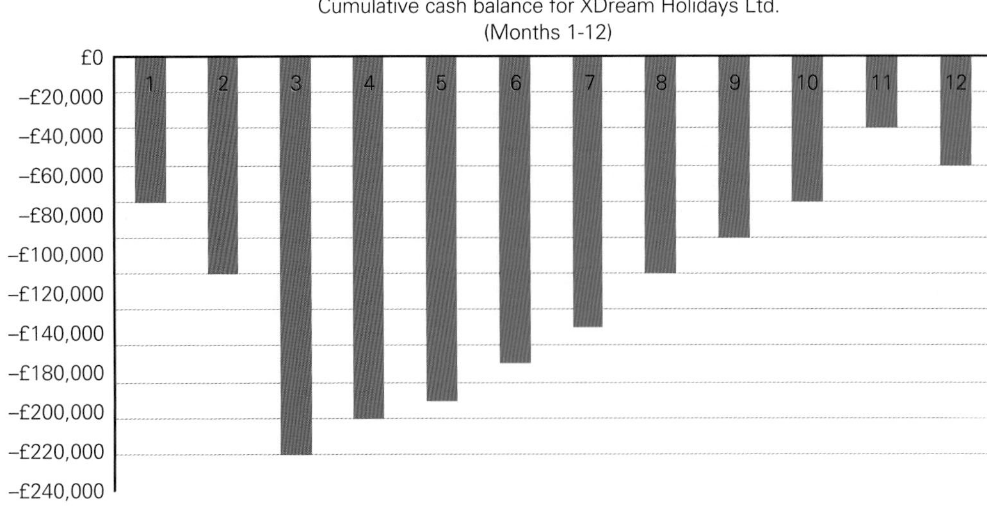

Figure 49.1 Cumulative cash balance for XDream Holidays Ltd (months 1–12)

much more comfortable; as one agent said: 'That price won't put off people in the segment you're targeting. You'll soon have rich City boys wanting to spend their bonuses with you on £10,000 trips parachuting onto Caribbean islands.'

Reassured by this, Karl started work on a cash flow forecast. They thought about an internet-only operation, but decided customers would like the reassurance of a proper office to come and visit. Now the remaining hurdle was raising finance; their £20,000 in savings would be nothing like enough to get the business going. In preparation, Natalia went to Companies House to establish XDream Holidays Ltd. Karl started to think about giving notice to quit their jobs. The dream was starting to come true.

Questions

Question 1

a) Natalia spotted the parachute business opportunity through her personal experience. State two other ways of identifying a business opportunity. (2)

b) Briefly explain whether you would regard Karl's research among travel agents as qualitative or quantitative. (2)

c) What is meant in the case by the term 'segment'? (2)

d) Calculate the break-even point for XDream Holidays in Wales. (4)

e) What profit per week can Karl and Natalia expect if they achieve their target of 12 customers? (4)

f) Explain two possible reasons for setting up the business as a limited organisation. (6)

Question 2

a) Examine the factors Karl and Natalia should consider when deciding where to locate their new business. (10)

b) Discuss whether Karl or Natalia showed the most enterprise. (15)

c) Karl and Natalia have not yet undertaken a formal business plan. Discuss whether completing a business plan would guarantee the success of the start-up of XDream Holidays Ltd. (15)

50 Tackling AQA Unit 2

Introduction: the continuing story

In Unit 1 we considered a start-up business and the ways in which it planned to commence trading. This unit takes the story further. We are now looking at businesses that are small to medium-sized and actively trading. We could be examining a small business operating as a sole trader with a handful of workers, or a private limited company with several hundred employees and sales amounting to several million pounds each year.

Unit 2 looks at the functional decisions that the owners and managers of businesses can take to improve the performance of the business. These will be short-term tactical decisions such as improving the utilisation of resources or altering the marketing mix. These decisions will relate to one of the functional areas of the business such as marketing or operations management.

What subject matter does Unit 2 cover?

Unit 2 covers the internal functional areas of a small to medium-sized business: finance, marketing, operations management and people in business. This unit builds on Unit 1 and, while there will be no direct questions on Unit 1 material, it may require you to remember and understand it. For example, in Unit 2 you might encounter a question asking you to calculate and comment on the variances in a particular budget. This would be impossible to do without drawing on your knowledge of the structure of budgets, which was part of financial planning in Unit 1.

The Unit 2 specification breaks down into four functional areas with which you must be completely familiar. Every Unit 2 paper will ask questions on *all* of these functional areas.

1. *Finance:* this considers how a business can measure its financial performance (most notably profits or losses) and the financial actions that it can take to improve it.
2. *People in business:* once again this element combines measures of the performance (of the workforce) and a range of methods by which managers might improve the workforce's performance.
3. *Operations management:* this element of Unit 2 examines the targets that operations managers might pursue and tactical actions that they might take to achieve these targets, thereby improving their performance.
4. *Marketing:* this focuses on designing an effective marketing mix and the issues that this involves. It also covers matters relating to a business's competitiveness – what makes a business competitive and how can it be improved. This offers some opportunities to consider a range of different functional actions.

Key features of the Unit 2 paper

Unit 2 papers will vary a little in style from paper to paper. For example, there will not always be exactly the same number of marks for questions on each of the four functional areas. However, the marks will be similar and those awarded for questions on each functional area will roughly balance out over time.

As with Unit 1, there will be a number of common features that you will encounter on each Unit 2 examination paper.

- There will be two data response questions. Each of these will contain some text and it is likely that each will include some numerical information. Each data response question will have about four individual questions.
- Each of the data response questions will relate to a specific business. This business could be real or imaginary. In any case, it will be small or medium-sized.
- The mix of subject matter on each data response question will vary from paper to paper according to the nature of the business chosen.
- The questions will have a build-up of examination skills (knowledge, application, analysis and evaluation), but even the opening question will require more than simple knowledge. Most questions on this paper, unlike on Unit 1, will require you to write analytically and to evaluate.
- It is highly likely that there will be a calculation, and not just on finance. Each of the functional areas offers some opportunities for calculations and you should prepare for such questions.
- The questions calling for evaluation could relate to more than one internal function of a business, especially if they are about competitiveness. They may be quite 'open', offering you some freedom on the material that you choose to draw upon.
- Key themes on the Unit 2 examination papers will be measuring the performance of a business and considering means of improving performance through tactical, functional decisions.

Key features of AQA Unit 2

- Based on two data response questions, each having about four sub-questions
- Covers all of the Unit 2 specification
- All questions on the paper are compulsory
- 80 marks in total for this paper
- The time available is 1 hour and 30 minutes
- This paper carries 60 of the marks for AS Business studies and 30% of the marks for the entire A level.

How should I prepare for and tackle Unit 2?

Revision

As with Unit 1, thorough revision is an excellent starting point. Unlike Unit 1, there will not be simple questions asking you for definitions, but mastering these is still important. A relevant definition is an excellent way to open the answer to even the most challenging of questions.

Comprehensive knowledge of the subject matter will also help you to tackle the high-mark evaluation questions. In an 'open' question you are able to bring in information that is most relevant to the question and to develop it effectively, offering the potential for high marks. If there are gaps in your knowledge of the Unit 2 specification, you will be less able to do this and your responses may be less impressive as a consequence.

Mastering the numerical aspects of the Unit 2 specification is also very important. You must be able to carry out relevant calculations such as capacity utilisation, unit costs and profit margins, but also to understand their significance as measures of performance. You should be prepared to use the results of calculations or data that you are given as the basis for suggesting, explaining and possibly justifying methods of improving performance.

You must also look at the theories and concepts you have studied as part of Unit 2, and be able to explain why and how they might affect a business's performance. This will enable you to develop relevant arguments as part of your answers to the higher mark allocation questions.

Writing good-quality answers on Unit 2

Unit 2 is different to Unit 1 in that it requires you to write more extended answers in which you develop arguments and make and justify judgements and decisions. These are challenging skills that take time and effort to develop. It is essential that you tackle a range of appropriate questions as you study each unit of Unit 2 in this textbook. You will find suitable questions in each 'Workbook' section at the end of the unit. There is a mock exam paper in the book (Unit 51) which you can use to test yourself. Tackling this should be a central part of your revision programme.

So, what might a good-quality answer to a Unit 2 question look like? It would have a number of important features.

- You will have developed a small number of arguments as fully as possible. So, for example, a question asking you to analyse how a particular business might improve its competitiveness would be best answered by selecting two (or at the most three) of the most appropriate ways that *this* business could achieve this objective. You might argue that this would involve the business reducing its prices and increasing its capacity utilisation. A good answer would explain *fully* how each of these actions might improve the business's performance.
- A good answer to a Unit 2 high-mark-allocation question will be presented in the format of a small number of substantial paragraphs. This allows you to develop your arguments in the way outlined above. Examiners are looking for quality of arguments, not quantity.
- Another feature of a good answer on Unit 2 will be the effective use of numerical information in answering all types of question. Numerical information – for example, on unit costs – can be most helpful if reaching and justifying decisions. The best answers will use this whenever possible.
- There will also be consistent evidence in a high-quality answer that the student has read and understood the stimulus material presented as part of the question, and is using it to develop answers. This could include the relevant use of numerical data or of particular aspects of the business's activities to construct arguments.
- Effective use of time: some of the opening questions on each data response question will require relatively brief answers. High-quality responses will not spend too long on these. More guidance on managing your time in the Unit 2 examination is given below.

Table 50.1 Unit 2 examination skills

Skill	Marks/80	Percentage
Marks for knowledge	21	26
Marks for applying answers to case study	19	23
Marks for analysis	23	29
Marks for making judgements or decisions	17	22

Using time effectively

Answering past papers is essential to develop a number of important skills, and this includes managing time effectively. The Unit 2 paper lasts 90 minutes and is worth 80 marks. You should allow 45 minutes to answer each data response question (which is worth 40 marks). If you spend five minutes during the examination reading each set of data response materials and any data, that allows you to spend one minute on a question for each mark allocated to it. This is the same as for Unit 1. It is important that you follow this rule to make sure you have enough time to tackle the high-mark questions at the end of the paper, which will have a major effect in determining your mark. So, only spend a maximum of five minutes on a five-mark opening question, no matter how much you know about it! The spaces in the answer booklet will also guide you as to how long to spend answering a question.

Key points to remember for Unit 2

- The paper has questions on all four functions and *thorough revision* of each of these functions is essential.
- *Using numerical information* to judge the performance of businesses and to justify actions intended to improve performance will be an important part of tackling this paper.
- *Developing a small number of arguments* as fully as possible is important as evidence of analysis and as a basis for making judgements.
- Most of the marks on this paper are for high-mark-allocation questions testing analysis and evaluation. It is essential that you *manage your time carefully* so that you can respond fully to these questions, and that you *practise answering such questions*.
- *Be prepared to respond to open questions* drawing on a number of different areas or functions of the Unit 2 specification.

51 Mock exam for Unit 2

This exam is based on unseen material (i.e. neither the candidates nor the teachers know in advance what the text will be about). There are two sets of questions, each based on text that is about 300–400 words long. The exam lasts 90 minutes and the mark total is 80. Therefore, there are 10 minutes for reading and one minute per mark when answering the questions (2-mark question: 2-minute answer; 12-mark question: 12-minute answer).

Usually, one set of questions will be based on a newspaper article about a real business situation and the other questions based on a made-up case study. Candidates need to be used to reading articles from newspapers such as *The Guardian*, *The Times*, *The Telegraph* and the *Financial Times*.

The mock exam below follows the exact style of the AQA exam.

Mock exam for AQA Unit 2 (80 marks; 90 minutes)

Answer all questions.

Questions

Question 1

Read the article below then answer the questions that follow.

What sort of boss gives a monkey's about his staff?

A survey by a management consultancy found that three-quarters of senior executives would do an annual cutback of their workforce to boost productivity and performance. One in six think they could get rid of 20 per cent of employees without damaging performance or morale; nearly half reckon firing up to 5 per cent a year would be a good thing.

Even though only 4 per cent actually carry out this threat, it is still a revealing finding. This is what executives really think of their 'most valued asset'. Not only that, it utterly ignores their own contribution to their employees' underperformance, raising so many questions it's hard to know where to begin.

But let's try. In another survey, the Chartered Institute of Personnel and Development (CIPD) noted that if Britain at work was a marriage, it was 'a marriage under stress, characterised by poor communications and low levels of trust'. Only 38 per cent of employees feel senior managers and directors treat them with respect, and 66 per cent don't trust them. Around a quarter of employees rarely or never look forward to going to work, and almost half are leaving or trying to. 'The findings suggest many managers aren't doing enough to keep their staff interested,' said the CIPD's Mike Emmott. The result: underperformance, low productivity and high staff turnover.

The last UK survey for Gallup's Employee Engagement Index makes similarly grim reading. In 2005 just 16 per cent of UK employees were 'positively engaged' – loyal and committed to the organisation. The rest were unengaged or actively disengaged – physically present but psychologically absent. And it is getting worse: since 2001 the proportion of engaged employees has fallen, while those actively disengaged have increased to 24 per cent.

Gallup puts the cost to the economy of active disengagement at £40bn, as employees express their disenchantment by going sick, not trying, leaving, or threatening strikes. The culprit, says Gallup, is poor management. 'Workers say they don't know what is expected of them, managers don't care about them as people, their jobs aren't a good fit for their talents and their views count for little'.

Adapted from an article by Simon Caulkin, the *Observer*, 28 January 2007. For the full article, go to www.guardian.co.uk/business/2007/jan/28/theobserver.observerbusiness4

a) Explain how an annual cutback of a workforce could 'boost productivity'. (4)

b) Use a motivation theory of your choosing to analyse the methods and attitudes of the senior executives/senior managers highlighted in this article. (9)

c) The article blames managers for the poor performance of staff. Discuss how organisational structure might affect the performance of a large business. (12)

d) Some business experts believe that poor staff morale and performance can undermine a firm's ability to develop effective customer service and quality management. To what extent do you agree with this view? (15)

Question 2

Read the case material below then answer the questions that follow.

Coney Cycles

Ten years ago 19-year-old Dean Coney inherited a bicycle shop when his father died. It was located in Ealing, West London. The business had barely broken even for years, so Dean thought about closing it down. He didn't, largely because of his own passion for racing bikes. He worked hard at modernising the shop, but for the first four years it was a struggle to take any pay out of the business.

Then the shop started to get busy. Commuters were turning to bikes to avoid the London congestion charge and the overcrowding on public transport. Furthermore, the increasing focus on personal health and fitness was turning whole families towards bikes. Between 2002 and 2007, the use of bikes doubled in London. All Dean had to do was to take his share of the growing market.

A threat, though, was that Halfords saw the same opportunity. It used heavy TV advertising to promote the expanded cycling sections in its 400 stores and opened a new Superstore a mile away. After buying and reading a couple of business books, he decided to start marketing his shop actively. He bought long-term contracts on poster sites in Ealing High Road and started the 'Coney Cycling Club', organising Sunday cycles in the country. On summer Sundays there were often 50 to 60 people taking their bikes by train or minivan, with Dean taking the opportunity to talk bikes and biking with his customers. No one would turn up on a Sunday with their latest bike from Halfords, so people were hooked into staying with Coney Cycles. Dean's bikes were never going to be cheaper than Halfords', but he made sure to stock high quality makes to match the high prices.

Over the past year a further issue has been staffing. When he started, he could run the shop on his own. Now he needed two full-time staff and four part-timers for hectic spring Saturdays and for the run-up to Christmas. He chose to only recruit those with a clear love of bikes, then he trained them carefully on different brands. All newcomers were taken to the Brompton Bicycle factory in West London, to see the manufacturing process. The close links formed with suppliers such as Brompton was a key part of Dean's approach to the business.

Now, for the first time, Dean feels in a position to open a second bicycle shop, about three miles away in Acton. He is confident that the finances of the business are strong enough to take the strain.

Table 51.1 Coney Cycles: Forecasts for July–September this year

Sales	1,000 bikes at an average of £250 each
Variable costs	£150 per bike
Total costs	£220,000
Net cash flow	(£40,000)

a) i) Calculate Coney Cycles' forecast fixed costs for July–September. (2)

ii) Calculate the forecast percentage net profit margin in the July–September period. (3)

iii) Analyse two actions Dean could take to try to increase this percentage profit margin. (8)

b) i) Calculate the difference between Coney Cycle's profit and its net cash flow for the period July–September. (2)

ii) Discuss what the reasons may be for this difference. (11)

c A former member of Dean's staff was overheard saying that 'he hasn't a clue about marketing; Halfords will steamroller him into the ground within five years'. To what extent do you agree with this view? (14)

That is the end of the exam.

52 Answers and commentary on mock exam papers

Mock exam Unit 1 (for full exam paper, see Unit 49)

1a) Natalia spotted the parachute business opportunity through her personal experience. State two other ways of identifying a business opportunity. (2)

- Market research, e.g. primary research among young, wealthy adults might have revealed their desire for more exciting holiday experiences.
- Creative or innovative thinking, i.e. spotting an opportunity for a product or service that others didn't know they wanted.

1b) Briefly explain whether you would regard Karl's research among travel agents as qualitative or quantitative. (2)

- Qualitative research is in-depth among relatively few respondents.
- Quantitative needs to be among a large enough sample size to be statistically valid.
- Interviewing eight travel agents in Birmingham and Manchester sounds very valuable, but the sample size is too small to be sure that the answers represent the whole market.
- Therefore the research was qualitative.

1c) What is meant in the case by the term 'segment'? (2)

- A slice of the market that has common characteristics, e.g. under 16 or, in this case, wealthy young adults (especially men).

1d) Calculate the break-even point for XDream Holidays in Wales. (4)

Break-even point = Fixed costs/contribution per unit (1)

Contribution per unit = £1,500 − £500 = £1,000 (1)

Fixed costs £8,000/£1,000 (1) = 8 customers (1)

1e) What profit per week can Karl and Natalia expect if they achieve their target of 12 customers? (4)

Profit = Total revenue − Total costs (1)

Revenue = £18,000 (1)

Total costs = ([£500 × 12 = £6,000] + £8,000) = £14,000 (1)

Profit = £4,000 (1)

1f) Explain two possible reasons for setting up the business as a limited organisation. (6)

See Table 52.1 for marking guidelines. Possible answers include:

- Karl and Natalia come from a stable, salaried background (working at a solicitors) so it is understandable that they would want the nearest thing in business to a secure business organisation; certainly Ltd status guarantees that the couple need not lose any more money in future.
- If their own £20,000 will provide 'nothing like enough' to get the business going, it is likely that the business will need more share capital as well as loan capital. Therefore an unlimited liability status would be unhelpful.

Table 52.1 Marking grid for (f) (out of 6)

Content	Application	Analysis
2	2	2
Good understanding shown of relevant terms	Relevant issues applied in detail to the case	Analysis of question set, using relevant theory
1	1	1
Some understanding of the relevant terms	Relevant issues applied to the case	One point used in a limited way to analyse the question

2a) Examine the factors Karl and Natalia should consider when deciding where to locate their new business. (10)

See Table 52.2. Possible answers include:

- Given the tightly defined market segment (rich City young adults) it should be quite easy to see the ideal location ...
- ... Either near the workplace of typical City types, or in the type of place that these people live.
- But it's also very important to bear in mind the costs involved. The posher the district the higher the rental value; therefore the 'best' location might not be the best value.
- But if the shop's real purpose is to boost the image and credibility of XDream Holidays, a posh location may be uneconomic, yet fulfil a really useful image-related purpose.

Table 52.2 Marking grid for (a) (out of 10)

Content	Application	Analysis
2	3	3–5
Good understanding shown of relevant terms	Relevant issues applied in detail to the case	Analysis of question set, using relevant theory
1	1–2	1–2
Some understanding of the relevant terms	Relevant issues applied to the case	One point used in a limited way to analyse the question

2b) Discuss whether Karl or Natalia showed the most enterprise. (15)

See Table 52.3. Possible answers include:

- Karl showed initiative, in going along to eight travel agents; another person might only have bothered to visit a few in one city, so the fact that he went to Birmingham and Manchester suggests that he is also hardworking; the latter quality is also implied by starting to do a cash flow forecast; the cash flow forecast also suggests that he understands the importance of finance within the context of business start-up.
- Natalia seems to have been the more creative of the pair (came up with the idea and the vision of how it would work and how it would fit with their lifestyles); she also showed a lot of initiative and hard work in the early stages, such as the research at airfields; overall she seemed the more willing to push ahead with a relatively risky venture.
- Natalia showed more of the characteristics of an entrepreneur, as she had Karl's qualities plus the creative spark; overall, though, their characteristics seem quite complementary, with Natalia being the more enterprising of the pair.

Table 52.3 Marking grid for (b) (out of 15)

Content	Application	Analysis	Evaluation
3	3	3–4	3–5
Good understanding shown of relevant terms	Relevant issues applied in detail to the case	Analysis of question set, using relevant theory	Judgement shown in discussing the issues raised, reaching a balanced conclusion
1–2	1–2	1–2	1–2
Some understanding of the relevant terms	Relevant issues applied to the case	An attempt at building an argument, but weakly	Some judgement shown in text or conclusions

2c) Karl and Natalia have not yet undertaken a formal business plan. Discuss whether completing a business plan would guarantee the success of the start-up of XDream Holidays Ltd. (15)

See Table 52.4. Possible answers include:

- A business plan would set out the business goals plus the forecasts and plans for achieving them, including financial, marketing, staffing and practical (operational) plans.
- This would force Natalia and Karl to think the whole thing through, and may reveal gaps or problems that they need to know now rather than later.
- For the same reason, a detailed business plan will help reassure investors or lenders that the business is relatively safe. If the investor wonders whether insurance charges (as parachuting is so risky) have been fully costed, a quick check of the business plan should provide reassurance.
- Unfortunately, even the best business ideas backed by thorough business plans can go wrong; economic circumstances can change, e.g. XDream Holidays would have looked a great idea in 2007, but would look faintly ludicrous in December 2008 at a time of recession and redundancies; therefore the idea that a business plan could *guarantee* success is laughable.
- Quite simply, no new business idea is guaranteed to succeed, and there is no method of achieving guaranteed success. A well-considered business plan would push a new business slightly away from 'likely to fail' towards 'likely to succeed'; a 'guarantee' of success remains a long, long way from that.

Table 52.4 Marking grid for (c) (out of 15)

Content	Application	Analysis	Evaluation
3	3	3–4	3–5
Good understanding shown of relevant terms	Relevant issues applied in detail to the case	Analysis of question set, using relevant theory	Judgement shown in discussing the issues raised, reaching a balanced conclusion
1–2	1–2	1–2	1–2
Some understanding of the relevant terms	Relevant issues applied to the case	An attempt at building an argument, but weakly	Some judgement shown in text or conclusions

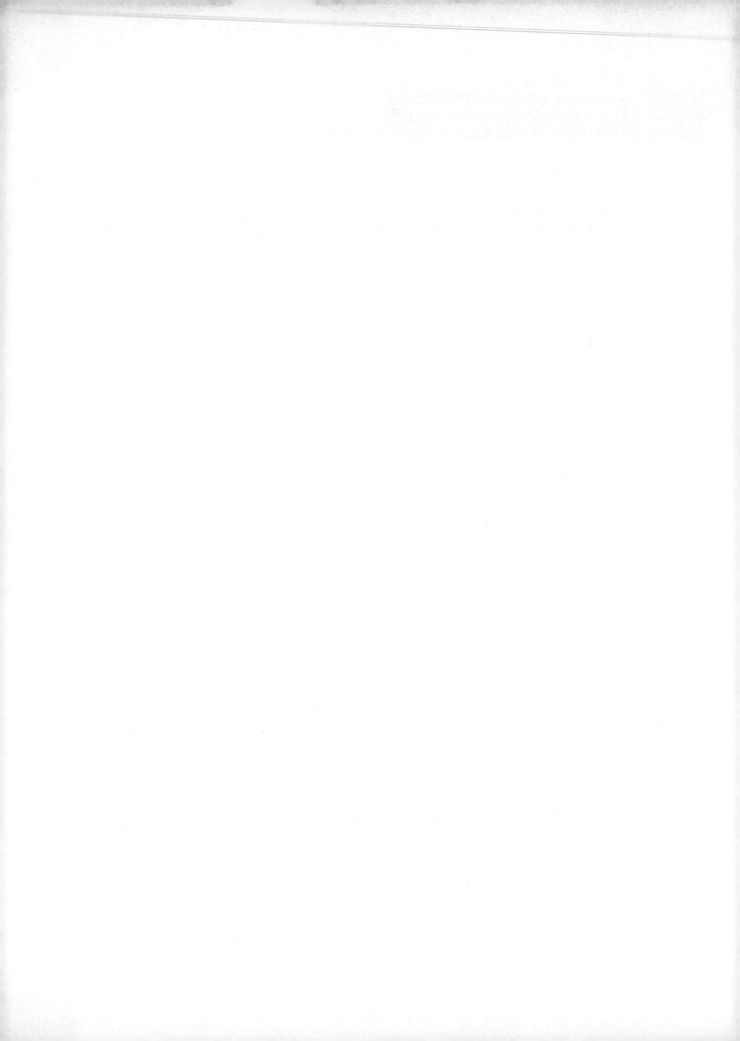

Index

Note: page numbers in **bold** refer to keyword definitions.